THE
AUTOBIOGRAPHY
OF
ST. TERESA OF AVILA

ST. TERESA OF JESUS
1515-1582

THE
AUTOBIOGRAPHY
OF
ST. TERESA OF AVILA

THE LIFE OF ST. TERESA OF JESUS
WRITTEN BY HERSELF

Including
THE RELATIONS
OR MANIFESTATIONS OF HER SPIRITUAL STATE WHICH
ST. TERESA SUBMITTED TO HER CONFESSORS.

Translated from the Spanish by
David Lewis

Compared with the Original Autograph Text and
Re-Edited with Additional Notes and Introduction by the
Very Rev. Fr. Benedict Zimmerman, O.C.D.
PRIOR OF ST. LUKE'S, WINCANTON

TAN BOOKS AND PUBLISHERS, INC.
Rockford, Illinois 61105

Nihil Obstat: Henry S. Bowden
                   Censor Deputatus

Re-Imprimatur: ✠ Edmund Canon Surmont
                   Vicar General
                   Westminster
                   November 28, 1910

This translation first published in approximately 1911. This edition published in 1997 by TAN Books and Publishers, Inc., being photographically reproduced from the Fifth Edition which was published in 1916 by Benziger Brothers, New York by arrangement with Thomas Baker, London.

Library of Congress Catalog Card No.: 97-60908

ISBN 0-89555-603-0

Cover illustration: Contemporary portrait of St. Teresa of Avila by Fray Juan de la Miseria, Discalced Carmelites, Seville.

Printed and bound in the United States of America.

TAN BOOKS AND PUBLISHERS, INC.
P.O. Box 424
Rockford, Illinois 61105
1997

Misericordias Domini in aeternum cantabo.
"The mercies of the Lord I will sing forever."

—Motto of St. Teresa of Avila
(*Psalm* 88:2)

CONTENTS.

CONTENTS.

CONTENTS.

INTRODUCTION.

St. Teresa was born at Avila on Wednesday, March 28, 1515,[1] and baptized on April 4, in the parish church of San Juan, the very day on which the first Mass was celebrated in the new church of the convent of the Incarnation.[2] Her god-father was Vela Nuñez, and the god-mother Doña Maria del Aguila. The name she received in baptism, Teresa, of frequent occurrence in Spain in the fourteenth and fifteenth centuries, was common to the families of both her father and mother ; for her great-grandmother on the father's side was Teresa Sanchez, and her grandmother on her mother's side was Teresa de las Cuevas.

Her father, Don Alonso Sanchez de Cepeda, son of Don Juan Sanchez de Toledo, had been married twice, first in 1504, to Doña Catalina del Peso, by whom he had three children—Don Juan Vasquez de Cepeda, Don Pedro de Cepeda, and a daughter, Doña Maria de Cepeda, who married Don Martin de Guzman, and is frequently mentioned in the writings of her saintly half-sister. Don Alonso having become a widower in 1507, married secondly Doña Beatriz Davila y Ahumada, who was in the fourth degree related to his first wife, so that a dispensation became necessary, which was granted October 17, 1509. This second marriage was blessed with nine children, who, according to the custom of those days, took the name either of the father or the mother, as it pleased them. They were : Don Fernando de Ahumada, Don Rodrigo de Cepeda, our saint, whose full name was Doña Teresa Sanchez Cepeda Davila y Ahumada, Don Lorenzo de Cepeda, Don Antonio and Don Pedro de Ahumada, Don Jeronimo de Cepeda, Don Agustin and Doña Juana de Ahumada.

Don Alonso, the father, was pious, stern, and austere ; if not exactly rich, at least so far well-to-do that he was able to provide liberally for each of his twelve children, as may be seen from his testament and the two inventories of his property, the first of which was drawn up after the death of his first wife and the other after

---

[1] Don Vicente de la Fuente, *Obras de Santa Teresa de Jesús*, vol. vi. p. 1 (Madrid, 1881).　　　　[2] *Ibid.* vol. vi. 1.

his own death.[3] St. Teresa, who has left a beautiful character sketch of him, delighted in speaking of him, and always did so in terms of the highest veneration. He was fond of good books, of which he collected a considerable number, so that his children might read them too. Some of these books are enumerated in the inventory of 1508 ; they were : *Portrait of the Life of Christ*, Cicero *de officiis*, Guzman's *Treatise on the Mass, On the seven sins, The Conquest of America*, Boethius's *Consolation, Proverbs of Seneca*, Virgil, Juan de Mena's *Trecientas* and *Coronación*, and a Calendar. During the following thirty years he must have enlarged his library, but in the inventory made after his death only two books are mentioned, the Gospels and a volume of sermons.

Doña Beatriz died young, and the eldest daughter, Maria de Cepeda, took charge of her younger sisters, and was as a second mother to them till her marriage, which took place in 1531, when the Saint was in her sixteenth year. But as she was too young to be left in charge of her father's house, and as her education was not finished, she was sent to the Augustinian monastery, the nuns of which received young girls, and brought them up in the fear of God.[4] The Saint's own account is that she was too giddy and careless to be trusted at home, and that it was necessary to put her under the care of those who would watch over her and correct her ways. She remained a year and a half with the Augustinian nuns, and all the while God was calling her to Himself. She was not willing to listen to His voice ; she would ask the nuns to pray for her that she might have light to see her way ; " but for all this," she writes, " I wished not to be a nun." [5] By degrees her will yielded, and she had some inclination to become a religious at the end of the eighteen months of her stay, but that was all. She became ill ; her father removed her, and the struggle within herself continued,—on the one hand, the voice of God calling her ; on the other, herself labouring to escape from her vocation.

At last, after a struggle which lasted three months, she made up her mind, and against her inclination, to give up the world. She asked her father's leave, and was refused. She besought him through her friends, but to no purpose. " The utmost I could get from him," she says, " was that I might do as I pleased after his death." [6] How long this contest with her father lasted is not known, but it is probable that it lasted many months, for the Saint was always most careful of the feelings of others, and would certainly

---

[3] Manuel Serrano y Sanz, *Apuntes para una biblioteca de Escritoras Españolas*, vol. ii. pp. 479–542 (Madrid, 1905).

[4] *Reforma de los Descalços*, lib. i. chap. vii. 3

[5] Ch. iii. 2.

[6] Ch. iii. 9.

have endured much rather than displease a father whom she loved so much, and who also loved her more than his other children.[7] But she had to forsake her father, and so she left her father's house by stealth, taking with her one of her brothers, whom she had persuaded to give himself to God in religion. The brother and sister set out early in the morning, the former for the monastery of the Dominicans, and the latter for the convent of the Incarnation, in Avila. The nuns received her into the house, but sent word to her father of his child's escape. Don Alonso, however, yielded at once, and consented to the sacrifice which he was compelled to make.

The Carmelite Order, to which the convent of the Incarnation belongs, had come from Palestine to Europe in the middle of the thirteenth century. The Rule, originally intended for hermits, was then slightly altered, but remained so strict that its observance became more and more difficult. It was mitigated in 1432, whereupon the Order began to flourish anew until, towards the end of the fifteenth century, a period of decadence set in, owing to the almost universal disinclination to religious life, which lasted until the Council of Trent infused new vigour into ecclesiastical institutions. In the year 1452 a community of Beguines near Guelders petitioned the General, Blessed John Soreth, for incorporation into his Order, which was readily granted and confirmed by the Apostolic See. Soreth gave them some regulations—still unpublished—but for the rest referred them to the Constitutions of the Friars. There being an essential difference between the vocation of one destined to the priesthood, who has to frequent university lectures, or move about in the exercise of his sacred ministry, and that of a nun, it follows that the Constitutions of the friars left the nuns rather more freedom in the matter of enclosure than is generally thought compatible with the aims of a strict Order. Convents of Carmelite nuns were founded in various countries ; Spain at the time of St. Teresa must have had six or eight, but unfortunately very little is known of their origin and history ; the only one of which we possess reliable information being that of Avila.[8] It was not an offshoot of some other foundation, but was of indigenous growth, if this expression may be used.

In the year 1467 some pious ladies of Avila determined to found a Beguinage, or, as it was called, a *Beaterio*, the number of Beatas being limited to fourteen, in honour of our Lord, our Lady, and the twelve apostles. On June 25, 1479, they went to live in

---

[7] Ch. i. 3.

[8] Don Enrique Ballesteros, *Estudio histórico de Avila* (Avila, 1896), supplemented by researches made by the present writer in the National Archives at Madrid. See also in the *Œuvres complètes de Sainte Térèse* (by the French Carmelite nuns), vol. i. p. 65 ; iii. pp. 290, 572 sqq. (Paris 1907, sqq.).

a house in the Calle del Lomo, near the Puerta San Vicente, close to an ancient synagogue which the bishop, Don Alonso de Fonseca, had converted into a church and placed at their disposal. There were two parties among the Beatas : some with the Prioress, Doña Elvira Gonzalez de Medina, were in favour of continuing the somewhat free life of Beatas or Beguines, while others, led by Doña Beatriz Higuera, would have preferred real religious life with the three vows. Consequently they left Avila and went to Alba de Tormes, returning only at the death of Doña Elvira in 1486, when Doña Beatriz was elected Prioress. A Papal Brief having left the community the choice between the adoption of the Rule of St. Dominic or that of the Carmelites, they decided in favour of the latter, probably because the friars of that Order had acted as their confessors and directors, the two religious houses being in proximity. Thus the convent was founded, and took for its title the " Incarnation," or, as we should say, the Annunciation, a title borne also by the Carmelite convents of Antiquera, Sevilla, and Valencia. Doña Beatriz remained at the head of the community forty years, during which it increased so rapidly that the building in the Calle del Lomo soon proved inadequate. In 1510 permission was obtained in Rome for the acquisition of a new and more spacious site, but before any further steps could be taken the convent became involved in a long lawsuit with Don Nuño Gonzalez who, probably as founder or benefactor of the original Beaterio, claimed the right of patronage. The convent was successful in every instance, but was nearly crushed by the costs, and the expense of the building operations, so that it had to alienate considerable property. The revenues were totally insufficient for the ever-increasing number of nuns. About the time of St. Teresa's entrance there were 140. When the General, John Baptist Rubeo, made a canonical visitation at Avila, April 1567, he forbade the reception of novices until the number of the nuns should have been reduced by death and translation, so as to restore the balance between income and expenditure.

The date of St. Teresa's entrance has long been under dispute. Some of her biographers and editors, notably P. Marcel Bouix, S.J., relying upon the passage in her *Life*,[9] where she says that she was not yet twenty years old when she had her first spiritual experience some months after her profession, concluded that the profession must have taken place in 1534, and the entrance into the convent on November 2, 1533. But there is evidence that St. Teresa's calculation of years is often at fault, as when she affirms[10] that she was less than twelve years old at the death of her mother, whereas we gather, from the date of the testament of

---

[9] Ch. iv. 9. [10] Ch. i. 7.

the latter, that she was not far from fourteen. Another opinion is that she took the habit in 1535 and the vows in 1536 (during the priorship of Doña Maria de Luna), and this is borne out by evidence so overwhelming that it seems indisputable ; we therefore have adopted it in this edition, and have corrected some other dates, dependent on that of the profession, where Mr. Lewis had followed the chronology of P. Bouix. To begin with, we have the positive statement of her most intimate friends, Julian d'Avila, Fr. Ribera, S.J., and Fr. Jerome Gratian. Likewise, Doña Maria Pinel, nun of the Incarnation, says : " She took the habit on November 2, 1535," and elsewhere refutes a contrary opinion. This is corroborated by various passages in St. Teresa's own writings. Thus, in *Rel.* vii., composed in 1575, she says : " This nun took the habit forty years ago " ; again in the passage of the *Life*, written about the end of 1564 or the beginning of the following year,[11] she refers to her having been a nun for twenty-eight years, which points to her profession in 1536.

A third opinion, placing her entrance into the convent in the year 1536 and the profession in 1537, has been propounded by the author of the *Reforma de los Descalços* on the strength of two documents bearing the date of October 31, 1536 ; one is St. Teresa's renunciation of her right to paternal inheritance, and the other the deed of dowry drawn up before a public notary. But neither of these documents is necessarily connected with the entrance into the convent, so long as it was completed before profession. For the Constitutions, then in vigour, say : " We advise that a person about to be received into the convent settle everything he (or she) may have had in the world before taking the habit, unless for some reasonable cause the General or the Provincial should ordain differently." There was indeed good reason, in the case of St. Teresa, to postpone these legal matters. Her father was much opposed to her becoming a nun ; but, in view of his well-known piety, it might have been expected that before the end of the year of probation he would grant his consent (which in the event he did the very day she took the habit), and make arrangements for the dowry. We therefore refer these two documents, not to the date of her entrance, but to that of her profession.

One little detail concerning her haste in entering the convent has been preserved by the *Reforma* and the Bollandists,[12] though neither seem to have understood its meaning. On leaving the convent of the Incarnation for that of St. Joseph in 1563, St. Teresa handed the Prioress of the former a receipt for her bedding, habit, and discipline. This almost ludicrous scrupulosity was in conformity with a decision of the general chapter of 1342, which said,

[11] Ch. xxxvi. 10.
[12] *Reforma*, lib. i. cap. xlvii. *Bollandists*, No. 366.

"*Ingrediens ad sui ipsius instantiam habeat lectisternia pro se ipso, sin autem, recipiens solvat lectum illum*.[13] As St. Teresa entered the convent without the knowledge of her father, she did not bring this insignificant trousseau with her; accordingly the Prioress became responsible for it, and obtained a receipt when St. Teresa went to the new convent. The dowry granted by Don Alonso to his daughter consisted of twenty-five measures, partly wheat, partly barley, or, in lieu thereof, two hundred ducats per annum. Few of the nuns of the Incarnation could have brought a better, or even an equal, dowry.

A little incident is related concerning the beginning of her religious life. She was told that a *zahori*, an old man credited with the knowledge of the future, had prophesied that the convent of the Incarnation was to give to the Church a "Saint Teresa." There lived in the convent a very old nun, Teresa Alvarez, whose name appears in documents of 1498, 1521, and 1538. A friendly dispute arose between the two as to who was the future Saint, each claiming the honour for herself. Doña Maria Espinel relates a similar anecdote with regard to another nun, Teresa de Quesada, much younger than her saintly namesake. If she did not attain sanctity she at least strove hard in its pursuit. During some years she embraced the Reform, became even Prioress of Medina del Campo, but ultimately returned to the Incarnation, where she died in the odour of sanctity.[14]

Unfortunately, very little is known about the life St. Teresa led at the Incarnation. From what she says in her book one would think that her time—when she was not ill—was almost entirely taken up by worldly conversation with friends and relatives, and, after she had come to a more serious frame of mind, by prayer. Beyond a few anecdotes about her relations with the other nuns, no account of her daily life has come down to us. But we are entitled to supplement so incomplete a picture. A person endowed with her gifts, her admirable qualities, of ceaseless activity, marvellously fit to organise and administrate as we know her to have been from 1560 to the last day, cannot have led an aimless life from 1536 to 1560. True, she says that she had never accepted any office,[15] and among the papers once belonging to the convent of the Incarnation and now preserved at the National Archives at Madrid, there is not one bearing her name [16]; but even without

[13] B. Zimmerman, *Monumenta historica Carmelitana*, vol. i. p. 141 (Lerini 1907).

[14] *Relaciones Históricas de los Siglos XVI. y XVII.* (Sociedad de los bibliófilos españoles) vol. xxxii. p. 327.

[15] Ch. xxxv. 8.

[16] It is, of course, possible that at the time of her beatification the documents relating to her may have been collected, and may even now be preserved elsewhere, *e.g.* in the archives of the Sacred Congregation of Rites in Rome.

occupying an official position she must have utilised her time to the last minute. She was skilled in every branch of housework, knew the details of kitchen and household, was an expert in cutting, and indefatigable with the distaff and the needle ; her embroideries still command the admiration of the connoisseur ; she was well read, had a talent for poetry, an eye for painting, and an ear for music. And above all—as she says herself—she never dispensed herself without urgent need from any of the numerous monastic duties and observances. Moreover, she exercised a powerful influence over all those who came into contact with her, guiding and directing many nuns in their spiritual life, and tendering advice and consolation to whoever approached her, while some of the junior sisters, and also some pensioners, were placed under her personal supervision and care. Such a life cannot be termed idle or dreamy.

In the monastery of the Incarnation the Saint was led on, without her own knowledge, to states of prayer so high that she became alarmed about herself. In the purity and simplicity of her soul, she feared that the supernatural visitations of God might, after all, be nothing else but delusions of Satan.[17] She was so humble that she could not believe graces so great could be given to a sinner like herself. The first person she consulted in her trouble seems to have been a layman, related to her family, Don Francisco de Salcedo. He was a married man, given to prayer, and a diligent frequenter of the theological lectures in the monastery of the Dominicans. Through him she obtained the help of a holy priest, Gaspar Daza, to whom she made known the state of her soul. The priest, hindered by his other labours, declined to be her director, and the Saint admits that she could have made no progress under his guidance.[18] She now placed herself in the hands of Don Francis, who encouraged her in every way, and, for the purpose of helping her onwards in the way of perfection, told her of the difficulties he himself had met with, and how by the grace of God he had overcome them.

But when the Saint told him of the great graces which God bestowed upon her, Don Francis became alarmed ; he could not reconcile them with the life the Saint was living, according to her own account. He never thought of doubting the Saint's account, and did not suspect her of exaggerating her imperfections in the depths of her humility: " he thought the evil spirit might have something to do " with her,[19] and advised her to consider carefully her way of prayer.

Don Francis now applied again to Gaspar Daza, and the two friends consulted together ; but, after much prayer on their part

[17] Ch. xxiii. 2. [18] Ch. xxiii. 8.
[19] *Ibidem* § 12.

and on that of the Saint, they came to the conclusion that she " was deluded by an evil spirit," and recommended her to have recourse to the fathers of the Society of Jesus, lately settled in Avila.

The Saint, now in great fear, but still hoping and trusting that God would not suffer her to be deceived, made preparations for a general confession, and committed to writing the whole story of her life, and made known the state of her soul to F. Juan de Padranos, one of the fathers of the Society. F. Juan understood it all, and comforted her by telling her that her way of prayer was sound and the work of God. Under his direction she made great progress, and for the further satisfaction of her confessor, and of Don Francis, who seems to have still retained some of his doubts, she told everything to St. Francis de Borja, who on one point changed the method of direction observed by F. Juan. That father recommended her to resist the supernatural visitations of the spirit as much as she could, but she was not able, and the resistance pained her [20]; St. Francis told her she had done enough, and that it was not right to prolong that resistance.[21]

The account of her life which she wrote before she applied to the Jesuits for direction has not been preserved ; but it is possible that it was made more for her own security than for the purpose of being shown to her confessor.

The next account is *Relation* i., made for St. Peter of Alcantara, and was probably seen by many ; for that Saint had to defend her, and maintain that the state of her soul was the work of God, against those who thought that she was deluded by Satan. Her own confessor was occasionally alarmed, and had to consult others, and thus, by degrees, her state became known to many ; and there were some who were so persuaded of her delusions, that they wished her to be exorcised as one possessed of an evil spirit,[22] and at a later time her friends were afraid that she might be denounced to the Inquisitors.[23]

During the troubles that arose when it became known that the Saint was about to found the monastery of St. Joseph, and therein establish the original rule of her Order in its primitive simplicity and austerity, she went for counsel to the Father Pedro Ibañez, the Dominican, a most holy and learned priest. That father not only encouraged her, and commended her work, but also ordered her to give him in writing the story of her spiritual life. The Saint readily obeyed, and began *Relation* ii. in the monastery of the Incarnation, and finished it in the house of Doña Luisa de la Cerda, in Toledo, in the month of June 1562.

But as the Saint carried a heavy burden laid on her by God, a

[20] Ch. xxiv. 1.
[22] Ch. xxix. 4.

[21] *Ibidem* § 4.
[23] Ch. xxxiii. 6.

constant fear of delusion, she had recourse, shortly after the foundation of St. Joseph's convent,[24] to the Inquisitor Soto, who advised her to write a history of her life, send it to Juan of Avila, the "Apostle of Andalucia," and abide by his counsel. About the same time her confessor, Fray Garcia de Toledo, charged her to write the history of the foundation of her little convent, together with many other things.[25] She therefore set to work to write the book now before the reader, beginning probably in spring 1563, and completing it in the course of 1565.

But here we find ourselves in presence of a difficult and complicated question : How many versions of her *Life* did she write ? At the end of the volume she says, " This book was finished in June, in the year MDLXII." Bañes wrote underneath : " This date refers to the first account which the holy Mother Teresa wrote of her life ; it was not then divided into chapters. Afterwards she made this copy, and inserted in it many things which had taken place subsequent to this date, such as the foundation of the monastery of St. Joseph of Avila." The letter with which the book concludes, and which bears neither the name of the addressee nor a date, has been assigned to the year 1562, and supposed to be addressed to Father Ibañez. This, in consequence of another remark of Bañez who, in the deposition for the process of canonisation, written in 1591, says : " Of one of her books, namely, the one in which she recorded her life and the kind of prayer whereby God had led her, I can say that she composed it to the end that her confessors might know her better and instruct her, and also that it might encourage and animate those who learn from it the great mercy God had shown her, a great sinner, as she humbly acknowledged herself to be. This book was already written when I made her acquaintance, her previous confessors having given her permission to that effect. Among these was a Licentiate of the Dominican Order, the Rev. Father Pedro Ibañez, reader of Divinity at Avila. She afterwards completed and recast this book." [26] These two notes of Bañez have led the biographers of the Saint to think that she wrote her Life twice : first in 1561 and the following year, completing it during her sojourn at Toledo in June 1562 ; and secondly between 1563 and 1565 at St. Joseph's convent, Avila. But there are serious objections to such a conclusion. To begin with, the letter at the end of the *Life* cannot have been written in 1562, but only in 1565, and consequently after the death of Ibañez. It must therefore have been addressed to somebody else, probably to Fray Garcia de Toledo. The reason why it cannot have been written in 1562 is that in it the Saint requests the addressee to forward the book to Father Juan d'Avila,

---

[24] *Relation* vii. 8–10.   [25] *Foundations*, Prologue.
[26] Fuente, vol. vi. p. 174.

but it was only in spring, 1563, that she was advised by Soto to seek advice from the "Apostle of Andalucia." Again, if as early as 1562 the Saint had requested some one to forward her *Life* to him it would be astonishing that she allowed six years to pass before she took any further steps to see her request carried out; for, in 1568, she wrote twice to Doña Luisa de la Cerda,[27] urging her to send it on; this was done at last, and in September of the same year Juan d'Avila gave his opinion, as we shall see later on.

Bañez does not say whether he ever saw the alleged first version of the *Life*, though he gives some particulars, viz. that it was not divided into chapters, and did not contain many matters which are fully treated in the second *Life*.

But whether it was really a first attempt at a Life or a mere Relation, perhaps of considerably greater bulk than any of those printed at the end of this volume—there can be no dispute about its purpose.[28] St. Teresa speaks of it in the following terms: "I had recourse to my Dominican father (Ibañez); I told him all about my visions, my way of prayer, the great graces our Lord had given me, as clearly as I could, and begged him to consider the matter well, and tell me if there was anything therein at variance with the Holy Writings, and give me his opinion on the whole matter."[29] The account thus rendered had the object of enabling Father Ibañez to give her light upon the state of her soul. But while she was drawing it up, a great change came over her. During St. Teresa's sojourn at Toledo she became from a pupil an experienced master in mystical knowledge. "When I was there a religious" (probably Father Garcia de Toledo) "with whom I had conversed occasionally some years ago, happened to arrive. When I was at Mass in a monastery of his Order, I felt a longing to know the state of his soul."[30] Three times the Saint rose from her seat, three times she sat down again, but at last she went to see him in a confessional, not to ask for any light for herself, but to give him what light she could, for she wished to induce him to surrender himself more perfectly to God, and this she accomplished by telling him how she had fared since their last meeting. No one who reads this remarkable chapter can help being struck by the change that has come over Teresa: the period of her schooling is at an end, and she is now the great teacher of mystical theology. Her humility

[27] Letters of May 18 and 27, 1568.
[28] If the former, it must have been very much shorter than the second edition, and can scarcely have contained more than the first nine chapters (perhaps verbatim) and an account of the visions, locutions, etc., contained in chapters xxiii.-xxxi., without comment.
[29] Ch. xxxiii. § 7.
[30] Ch. xxxiv. § 8.

does not allow her to speak with the same degree of openness upon her achievements as she did when making known her failings, yet she cannot conceal the gift of Wisdom she had received and the use she made of it.

St. Teresa's development, if extraordinary considering the degree of spirituality she reached, was nevertheless gradual and regular. With her wonderful power of analysis, she has given us not only a clear insight into her interior progress, but also a sketch of the development of her understanding of supernatural things. " It is now (*i.e.* about the end of 1563) some five or six years, I believe, since our Lord raised me to this state of prayer, in its fulness, and that more than once,—and I never understood it, and never could explain it ; and so I was resolved, when I should come thus far in my story, to say very little or nothing at all." [31] In the following chapter she adds : " You, my father, will be delighted greatly to find an account of the matter in writing, and to understand it ; for it is one grace that our Lord gives grace ; and it is another grace to understand what grace and what gift it is ; and it is another and further grace to have the power to describe and explain it to others. Though it does not seem that more than the first of these— the giving of grace—is necessary, it is a great advantage and a great grace to understand it." [32] These words contain the clue to much that otherwise would be obscure in the life of our Saint : great graces were bestowed upon her, but at first she neither understood them herself nor was she able to describe them. Hence the inability of her confessors and spiritual advisers to guide her. Her natural gifts, great though they were, did not help her much. " Though you, my father, may think that I have a quick understanding, it is not so ; for I have found out in many ways that my understanding can take in only, as they say, what is given it to eat. Sometimes my confessor used to be amazed at my ignorance : and he never explained to me—nor, indeed, did I desire to understand—how God did this, nor how it could be. Nor did I ever ask." [33] At first she was simply bewildered by the favours shown her, and afterwards she could not help knowing, despite the fears of her over-anxious friends, that they did come from God, and so far from imperilling her soul made a different woman of her, but even then she was not able to explain to others what she experienced in herself. But shortly before the foundation of St. Joseph's convent she received the last of the three graces mentioned above, the Gift of Wisdom, and the scene at Toledo is the first manifestation of it.

This explains the difference of the *Life* such as we know it from the first version or the *Relation* preceding it. Whatever this writing was, it still belonged to the period of her spiritual

[31] Ch. xvi. § 2. [32] Ch. xvii. § 7.
[33] Ch. xxviii. § 10.

education, whereas the volume before us is the first-fruit of her spiritual Mastership. The new light that had come to her induced her confessors to demand a detailed work embodying everything she had learned from her heavenly Teacher.[34] The treatise on mystical theology contained in Chapters X. to XXI., the investigation of divine Locutions, Visions and Revelations in the concluding portion of the work could have had no place in any previous writing. While her experiences before she obtained the Gift of Wisdom influenced but three persons (one of them being her father), a great many profited by her increased knowledge. The earlier writings were but confidential communications to her confessors, and if they became known to larger circles this was due to indiscretion. But her *Life* was written from the beginning with a view to publication. Allusions to this object may be found in various places [35] as well as in the letter appended to the book, but the decisive utterances must be sought for elsewhere, namely, in the *Way of Perfection*. This work was written immediately after the *Life*, while the Saint was as yet at the convent of St. Joseph's. It was rewritten later on, and both versions are still preserved, and have been published ; the one contained in the MS. of the Escorial leaves no doubt as to the intentions of St. Teresa in writing her *Life*. " I have written a few days ago a certain Relation of my Life. But since it might happen that my confessor may not permit you [the Sisters of St. Joseph's] to read it, I will put here some things concerning prayer which are conformable to what I have said there, as well as some other things which appear to me to be necessary." [36] Again : " As all this is better explained in the book which I say I have written, there is no need for me to speak of it with so much detail. I have said there all I know. Those of you who have been led by God to this degree of contemplation (and I say that some have been led so far), should procure the book because it is important for you, after I am dead." [37] At the end she writes : " Since the Lord has taught you the way and has inspired me as to what I should put in the book which I say has been written, how they should behave who have arrived at this fountain of living water and what the soul feels there, and how God satiates her and makes her lose the thirst for things of this world and causes her to grow in things pertaining to the service of God ; that book, therefore, will be of great help for those who have arrived at this state, and will give them much light. Procure it. For Father Domingo Bañez, presentado of the Order of St. Dominic who, as I say, is my confessor, and to whom I shall give this, has it : if he judges that you

[34] Ch. xviii. § 11.
[35] Ch. x. §§ 11 and 12.
[36] *Way of Perfection*, at the end of the Introduction.
[37] *Ibid.* ch. xxv. 3.

should see this, and gives it to you, he will also give you the other." [38]
While the first and second of these quotations may be found,
somewhat weakened, in the final version of the *Way of Perfection*,
the last one is entirely omitted. Nor need this surprise us, for
Father Bañez had his own ideas about the advisability of the
publication of the *Life*.

St. Teresa wrote her *Life* slowly. It was begun in spring,
1563 [39], and completed in May or June 1565. She complains that
she can only work at it by stealth on account of her duties at the
distaff [40]; but the book is written with so much order and method,
the manuscript is so free from mistakes, corrections, and erasures,
that we may conclude that, while spinning, she worked it out in her
mind, so that the apparent delay proved most advantageous.

The book being at length completed, St. Teresa gave it to the
addressee of the letter appended to it—whoever that was—with a
request to forward it to the Venerable Juan d'Avila. She did
not know him personally, and therefore had recourse to her friends,
Gaspar Daza and Don Francis de Salcedo, who obtained the consent
of the " Apostle of Andalucia " to undertake the revision.[41] Accordingly the Saint sent the work to Doña Luisa de la Cerda, who was
living at no great distance from that remarkable man. But there
followed a considerable delay, perhaps because Doña Luisa was
reading the book herself, and it required two urgent letters of the
Saint before she could be persuaded to part with it ; in the meantime St. Teresa was in fears Father Juan might die before he could
give his decision. However, his answer arrived in due time, and
cannot but have greatly comforted the Saint. It was as follows [42]:

" The grace and peace of Jesus Christ be with you always.

" 1. When I undertook to read the book sent me, it was not
so much because I thought myself able to judge of it, as because
I thought I might, by the grace of our Lord, learn something
from the teachings it contains : and praised be Christ ; for, though
I have not been able to read it with the leisure it requires, I have
been comforted by it, and might have been edified by it, if the

[38] *Ibid.* ch. lxxiii. (Escorial). The English version [ch. xlii. 8] follows here
the edition of Valladolid.

[39] In the Prologue to the *Foundations* St. Teresa says that Father Garcia
de Toledo ordered her to rewrite the book the same year in which St. Joseph's
Convent was founded, *i.e.* 1562, but seeing that she only spent a few hours
there and that the principal difficulties only arose after her return to the
Incarnation, it appears more probable that Father Garcia's command was
not made until the spring of the following year, when she went to live at
St. Joseph's.

[40] Ch. x. § 11.

[41] *Œuvres complètes*, vol. i. p. 437.

[42] *Letters of Blessed John of Avila*, translated by the Benedictines of
Stanbrook, 1904, p. 17 sqq.

fault had not been mine. And although, indeed, I may have been comforted by it, without saying more, yet the respect due to the subject and to the person who has sent it will not allow me, I think, to let it go back without giving my opinion on it, at least in general.

" 2. The book is not fit to be in the hands of everybody, for it is necessary to correct the language in some places, and explain it in others ; and there are some things in it useful for your spiritual life, and not so for others who might adopt them, for the special ways by which God leads some souls are not meant for others. These points, or the greater number of them, I have marked for the purpose of arranging them when I shall be able to do so, and I shall not fail to send them to you ; for if you are aware of my infirmities and necessary occupations, I believe they would make you pity me rather than blame me for the omission.

" 3. The doctrine of prayer is for the most part sound, and you may rely on it, and observe it ; and the raptures I find to possess the tests of those which are true. What you say of God's way of teaching the soul, without respect to the imagination and without interior locutions, is safe, and I find nothing to object to it. St. Augustine speaks well of it.

" 4. Interior locutions in these days have been a delusion of many, and exterior locutions are the least safe. It is easy enough to see when they proceed from ourselves, but to distinguish between those of a good and those of an evil spirit is more difficult. There are many rules given for finding out whether they come from our Lord or not, and one of them is, that they should be sent us in a time of need, or for some good end, as for the comforting a man under temptation or in doubt, or as a warning of coming danger. As a good man will not speak unadvisedly, neither will God ; so, considering this, and that the locutions are agreeable to the holy writings and the teaching of the Church, my opinion is that the locutions mentioned in the book came from God.

" 5. Imaginary or bodily visions are those which are most doubtful, and should in no wise be desired, and if they come undesired still they should be shunned as much as possible, yet not by treating them with contempt, unless it be certain that they come from an evil spirit ; indeed, I was filled with horror, and greatly distressed, when I read of the gestures of contempt that were made.[43] People ought to entreat our Lord not to lead them by the way of visions, but to reserve for them in heaven the blessed vision of Himself and the saints, and to guide them here along the beaten path as He guides His faithful servants, and they must take other good measures for avoiding these visions.

" 6. But if the visions continue after all this is done, and if the soul derives good from them, and if they do not lead to vanity,

[43] See *Life*, ch. xxix. 6.

but to deeper humility, and if the locutions be at one with the teaching of the Church, and if they continue for any time, and that with inward satisfaction—better felt than described—there is no reason then for avoiding them. But no one ought to rely on his own judgment herein ; he should make everything known to him who can give him light. That is the universal remedy to be had recourse to in such matters, together with hope in God, Who will not let a soul that wishes to be safe lie under a delusion, if it be humble enough to yield obedience to the opinion of others.

" 7. Nor should any one cause alarm by condemning them forthwith, because he sees that the person to whom they are granted is not perfect, for it is nothing new that our Lord in His goodness makes wicked people just, yea, even grievous sinners, by giving them to taste most deeply of His sweetness. I have seen it so myself. Who will set bounds to the goodness of our Lord ?— especially when these graces are given, not for merit, nor because one is stronger ; on the contrary, they are given to one because he is weaker ; and as they do not make one more holy, they are not always given to the most holy.

" 8. They are unreasonable who disbelieve these things merely because they are most high things, and because it seems to them incredible that infinite Majesty humbles Himself to these loving relations with one of His creatures. It is written, God is love, and if He is love, then infinite love and infinite goodness, and we must not be surprised if such a love and such a goodness breaks out into such excesses of love as disturb those who know nothing of it. And though many know of it by faith, still, as to that special experience of the loving, and more than loving, converse of God with whom He will, if not had, how deep it reaches can never be known ; and so I have seen many persons scandalised at hearing of what God in His love does for His creatures. As they are themselves very far away from it, they cannot think that God will do for others what He is not doing for them. As this is an effect of love, and that a love which causes wonder, reason requires we should look upon it as a sign of its being from God, seeing that He is wonderful in His works, and most especially in those of His compassion ; but they take occasion from this to be distrustful, which should have been a ground of confidence, when other circumstances combine as evidences of these visitations being good.

" 9. It seems from the book, I think, that you have resisted, and even longer than was right. I think, too, that these locutions have done your soul good, and in particular that they have made you see your own wretchedness and your faults more clearly, and amend them. They have lasted long, and always with spiritual profit. They move you to love God, and to despise yourself, and to do penance. I see no reasons for condemning them, I incline rather to regard them as good, provided you are careful not to rely altogether on them, especially if they are unusual, or bid you do something out of the way, or are not very plain. In all these and the like cases you must withhold your belief in them, and at once seek for direction.

"10. Also it should be considered that, even if they do come from God, Satan may mix with them suggestions of his own; you should therefore be always suspicious of them. Also, when they are known to be from God, men must not rest much on them, seeing that holiness does not lie in them, but in a humble love of God and our neighbour; everything else, however good, must be feared, and our efforts directed to the gaining of humility, goodness, and the love of our Lord. It is seemly, also, not to worship what is seen in these visions, but only Jesus Christ, either as in heaven or in the Sacrament, or, if it be in a vision of the saints, then to lift up the heart to the Holy One in heaven, and not to that which is presented to the imagination: let it suffice that the imagination may be made use of for the purpose of raising me up to that which it makes me see.

"11. I say, too, that the things mentioned in this book befall other persons even in this our day, and that there is a great certainty that they come from God, Whose arm is not shortened that He cannot do now what He did in times past, and that in weak vessels, for His own glory.

"12. Go on your road, but always suspecting robbers, and asking for the right way; give thanks to our Lord, Who has given you His love, the knowledge of yourself, and a love of penance and the cross, making no account of these other things. However, do not despise them either, for there are signs that most of them come from our Lord, and those that do not come from Him will not hurt you if you ask for direction.

"13. I cannot believe that I have written this in my own strength, for I have none, but it is the effect of your prayers. I beg of you, for the love of Jesus Christ our Lord, to burden yourself with a prayer for me; He knows that I am asking this in great need, and I think that is enough to make you grant my request. I ask your permission to stop now, for I am bound to write another letter. May Jesus be glorified in all and by all! Amen.

"Your servant for Christ's sake.

"JUAN DE AVILA.

"MONTILLA, *Sep.* 12, 1568."

Her confessors, having seen the book, "commanded her to make copies of it," [44] one of which has been traced into the possession of the Duke and Duchess of Alva.

[44] *Rel.* vii. 9.

The Princess of Eboli, in 1569, obtained a copy from the Saint herself, after much importunity ; but it was more out of vanity or curiosity, it is to be feared, than from any real desire to learn the story of the Saint's spiritual life, that the Princess desired the boon. She and her husband promised to keep it from the knowledge of others, but the promise given was not kept. The Saint heard within a few days later that the book was in few hands of the servants of the Princess, who was angry with the Saint because she had refused to admit, at the request of the Princess, an Augustinian nun into the Order of Carmel in the new foundation of Pastrana. The contents of the book were bruited abroad, and the visions and revelations of the Saint were said to be of a like nature with those of Magdalen of the Cross, a deluded and deluding nun. The gossip in the house of the Princess was carried to Madrid, and the result was that the Inquisition began to make a search for the book.[45] It is not quite clear, however, that it was seized at this time.

The Princess became a widow in July 1573, and insisted on becoming a Carmelite nun in the house she and her husband, Ruy Gomez, had founded in Pastrana. When the news of her resolve reached the monastery, the mother-prioress, Isabel of St. Dominic, exclaimed, " The Princess a nun ! I look on the house as ruined." The Princess came, and insisted on her right as foundress ; she had compelled a friar to give her the habit before her husband was buried, and when she came to Pastrana she began her religious life by the most complete disobedience and disregard of common propriety. Don Vicente's description of her is almost literally correct, though intended only for a general summary of her most childish conduct :

" On the death of the Prince of Eboli, the Princess would become a nun in her monastery of Pastrana. The first day she had a fit of violent fervour ; on the next she relaxed the rule ; on the third she broke it, and conversed with secular people within the cloisters. She was also so humble that she required the nuns to speak to her on their knees, and insisted upon their receiving into the house as religious whomsoever she pleased. Hereupon complaints were made to St. Teresa, who remonstrated with the Princess, and showed her how much she was in the wrong, whereupon she replied that the monastery was hers ; but the Saint proved to her that the nuns were not, and had them removed to Segovia."

The nuns were withdrawn from Pastrana in April 1574, and then the anger of the Princess prevailed ; she sent the *Life* of the Saint, which she had still in her possession, to the Inquisition, and denounced it as a book containing visions, revelations, and dangerous doctrines, which the Inquisitors should look into and examine.

[45] *Reforma de los Descalços*, lib. ii. cap. xxviii. 6.

The book was forthwith given to theologians for examination, and two Dominican friars, of whom Bañes was one, were delegated censors of it by the Inquisition.[46]

Fr. Bañes did not know the Saint when he undertook her defence in Avila against the authorities of the city, eager to destroy the monastery of St. Joseph [47]; but from that time forth he was one of her most faithful friends, strict and even severe, as became a wise director who had a great Saint for his penitent. He testifies in the process of her beatification that he was firm and sharp with her; while she herself was the more desirous of his counsel, the more he humbled her, and the less he appeared to esteem her.[48] When he found that copies of her *Life* were in the hands of secular people,—he had probably also heard of the misconduct of the Princess of Eboli,—he showed his displeasure to the Saint, and told her he would burn the book, it being unseemly that the writings of women should be made public. The Saint left it in his hands, but Fr. Bañes, struck with her humility, had not the courage to burn it; he sent it to the Holy Office in Madrid.[49] Thus the book was in a sense denounced twice,—once by an enemy, the second time by a friend, to save it. Both the Saint and her confessor, Fr. Bañes, state that the copy given up by the latter was sent to the Inquisition in Madrid, and Fr. Bañes says so twice in his deposition. The Inquisitor Soto returned the copy to Fr. Bañes, desiring him to read it, and give his opinion thereon. Fr. Bañes did so, and wrote his "censure" of the book on the blank leaves at the end. That censure still remains, and is one of the most important, because given during the lifetime of the Saint, and while many persons were crying out against her. Bañes wished it had been published when the Saint's *Life* was given to the world by Fr. Luis de Leon; but notwithstanding its value, and its being preserved in the book which is in the handwriting of the Saint, no one before Don Vicente made it known. It was easy enough to praise the writings of St. Teresa, and to admit her sanctity, after her death. Fr. Bañes had no external help in the applause of the many, and he had to judge the book as a theologian, and the Saint as one of his ordinary penitents. When he wrote, he wrote like a man whose whole life was spent, as he tells us himself, "in lecturing and disputing." [50]

[46] Jerome Gratian, *Lucidario*, ch. iv.

[47] *Life*, ch. xxxvi. 15.

[48] The Saint says of herself, *Rel.* vii. 18, that "she took the greatest pains not to submit the state of her soul to any one who she thought would believe that these things came from God, for she was instantly afraid that the devil would deceive them both."

[49] *Rel.* vii. 16.

[50] "Como hombre criado toda mi vida en leer y disputar " (*Fuente*, vol. vi. 171, Deposition in view of the beatification).

That censure is as follows :

" 1. This book, wherein Teresa of Jesus, Carmelite nun, and foundress of the Barefooted Carmelites, gives a plain account of the state of her soul, in order to be taught and directed by her confessors, has been examined by me, and with much attention, and I have not found anywhere in it anything which, in my opinion, is erroneous in doctrine. On the contrary, there are many things in it highly edifying and instructive for those who give themselves to prayer. The great experience of this religious, her discretion also and her humility, which made her always seek for light and learning in her confessors, enabled her to speak with an accuracy on the subject of prayer that the most learned men, through their want of experience, have not always attained to. One thing only there is about the book that may reasonably cause any hesitation till it shall be very carefully examined : it contains many visions and revelations, matters always to be afraid of, especially in women, who are very ready to believe of them that they come from God, and to look on them as proofs of sanctity, though sanctity does not lie in them. On the contrary, they should be regarded as dangerous trials for those who are aiming at perfection, because Satan is wont to transform himself into an angel of light,[51] and to deceive souls which are curious and of scant humility, as we have seen in our day : nevertheless, we must not therefore lay down a general rule that all revelations and visions come from the devil. If it were so, St. Paul could not have said that Satan transforms himself into an angel of light, if the angel of light did not sometimes enlighten us.

" 2. Saints, both men and women, have had revelations, not only in ancient, but also in modern times ; such were St. Dominic, St. Francis, St. Vincent Ferrer, St. Catherine of Siena, St. Gertrude, and many others that might be named ; and as the Church of God is, and is to be, always holy to the end, not only because her profession is holiness, but because there are in her just persons and perfect in holiness, it is unreasonable to despise visions and revelations, and condemn them in one sweep, seeing they are ordinarily accompanied with much goodness and a Christian life. On the contrary, we should follow the saying of the Apostle in 1 Thess. v. 19–22 : ' Spiritum nolite extinguere. Prophetias nolite spernere. Omnia [autem] probate : quod bonum est tenete. Ab omni specie mala abstinete vos.' He who will read St. Thomas on that passage will see how carefully they are to be examined who, in the Church of God, manifest any particular gift that may be profitable or hurtful to our neighbour, and how watchful the examiners ought to be lest the fire of the Spirit of God should be quenched in the

---

[51] 2 Cor. xi. 14 : " Ipse enim Satanas transfigurat se in angelum lucis."

good, and others cowed in the practices of the perfect Christian life.

" 3. Judging by the revelations made to her, this woman, even though she may be deceived in something, is at least not herself a deceiver, because she tells all the good and the bad so simply and with so great a wish to be correct, that no doubt can be made as to her good intention ; and the greater the reason for trying spirits of this kind, because there are persons in our day who are deceivers with the appearance of piety, the more necessary it is to defend those who, with the appearance, have also the reality of piety. For it is a strange thing to see how lax and worldly people delight in seeing those discredited who have an appearance of goodness. God complained of old, by the Prophet Ezekiel, ch. xiii., of those false prophets who made the just to mourn and who flattered sinners, saying : ' Mœrere fecistis cor justi mendaciter, quem Ego non contristavi : et comfortastis manus impii.' In a certain sense this may be said of those who are going on by the way of prayer and perfection, telling them that this way is singular and full of danger, that many who went by it have fallen into delusions, and that the safest way is that which is plain and common, travelled by all.

" 4. Words of this kind, clearly, sadden the hearts of those who would observe the counsels of perfection in continual prayer, so far as it is possible for them, and in much fasting, watching, and disciplines ; and, on the other hand, the lax and the wicked take courage and lose the fear of God, because they consider the way on which they are travelling as the safer : and this is their delusion,—they call that a plain and safe road which is the absence of the knowledge and consideration of the dangers and precipices amidst which we are all of us journeying in this world. Nevertheless, there is no other security than that which lies in our knowing our daily enemies, and in humbly imploring the compassion of God, if we would not be their prisoners. Besides, there are souls whom God, in a way, constrains to enter on the way of perfection, and who, if they relaxed in their fervour, could not keep a middle course, but would immediately fall into the other extreme of sins, and for souls of this kind it is of the utmost necessity that they should watch and pray without ceasing ; and, in short, there is nobody whom lukewarmness does not injure. Let every man examine his own conscience, and he will find this to be the truth.

" 5. I firmly believe that if God for a time bears with the lukewarm, it is owing to the prayers of the fervent, who are continually crying, ' et ne nos inducas in tentationem.' I have said this, not for the purpose of honouring those whom we see walking in the way of contemplation ; for it is another extreme into which the world falls, and a covert persecution of goodness, to pronounce those holy forthwith who have the appearance of it. For that would be to furnish them with motives for vainglory, and would do little honour to goodness; on the contrary, it would expose it to great risks, because, when they fall who have been objects of praise, the honour of goodness suffers more than if those people had not been so esteemed. And so I look upon this exaggeration of their holiness who are still living in the world to be a temptation of Satan. That we should have a good opinion of the servants of God is most just, but let us consider them always as people in danger, however good they may be, and that their goodness is not so evident that we can be sure of it even now.

" 6. Considering myself that what I have said is true, I have always proceeded cautiously in the examination of this account of the prayer and life of this nun, and no one has been more incredulous than myself as to her visions and revelations,—not so, however, as to her goodness and her good desires, for herein I have had great experience of her truthfulness, her obedience, mortification, patience, and charity towards her persecutors, and of her other virtues, which any one who will converse with her will discern; and this is what may be regarded as a more certain proof of her real love of God than these visions and revelations. I do not, however, undervalue her visions, revelations, and ecstasies; on the contrary, I suspect them to be the work of God, as they have been in others who were Saints. But in this case it is always safer to be afraid and wary; for if she is confident about them, Satan will take occasion to interfere, and that which was once, perhaps, the work of God, may be changed into something else, and that will be the devil's.

" 7. I am of opinion that this book is not to be shown to every one, but only to men of learning, experience, and Christian discretion. It perfectly answers the purpose for which it was written, namely, that the nun should give an account of the state of her soul to those who had the charge of it, in order that she might not fall into delusions. Of one thing I am very sure, so far as it is possible for a man to be,—she is not a deceiver; she deserves, therefore, for her sincerity, that all should be favourable to her in her good purposes and good works. For within the last thirteen years she has, I believe, founded a dozen monasteries of Barefooted Carmelite nuns, the austerity and perfection of which are exceeded by none other; of which they who have been visitors of them, as the Dominican Provincial, master in theology,[52] Fray Pedro Fernandez, the master Fray Hernando del Castillo, and many others, speak highly. This is what I think at present concerning the

---

[52] The other theologian appointed by the Inquisition, with Fray Bañes, to examine the *Life*.

censure of this book, submitting my judgment herein to that of Holy Church our mother, and her ministers.

"Given in the College of St. Gregory, Valladolid, on the sixth day of July, 1575.

"FRAY DOMINGO BAÑES."

The book remained in the keeping of the Inquisition, and the Saint never saw it again. But she heard of it from the Archbishop of Toledo, Cardinal Quiroga, President of the Supreme Court of the Inquisition, when she applied to him for licence to found a monastery in Madrid. Jerome Gratian was with her, and heard the Cardinal's reply. His Eminence said he was glad to see her; that a book of hers had been in the Holy Office for some years, and had been rigorously examined; that he had read it himself, and regarded it as containing sound and wholesome doctrine. He would grant the licence, and do whatever he could for the Saint. When she heard this, she wished to present a petition to the Inquisition for the restitution of her book; but Gratian thought it better to apply to the Duke of Alva for the copy which he had, and which the Inquisitors had allowed him to retain and read. The Duke gave his book to Fray Jerome, who had copies of it made for the use of the monasteries both of men and women.

Anne of Jesus, in 1586, founding a monastery of her Order in Madrid,—the Saint had died in 1582,—made inquiries about the original, and applied to the Inquisition for it, for she was resolved to publish the writings of her spiritual mother. The Inquisitors made no difficulty, and consented to the publication. In this she was seconded by the Empress Maria, daughter of Charles V., and widow of Maximilian II., who had obtained one of the copies which Jerome Gratian had ordered to be made. Fray Nicholas Doria, then Provincial, asked Fray Luis de Leon, the Augustinian, to edit the book, who consented. He was allowed to compare the copy furnished him with the original, which was afterwards presented to the king; but his edition has not been considered accurate, notwithstanding the facilities given him, and his great reverence for the Saint. It was published in Salamanca, A.D. 1588.

With the *Life* of the Saint Fray Luis de Leon received certain papers in the handwriting of the Saint, which he published as an additional chapter. Whether he printed all he received, or merely made extracts, may be doubtful, but anyhow that chapter is singularly incomplete. Don Vicente de la Fuente omitted the additional chapter of Fray Luis de Leon, contrary to the practice of his predecessors. But he has done more, for he has traced the paragraphs of that chapter to their sources, and has given us now a collection of papers which form almost another *Life* of the Saint, to which he has given their old name of *Relations*,[53] the name which the Saint herself had given them.[54] Some of them are usually printed among the Saint's letters, and portions of some of the others are found in the *Lives* of the Saint written by Ribera and Yepes, and in the Chronicle of the Order ; the rest was published for the first time by Don Vicente : the arrangement of the whole is due to him.

The *Relations* are ten in the Spanish edition, and eleven in the translation. The last, the eleventh, has hitherto been left among the letters, and Don Vicente, seemingly not without some hesitation, so left it ; but as it is of the like nature with the *Relations*, it has now been added to them.

St. Teresa's canonisation took place before the stringent laws of Urban VIII. came into force. Consequently, the writings of the Saint were not then inquired into, the Holy See contenting itself with the approbations granted by the Spanish Inquisition, and by the congregation of the Rota in Rome. A certain number of passages selected from various works having been denounced by some Roman theologians as being contrary to the teaching of St. Thomas Aquinas and other authorities, Diego Alvarez, a Dominican, and John Rada, a Franciscan, were commissioned to examine the matter and report on it. The twelve censures with the answers of the two theologians and the final judgment of the Rota seem to have remained unknown to the Bollandists.[55] The " heavenly doctrine " of St. Teresa is alluded to not only in the Bull of canonisation, but even in the Collect of the Mass of the Saint.

The original text, in the handwriting of the Saint, is preserved in the Escorial, not in the library but in a room set apart for the most precious relics. In 1873 the Sociedad Foto-Tipográfica-Católica of Madrid published a photographic reproduction of it in 412 pages in folio, which establishes the true text once for all. Don Vicente de la Fuente prepared a transcript of this, which, however, is far from accurate, even allowing for the adoption, on principle, of the modern form of spelling. A minute comparison of the autograph with the transcript reveals the startling fact that nearly a thousand inaccuracies have been allowed to creep in. Most of these variants are immaterial, but there are some which ought not to have been overlooked. Mr. Lewis possessed a copy of the facsimile, but his translation having been made from Fuente's edition of 1861-2, some passages misread or misunderstood by

[53] *Reforma de los Descalços*, lib. v. cap. xxxiv. 4 : " Relaciones de su espiritu."

[54] *Rel.* ii. 18.

[55] See *Historia Generalis Fratrum Discalceatorum Ordinis B. Virginis Mariæ de Monte Carmelo Congregationis S. Eliæ*, vol. i. pp. 340-358 ad ann. 1604 (Romæ, 1668).

him have been corrected in the present reprint. The heading of the chapters, St. Teresa's own work, have been inserted in the proper places. In some instances, where she says " this is most admirable " or something to the same effect, Bañez, before handing the manuscript to the Inquisition, appears to have exercised editorial privileges.

The *Life* of St. Teresa has been frequently translated into English :

1. " The Lyf of the Mother Teresa of Jesus, Foundresse of the Monasteries of the Discalced or Bare-footed Carmelite Nunnes and Fryers of the First Rule.

" Written by herself at the commaundement of her ghostly father, and now translated into English out of Spanish. By W. M. [William Malone ?] of the Society of Jesus.

" Imprinted in Antwerp by Henry Jaye. Anno MDCXI., small quarto."

Some thirty years afterwards Sir Tobias Matthew, dissatisfied, as he says, with the former translation, published another, with the following title ; the volume is a small octavo in form :

" 2. The Flaming Hart, or the Life of the glorious St. Teresa, Foundresse of the Reformation of the Order of the All-Immaculate Virgin Mother, our B. Lady of Mount Carmel.

" This History of her Life was written by the Saint in Spanish, and is newly translated into English in the year of our Lord God 1642.

> ' Aut mori aut pati :
> Either to dye or else to suffer.'—*Chap.* xl.

" Antwerpe, printed by Joannes Meursius. Anno MDCXLII."

The next translation was published in 1671, without the name of the translator, or of the printer, or of the place of publication. It is in quarto, and bears the following title :

" The Life of the Holy Mother St. Teresa, Foundress of the Reformation of the Discalced Carmelites according to the Primitive Rule. Printed in the year MDCLXXI."

This translation, commonly ascribed to Abraham Woodhead, is only partly his work. Father Bede of St. Simon Stock (Walter Joseph Travers), a Discalced Carmelite, labouring on the English mission from 1660 till 1692, was anxious to complete the translation of St. Teresa's works into English. He had not proceeded very far when he learnt that " others were engaged in the same task." On inquiry he found that " a new translation was contemplated by two graduates of the University of Cambridge, converts to the Faith, most learned and pious men, who were leading a solitary life, spending their time and talents in the composition of controversial and devotional works for the good of their neighbour and the glory of God." One of these two was Woodhead, who, however, was an Oxford man, but the name of the other, who must have been a Cambridge man, is not known. They undertook the translation while Father Bede provided the funds and bore the risks of what was then a dangerous work. As there existed already two English translations of the *Life*, the first volume to appear (1669) contained the *Book of Foundations*, to which was prefixed the history of the foundation of St. Joseph's from the *Life*. When, therefore, the new translation of the latter appeared in 1671, this portion of the book was omitted.[56] The translation was made direct from the Spanish but " uniformly with the Italian edition."

The fourth translation is that of the Very Reverend John Dalton, Canon of Northampton. The title is :

" The Life of St. Teresa, written by herself, and translated from the Spanish by the Rev. John Dalton. London, MDCCCLI."

The present translation, the fifth, is due to David Lewis, M.A. (born November 12, 1814, died January 23, 1895). It appeared in 1870, and was reprinted in 1888 under the supervision of the translator, and in 1904 under that of the present writer. The translation is so excellent that, apart from a few mistakes (which have been corrected) the entire text has been reproduced, not only of the *Life* but also of the *Relations*. These, however, are not quite as complete as the *Life* ; of late years many have been discovered which were unknown to Fuente in 1861, and consequently to Mr. Lewis in 1870. The French Carmelite nuns, in their recent edition and translation of the works of St. Teresa,[57] have adopted an entirely new arrangement of the whole collection of *Relations*, placing every paragraph in strictly chronological order. The light thus thrown on the development of the Saint adds greatly to our knowledge of her life. Much as we should have liked to follow their lead, practical considerations have compelled us to adhere to the established order ; the only change we were able to make was the insertion of the exact dates where these could be ascertained.

We enjoyed greater freedom in revising and re-editing the foot-notes. Here again Mr. Lewis's work was excellent, but since his time so much has been done towards elucidating the history of St. Teresa and that of her contemporaries that many of the historical notes had become insufficient or unreliable. Critical observations. too, for which Mr. Lewis relied on the labours of the authors of the *Reforma*, on Fuente and Bouix are now based on the autograph and on other authentic documents. In all these points we have freely utilised the most recent works, such as Morel-Fatio's *Essai* on the authors and editions read and quoted by the Saint, the

[56] See *Carmel in England*, by Rev. B. Zimmerman, pp. 240 sqq. (London, 1899).
[57] See note 8 supra.

valuable collection of documents published by the French Carmelite nuns, and, if we may be pardoned for mentioning it, our own personal researches in the archives and libraries in Spain and elsewhere. By these means many an obscure question has been solved, but much remains to be done yet. The bulk of Mr. Lewis's masterly Preface has been embodied in this Introduction.

St. Teresa's life and character having always been a favourite study of men and women of various schools of thought, it may be useful to notice here a few recent English and foreign works on the subject :

The Life of Saint Teresa, by the author of *Devotions before and after Holy Communion* (*i.e.* Miss Maria Trench), London, 1875.

The Life of Saint Teresa of the Order of our Lady of Mount Carmel. Edited with a preface by the Archbishop of Westminster (Cardinal Manning), London, 1865. (By Miss Elizabeth Lockhart, afterwards first abbess of the Franciscan convent, Notting Hill.) Frequently reprinted.

The Life and Letters of St. Teresa, by Henry James Coleridge, S.J. Quarterly Series. 3 vols. (1881, 1887, 1888).

And, from another point of view :

The Life of St. Teresa, by Gabriela Cunninghame-Graham, 2 vols., London, 1894.

Saint Teresa of Spain, by Helen Hester Colvill, London, 1909.

Histoire de Sainte Thérèse d'après les Bollandistes. 2 vols., Nantes, 1882. Frequently reprinted. The author is Mlle Adelaide Lecornu (born July 5, 1852, died at the Carmelite convent at Caen, December 14, 1901. Her name in religion was Adelaide-Jéronyme-Zoe-Marie du Sacré-Cœur).

An excellent character sketch of the Saint has appeared in the " Les Saints " series (Paris, Lecoffre, 1901) :

Sainte Thérèse, par Henri Joly.

Although the attempt at explaining the extraordinary phenomena in the life of St. Teresa by animal magnetism and similar theories had already been exploded by the Bollandists, it has lately been revived by Professor Don Arturo Perales Gutierrez of Granada, and Professor Don Fernando Segundo Brieva Salvatierra of Madrid, who considered her a subject of hysterical derangements. The discussion carried on for some time, not only in Spain but also in France, Germany, and other countries, has been ably summed up and disposed of by P. Grégoire de S. Joseph : *La prétendue Hystérie de Sainte Thérèse*. Lyons.

The *Bibliographie Térèsienne*, by Henry de Curzon (Paris, 1902) is, unfortunately, too incomplete, not to say slovenly, to be of much use.

Finally, it is necessary to say a word about the spelling of the name Teresa. In Spanish and Italian it should be written without an *h*, as these languages do not admit the use of *Th* ; in English, likewise, where this combination of letters represents a special sound, the name should be spelt with *T* only. But the present fashion of thus writing it in Latin, German, French, and other languages, which generally maintain the etymological spelling, is intolerable. The name is Greek, and was placed on the calendar in honour of a noble Spanish lady, St. Therasia, who became the wife of a Saint, Paulinus of Nola, and a Saint herself. See *Sainte Thérèse, Lettres au R. P. Bouix*, by the Abbé Postel, Paris, 1864. The derivation of the name from the Hebrew Thersa can no longer be defended (Father Jerome-Gratian, in Fuente, *Obras*, vol. vi. pp. 369 sqq.).

BENEDICT ZIMMERMAN,
Prior O.C.D.

St. Luke's Priory,
Wincanton, Somerset.
15th October, 1910.

A letter from St. Peter of Alcantara to St. Teresa on founding her houses without revenues. April 14, 1562.—*Yepes*, bk. ii. ch. vii. See *Life*, ch. xxxv. 6.

MADAM, may your soul be dilated by the Holy Ghost !

I have received your letter, which was delivered to me by Señor Gonsalvo de Aranda. I most certainly think that you are seeking advice from learned men about a question which it is quite out of their province to answer. If the matter concerned the law, or cases of conscience, it would be well to take the opinion of lawyers, or theologians, but no one should decide about a life of perfection except those who themselves live it, for as a rule people's conscience and opinions are no higher than their actions. As regards the evangelical counsels, we must not question whether it would be well to follow them or no, or whether they are practicable or not ; such a doubt contains the germ of infidelity. A counsel given by God cannot but be good nor can it be difficult to practise, save by the faithless and by those who, being ruled solely by human prudence, have little trust in Him. He Who gave the counsel will give the needed help, since He is able to do so. No good man gives counsel that he does not wish to be beneficial, although man's nature is evil. How far more does He, Who is supremely good and powerful, desire and ensure that His counsels should profit those who follow them !

If, then, you wish to practise Christ's counsel of greater perfection, do so, for He gave it not only to men but also to women, and He will see that all prospers with you, as has been the case with all who have observed it. But, if you choose to take the advice of learned but unspiritual persons, and to ensure yourself a good income, see whether either of them benefit you more than dispensing with both, for the sake of following Christ's counsel. If we see a want of necessaries in communities of nuns who practise poverty, it is because they are poor against their will and because they cannot help it, and not because they wish to follow the counsel of our Lord. I do not commend poverty in itself, but the suffering it with patience for the love of Christ, and I praise far more the desiring, seeking, embracing it, out of love. If I held a deliberate opinion to the contrary, I should consider that I was unsound in the faith. On this point, as on all others, I believe what Christ our Lord declared, and I hold firmly that His counsels are wholly right, being the counsels of God, and that, though they do not oblige under pain of sin, yet a man must necessarily be more perfect if he follows them than if he does not :— I mean that, on this point at least, he must be more perfect, holy, and pleasing to God. I believe that, as His Majesty declares, the poor in spirit are blessed, that is, those who are willingly poor : this I have witnessed for myself, yet I believe God's word rather than my own experience. Those who are truly poor at heart are, by the grace of God, blessed in their lives, as are all who love, trust, and hope in God.

Madam, may His Majesty give you light to understand these truths and to act upon them. Give no credence to those who contradict them, either from want of light or faith, or because they have not tasted and seen how sweet the Lord is to them who fear and love Him, and who renounce, for love of Him, all the things of this world, which do not help them to love Him more. Such people are averse to bearing the cross of Christ, nor do they believe in the glory which comes after it. May He Himself enlighten you, that you may not feel dubious about such manifest truths nor take the advice of any one but those who imitate Christ. For although people save their souls by keeping to what is of obligation, yet, as a rule, they understand no more than they practise. Though they may give good counsel, yet Christ our Lord gives better. He knows what He is advocating and when the end comes He repays, although not in this world's coin, those who have trusted in Him.

Your humble chaplain,
FRAY PETER OF ALCANTARA.

ANNALS OF THE SAINT'S LIFE.

1515. St. Teresa is born in Avila, March 28.[1]

1522. She desires martyrdom, and leaves her father's house with one of her brothers.

1528. Death of her mother.

1529. Reads romances of chivalry, and is misled by a thoughtless cousin.

1531. Her sister Maria's marriage, and her removal from home to the Augustinian monastery, where she remains till the autumn of next year.

1535. Nov. 2, enters the monastery of the Incarnation.

1536. Makes her profession, probably on Nov. 3.

1537. Goes to Castellanos de la Cañada, to her sister's house, where she remains till the spring of 1538, when she goes to Bezadas.

1539. Returns to Avila on Palm Sunday. In July seriously ill, and in a trance for four days, when in her father's house. Paralysed for more than two years.

1542. Is cured of her paralysis by St. Joseph. Begins to grow lukewarm, and gives up mental prayer.

[1] In the same year St. Philip was born in Florence. St. Teresa died in 1582, and St. Philip in 1595 ; but they were canonised on the same day, with St. Isidore, St. Ignatius, and St. Francis Xavier. The three latter were joined together in the three final consistories held before the solemn proclamation of their sanctity, and St. Teresa and St. Philip were joined together in the same way in the final consistories held specially, as usual, for them.

1544. Feb. 1. Death of her father. She places herself under the direction of Fr. Vicente Barón.

1555. Ceases to converse with secular people, moved thereto by the sight of a picture of our Lord on the cross (ch. ix. 1). The Jesuits come to Avila and the Saint confesses to F. Juan de Padranos.

1556. Beginning of the supernatural visitations.

1557. St. Francis de Borja comes to Avila, and approves of the spirit of the Saint.

1558. First rapture of the Saint (ch. xxiv. 7). The vision of Hell (ch. xxxii. 1). Father Alvarez ordained priest.

1559. She takes F. Alvarez for her confessor. The transpiercing of her heart (ch. xxix. 17). Vision of our Lord risen from the dead (ch. xxvii. 3, ch. xxviii. 2).

1560. The vow of greater perfection. St. Peter of Alcantara approves of her spirit, and St. Luis Beltran encourages her to proceed with her plan of founding a new monastery.

1561. F. Gaspar de Salazar, S.J., comes to Avila ; her sister Doña Juana comes to Avila from Alba de Tormes to help the Saint in the new foundation (ch. xxxiii. 13). Restores her nephew to life (ch. xxxv. 14, note). Fray Ibañez bids her write her Life. Receives a sum of money from her brother in Peru, which enables her to go on with the building of the new house.

1562. Goes to Toledo, to the house of Doña Luisa de la Cerda, and finishes the account of her Life. Makes the acquaintance of Fray Garcia of Toledo, Dominican. Receives a visit from Maria of Jesus. Has a revelation that her sister, Doña Maria, will die suddenly (ch. xxxiv. 24). Returns to Avila and takes possession of the new monastery, August 24. Troubles in Avila. The Saint ordered back to the monastery of the Incarnation.

1563. Mid-Lent. Obtains permission to live at St. Joseph's as a Discalced nun. Nominated Prioress. Writes her Life and the history of the foundation at the bidding of the Inquisitor Soto, Fray Garcia, and Fray Domingo Bañes.

1565. May or June, completes the *Life*, and sends it to her confessor. Begins the *Way of Perfection*.

1568. The *Life* revised and approved by Blessed John of Avila.

Further dates will be found in the *Book of Foundations*.

THE LIFE

OF THE

HOLY MOTHER TERESA OF JESUS.

WRITTEN BY HERSELF.

I H S

PROLOGUE.

As I have been commanded and left at liberty to describe at length my way of prayer, and the workings of the grace of our Lord within me, I could wish that I had been allowed at the same time to speak distinctly and in detail of my grievous sins and wicked life. But it has not been so willed ; on the contrary, I am laid herein under great restraint ; and therefore, for the love of our Lord, I beg of every one who shall read this story of my life [1] to keep in mind how wicked it has been ; and how, among the Saints who were converted to God, I have never found one in whom I can have any comfort. For I see that they, after our Lord had called them, never fell into sin again ; I not only became worse, but, as it seems to me, deliberately withstood the graces of His Majesty, because I saw that I was thereby bound to serve Him more earnestly, knowing, at the same time, that of myself I could not pay the least portion of my debt.

[1] The Saint, in a letter written Nov. 19, 1581, to Don Pedro de Castro, then Canon of Avila, speaking of this book, calls it the book " Of the Compassions of God "—*Y ansi intitulé ese libro De las Misericordias de Dios.* " Vitam igitur suam internam et supernaturalem magis pandit quam narrat actiones suas mere humanas " (*Bollandists*, n. 2).

May He be blessed for ever Who waited for me so long! I implore Him with my whole heart to send me His grace, so that in all clearness and truth I may give this account of myself which my confessors command me to give; and even our Lord Himself, I know it, has also willed it should be given for some time past, but I had not the courage to attempt it. And I pray it may be to His praise and glory, and a help to my confessors; who, knowing me better, may succour my weakness, so that I may render to our Lord some portion of the service I owe Him. May all creatures praise Him for ever! Amen.

I H S

CHAPTER I.

CHILDHOOD AND EARLY IMPRESSIONS. THE BLESSING OF PIOUS PARENTS. DESIRE OF MARTYRDOM. DEATH OF THE SAINT'S MOTHER.

In which she tells how the Lord began to dispose this soul from childhood for virtue, and how she was helped by having virtuous parents.

1. I HAD a father and mother who were devout and feared God. Our Lord also helped me with His grace. All this would have been enough to make me good, if I had not been so wicked. My father was very much given to the reading of good books; and so he had them in Spanish, that his children might read them. These books, with my mother's carefulness to make us say our prayers, and to bring us up devout to our Lady and to certain Saints, began to make me think seriously when I was, I believe, six or seven years old. It helped me, too, that I never saw my father and mother respect anything but goodness. They were

very good themselves. My father was a man of great charity towards the poor, and compassion for the sick, and also for servants ; so much so, that he never could be persuaded to keep slaves, for he pitied them so much : and a slave belonging to one of his brothers being once in his house, was treated by him with as much tenderness as his own children. He used to say that he could not endure the pain of seeing that she was not free. He was a man of great truthfulness ; nobody ever heard him swear or speak ill of any one ; his life was most pure.

2. My mother also was a woman of great goodness, and her life was spent in great infirmities. She was singularly pure in all her ways. Though possessing great beauty, yet was it never known that she gave reason to suspect that she made any account whatever of it ; for, though she was only three-and-thirty years of age when she died, her apparel was already that of a woman advanced in years. She was very calm, and had great sense. The sufferings she went through during her life were grievous, her death most Christian.[1]

3. We were three sisters and nine brothers.[2] All,

---

[1] See ch. xxxvii. 1, where the Saint says that she saw them in a vision both in Heaven.

[2] Don Alonso Sanchez de Cepeda, father of the Saint, married first Doña Catalina del Peso y Henao, and had three children—one daughter, Maria de Cepeda, and two sons. After the death of Catalina, he married Doña Beatriz Davila y Ahumada, by whom he had nine children—seven boys and two girls. The third of these, and the eldest of the daughters, was the Saint, Doña Teresa Sanchez Cepeda Davila y Ahumada. In the Monastery of the Incarnation, where she was a professed nun for twenty-six years, she was known as Doña Teresa ; but in the year 1563, when she left her monastery for the new foundation of St. Joseph, of the Reform of the Carmelites, she took for the first time the name of Teresa of Jesus. The saint was born March 28, 1515, and baptized on the 4th of April, in the Church of San Juan ; on which day Mass was said for the first time in the new Monastery of the Incarnation, where the Saint made her profession. Her godfather was Vela Nuñez, and her godmother Doña Maria del Aguila. The Bollandists and Father Bouix say that she was baptized on the very day of her birth. But the testimony of Doña Maria de Pinel, a nun in the Monastery of the Incarnation, is clear : and Don Vicente de la Fuente, quoting it, vol. vi. p. 4, says that this delay of baptism was nothing singular in those days, provided there was no danger of death.

by the mercy of God, resembled their parents in goodness except myself, though I was the most cherished
of my father. And, before I began to offend God, I
think he had some reason,—for I am filled with
sorrow whenever I think of the good desires with which
our Lord inspired me, and what a wretched use I made
of them. Besides, my brothers never in any way
hindered me in the service of God.

4. One of my brothers was nearly of my own age[3];
and he it was whom I most loved, though I was very
fond of them all, and they of me. He and I used to
read Lives of Saints together. When I read of martyrdom undergone by the Saints for the love of God, it
struck me that the vision of God was very cheaply
purchased; and I had a great desire to die a martyr's
death— not out of any love of Him of which I was
conscious, but that I might most quickly attain to the
fruition of those great joys of which I read that they
were reserved in Heaven; and I used to discuss with
my brother how we could become martyrs. We
settled to go together to the country of the Moors,[4]
begging our way for the love of God, that we might
be there beheaded[5]; and our Lord, I believe, had
given us courage enough, even at so tender an age, if
we could have found the means to proceed; but our
greatest difficulty seemed to be our father and mother.

---

[3] Rodrigo de Cepeda, four years older than the Saint, entered the army,
and, serving in South America, died in the wilderness of Chaco. St. Teresa
always considered him a martyr, because he died in defence of the Catholic
faith (Ribera, lib. i. cap. iii.). Before he sailed for the Indies, he made his
will, and left all his property to the Saint, his sister (Reforma de los Descalços,
vol. i. lib. i. cap. iii. § 4).

[4] The Bollandists incline to believe that St. Teresa may not have intended
to quit Spain, because all the Moors were not at that time driven out of the
country. The Bull of the Saint's canonization, and the Lections of the
Breviary, say that she left her father's house, ut in Africam trajiceret.

[5] The two children set out on their strange journey—one of them seven,
the other eleven, years old—-through the Adaja Gate; but when they had
crossed the bridge, they were met by one of their uncles, Don Francisco
Alvarez de Cepeda, who brought them back to their mother, who had already
sent through Avila in quest of them. Rodrigo, like Adam, excused himself,
and laid the blame on the woman (Ribera, lib. i. cap. iv.).

5. It astonished us greatly to find it said in what we were reading that pain and bliss were everlasting. We happened very often to talk about this ; and we had a pleasure in repeating frequently, " For ever, ever, ever." Through the constant uttering of these words, our Lord was pleased that I should receive an abiding impression of the way of truth when I was yet a child.

6. As soon as I saw it was impossible to go to any place where people would put me to death for the sake of God, my brother and I set about becoming hermits ; and in an orchard belonging to the house we contrived, as well as we could, to build hermitages, by piling up small stones one on the other, which fell down immediately ; and so it came to pass that we found no means of accomplishing our wish. Even now I have a feeling of devotion when I consider how God gave me in my early youth what I lost by my own fault. I gave alms as I could—and I could but little. I contrived to be alone, for the sake of saying my prayers [6]—and they were many—especially the Rosary, to which my mother had a great devotion, and had made us also in this like herself. I used to delight exceedingly, when playing with other children, in the building of monasteries, as if we were nuns ; and I think I wished to be a nun, though not so much as I did to be a martyr or a hermit.

7. I remember that, when my mother died,[7] I was about twelve years old—a little less. When I began to understand my loss, I went in my affliction to an image of our Lady,[8] and with many tears implored her

---

[6] She was also marvellously touched by the story of the Samaritan woman at the well, of whom there was a picture in her room (*Ribera*, lib. i. cap. iv.). She speaks of this repeatedly. (See ch. xxx. 24 ; *Foundations*, xxxi. 42 ; *Int. Castle*, M. vi. ch. xi. 5 ; *Way of Perfection*, xix. 4.)

[7] The last will and testament of Doña Beatriz de Ahumada was made Nov. 24, 1528 : and she must have died soon after ; the Saint was nearly fourteen years old at that time.

[8] Our Lady of Charity, in the church of the hospital where the poor and pilgrims were received ; this statue is now in the cathedral of Avila.

to be my mother. I did this in my simplicity, and I believe that it was of service to me ; for I have by experience found the royal Virgin help me whenever I recommended myself to her ; and at last she has brought me back to herself. It distresses me now, when I think of, and reflect on, that which kept me from being earnest in the good desires with which I began.

8. O my Lord, since Thou art determined to save me—may it be the pleasure of Thy Majesty to effect it !—and to bestow upon me so many graces, why has it not been Thy pleasure also—not for my advantage, but for Thy greater honour—that this habitation, wherein Thou hast continually to dwell, should not have contracted so much defilement ? It distresses me even to say this, O my Lord, because I know the fault is all my own, seeing that Thou hast left nothing undone to make me, even from my youth, wholly Thine. When I would complain of my parents, I cannot do it ; for I saw nothing in them but all good, and carefulness for my welfare. Then, growing up, I began to discover the natural gifts which our Lord had given me—they were said to be many ; and, when I should have given Him thanks for them, I made use of every one of them, as I shall now explain, to offend Him.

CHAPTER II.

EARLY IMPRESSIONS. DANGEROUS BOOKS AND COM-
PANIONS. THE SAINT IS PLACED IN A CONVENT.

How she lost these virtues and how important it is to deal from childhood with virtuous persons.

1. WHAT I shall now speak of was, I believe, the beginning of great harm to me. I often think how

wrong it is of parents not to be very careful that their children should always, and in every way, see only that which is good ; for though my mother was, as I have just said, so good herself, nevertheless I, when I came to the use of reason, did not derive so much good from her as I ought to have done—almost none at all ; and the evil I learned did me much harm. She was very fond of books of chivalry ; but this pastime did not hurt her so much as it hurt me, because she never wasted her time on them ; only we, her children, were left at liberty to read them ; and perhaps she did this to distract her thoughts from her great sufferings, and occupy her children, that they might not go astray in other ways. It annoyed my father so much that we had to be careful he never saw us. I contracted a habit of reading these books ; and this little fault which I observed in my mother was the beginning of lukewarmness in my good desires, and the occasion of my falling away in other respects. I thought there was no harm in it when I wasted many hours night and day in so vain an occupation, even when I kept it secret from my father. So completely was I mastered by this passion that I thought I could never be happy without a new book.

2. I began to make much of dress, to wish to please others by my appearance. I took pains with my hands and my hair, used perfumes, and all vanities within my reach—and they were many, for I was very much given to them. I had no evil intention, because I never wished any one to offend God for me. This fastidiousness of excessive neatness [1] lasted some years ; and so also did other practices, which I thought

---

[1] The Saint throughout her life was extremely careful of cleanliness. In one of her letters to Father Jerome Gratian of the Mother of God (Feb., 1581), she begs him, for the love of God, to see that the Fathers had clean cells and table ; and the Ven. Mother Anne of St. Bartholomew, in her life (Bruxelles, 1708, p. 40), says that she changed the Saint's linen on the day of her death, and was thanked by her for her carefulness. " Her soul was so pure," says the Ven. Mother, " that she could not bear anything that was not clean."

then were not at all sinful ; now, I see how wrong all this must have been.

3. I had some cousins ; for into my father's house no others were allowed an entrance. In this he was very cautious ; and would to God he had been cautious about them !—for I see now the danger of conversing, at an age when virtue should begin to grow, with persons who, knowing nothing themselves of the vanity of the world, provoke others to throw themselves into the midst of it. These cousins were nearly of mine own age—a little older, perhaps. We were always together ; and they had a great affection for me. In everything that gave them pleasure, I kept the conversation alive—listened to the stories of their affections and childish follies, good for nothing ; and, what was still worse, my soul began to give itself up to that which was the cause of all its disorders. If I were to give advice, I would say to parents that they ought to be very careful whom they allow to mix with their children when young ; for much mischief thence ensues, and our natural inclinations are unto evil rather than good.

4. So it was with me ; for I had a sister much older than myself,[2] from whose modesty and goodness, which were great, I learned nothing ; and learned every evil from a relative who was often in the house. She was so light and frivolous that my mother took great pains to keep her out of the house, as if she foresaw the evil I should learn from her ; but she could not succeed, there being so many reasons for her coming. I was very fond of this person's company, gossiped and talked with her ; for she helped me in all the amusements I liked, and, what is more, found some for me, and communicated to me her own con-

---

[2] Doña Maria de Cepeda, half-sister of the Saint. She was married to Don Martin de Guzman y Barrientos, and the contract for the dowry was signed Jan. 11, 1531 (*Reforma de los Descalços*, lib. i. cap. vii. § 4). The Saint was then sixteen years old, not fourteen as she says.

versations and her vanities. Until I knew her, I mean, until she became friendly with me, and communicated to me her own affairs—I was then about fourteen years old, a little more, I think—I do not believe that I turned away from God in mortal sin, or lost the fear of Him, though I had a greater fear of disgrace. This latter fear had such sway over me, that I never wholly forfeited my good name—and, as to that, there was nothing in the world for which I would have bartered it, and nobody in the world I liked well enough who could have persuaded me to do it. Thus I might have had the strength never to do anything against the honour of God, as I had it by nature not to fail in that wherein I thought the honour of the world consisted ; and I never observed that I was failing in many other ways. In vainly seeking after it I was extremely careful ; but in the use of the means necessary for preserving it I was utterly careless. I was anxious only not to be lost altogether.

5. This friendship distressed my father and sister exceedingly. They often blamed me for it ; but, as they could not hinder that person from coming into the house, all their efforts were in vain ; for I was very adroit in doing anything that was wrong. Now and then, I am amazed at the evil one bad companion can do,—nor could I believe it if I did not know it by experience,—especially when we are young : then is it that the evil must be greatest. Oh, that parents would take warning by me, and look carefully to this ! So it was ; the conversation of this person so changed me, that no trace was left of my soul's natural disposition to virtue, and I became a reflection of her and of another who was given to the same kind of amusements.

6. I know from this the great advantage of good companions ; and I am certain that if at that tender age I had been thrown among good people, I should have persevered in virtue ; for if at that time I had

found any one to teach me the fear of God, my soul would have grown strong enough not to fall away. Afterwards, when the fear of God had utterly departed from me, the fear of dishonour alone remained, and was a torment to me in all I did. When I thought that nobody would ever know, I ventured upon many things that were neither honourable nor pleasing unto God.

7. In the beginning these conversations did me harm—I believe so. The fault was perhaps not hers, but mine ; for afterwards my own wickedness was enough to lead me astray, together with the servants about me, whom I found ready enough for all evil. If any one of these had given me good advice I might perhaps have profited by it ; but they were blinded by interest, as I was by passion. Still, I was never inclined to much evil—for I hated naturally anything dishonourable—but only to the amusement of a pleasant conversation. The occasion of sin, however, being present, danger was at hand, and I exposed to it my father and brothers. God delivered me out of it all, so that I should not be lost, in a manner visibly against my will, yet not so secretly as to allow me to escape without the loss of my good name and the suspicions of my father.

8. I had not spent, I think, three months in these vanities when they took me to a monastery[3] in the city where I lived, in which children like myself were brought up, though their way of life was not so wicked as mine. This was done with the utmost concealment of the true reason, which was known only to myself and one of my kindred. They waited for an opportunity which would make the change seem nothing out of the way ; for, as my sister was married, it was

---

[3] The Augustinian convent of Santa Maria de Gracia. It was founded in 1509 by the Venerable Fray Juan de Sevilla, Vicar-General of the Order (*Reforma de los Descal'os*, lib. i. cap. vii. n. 2). There were forty nuns in the house at this time (*De la Fuente*).

not fitting I should remain alone, without a mother, in the house.

9. So excessive was my father's love for me, and so deep my dissembling, that he never would believe me to be so wicked as I was ; and hence I was never in disgrace with him. Though some remarks were made, yet, as the time had been short, nothing could be positively asserted ; and, as I was so much afraid about my good name, I had taken every care to be secret ; and yet I never considered that I could conceal nothing from Him Who seeth all things. O my God, what evil is done in the world by disregarding this, and thinking that anything can be kept secret that is done against Thee ! I am quite certain that great evils would be avoided if we clearly understood that what we have to do is, not to be on our guard against men, but on our guard against displeasing Thee.

10. For the first eight days I suffered much, but more from the suspicion that my vanity was known, than from being in the monastery ; for I was already weary of myself—and, though I offended God, I never ceased to have a great fear of Him, and contrived to go to confession as quickly as I could. I was very uncomfortable ; but within eight days, I think sooner, I was much more contented than I had been in my father's house. All the nuns were pleased with me ; for our Lord had given me the grace to please every one, wherever I might be. I was therefore made much of in the monastery. Though at this time I hated to be a nun, yet I was delighted at the sight of nuns so good ; for they were very good in that house—very prudent, observant of the rule, and recollected.

11. Yet, for all this, the devil did not cease to tempt me ; and people in the world sought means to trouble my rest with messages and presents. As this could not be allowed, it was soon over, and my soul began to return to the good habits of my earlier years ; and I recognized the great mercy of God to those

whom He places among good people. It seems as if
His Majesty had sought and sought again how to
convert me to Himself. Blessed be thou, O Lord, for
having borne with me so long! Amen.

12. Were it not for my many faults, there was
some excuse for me, I think, in this: that the conversation I shared in was with one who, I thought, would
do well in the estate of matrimony [4]; and I was told
by my confessors, and others also, whom in many
points I consulted, used to say, that I was not offending
God. One of the nuns [5] slept with us who were seculars,
and through her it pleased our Lord to give me light,
as I shall now explain.

CHAPTER III.

THE BLESSING OF BEING WITH GOOD PEOPLE.   HOW
CERTAIN ILLUSIONS WERE REMOVED.

*In which she sets forth how good company was the
means of her resuming good intentions, and in what
manner God began to give her some light on the deception
to which she was subjected.*

1. I BEGAN gradually to like the good and holy conversation of this nun. How well she used to speak of
God! for she was a person of great discretion and
sanctity. I listened to her with delight. I think
there never was a time when I was not glad to listen
to her. She began by telling me how she came to be

---

[4] Some have erroneously inferred from these words that the Saint at this
time intended, or wished, to be married. But it is more probable that the
Saint had listened only to the story of her cousin's intended marriage; for
in ch. v. 12 she says that our Lord had always kept her from seeking to be
loved of men.

[5] Doña Maria Brizeño, mistress of the secular children who were educated
in the monastery. Born in 1498, she entered the convent in 1514 and died
at an advanced age in 1592.

a nun through the mere reading of the words of the Gospel : " Many are called, and few are chosen." [1] She would speak of the reward which our Lord gives to those who forsake all things for His sake. This good companionship began to root out the habits which bad companionship had formed, and to bring my thoughts back to the desire of eternal things, as well as to banish in some measure the great dislike I had to be a nun, which had been very great ; and if I saw any one weep in prayer, or devout in any other way, I envied her very much ; for my heart was now so hard, that I could not shed a tear, even if I read the Passion through. This was a grief to me.

2. I remained in the monastery a year and a half, and was very much the better for it. I began to say many vocal prayers, and to ask all the nuns to pray for me, that God would place me in that state wherein I was to serve Him ; but, for all this, I wished not to be a nun, and that God would not be pleased I should be one, though at the same time I was afraid of marriage. At the end of my stay there I had a greater inclination to be a nun, yet not in that house, on account of certain devotional practices which I understood prevailed there, and which I thought overstrained. Some of the younger ones encouraged me in this my wish ; and, if all had been of one mind, I might have profited by it. I had also a great friend [2] in another monastery ; and this made me resolve, if I was to be a nun, not to be one in any other house than where she was. I looked more to the pleasure of sense and vanity than to the good of my soul. These good thoughts of being a nun came to me from time to time.

---

[1] St. Matt. xx. 16 : " Multi enim sunt vocati, pauci vero electi."

[2] Juana Suarez, a nun of the convent of the Incarnation at Avila. She was much older than her kinswoman, Teresa de Ahumada, and did not belong to the nobility. Her name occurs for the first time on a document of 1521, as one of the younger of the professed nuns (Juana Xuarez Mexia), and again in 1530, 1532, 1557, and 1563, after which date it disappears. Thus it will be seen that she through whom Saint Teresa was brought to Carmel was the witness of her prolonged struggles and final victory.

They left me very soon ; and I could not persuade myself to become one.

3. At this time, though I was not careless about my own good, our Lord was much more careful to dispose me for that state of life which was best for me. He sent me a serious illness, so that I was obliged to return to my father's house.

4. When I became well again, they took me to see my sister [3] in her house in the country village where she dwelt. Her love for me was so great that, if she had had her will, I should never have left her. Her husband also had a great affection for me—at least, he showed me all kindness. This too I owe rather to our Lord, for I have received kindness everywhere ; and all my service in return is, that I am what I am !

5. On the road lived a brother of my father [4]—a prudent and most excellent man, then a widower. Him too our Lord was preparing for Himself. In his old age, he left all his possessions and became a religious. He so finished his course that I believe him to have the vision of God. He would have me stay with him some days. His practice was to read good books in Spanish ; and his ordinary conversation was about God and the vanity of the world. These books he made me read to him ; and, though I did not much like them, I appeared as if I did ; for in giving pleasure to others I have been most particular, though it might be painful to myself—so much so, that what in others might have been a virtue was in me a great fault, because I was often extremely indiscreet. O my God, in how many ways did His Majesty prepare me for the state wherein it was His will I should serve Him !—how, against

---

[3] Doña Maria de Cepeda, married to Don Martin Guzman y Barrientos. They lived in Castellanos de la Cañada, where they had considerable property ; but in the later years of their lives they were in straitened circumstances. See below, ch. xxxiv. 24.

[4] Don Pedro Sanchez de Cepeda, who lived in Hortigosa, four leagues from Avila ; he had been married with Doña Catalina del Aguila, on whose death he entered a monastery.

my own will, He constrained me to do violence to
myself! May He be blessed for ever! Amen.

6. Though I remained here but a few days, yet,
through the impression made on my heart by the
words of God both heard and read, and by the good
conversation of my uncle, I came to understand the
truth I had heard in my childhood, that all things are
as nothing, the world vanity, and passing rapidly away.
I also began to be afraid that, if I were then to die, I
should go down to hell. Though I could not bend
my will to be a nun, I saw that the religious state was
the best and safest. And thus, by little and little,
I resolved to force myself into it.

7. The struggle lasted three months. I used to
press this reason against myself : The trials and
sufferings of living as a nun cannot be greater than
those of purgatory, and I have well deserved to be in
hell. It is not much to spend the rest of my life as
if I were in purgatory, and then go straight to Heaven
—which was what I desired. I was more influenced
by servile fear, I think, than by love, to enter religion.

8. The devil put before me that I could not endure the trials of the religious life, because of my delicate nurture. I defended myself against him by
alleging the trials which Christ endured, and that it
was not much for me to suffer something for His sake ;
besides, He would help me to bear it. I must have
thought so, but I do not remember this consideration.
I endured many temptations during these days. I
was subject to fainting-fits, attended with fever—
for my health was always weak. I had become by
this time fond of good books, and that gave me life.
I read the Epistles of St. Jerome,[5] which filled me with
so much courage, that I resolved to tell my father of
my purpose—which was almost like taking the habit ;

---

[5] Translated into Spanish by Juan de Molina, and published in 1520
(Valencia) and frequently reprinted. See the *Essai sur les Lectures de Sainte
Thérèse*, by A. Morel Fatio (Bulletin Hispanique, Paris 1908).

for I was so jealous of my word that I would never, for any consideration, recede from a promise when once my word had been given.

My father's love for me was so great that I could never obtain his consent; nor could the prayers of others, whom I persuaded to speak to him, be of any avail. The utmost I could get from him was that I might do as I pleased after his death. I now began to be afraid of myself, and of my own weakness—for I might go back. So, considering that such waiting was not safe for me, I obtained my end in another way, as I shall now relate.

CHAPTER IV.

OUR LORD HELPS HER TO BECOME A NUN.
HER MANY INFIRMITIES.

She explains how, with the assistance of God, she compelled herself to take the habit, and how His Majesty began to send her many infirmities.

1. IN those days, when I was thus resolved, I had persuaded one of my brothers,[1] by speaking to him of the vanity of the world, to become a friar; and we agreed together to set out one day very early in the morning for the monastery where that friend of mine lived for whom I had so great an affection[2]: though I would have gone to any other monastery, if I thought I should serve God better in it, or to any one my father liked, so strong was my resolution now to become

---

[1] Don Antonio de Ahumada, born about 1520, took the habit in the Dominican monastery at Avila, but left it and joined the Hieronymites. Illness compelled him to return to his father's house. Restored to health, he chose the military life (probably after his father's death) and was wounded at the battle of Iñaquito; he died at Quito, Jan. 20, 1546.

[2] Juana Suarez, in the Convent of the Incarnation, Avila.

a nun—for I thought more of the salvation of my soul now, and made no account whatever of mine own ease. I remember perfectly well, and it is quite true, that the pain I felt when I left my father's house was so great, that I do not believe the pain of dying will be greater—for it seemed to me as if every bone in my body were wrenched asunder[3] ; for, as I had no love of God to destroy my love of father and of kindred, this latter love came upon me with a violence so great that, if our Lord had not been my keeper, my own resolution to go on would have failed me. But He gave me courage to fight against myself, so that I executed my purpose.[4]

2. When I took the habit[5] our Lord at once made me understand how He helps those who do violence to themselves in order to serve Him. No one observed this violence in me ; they saw nothing but the greatest good-will. At that moment, because I was entering on that state, I was filled with a joy so great that it has never failed me to this day ; and God converted the aridity of my soul into the greatest tenderness. Everything in religion was a delight unto me ; and it is true that now and then I used to sweep the house during those hours of the day which I had formerly spent on my amusements and my dress ; and, calling to mind that I was delivered from such follies, I was filled with a new joy that surprised me, nor could I understand whence it came.

3. Whenever I remember this, there is nothing in the world, however hard it may be, that, if it were proposed to me, I would not undertake without any

---

[3] See *Relation* vi. 3.

[4] The nuns sent word to the father of his child's escape, and of her desire to become a nun, but without any expectation of obtaining his consent. He came to the convent forthwith, and " offered up his Isaac on Mount Carmel " (*Reforma*, lib. i. cap. viii. 5).

[5] She took the habit at the Monastery of the Incarnation Nov. 2, 1535 and made her profession in 1536. These dates, which have often been disputed, are supported by abundant documentary evidence, and must be taken as definitely established.

hesitation whatever ; for I know now, by experience in many things, that if from the first I resolutely persevere in my purpose, even in this life His Majesty rewards it in a way which he only understands who has tried it. When the act is done for God only, it is His will before we begin it that the soul, in order to the increase of its merits, should be afraid ; and the greater the fear, if we do but succeed, the greater the reward, and the sweetness thence afterwards resulting. I know this by experience, as I have just said, in many serious affairs ; and so, if I were a person who had to advise anybody, I would never counsel any one, to whom good inspirations from time to time may come, to resist them through fear of the difficulty of carrying them into effect ; for if a person lives detached for the love of God only, that is no reason for being afraid of failure, for He is omnipotent. May He be blessed for ever ! Amen.

4. O supreme Good, and my Rest, those graces ought to have been enough which Thou hadst given me hitherto, seeing that Thy compassion and greatness had drawn me through so many windings to a state so secure, to a house where there are so many servants of God, from whom I might learn how I may advance in Thy service. I know not how to go on, when I call to mind the circumstances of my profession, the great resolution and joy with which I made it, and my betrothal unto Thee. I cannot speak of it without tears ; and my tears ought to be tears of blood, my heart ought to break, and that would not be much to suffer because of the many offences against Thee which I have committed since that day. It seems to me now that I had good reasons for not wishing for this dignity, seeing that I have made so sad a use of it. But Thou, O my Lord, hast been willing to bear with me for almost twenty years of my evil using of Thy graces, till I might become better. It seems to me, O my God, that I did nothing but promise never to

keep any of the promises then made to Thee. Yet such was not my intention ; but I see that what I have done since is of such a nature, that I know not what my intention was. So it was and so it happened, that it may be the better known, O my Bridegroom, Who Thou art and what I am.

5. It is certainly true that very frequently the joy I have in that the multitude of Thy mercies is made known in me, softens the bitter sense of my great faults. In whom, O Lord, can they shine forth as they do in me, who by my evil deeds have shrouded in darkness Thy great graces, which Thou hadst begun to work in me ? Woe is me, O my Maker ! If I would make an excuse, I have none to offer ; and I only am to blame. For if I could return to Thee any portion of that love which Thou hadst begun to show unto me, I would give it only unto Thee, and then everything would have been safe. But, as I have not deserved this, nor been so happy as to have done it, let Thy mercy, O Lord, rest upon me.

6. The change in the habits of my life, and in my food, proved hurtful to my health ; and though my happiness was great, that was not enough. The fainting-fits began to be more frequent, and my heart was so seriously affected that every one who saw it was alarmed ; and I had also many other ailments. And thus it was I spent the first year, having very bad health, though I do not think I offended God in it much. And as my illness was so serious—I was almost insensible at all times, and frequently wholly so—my father took great pains to find some relief ; and as the physicians who attended me had none to give, he had me taken to a place which had a great reputation for the cure of other infirmities. They said I should find relief there.[6] That friend of whom I have

[6] Her father took her from the monastery in the autumn of 1537, bringing her first to her uncle's house in Hortigosa, and then to Castellanos de la Cañada, to the house of her sister, Doña Maria, where she remained till the spring, when she went to Bezadas for her cure, which began in May 1538.

spoken as being in the house went with me.   She was one of the elder nuns.   In the house where I was a nun, there was no vow of enclosure.[7]

7. I remained there nearly a year, for three months of it suffering most cruel tortures—effects of the violent remedies which they applied. I know not how I endured them ; and indeed, though I submitted myself to them, they were, as I shall relate,[8] more than my constitution could bear.

8. I was to begin the treatment in the spring, and went thither when winter commenced. The intervening time I spent with my sister, of whom I spoke before,[9] in her house in the country, waiting for the month of April, which was drawing near, that I might not have to go and return.   The uncle of whom I have made mention before,[10] and whose house was on our road, gave me a book called *Tercer Abecedario*,[11] which treats of the prayer of recollection. Though in the first year I had read good books—for I would read no others, because I understood now the harm they had done me—I did not know how to make my prayer, nor how to recollect myself. I was therefore much pleased with the book, and resolved to follow the way of prayer it described with all my might.   And as our Lord had already bestowed upon me the gift of tears, and I found pleasure in reading, I began to spend a certain time in solitude, to go frequently to confession, and make a beginning of that way of prayer, with this book for my guide ; for I had no master—I mean, no confessor—who understood me, though I sought for such a one for twenty years afterwards : which did me much harm, in that I frequently went back-

---

[7] That is, the Provincial could give leave to the nuns to absent themselves. The new regulations of the Council of Trent were enforced in 1567.
[8] Ch. v. 15.   [9] Ch. iii. 4.   [10] Ch. iii. 5.
[11] By Fray Francisco de Osuna, of the Order of St. Francis. A large work in six parts (*Abecedario Espiritual*), the first of which appeared about 1525, the two last, after the death of the author, in 1542 and 1554. The third part, of which Saint Teresa speaks, appeared for the first time at Toledo in 1527. The work has become extremely rare.

wards, and might have been utterly lost ; for, anyhow, a director would have helped me to escape the risks I ran of sinning against God.

9. From the very beginning, God was most gracious unto me. Though I was not so free from sin as the book required, I passed that by ; such watchfulness seemed to me almost impossible. I was on my guard against mortal sin—and would to God I had always been so !—but I was careless about venial sins, and that was my ruin. Yet, for all this, at the end of my stay there—I spent nearly nine months in the practice of solitude—our Lord began to comfort me so much in this way of prayer, as in His mercy to raise me to the prayer of quiet, and now and then to that of union, though I understood not what either the one or the other was, nor the great esteem I ought to have had of them. I believe it would have been a great blessing to me if I had understood the matter. It is true that the prayer of union lasted but a short time : I know not if it continued for the space of an *Ave Maria* ; but the fruits of it remained ; and they were such that, though I was then not twenty years of age,[12] I seemed to despise the world utterly ; and so I remember how sorry I was for those who followed its ways, though only in things lawful.

10. I used to labour with all my might to imagine Jesus Christ, our Good and our Lord, present within me. And this was the way I prayed. If I meditated on any mystery of His life, I represented it to myself as within me, though the greater part of my time I spent in reading good books, which was all my comfort ; for God never endowed me with the gift of making reflections with the understanding, or with that of using the imagination to any good purpose : my imagination is so sluggish [13] that, even if I would think of, or picture to myself, as I used to labour to picture, our Lord's Humanity, I never could do it.

[12] She was twenty-three years old.   [13] See ch. ix. 4, 7.

11. And though men may attain more quickly to the state of contemplation, if they persevere, by this way of inability to exert the intellect, yet is the process more laborious and painful ; for if the will have nothing to occupy it, and if love have no present object to rest on, the soul is without support and without employment—its isolation and dryness occasion great pain, and the thoughts assail it most grievously. Persons in this condition must have greater purity of conscience than those who can make use of their understanding ; for he who can use his intellect in the way of meditation on what the world is, on what he owes to God, on the great sufferings of God for him, his own scanty service in return, and on the reward God reserves for those who love Him, learns how to defend himself against his own thoughts, and against the occasions and perils of sin. On the other hand, he who has not that power is in greater danger, and ought to occupy himself much in reading, seeing that he is not in the slightest degree able to help himself.

12. This way of proceeding is so exceedingly painful, that if the master who teaches it insists on cutting off the succours which reading gives, and requires the spending of much time in prayer, then, I say, it will be impossible to persevere long in it : and if he persists in his plan, health will be ruined, because it is a most painful process. Reading is of great service towards procuring recollection in any one who proceeds in this way ; and it is even necessary for him, however little it may be that he reads, if only as a substitute for the mental prayer which is beyond his reach.[14]

13. Now I seem to understand that it was the good providence of our Lord over me that found no one to teach me. If I had, it would have been impossible for me to persevere during the eighteen years of trial and of those great aridities, because of my inability to meditate. During all this time, it was only after

[14] Ch. xxvi. 6.

Communion that I ever ventured to begin my prayer without a book—my soul was as much afraid to pray without one, as if it had to fight against a host. With a book to help me—it was like a companion, and a shield whereon to receive the blows of many thoughts —I found comfort, for it was not usual with me to be in aridity ; but I always was so when I had no book ; for my soul was disturbed, and my thoughts wandered at once. With one, I began to collect my thoughts, and, using it as a decoy, kept my soul in peace, very frequently by merely opening a book—there was no necessity for more. Sometimes I read but little, at other times much—according as our Lord had pity on me.

14. It seemed to me, in these beginnings of which I am speaking, that there could be no danger capable of withdrawing me from so great a blessing, if I had but books, and could have remained alone ; and I believe that, by the grace of God, it would have been so, if I had had a master or any one to warn me against those occasions of sin in the beginning, and, if I fell, to bring me quickly out of them. If the devil had assailed me openly then, I believe I should never have fallen into any grievous sin ; but he was so subtle, and I so weak, that all my good resolutions were of little service— though, in those days in which I served God, they were very profitable in enabling me, with that patience which His Majesty gave me, to endure the alarming illnesses which I had to bear. I have often thought with wonder of the great goodness of God, and my soul has rejoiced in the contemplation of His great magnificence and mercy. May He be blessed for ever !— for I see clearly that He has not omitted to reward me, even in this life, for every one of my good desires. My good works, however wretched and imperfect, have been made better and perfected by Him Who is my Lord : He has rendered them meritorious. As to my evil deeds and my sins, He hid them at once. The

eyes of those who saw them He made even blind, and He has blotted them out of their memory. He gilds my faults, makes virtue to shine forth, giving it to me Himself, and compelling me to possess it, as it were, by force.

15. I must now return to that which has been enjoined me. I say, that if I had to describe minutely how our Lord dealt with me in the beginning, it would be necessary for me to have another understanding than that I have : so that I might be able to appreciate what I owe to Him, together with my own ingratitude and wickedness ; for I have forgotten it all.

May He be blessed for ever Who has borne with me so long ! Amen.

CHAPTER V.

ILLNESS AND PATIENCE OF THE SAINT. THE STORY OF A PRIEST WHOM SHE RESCUED FROM A LIFE OF SIN.

She continues to speak of the great infirmities she suffered, and the patience God gave her to bear them, and how He turned evil into good, as is seen from something that happened in the place where she went for a cure.

1. I FORGOT to say how, in the year of my novitiate, I suffered much uneasiness about things in themselves of no importance ; but I was found fault with very often when I was blameless. I bore it painfully and with imperfection ; however, I went through it all, because of the joy I had in being a nun. When they saw me seeking to be alone, and even weeping over my sins at times, they thought I was discontented, and said so.

2. All religious observances had an attraction for me, but I could not endure any which seemed to make

me contemptible. I delighted in being thought well of by others, and was very exact in everything I had to do. All this I thought was a virtue, though it will not serve as an excuse for me, because I knew what it was to procure my own satisfaction in everything, and so ignorance does not blot out the blame. There may be some excuse in the fact that the convent was not founded in great perfection. I, wicked as I was, followed after that which I saw was wrong, and neglected that which was good.

3. There was then in the house a nun labouring under a most grievous and painful disorder, for there were open ulcers in her body, caused by certain obstructions, through which her food was rejected. Of this sickness she soon died. All her sisters, I saw, were afraid of her malady. I envied her patience very much ; I prayed to God that He would give me a like patience ; and then, whatever sickness it might be His pleasure to send, I do not think I was afraid of any, for I was resolved on gaining eternal good, and determined to gain it by any and by every means.

4. I am surprised at myself, because then I had not, as I believe, that love of God which I think I had after I began to pray. Then, I had only light to see that all things that pass away are to be lightly esteemed, and that the good things to be gained by despising them are of great price, because they are for ever. His Majesty heard me also in this, for in less than two years I was so afflicted myself that the illness which I had, though of a different kind from that of the sister, was, I really believe, not less painful and trying for the three years it lasted, as I shall now relate.

5. When the time had come for which I was waiting in the place I spoke of before [1]—I was in my sister's

---

[1] Ch. iv. 6. The person to whom she was taken was a woman famous for certain cures she had wrought, but whose skill proved worse than useless to the Saint (*Reforma*, lib. i. cap. xi. 2).

house, for the purpose of undergoing the medical treatment—they took me away with the utmost care of my comfort ; that is, my father, my sister, and the nun, my friend, who had come from the monastery with me—for her love for me was very great. At that moment Satan began to trouble my soul; God, however, brought forth a great blessing out of that trouble.

6. In the place to which I had gone for my cure lived a priest of good birth and understanding, with some learning, but not much. I went to confession to him, for I was always fond of learned men, although confessors indifferently learned did my soul much harm ; for I did not always find confessors whose learning was as good as I could wish it was. I know by experience that it is better, if the confessors are good men and of holy lives, that they should have no learning at all, than a little ; for such confessors never trust themselves without consulting those who are learned—nor would I trust them myself : and a really learned confessor never deceived me.[2] Neither did the others willingly deceive me, only they knew no better ; I thought they were learned, and that I was not under any other obligation than that of believing them, as their instructions to me were lax, and left me more at liberty—for if they had been strict with me, I am so wicked, I should have sought for others. That which was a venial sin, they told me was no sin at all ; of that which was most grievously mortal, they said it was venial.[3]

7. This did me so much harm, that it is no wonder I should speak of it here as a warning to others, that they may avoid an evil so great ; for I see clearly that

---

[2] Schram, *Theolog. Mystic.,* § 483. " Magni doctores scholastici, si non sint spirituales, vel omni rerum spiritualium experientia careant, non solent esse magistri spirituales idonei—nam theologia scholastica est perfectio intellectus ; mystica, perfectio intellectus et voluntatis : unde bonus theologus scholasticus potest esse malus theologus mysticus. In rebus tamen difficilibus, dubiis, spiritualibus, præstat mediocriter spiritualem theologum consulere quam spiritualem idiotam."

[3] See *Way of Perfection,* ch. v. 2.

in the eyes of God I was without excuse, that the things I did being in themselves not good, this should have been enough to keep me from them. I believe that God, by reason of my sins, allowed those confessors to deceive themselves and to deceive me. I myself deceived many others by saying to them what had been said to me.

8. I continued in this blindness, I believe, more than seventeen years, till a most learned Dominican Father[4] undeceived me in part, and those of the Company of Jesus made me altogether so afraid, by insisting on the erroneousness of these principles, as I shall hereafter show.[5]

9. I began, then, by going to confession to that priest of whom I spoke before.[6] He took an extreme liking to me, because I had then but little to confess in comparison with what I had afterwards ; and I had never much to say since I became a nun. There was no harm in the liking he had for me, but it ceased to be good, because it was in excess. He clearly understood that I was determined on no account whatever to do anything whereby God might be seriously offended. He, too, gave me a like assurance about himself, and accordingly our conferences were many. But at that time, through the knowledge and fear of God which filled my soul, what gave me most pleasure in all my conversations with others was to speak of God ; and, as I was so young, this made him ashamed ; and then, out of that great good-will he bore me, he began to tell me of his wretched state. It was very sad, for he had been nearly seven years in a most perilous condition, because of his affection for, and conversation with, a woman of that place ; and yet he used to say Mass. The matter was so public that his honour and good name were lost, and no one ventured to speak to him about it. I was extremely sorry for him, because I

---

[4] F. Vicente Baron.   [5] See ch. xxiii.
[6] § 6.   See also ch. xxxvii. 6.

liked him much. I was then so imprudent and so blind as to think it a virtue to be grateful and loyal to one who liked me. Cursed be that loyalty which reaches so far as to go against the law of God. It is a madness common in the world, and it makes me mad to see it. We are indebted to God for all the good that men do to us, and yet we hold it to be an act of virtue not to break a friendship of this kind, though it lead us to go against Him. Oh, blindness of the world! Let me, O Lord, be most ungrateful to the world ; never at all unto Thee. But I have been altogether otherwise through my sins.

10. I procured further information about the matter from members of his household ; I learned more of his ruinous state, and saw that the poor man's fault was not so grave, because the miserable woman had had recourse to enchantments, by giving him a little image made of copper, which she had begged him to wear for love of her around his neck ; and this no one had influence enough to persuade him to throw away. As to this matter of enchantments, I do not believe it to be altogether true ; but I will relate what I saw, by way of warning to men to be on their guard against women who will do things of this kind. And let them be assured of this, that women—for they are more bound to purity than men—if once they have lost all shame before God, are in nothing whatever to be trusted ; and that in exchange for the gratification of their will, and of that affection which the devil suggests, they will hesitate at nothing.

11. Though I have been so wicked myself, I never fell into anything of this kind, nor did I ever attempt to do evil ; nor, if I had the power, would I have ever constrained any one to like me, for our Lord kept me from this. But if He had abandoned me, I should have done wrong in this, as I did in other things—for there is nothing in me whereon any one may rely.

12. When I knew this, I began to show him greater

affection : my intention was good, but the act was wrong, for I ought not to do the least wrong for the sake of any good, how great soever it may be. I spoke to him most frequently of God ; and this must have done him good—though I believe that what touched him most was his great affection for me, because, to do me a pleasure, he gave me that little image of copper, and I had it at once thrown into a river. When he had given it up, like a man roused from deep sleep, he began to consider all that he had done in those years ; and then, amazed at himself, lamenting his ruinous state, that woman came to be hateful in his eyes. Our Lady must have helped him greatly, for he had a very great devotion to her Conception, and used to keep the feast thereof with great solemnity. In short, he broke off all relations with that woman utterly, and was never weary of giving God thanks for the light He had given him ; and at the end of the year from the day I first saw him, he died.

13. He had been most diligent in the service of God ; and as for that great affection he had for me, I never observed anything wrong in it, though it might have been of greater purity. There were also occasions wherein he might have most grievously offended, if he had not kept himself in the near presence of God. As I said before,[7] I would not then have done anything I knew was a mortal sin. And I think that observing this resolution in me helped him to have that affection for me ; for I believe that all men must have a greater affection for those women whom they see disposed to be good : and even for the attainment of earthly ends, women must have more power over men because they are good, as I shall show hereafter. I am convinced that the priest is in the way of salvation. He died most piously, and completely withdrawn from that occasion of sin. It seems that it was the will of our Lord he should be saved by these means.

[7] § 9.

14. I remained three months in that place, in the most grievous sufferings ; for the treatment was too severe for my constitution. In two months—so strong were the medicines—my life was nearly worn out ; and the severity of the pain in the heart,[8] for the cure of which I was there, was much more keen : it seemed to me, now and then, as if it had been seized by sharp teeth. So great was the torment that it was feared it might end in madness. There was a great loss of strength, for I could eat nothing whatever, only drink. I had a great loathing for food, and a fever that never left me. I was so reduced, for they had given me purgatives daily for nearly a month, and so parched up, that my sinews began to shrink. The pains I had were unendurable, and I was overwhelmed in a most deep sadness, so that I had no rest either night or day.

15. This was the result ; and thereupon my father took me back. Then the physicians visited me again. All gave me up ; they said I was also consumptive. This gave me little or no concern ; what distressed me were the pains I had—for I was in pain from my head down to my feet. Now, nervous pains, according to the physicians, are intolerable ; and all my nerves were shrunk. Certainly, if I had not brought this upon myself by my sins, the torture would have been unendurable.

16. I was not more than three months in this cruel distress, for it seemed impossible that so many ills could be borne together. I now am astonished at myself, and the patience His Majesty gave me—for it clearly came from Him—I look upon as a great mercy of our Lord. It was a great help to me to be patient, that I had read the story of Job, in the *Morals* of St. Gregory (our Lord seems to have prepared me thereby); and that I had begun the practice of prayer, so that I might bear it all, conforming my will to the will of God. All my conversation was with God. I had

---

[8] Ch. iv. 6.

continually these words of Job in my thoughts and in my mouth : " If we have received good things of the hand of our Lord, why should we not receive evil things ? " [9]   This seemed to give me courage.

17. The feast of our Lady, in August, came round ; from April until then I had been in great pain, but more especially during the last three months.   I made haste to go to confession, for I had always been very fond of frequent confession.   They thought I was driven by the fear of death ; and so my father, in order to quiet me, would not suffer me to go.   Oh, the unreasonable love of flesh and blood ! Though it was that of a father so Catholic and so wise—he was very much so, and this act of his could not be the effect of any ignorance on his part—what evil it might have done me !

18. That very night my sickness became so acute that for about four days I remained insensible.   They administered the Sacrament of Extreme Unction, and every hour, or rather every moment, thought I was dying ; they did nothing but repeat the *Credo*, as if I could have understood anything they said.   They must have regarded me as dead more than once, for I found afterwards drops of wax on my eyelids.   My father, because he had not allowed me to go to confession, was grievously distressed.   Loud cries and many prayers were made to God : blessed be He Who heard them.

19. For a day and a half the grave was open in my monastery, waiting for my body [10] ; and the friars of our Order, in a house at some distance from this place, performed funeral solemnities.   But it pleased our

---

[9] Job ii. 10 : " Si bona suscepimus de manu Dei, mala quare non suscipiamus ? " The *Moralia* had been translated by Alonso Alvarez de Toledo, and published in 1514.   The volume used and annotated by Saint Teresa (edition of Sevilla, 1527) is still preserved at the convent of St. Joseph, Avila.

[10] Some of the nuns of the Incarnation were in the house, sent thither from the convent ; and, but for the father's disbelief in her death, would have taken her home for burial (*Ribera*, lib. i. cap. iv.).

Lord I should come to myself. I wished to go to confession at once. I communicated with many tears ; but I do not think those tears had their source in that pain and sorrow only for having offended God, which might have sufficed for my salvation—unless, indeed, the delusion which I laboured under were some excuse for me, and into which I had been led by those who had told me that some things were not mortal sins which afterwards I found were so certainly.

20. Though my sufferings were unendurable, and my perceptions dull, yet my confession, I believe, was complete as to all matters wherein I understood myself to have offended God.   This grace, among others, did His Majesty bestow on me, that ever since my first Communion never in confession have I failed to confess anything I thought to be a sin, though it might be only a venial sin. But I think that undoubtedly my salvation was in great peril, if I had died at that time— partly because my confessors were so unlearned, and partly because I was so very wicked.   It is certainly true that when I think of it, and consider how our Lord seems to have raised me up from the dead, I am so filled with wonder that I almost tremble with fear.[11]

21. And now, O my soul, it were well for thee to look that danger in the face from which our Lord delivered thee ; and if thou dost not cease to offend Him out of love, thou shouldst do so out of fear.   He might have slain thee a thousand times, and in a far more perilous state.   I believe I exaggerate nothing if I say a thousand times again, though he may rebuke me who has commanded me to restrain myself in recounting my sins ; and they are glossed over enough. I pray him, for the love of God, not to suppress one of

---

[11] *Ribera*, lib. i. cap. iv., says he heard Fray Bañes, in a sermon, say that the Saint told him she had, during these four days, seen hell in a vision. And the chronicler says that though there was bodily illness, yet it was a trance of the soul at the same time (vol. i. lib. i. cap. xii. 3).

my faults, because herein shines forth the magnificence of God, as well as His long-suffering towards souls. May He be blessed for evermore, and destroy me utterly rather than let me cease to love Him any more!

CHAPTER VI.

THE GREAT DEBT SHE OWED TO OUR LORD FOR HIS MERCY TO HER. SHE TAKES ST. JOSEPH FOR HER PATRON.

Of the great debt she owes God for giving her conformity of will in her trials, and how she turned towards the glorious St. Joseph as her helper and advocate, and how much she profited thereby.

1. AFTER those four days, during which I was insensible, so great was my distress, that our Lord alone knoweth the intolerable sufferings I endured. My tongue was bitten to pieces ; there was a choking in my throat because I had taken nothing, and because of my weakness, so that I could not swallow even a drop of water ; all my bones seemed to be out of joint, and the disorder of my head was extreme. I was bent together like a coil of ropes—for to this was I brought by the torture of those days—unable to move either arm, or foot, or hand, or head, any more than if I had been dead, unless others moved me ; I could move, however, I think, one finger of my right hand. Then, as to touching me, that was impossible, for I was so bruised that I could not endure it. They used to move me in a sheet, one holding one end and another the other. This lasted till Palm Sunday.[1]

[1] March 30, 1539.

2. The only comfort I had was this—if no one came near me, my pains frequently ceased ; and then, because I had a little rest, I considered myself well, for I was afraid my patience would fail ; and thus I was exceedingly happy when I saw myself free from those pains which were so sharp and constant, though in the cold fits of an intermittent fever, which were most violent, they were still unendurable. My dislike of food was very great.

3. I was now so anxious to return to my monastery, that I had myself conveyed thither in the state I was in. There they received alive one whom they had waited for as dead ; but her body was worse than dead ; the sight of it could only give pain. It is impossible to describe my extreme weakness, for I was nothing but bones. I remained in this state, as I have already said,[2] more than eight months ; and was paralytic, though getting better, for about three years. I praised God when I began to crawl on my hands and knees. I bore all this with great resignation, and, if I except the beginning of my illness, with great joy ; for all this was as nothing in comparison with the pains and tortures I had to bear at first. I was resigned to the will of God, even if He left me in this state for ever. My anxiety about the recovery of my health seemed to be grounded on my desire to pray in solitude, as I had been taught ; for there was no means of doing so in the infirmary. I went to confession most frequently, spoke much about God, and in such a way as to edify every one ; and they all marvelled at the patience which our Lord gave me — for if it had not come from the hand of His Majesty, it seemed

---

[2] Ch. v. 17. The Saint left her monastery in the autumn of 1537 and in May 1538 went from her sister's house to Bezadas ; in July she was brought back to her father's house in Avila, wherein she remained till Palm Sunday, 1539, when she returned to the Monastery of the Incarnation. She had been seized with paralysis there, and laboured under it nearly three years, from 1539–1542, when she was miraculously healed through the intercession of St. Joseph.

impossible to endure so great an affliction with so great a joy.

4. It was a great thing for me to have had the grace of prayer which God had wrought in me ; it made me understand what it is to love Him. In a little while I saw these virtues renewed within me ; still they were not strong, for they were not sufficient to sustain me in justice. I never spoke ill in the slightest degree whatever of any one, and my ordinary practice was to avoid all detraction ; for I used to keep most carefully in mind that I ought not to assent to, nor say of another, anything I should not like to have said of myself. I was extremely careful to keep this resolution on all occasions ; though not so perfectly, upon some great occasions that presented themselves, as not to break it sometimes. But my ordinary practice was this : and thus those who were about me, and those with whom I conversed, became so convinced that it was right that they adopted it as a habit. It came to be understood that where I was, absent persons were safe ; so they were also with my friends and kindred, and with those whom I instructed. Still, for all this, I have a strict account to give unto God for the bad example I gave in other respects. May it please His Majesty to forgive me, for I have been the cause of much evil ; though not with intentions as perverse as were the acts that followed.

5. The longing for solitude remained, and I loved to discourse and speak of God ; for if I found any one with whom I could do so, it was a greater joy and satisfaction to me than all the refinements—or rather, to speak more correctly, the real rudeness—of the world's conversation. I comunicated and confessed more frequently still, and desired to do so ; I was extremely fond of reading good books ; I was most deeply penitent for having offended God ; and I remember that very often I did not dare to pray, because I was afraid of that most bitter anguish which I felt

for having offended God, dreading it as a great chastisement. This grew upon me afterwards to so great
a degree, that I know of no torment wherewith to
compare it ; and yet it was neither more nor less
because of any fear I had at any time, for it came upon
me only when I remembered the consolations of our
Lord which He gave me in prayer, the great debt I
owed Him, the evil return I made : I could not bear it.
I was also extremely angry with myself on account of
the many tears I shed for my faults, when I saw how
little I improved, seeing that neither my good resolutions nor the pains I took were sufficient to keep me
from falling whenever I had the opportunity.   I looked
on my tears as a delusion ; and my faults, therefore,
I regarded as the more grievous, because I saw the
great goodness of our Lord to me in the shedding
of those tears, and together with them such deep
compunction.

6. I took care to go to confession as soon as I
could ; and, as I think, did all that was possible on
my part to return to a state of grace.   But the whole
evil lay in my not thoroughly avoiding the occasions
of sin, and in my confessors, who helped me so little.
If they had told me that I was travelling on a
dangerous road, and that I was bound to abstain from
those conversations, I believe, without any doubt, that
the matter would have been remedied, because I could
not bear to remain even for one day in mortal sin, if
I knew it.

7. All these tokens of the fear of God came to me
through prayer ; and the greatest of them was this,
that fear was swallowed up of love—for I never thought
of chastisement.   All the time I was so ill, my strict
watch over my conscience reached to all that is mortal
sin.

8. O my God !   I wished for health, that I might
serve Thee better ; that was the cause of all my ruin.
For when I saw how helpless I was through paralysis,

being still so young, and how the physicians of this world had dealt with me, I determined to ask those of heaven to help me—for I wished, nevertheless, to be well, though I bore my illness with great joy. Sometimes, too, I used to think that if I recovered my health, and yet were lost for ever, I was better as I was. But, for all that, I thought I might serve God much better if I were well. This is our delusion ; we do not resign ourselves absolutely to the disposition of our Lord, Who knows best what is for our good.

9. I began by having Masses and prayers said for my intention—prayers that were highly sanctioned ; for I never liked those other devotions which some people, especially women, make use of with a ceremoniousness to me intolerable, but which moves them to be devout. I have been given to understand since that they were unseemly and superstitious ; and I took for my patron and lord the glorious St. Joseph, and recommended myself earnestly to him. I saw clearly that both out of this my present trouble, and out of others of greater importance, relating to my honour and the loss of my soul, this my father and lord delivered me, and rendered me greater services than I knew how to ask for. I cannot call to mind that I have ever asked him at any time for anything which he has not granted ; and I am filled with amazement when I consider the great favours which God hath given me through this blessed Saint ; the dangers from which he hath delivered me, both of body and of soul. To other Saints our Lord seems to have given grace to succour men in some special necessity ; but to this glorious Saint, I know by experience, to help us in all : and our Lord would have us understand that, as He was Himself subject to him upon earth—for St. Joseph, having the title of father, and being His guardian, could command Him—so now in heaven He performs all his petitions. I have asked others to recommend

themselves to St. Joseph, and they too know this by experience ; and there are many who are now of late devout to him,[3] having had experience of this truth.

10. I used to keep his feast with all the solemnity I could, but with more vanity than spirituality, seeking rather too much splendour and effect, and yet with good intentions. I had this evil in me, that if our Lord gave me grace to do any good, that good became full of imperfections, and of many faults ; but as for doing wrong, the indulgence of curiosity and vanity, I was very skilful and active therein. Our Lord forgive me !

11. Would that I could persuade all men to be devout to this glorious Saint ; for I know by long experience what blessings he can obtain for us from God. I have never known any one who was really devout to him, and who honoured him by particular services, who did not visibly grow more and more in virtue ; for he helps in a special way those souls who commend themselves to him. It is now some years since I have always on his feast asked him for something, and I always have it. If the petition be in any way amiss, he directs it aright for my greater good

12. If I were a person who had authority to write, it would be a pleasure to me to be diffusive in speaking most minutely of the graces which this glorious Saint has obtained for me and for others. But that I may not go beyond the commandment that is laid upon me, I must in many things be more brief than I could wish, and more diffusive than is necessary in others ; for, in

---

[3] Of the devotion to St. Joseph, F. Faber (*The Blessed Sacrament*, bk. ii. p. 199, 3rd ed.) says that "it spread over the Church. Gerson was raised up to be its doctor and theologian, and St. Teresa to be its Saint, and St. Francis of Sales to be its popular teacher and missionary. The houses of Carmel were like the holy house of Nazareth to it ; and the colleges of the Jesuits, its peaceful sojourns in dark Egypt." The assertion, frequently made, that the veneration of St. Joseph was brought by the Carmelites from the East is, however, not borne out by evidence.

short, I am a person who, in all that is good, has but little discretion. But I ask, for the love of God, that he who does not believe me will make the trial for himself—when he will see, by experience, the great good that results from commending oneself to this glorious patriarch, and being devout to him. Those who give themselves to prayer should in a special manner have always a devotion to St. Joseph; for I know not how any man can think of the Queen of the angels, during the time that she suffered so much with the infant Jesus, without giving thanks to St. Joseph for the services he rendered them then. He who cannot find any one to teach him how to pray, let him take this glorious Saint for his master, and he will not wander out of the way.

13. May it please our Lord that I have not done amiss in venturing to speak about St. Joseph; for, though I publicly profess my devotion to him, I have always failed in my service to him and imitation of him. He was like himself when he made me able to rise and walk, no longer a paralytic; and I, too, am like myself when I make so bad a use of this grace.

14. Who could have said that I was so soon to fall, after such great consolations from God—after His Majesty had implanted virtues in me which of themselves made me serve Him—after I had been, as it were, dead, and in such extreme peril of eternal damnation—after He had raised me up, soul and body, so that all who saw me marvelled to see me alive? What can it mean, O my Lord? The life we live is so full of danger! While I am writing this—and it seems to me, too, by Thy grace and mercy—I may say with St. Paul, though not so truly as he did: "It is not I who live now, but Thou, my Creator, livest in me." [4] For some years past, so it seems to me, Thou

---

[4] Galat. ii. 20 : "Vivo autem, jam non ego ; vivit vero in me Christus."

hast held me by the hand ; and I see in myself desires and resolutions—in some measure tested by experience in many ways, during that time—never to do anything, however slight it may be, contrary to Thy will, though I must have frequently offended Thy Divine Majesty without being aware of it ; and I also think that nothing can be proposed to me that I should not with great resolution undertake for Thy love. In some things Thou hast Thyself helped me to succeed therein. I love neither the world, nor the things of the world ; nor do I believe that anything that does not come from Thee can give me pleasure ; everything else seems to me a heavy cross.

15. Still, I may easily deceive myself, and it may be that I am not what I say I am; but Thou knowest, O my Lord, that, to the best of my knowledge, I lie not. I am afraid, and with good reason, lest Thou shouldst abandon me ; for I know now how far my strength and little virtue can reach, if Thou be not ever at hand to supply them, and to help me never to forsake Thee. May His Majesty grant that I be not forsaken of Thee even now, when I am thinking all this of myself !

16. I know not how we can wish to live, seeing that everything is so uncertain. Once, O Lord, I thought it impossible to forsake Thee so utterly ; and now that I have forsaken Thee so often, I cannot help being afraid ; for when Thou didst withdraw but a little from me, I fell down to the ground at once. Blessed for ever be Thou ! Though I have forsaken Thee, Thou hast not forsaken me so utterly but that Thou hast come again and raised me up, giving me Thy hand always. Very often, O Lord, I would not take it ; very often I would not listen when Thou wert calling me again, as I am going to show.

CHAPTER VII.

LUKEWARMNESS.   THE LOSS OF GRACE.   INCONVENI-
ENCE OF LAXITY IN RELIGIOUS HOUSES.

*Of the way whereby she lost the graces God had granted
her, and the wretched life she began to lead; she also
speaks of the danger arising from the want of a strict
enclosure in convents of nuns.*

1. So, then, going on from pastime to pastime, from
vanity to vanity, from one occasion of sin to another,
I began to expose myself exceedingly to the very
greatest dangers : my soul was so distracted by many
vanities that I was ashamed to draw near unto God in
an act of such special friendship as that of prayer.[1]
As my sins multiplied, I began to lose the pleasure and
comfort I had in virtuous things : and that loss contributed to the abandonment of prayer.   I see now
most clearly, O my Lord, that this comfort departed
from me because I had departed from Thee.

2. It was the most fearful delusion into which Satan
could plunge me—to give up prayer under the pretence
of humility.   I began to be afraid of giving myself to
prayer, because I saw myself so lost.   I thought it
would be better for me, seeing that in my wickedness
I was one of the most wicked, to live like the multitude—to say the prayers which I was bound to say,
and that vocally; not to practise mental prayer nor
commune with God so much; for I deserved to be
with the devils, and was deceiving those who were
about me, because I made an outward show of goodness.   And therefore the community in which I dwelt
is not to be blamed, for with my cunning I so managed
matters, that all had a good opinion of me ; and yet

[1] See *Way of Perfection*, ch. xxviii. 3.

I did not seek this deliberately by simulating devotion, for in all that relates to hypocrisy and ostentation—glory be to God!—I do not remember that I ever offended Him,[2] so far as I know. The very first movements herein gave me such pain, that the devil would depart from me with loss, and the gain remained with me ; and thus, accordingly, he never tempted me much in this way. Perhaps, however, if God had permitted Satan to tempt me as sharply herein as he tempted me in other things, I should have fallen also into this ; but His Majesty has preserved me until now. May He be blessed for evermore ! It was rather a heavy affliction to me that I should be thought so well of ; for I knew my own secret.

3. The reason why they thought I was not so wicked was this : they saw that I, who was so young and exposed to so many occasions of sin, withdrew myself so often into solitude for prayer, read much, spoke of God, that I liked to have His image painted in many places, to have an oratory of my own, and furnish it with objects of devotion, that I spoke ill of no one, and other things of the same kind in me which have the appearance of virtue. Yet all the while—I was so vain—I knew how to procure respect for myself by doing those things which in the world are usually regarded with respect.

4. In consequence of this, they gave me as much liberty as they did to the oldest nuns, and even more, and had great confidence in me ; for as to taking any liberty for myself, or doing anything without leave—such as conversing through the door, or in secret, or by night[3]—I do not think I could have brought myself to speak with anybody in the monastery in that way, and I never did it ; for our Lord held me back. It seemed to me—for I considered many things carefully and of set purpose—that it would be a very evil deed

[2] See *Relation* i. 18.
[3] The Rule enjoins silence from Compline until Prime of the next day.

on my part, wicked as I was, to risk the credit of so many nuns, who were all good—as if everything else I did was well done ! In truth, the evil I did was not the result of deliberation, as this would have been, if I had done it, although it was too much so.

5. Therefore, I think that it did me much harm to be in a monastery not enclosed. The liberty which those who were good might have with advantage—they not being obliged to do more than they do, because they had not bound themselves to enclosure—would certainly have led me, who am wicked, straight to hell, if our Lord, by so many remedies and means of His most singular mercy, had not delivered me out of that danger—and it is, I believe, the very greatest danger—namely, a monastery of women unenclosed—yea, more, I think it is, for those who will be wicked, a road to hell rather than a help to their weakness. This is not to be understood of my monastery ; for there are so many there who in the utmost sincerity, and in great perfection, serve our Lord, so that His Majesty, according to His goodness, cannot but be gracious unto them. Neither is it one of those which are most open : for all religious observances are kept in it ; and I am speaking only of others which I have seen and known.

6. I am exceedingly sorry for these houses, because our Lord must of necessity send His special inspirations not merely once, but many times, if the nuns therein are to be saved, seeing that the honours and amusements of the world are allowed among them, and the obligations of their state are so ill-understood. God grant they may not count that to be virtue which is sin, as I did so often ! It is very difficult to make people understand this ; it is necessary our Lord Himself should take the matter seriously into His own hands.

7. If parents would take my advice, now that they are at no pains to place their daughters where they may walk in the way of salvation without incurring a greater

risk than they would do if they were left in the world,
let them look at least at that which concerns their good
name. Let them marry them to persons of a much
lower degree rather than place them in monasteries of
this kind, unless they be of extremely good inclinations, and God grant that these inclinations may come
to good ! or let them keep them at home.[4] If they will
be wicked at home, their evil life can be hidden only for
a short time ; but in monasteries it can be hidden long,
and, in the end, it is our Lord that discovers it.   They
injure not only themselves, but all the nuns also.   And
all the while the poor things are not in fault ; for they
walk in the way that is shown them.   Many of them
are to be pitied ; for they wished to withdraw from the
world, and, thinking to escape from the dangers of it,
and that they were going to serve our Lord, have
found themselves in ten worlds at once, without knowing what to do, or how to help themselves.   Youth
and sensuality and the devil invite them and incline
them to follow certain ways which are of the essence
of worldliness.   They see these ways, so to speak, considered as safe there.

8. Now, these seem to me to be in some degree like
those wretched heretics who will make themselves
blind, and who will consider that which they do to be
good, and so believe, but without really believing ; for
they have within themselves something that tells them
it is wrong.

9. Oh, what utter ruin ! utter ruin of religious
persons—I am not speaking now more of women than
of men—where the rules of the Order are not kept ;
where the same monastery offers two roads : one of
virtue and observance, the other of inobservance, and
both equally frequented ! I have spoken incorrectly ;
they are not equally frequented ; for, on account of
our sins, the way of the greatest imperfection is the
most frequented ; and because it is the broadest, it is

[4] *Way of Perfection*, ch. viii. 1.

also the most in favour. The way of religious observance is so little used, that the friar and the nun who
would really begin to follow their vocation thoroughly
have reason to fear the members of their communities
more than all the devils together. They must be more
cautious, and dissemble more, when they would speak
of that friendship with God which they desire to have,
than when they would speak of those friendships and
affections which the devil arranges in monasteries. I
know not why we are astonished that the Church is in
so much trouble, when we see those, who ought to be an
example of every virtue to others, so disfigure the work
which the spirit of the Saints departed wrought in
their Orders. May it please His Divine Majesty to
apply a remedy to this, as He sees it to be needful!
Amen.

10. So, then, when I began to indulge in these
conversations, I did not think, seeing they were customary, that my soul must be injured and dissipated,
as I afterwards found it must be, by such conversations. I thought that, as receiving visits was so
common in many monasteries, no more harm would
befall me thereby than befell others, whom I knew to
be good. I did not observe that they were much better
than I was, and that an act which was perilous for me
was not so perilous for them ; and yet I have no doubt
there was some danger in it, were it nothing else but
a waste of time.

11. I was once with a person—it was at the very
beginning of my acquaintance with her—when our
Lord was pleased to show me that these friendships
were not good for me : to warn me also, and in my
blindness, which was so great, to give me light. Christ
stood before me, stern and grave, giving me to understand what in my conduct was offensive to Him. I
saw Him with the eyes of the soul more distinctly than
I could have seen Him with the eyes of the body. The
vision made so deep an impression upon me that,

though it is more than twenty-six years ago, I seem
to see Him present even now.   I was greatly astonished
and disturbed, and I resolved not to see that person
again.

12. It did me much harm that I did not then know
it was possible to see anything otherwise than with the
eyes of the body [5] ; so did Satan too, in that he helped
me to think so : he made me understand it to be
impossible, and suggested that I had imagined the
vision—that it might be Satan himself—and other
suppositions of that kind.   For all this, the impression
remained with me that the vision was from God, and
not an imagination ; but, as it was not to my liking, I
forced myself to lie to myself ; and, as I did not dare to
discuss the matter with any one, and as great importunity was used, I went back to my former conversation with the same person, and with others also, at
different times ; for I was assured that there was no
harm in seeing such a person, and that I gained, instead of losing, reputation by doing so.   I spent many
years in this pestilent amusement ; for it never appeared to me, when I was engaged in it, to be so bad
as it really was, though at times I saw clearly it was no
good.   But no one caused me the same distraction
which that person did of whom I am speaking ; and
that was because I had a great affection for her.

13. At another time, when I was with that person,
we saw, both of us, and others who were present also
saw, something like a great toad crawling towards us,
more rapidly than such a creature is in the habit of
crawling.   I cannot understand how a reptile of that
kind could, in the middle of the day, have come forth
from that place ; it never had done so before,[6] but the

[5] See ch. xxvii. 3.   As this passage cannot have been written later than
the second half of 1564, and, perhaps, was written earlier, the event, assuming
her count of years to be correct, would have taken place in 1537, that is,
before the Saint left the convent for her cure at Bezadas.

[6] In one of the parlours of the Monastery of the Incarnation at Avila a
painting of this is preserved to this day.

impression it made on me was such that I think it
must have had a meaning ; neither have I ever forgotten it. Oh the greatness of God ! with what care
and tenderness didst Thou warn me in every way !
and how little I profited by those warnings !

14. There was in that house a nun who was related
to me, now grown old, a great servant of God, and a
strict observer of the rule. She too warned me from
time to time ; but I not only did not listen to her, but
was even offended, thinking she was scandalized without cause. I have mentioned this in order that my
wickedness and the great goodness of God might be
understood, and to show how much I deserved hell for
ingratitude so great, and, moreover, if it should be our
Lord's will and pleasure that any nun at any time
should read this, that she might take warning by me.
I beseech them all, for the love of our Lord, to flee from
such recreations as these.

15. May His Majesty grant I may undeceive some
one of the many I led astray when I told them there
was no harm in these things, and assured them there
was no such great danger therein. I did so because
I was blind myself ; for I would not deliberately
lead them astray. By the bad example I set before
them—I spoke of this before [7]—I was the occasion
of much evil, not thinking I was doing so much
harm.

16. In those early days, when I was ill, and before I
knew how to be of use to myself, I had a very strong
desire to further the progress of others [8] : a most common temptation of beginners. With me, however, it
had good results. Loving my father so much, I longed
to see him in the possession of that good which I
seemed to derive myself from prayer. I thought that
in this life there could not be a greater good than

[7] Ch. vi. 4.
[8] See *Interior Castle*, M. v. ch. iii. 1 ; *Way of Perfection*, ch. xli. 8.

prayer ; and so, by roundabout ways, as well as I could, I contrived to make him enter upon it ; I gave him books for that end.   As he was so good—I said so before[9]—this exercise took such a hold upon him that in five or six years, I think it was, he made so great a progress that I used to praise our Lord for it. It was a very great consolation to me.   He had most grievous trials of diverse kinds, and he bore them all with the greatest resignation.   He came often to see me, for it was a comfort to him to speak of the things of God.

17. And now that I had become so dissipated, and had ceased to pray, and yet saw that he still thought I was what I used to be, I could not endure it, and so undeceived him.   I had been a year and more without praying, thinking it an act of greater humility to abstain.   This—I shall speak of it again[10]—was the greatest temptation I ever had, because it very nearly wrought my utter ruin[11] ; for, when I used to pray, if I offended God one day, on the following days I would recollect myself, and withdraw farther from the occasions of sin.

18. When that blessed man, having that good opinion of me, came to visit me, it pained me to see him so deceived as to think that I used to pray to God as before.   So I told him that I did not pray ; but I did not tell him why.   I put my infirmities forward as an excuse ; for, though I had recovered from that which was so troublesome, I have always been weak, even very much so ; and though my infirmities are somewhat less troublesome now than they were, they still afflict me in many ways ; specially, I have been suffering for twenty years from sickness every morning,[12] so that I could not take any food till past midday, and even occasionally not till later ; and now, since my Communions have become more frequent, it

---

[9] Ch. i. 1.   [10] Ch. xix. 9, 17.   [11] See § 2, above.
[12] See ch. xi. 23 ; *Interior Castle*, M. vi. ch. i. 14.

is at night, before I lie down to rest, that the sickness occurs, and with greater pain ; for I have to bring it on with a feather, or other means. If I do not bring it on, I suffer more ; and thus I am never, I believe, free from great pain, which is sometimes very acute, especially about the heart ; though the fainting-fits are now but of rare occurrence. I am also, these eight years past, free from the paralysis, and from other infirmities of fever, which I had so often. These afflictions I now regard so lightly, that I am even glad of them, believing that our Lord in some degree takes His pleasure in them.

19. My father believed me when I gave him that for a reason, as he never told a lie himself ; neither should I have done so, considering the relation we were in. I told him, in order to be the more easily believed, that it was much for me to be able to attend in choir, though I saw clearly that this was no excuse whatever ; neither, however, was it a sufficient reason for giving up a practice which does not require, of necessity, bodily strength, but only love and a habit thereof ; yet our Lord always furnishes an opportunity for it, if we but seek it. I say always ; for though there may be times, as in illness, and from other causes, when we cannot be much alone, yet it can never be but there must be opportunities when our strength is sufficient for the purpose ; and in sickness itself, and amidst other hindrances, true prayer consists, when the soul loves, in offering up its burden and in thinking of Him for Whom it suffers, and in the resignation of the will, and in a thousand ways which then present themselves. It is under these circumstances that love exerts itself ; for it is not necessarily prayer when we are alone ; and neither is it not prayer when we are not.

20. With a little care, we may find great blessings on those occasions when our Lord, by means of afflictions, deprives us of time for prayer ; and so I found it when I had a good conscience. But my father, having

that opinion of me which he had, and because of the
love he bore me, believed all I told him ; moreover,
he was sorry for me ; and, as he had now risen to great
heights of prayer himself, he never remained with me
long ; for when he had seen me he went his way,
saying that he was wasting time. As I was wasting
it in other vanities, I cared little about this.

21. My father was not the only person whom I prevailed upon to practise prayer, though I was walking in
vanity myself. When I saw persons fond of reciting
their prayers, I showed them how to make a meditation, and helped them and gave them books ; for from
the time I began myself to pray, as I said before,[13] I
always had a desire that others should serve God. I
thought, now that I did not myself serve our Lord
according to the light I had, that the knowledge His
Majesty had given me ought not to be lost, and that
others should serve Him for me.[14] I say this in order
to explain the great blindness I was in : going to ruin
myself, and labouring to save others.

22. At this time, that illness befell my father of
which he died[15] ; it lasted some days. I went to nurse
him, being more sick in spirit than he was in body,
owing to my many vanities—though not, so far as I
know, to the extent of being in mortal sin—through
the whole of that wretched time of which I am speaking ; for, if I knew myself to be in mortal sin, I would
not have continued in it on any account. I suffered
much myself during his illness. I believe I rendered
him some service in return for what he had suffered in
mine. Though I was very ill, I did violence to myself ;
and though in losing him I was to lose all the comfort
and good of my life—he was all this to me—I was so
courageous that I never betrayed my sorrows, concealing them till he was dead, as if I felt none at all.
It seemed as if my very soul were wrenched when I

---

[13] § 16.   [14] See *Interior Castle*, M. v. ch. iii. 2.
[15] Towards the end of 1543.

saw him at the point of death—my love for him was so deep.

23. It was a matter for which we ought to praise our Lord—the death that he died, and the desire he had to die ; so also was the advice he gave us after the last anointing, how he charged us to recommend him to God, and to pray for mercy for him, how he bade us serve God always, and consider how all things come to an end. He told us, with tears, how sorry he was that he had not served Him himself ; for he wished he was a friar—I mean, that he had been one in the strictest Order that is. I have a most assured conviction that our Lord, some fifteen days before, had revealed to him he was not to live ; for up to that time, though very ill, he did not think so ; but now, though he was somewhat better, and the physicians said so, he gave no heed to them, but employed himself in the ordering of his soul.

24. His chief suffering consisted in a most acute pain of the shoulders, which never left him : it was so sharp at times, that it put him into great torture. I said to him that, as he had so great a devotion to our Lord carrying His cross on His shoulders, he should now think that His Majesty wished him to feel somewhat of that pain which He then suffered Himself. This so comforted him that I do not think I heard him complain afterwards.

25. He remained three days without consciousness ; but on the day he died our Lord restored him so completely, that we were astonished : he preserved his understanding to the last ; for in the middle of the creed, which he repeated himself, he died.[16] He lay there like an angel—such he seemed to me, if I may

[16] Don Alfonso Sanchez de Cepeda, being seriously ill, made his last will Dec. 3, 1543, and died Feb. 1 of the following year. He was buried in the Franciscan church situated not far from the Convent of the Incarnation. When the Saint says that he expressed the wish of having been a friar of one of the strictest Orders she probably meant the Reformed Franciscans of St. Peter of Alcantara.

say so, both in soul and disposition : he was very
good.

26. I know not why I have said this unless it be
for the purpose of showing how much the more I am to
be blamed for my wickedness ; for after seeing such a
death, and knowing what his life had been, I, in order
to be in any wise like unto such a father, ought to have
grown better. His confessor, a most learned Dominican,[17] used to say that he had no doubt he went
straight to heaven.[18] He had heard his confession for
some years, and spoke with praise of the purity of his
conscience.

27. This Dominican father, who was a very good
man, fearing God, did me a very great service ; for I
confessed to him. He took upon himself the task of
helping my soul in earnest, and of making me see the
perilous state I was in.[19] He sent me to Communion
once a fortnight [20] ; and I, by degrees beginning to
speak to him, told him about my prayer. He charged
me never to omit it : that, anyhow, it could not do me
anything but good. I began to return to it—though I
did not cut off the occasions of sin—and never afterwards gave it up. My life became most wretched,
because I learned in prayer more and more of my
faults. On one side God was calling me, on the
other, I was following the world. All the things of God
gave me great pleasure ; and I was a prisoner to the
things of the world. It seemed as if I wished to
reconcile two contradictions, so much at variance one
with another as are the life of the spirit and the joys
and pleasures and amusements of sense.[21]

28. I suffered much in prayer ; for the spirit was
slave, and not master ; and so I was not able to shut

[17] F. Vicente Baron.   [18] See ch. xxxviii. 1.   [19] See ch. xix. 19.
[20] Frequent communion was not then customary. The Constitutions
of the Order prescribed ten or twelve communions a year, and allowed
the more fervent members' Communion on the great feasts or even on ordinary
Sundays.   [21] See ch. xiii. 7, 8.

myself up within myself—that was my whole method
of prayer—without shutting up with me a thousand
vanities at the same time. I spent many years in this
way ; and I am now astonished that any one could
have borne it without abandoning either the one or
the other. I know well that it was not in my power
then to give up prayer, because He held me in His
hand Who sought me that He might show me greater
mercies.

29. O my God ! if I might, I would speak of the
occasions from which God delivered me, and how I
threw myself into them again ; and of the risks I ran
of losing utterly my good name, from which He delivered me. I did things to show what I was ; and our
Lord hid the evil, and revealed some little virtue—if so
be I had any—and made it great in the eyes of all, so
that they always held me in much honour. For
although my follies came occasionally into light, people
would not believe it when they saw other things, which
they thought good. The reason is, that He Who
knoweth all things saw it was necessary it should be so,
in order that I might have some credit given me by
those to whom in after-years I was to speak of His
service. His supreme munificence regarded not my
great sins, but rather the desires I frequently had to
please Him, and the pain I felt because I had not the
strength to bring those desires to good effect !

30. O Lord of my soul ! how shall I be able to
magnify the graces which Thou, in those years, didst
bestow upon me ? Oh how, at the very time that I
offended Thee most, Thou didst prepare me in a
moment, by a most profound compunction, to taste of
the sweetness of Thy consolations and mercies ! In
truth, O my King, Thou didst administer to me the
most delicate and painful chastisement it was possible
for me to bear ; for Thou knewest well what would have
given me the most pain. Thou didst chastise my sins
with great consolations. I do not believe I am say-

ing foolish things, though it may well be that I am beside myself whenever I call to mind my ingratitude and my wickedness.

31. It was more painful for me, in the state I was in, to receive graces, when I had fallen into grievous faults, than it would have been to receive chastisement ; for one of those faults I am sure used to bring me low, shame and distress me, more than many diseases, together with many heavy trials, could have done. For, as to the latter, I saw that I deserved them ; and it seemed to me that by them I was making some reparation for my sins, though it was but slight, for my sins are so many. But when I see myself receive graces anew, after being so ungrateful for those already received, that is to me—and, I believe, to all who have any knowledge or love of God—a fearful kind of torment. We may see how true this is by considering what a virtuous mind must be. Hence my tears and vexation when I reflected on what I felt, seeing myself in a condition to fall at every moment, though my resolutions and desires then—I am speaking of that time—were strong.

32. It is a great evil for a soul to be alone in the midst of such great dangers ; it seems to me that if I had had any one with whom I could have spoken of all this, it might have helped me not to fall. I might, at least, have been ashamed before him—and yet I was not ashamed before God.

33. For this reason I would advise those who give themselves to prayer, particularly at first, to form friendships and converse familiarly with others who are doing the same thing. It is a matter of the last importance, even if it lead only to helping one another by prayer : how much more, seeing that it has led to much greater gain ! Now, if in their intercourse one with another, and in the indulgence of human affections even not of the best kind, men seek friends with whom they may refresh themselves, and for the purpose

of having greater satisfaction in speaking of their empty joys, I know no reason why it should not be lawful for him who is beginning to love and serve God in earnest to confide to another his joys and sorrows ; for they who are given to prayer are thoroughly accustomed to both.

34. For if that friendship with God which he desires be real, let him not be afraid of vain-glory ; and if the first movements thereof assail him, he will escape from it with merit ; and I believe that he who will discuss the matter with this intention will profit both himself and those who hear him, and thus will derive more light for his own understanding, as well as for the instruction of his friends. He who in discussing his method of prayer falls into vain-glory will do so also when he hears Mass devoutly, if he is seen of men, and in doing other good works, which must be done under pain of being no Christian ; and yet these things must not be omitted through fear of vain-glory.

35. Moreover, it is a most important matter for those souls who are not strong in virtue ; for they have so many people, enemies as well as friends, to urge them the wrong way, that I do not see how this point is capable of exaggeration. It seems to me that Satan has employed this artifice—and it is of the greatest service to him—namely, that men who really wish to love and please God should hide the fact, while others, at his suggestion, make open show of their malicious dispositions ; and this is so common, that it seems a matter of boasting now, and the offences committed against God are thus published abroad.

36. I do not know whether the things I am saying are foolish or not. If they be so, your reverence will strike them out. I entreat you to help my simplicity by adding a good deal to this, because the things that relate to the service of God are so feebly managed, that it is necessary for those who would serve Him to join shoulder to shoulder, if they are to advance at all ; for

it is considered safe to live amidst the vanities and pleasures of the world, and few there be who regard them with unfavourable eyes. But if any one begins to give himself up to the service of God, there are so many to find fault with him, that it becomes necessary for him to seek companions in order that he may find protection among them till he grows strong enough not to feel what he may be made to suffer. If he does not, he will find himself in great straits.

37. This, I believe, must have been the reason why some of the Saints withdrew into the desert. And it is a kind of humility in man not to trust to himself, but to believe that God will help him in his relations with those with whom he converses ; and charity grows by being diffused ; and there are a thousand blessings herein which I would not dare to speak of, if I had not known by experience the great importance of it. It is very true that I am the most wicked and the basest of all who are born of women ; but I believe that he who, humbling himself, though strong, yet trusteth not in himself, and believeth another who in this matter has had experience, will lose nothing. Of myself I may say that, if our Lord had not revealed to me this truth, and given me the opportunity of speaking very frequently to persons given to prayer, I should have gone on falling and rising till I tumbled into hell. I had many friends to help me to fall ; but as to rising again, I was so much left to myself that I wonder now I was not always on the ground. I praise God for His mercy ; for it was He only Who stretched out His hand to me. May He be blessed for ever ! Amen.

CHAPTER VIII.

THE SAINT CEASES NOT TO PRAY. PRAYER THE WAY
TO RECOVER WHAT IS LOST. ALL EXHORTED TO
PRAY. THE GREAT ADVANTAGE OF PRAYER, EVEN
TO THOSE WHO MAY HAVE CEASED FROM IT.

*Of the great advantages she derived from not entirely
abandoning prayer so as not to lose her soul ; and what
an excellent remedy this is, in order to win back what
one has lost. She exhorts everybody to practise prayer,
and shows what a gain it is, even if one should have given
it up for a time, to make use of so great a good.*

1. IT is not without reason that I have dwelt so long
on this portion of my life. I see clearly that it will
give no one pleasure to see anything so base ; and certainly I wish those who may read this to have me in
abhorrence, as a soul so obstinate and so ungrateful to
Him Who did so much for me. I could wish, too, I had
permission to say how often at this time I failed in my
duty to God, because I was not leaning on the strong
pillar of prayer. I passed nearly twenty years on this
stormy sea, falling and rising, but rising to no good purpose, seeing that I went and fell again. My life was
one of perfection ; but it was so mean that I scarcely
made any account whatever of venial sins, and though
of mortal sins I was afraid, I was not so afraid of them
as I ought to have been, because I did not avoid the
perilous occasions of them. I may say that it was the
most painful life that can be imagined, because I had
no sweetness in God and no pleasure in the world.

2. When I was in the midst of the pleasures of the
world, the remembrance of what I owed to God made
me sad, and when I was praying to God my worldly
affections disturbed me. This is so painful a struggle
that I know not how I could have borne it for a month,

let alone for so many years. Nevertheless, I can trace distinctly the great mercy of our Lord to me, while thus immersed in the world, in that I had still the courage to pray. I say courage, because I know of nothing in the whole world which requires greater courage than plotting treason against the King, knowing that He knows it, and yet never withdrawing from His presence ; for, granting that we are always in the presence of God, yet it seems to me that those who pray are in His presence in a very different sense ; for they, as it were, see that He is looking upon them, while others may be for days together without even once recollecting that God sees them.

3. It is true, indeed, that during these years there were many months, and, I believe, occasionally a whole year, in which I so kept guard over myself that I did not offend our Lord, gave myself much to prayer, and took some pains, and that successfully, not to offend Him. I speak of this now because all I am saying is strictly true ; but I remember very little of those good days, and so they must have been few, while my evil days were many. Still, the days that passed over without my spending a great part of them in prayer were few, unless I was very ill, or very much occupied.

4. When I was ill, I was well with God. I contrived that those about me should be so, too, and I made supplications to our Lord for this grace, and spoke frequently of Him. Thus, with the exception of that year of which I have been speaking, during eight and twenty years of prayer, I spent more than eighteen in that strife and contention which arose out of my attempts to reconcile God and the world. As to the other years, of which I have now to speak, in them the grounds of the warfare, though it was not slight, were changed ; but inasmuch as I was—at least, I think so— serving God, and aware of the vanity of the world, all has been pleasant, as I shall show hereafter.[1]

<hr />

[1] Ch. ix. 10.

5. The reason, then, of my telling this at so great a length is that, as I have just said,[2] the mercy of God and my ingratitude, on the one hand, may become known ; and, on the other, that men may understand how great is the good which God works in a soul when He gives it a disposition to pray in earnest, though it may not be so well prepared as it ought to be. If that soul perseveres in spite of sins, temptations, and relapses, brought about in a thousand ways by Satan, our Lord will bring it at last—I am certain of it—to the harbour of salvation, as He has brought me myself ; for so it seems to me now. May His Majesty grant I may never go back and be lost ! He who gives himself to prayer is in possession of a great blessing, of which many saintly and good men have written—I am speaking of mental prayer—glory be to God for it ! and, if they had not done so, I am not proud enough, though I have but little humility, to presume to discuss it.

6. I may speak of that which I know by experience ; and so, I say, let him never cease from prayer who has once begun it, be his life ever so wicked ; for prayer is the way to amend it, and without prayer such amendment will be much more difficult. Let him not be tempted by Satan, as I was, to give it up, on the pretence of humility[3] ; let him rather believe that His words are true Who says that, if we truly repent, and resolve never to offend Him, He will take us into His favour again,[4] give us the graces He gave us before, and occasionally even greater, if our repentance deserve it. And as to him who has not begun to pray, I implore him by the love of our Lord not to deprive himself of so great a good.

7. Herein there is nothing to be afraid of, but everything to hope for. Granting that such a one does

---

[2] § 1, above.   [3] Ch. vii. 17 ; ch. xix. 8.
[4] Ezech. xviii. 21 : " Si autem impius egerit pœnitentiam, . . . vita vivet, et non morietur. Omnium iniquitatum ejus . . . non recordabor."

not advance, nor make an effort to become perfect, so as to merit the joys and consolations which the perfect receive from God, yet he will by little and little attain to a knowledge of the road which leads to heaven. And, if he perseveres, I hope in the mercy of God for him, seeing that no one ever took Him for his friend that was not amply rewarded ; for mental prayer is nothing else, in my opinion, but being on terms of friendship with God, frequently conversing in secret with Him Who, we know, loves us. Now, true love and lasting friendship require certain dispositions : those of our Lord, we know, are absolutely perfect ; ours, vicious, sensual, and thankless ; and you cannot, therefore, bring yourselves to love Him, as He loves you, because you have not the disposition to do so ; and if you do not love Him, yet, seeing how much it concerns you to have His friendship, and how great is His love for you, rise above that pain you feel at being much with Him Who is so different from you.

8. O infinite Goodness of my God ! I seem to see Thee and myself in this relation to one another. O Joy of the angels ! when I consider it, I wish I could wholly die of love ! How true it is that Thou endurest those who will not endure Thee ! Oh, how good a friend art Thou, O my Lord ! how Thou comfortest and endurest, and also waitest for them to make themselves like unto Thee, and yet, in the meanwhile, art Thyself so patient of the state they are in ! Thou takest into account the occasions during which they seek Thee, and for a moment of penitence forgettest their offences against Thyself.

9. I have seen this distinctly in my own case, and I cannot tell why the whole world does not labour to draw near to Thee in this particular friendship. The wicked, who do not resemble Thee, ought to do so, in order that Thou mayest make them good, and for that purpose should permit Thee to remain with them at least for two hours daily, even though they may not

remain with Thee but, as I used to do, with a thousand distractions, and with worldly thoughts. In return for this violence which they offer to themselves for the purpose of remaining in a company so good as Thine—for at first they can do no more, and even afterwards at times—Thou, O Lord, defendest them against the assaults of evil spirits, whose power Thou restrainest, and even lessenest daily, giving to them the victory over these enemies. So it is, O Life of all lives, Thou slayest none that put their trust in Thee, and seek Thy friendship ; yea, rather, Thou sustainest their bodily life in greater vigour, and makest their soul to live.

10. I do not understand what there can be to make them afraid who are afraid to begin mental prayer, nor do I know what it is they dread. The devil does well to bring this fear upon us, that he may really hurt us ; if, by putting me in fear, he can make me cease from thinking of my offences against God, of the great debt I owe Him, of the existence of heaven and hell, and of the great sorrows and trials He underwent for me. That was all my prayer, and had been, when I was in this dangerous state, and it was on those subjects I dwelt whenever I could ; and very often, for some years, I was more occupied with the wish to see the end of the time I had appointed for myself to spend in prayer, and in watching the hour-glass, than with other thoughts that were good. If a sharp penance had been laid upon me, I know of none that I would not very often have willingly undertaken, rather than prepare myself for prayer by self-recollection. And certainly the violence with which Satan assailed me was so irresistible, or my evil habits were so strong, that I did not betake myself to prayer ; and the sadness I felt on entering the oratory was so great, that it required all the courage I had to force myself in. They say of me that my courage is not slight, and it is known that God has given me a courage beyond that of a woman ; but I have made a bad use of it. In the end,

our Lord came to my help ; and then, when I had done this violence to myself, I found greater peace and joy than I sometimes had when I had a desire to pray.

11. If, then, our Lord bore so long with me, who was so wicked—and it is plain that it was by prayer all my evil was corrected—why should any one, how wicked soever he may be, have any fear ? Let him be ever so wicked, he will not remain in his wickedness so many years as I did, after receiving so many graces from our Lord. Is there any one who can despair, when He bore so long with me, only because I desired and contrived to find some place and some opportunities for Him to be alone with me—and that very often against my will ? for I did violence to myself, or rather our Lord Himself did violence to me.

12. If, then, to those who do not serve God, but rather offend Him, prayer be all this, and so necessary, and if no one can really find out any harm it can do him, and if the omission of it be not a still greater harm, why, then, should they abstain from it who serve and desire to serve God ? Certainly I cannot comprehend it, unless it be that men have a mind to go through the troubles of this life in greater misery, and to shut the door in the face of God, so that He shall give them no comfort in it. I am most truly sorry for them, because they serve God at their own cost ; for of those who pray, God Himself defrays the charges, seeing that for a little trouble He gives sweetness, in order that, by the help it supplies, they may bear their trials.

13. But because I have much to say hereafter of this sweetness, which our Lord gives to those who persevere in prayer,[5] I do not speak of it here ; only this will I say : prayer is the door to those great graces which our Lord bestowed upon me. If this door be shut, I do not see how He can bestow them ; for even if He entered into a soul to take His delight therein, and to make that soul also delight in Him, there is no

[5] See ch. x. 2, and ch. xi. 22.

way by which He can do so ; for His will is, that such
a soul should be lonely and pure, with a great desire to
receive His graces.   If we put many hindrances in the
way, and take no pains whatever to remove them, how
can He come to us, and how can we have any desire
that He should show us His great mercies ?

14. I will speak now—for it is very important to
understand it—of the assaults which Satan directs
against a soul for the purpose of taking it, and of the
contrivances and compassion wherewith our Lord
labours to convert it to Himself, in order that men
may behold His mercy, and the great good it was for
me that I did not give up prayer and spiritual reading,
and that they may be on their guard against the
dangers against which I was not on my guard myself.
And, above all, I implore them for the love of our Lord,
and for the great love with which He goeth about
seeking our conversion to Himself, to beware of the
occasions of sin ; for once placed therein, we have no
ground to rest on—so many enemies then assail us,
and our own weakness is such, that we cannot defend
ourselves.

15. Oh, that I knew how to describe the captivity
of my soul in those days.   I understood perfectly that
I was in captivity, but I could not understand the
nature of it ; neither could I entirely believe that those
things which my confessors did not make so much of
were so wrong as I in my soul felt them to be.   One of
them—I had gone to him with a scruple—told me that,
even if I were raised to high contemplation, those occasions and conversations were not unfitting for me.
This was towards the end, when, by the grace of God, I
was withdrawing more and more from those great
dangers, but not wholly from the occasions of them.

16. When they saw my good desires, and how I
occupied myself in prayer, I seemed to them to have
done much ; but my soul knew that this was not doing
what I was bound to do for Him to Whom I owed so

much. I am sorry for my poor soul even now, because of its great sufferings, and the little help it had from any one except God, and for the wide door that man opened for it, that it might go forth to its pastimes and pleasures, when they said that these things were lawful.

17. Then there was the torture of sermons, and that not a slight one ; for I was very fond of them. If I heard any one preach well and with unction, I felt, without my seeking it, a particular affection for him, neither do I know whence it came. Thus, no sermon ever seemed to me so bad, but that I listened to it with pleasure ; though, according to others who heard it, the preaching was not good. If it was a good sermon, it was to me a most special refreshment. To speak of God, or to hear Him spoken of, never wearied me. I am speaking of the time after I gave myself to prayer. At one time I had great comfort in sermons, at another they distressed me, because they made me feel that I was very far from being what I ought to have been.

18. I used to pray to our Lord for help ; but, as it now seems to me, I must have committed the fault of not putting my whole trust in His Majesty, and of not thoroughly distrusting myself. I sought for help, took great pains ; but it must be that I did not understand how all is of little profit if we do not root out all confidence in ourselves, and place it wholly in God. I wished to live, but I saw clearly that I was not living, but rather wrestling with the shadow of death ; there was no one to give me life, and I was not able to take it. He Who could have given it me had good reasons for not coming to my aid, seeing that He had brought me back to Himself so many times, and I as often had left Him.

CHAPTER IX.

THE MEANS WHEREBY OUR LORD QUICKENED HER SOUL,
GAVE HER LIGHT IN HER DARKNESS, AND MADE
HER STRONG IN GOODNESS.

*By what means God began to rouse her soul and give
light in the midst of darkness, and to strengthen her
virtues so that she should not offend Him.*

1. MY soul was now grown weary ; and the miserable
habits it had contracted would not suffer it to rest,
though it was desirous of doing so. It came to pass
one day, when I went into the oratory, that I saw a
statue which they had put by there, and which had
been procured for a certain feast observed in the house.
It was a representation of Christ most grievously
wounded ; and so devotional, that the very sight of it,
when I saw it, moved me—so well did it show forth
that which He suffered for us. So keenly did I feel the
evil return I had made for those wounds, that I thought
my heart was breaking. I threw myself on the ground
beside it, my tears flowing plenteously, and implored
Him to strengthen me once for all, so that I might
never offend Him any more.

2. I had a very great devotion to the glorious
Magdalene, and very frequently used to think of her
conversion—especially when I went to Communion.
As I knew for certain that our Lord was then within
me, I used to place myself at His feet, thinking that
my tears would not be despised. I did not know what
I was saying ; only He did great things for me, in that
He was pleased I should shed those tears, seeing that
I so soon forgot that impression. I used to recommend
myself to that glorious Saint, that she might obtain
my pardon.

3. But this last time, before that picture of which I

am speaking, I seem to have made greater progress ; for I was now very distrustful to myself, placing all my confidence in God. It seems to me that I said to Him then that I would not rise up till He granted my petition. I do certainly believe that this was of great service to me, because I have grown better ever since.[1]

4. This was my method of prayer : as I could not make reflections with my understanding, I contrived to picture Christ as within me[2] ; and I used to find myself the better for thinking of those mysteries of His life during which He was most lonely. It seemed to me that the being alone and afflicted, like a person in trouble, must needs permit me to come near unto Him.

5. I did many simple things of this kind ; and in particular I used to find myself most at home in the prayer in the Garden, whither I went in His company. I thought of the bloody sweat, and of the affliction He endured there ; I wished, if it had been possible, to wipe away that painful sweat from His face ; but I remember that I never dared to form such a resolution —my sins stood before me so grievously. I used to remain with Him there as long as my thoughts allowed me, and I had many thoughts to torment me. For many years, nearly every night before I fell asleep, when I recommended myself to God, that I might sleep in peace, I used always to think a little of this mystery of the prayer in the Garden—yea, even before I was a nun, because I had been told that many indulgences were to be gained thereby. For my part, I believe that my soul gained very much in this way, because I began to practise prayer without knowing what it was ; and, now that it had become my constant habit, I was saved from omitting it, as I was from omitting to bless myself with the sign of the cross before I slept.

6. And now to go back to what I was saying of the torture which my thoughts inflicted upon me. This

---

[1] About the year 1555.   [2] See ch. iv. 10 ; ch. x. 1.

method of praying, in which the understanding makes
no reflections, hath this property : the soul must gain
much, or lose.   I mean, that those who advance without meditation make great progress, because it is done
by love.   But to attain to this involves great labour,
except to those persons whom it is our Lord's good
pleasure to lead quickly to the prayer of quiet.   I
know of some.   For those who walk in this way, a
book is profitable, that by the help thereof they may
the more quickly recollect themselves.   It was a help
to me also to look on fields, water, and flowers.³   In
them I saw traces of the Creator—I mean, that the
sight of these things was as a book unto me ; it roused
me, made me recollected, and reminded me of my
ingratitude and of my sins.   My understanding was so
dull that I could never represent in the imagination
either heavenly or high things in any form whatever,
until our Lord placed them before me in another
way.

7. I was so little able to put things before me by the
help of my understanding, that, unless I saw a thing
with my eyes, my imagination was of no use whatever.
I could not do as others do, who can put matters before
themselves so as to become thereby recollected.   I was
able to think of Christ only as man.   But so it was ;
and I never could form any image of Him to myself,
though I read much of His beauty, and looked at
pictures of Him.   I was like one who is blind, or in the
dark, who, though speaking to a person present, and
feeling his presence, because he knows for certain that
he is present—I mean, that he understands him to be
present, and believes it—yet does not see him.   It was
thus with me when I used to think of our Lord.   This
is why I was so fond of images.   Wretched are they
who, through their own fault, have lost this blessing ;
it is clear enough that they do not love our Lord—
for if they loved Him, they would rejoice at the sight of

---

³ See *Relation* i. 12.   ⁴ See chap. iv. 11.

His picture, just as men find pleasure when they see the portrait of one they love.

8. At this time, the *Confessions* of St. Augustine were given me. Our Lord seems to have so ordained it, for I did not seek them myself, neither had I ever seen them before. I had a very great devotion to St. Augustine, because the monastery in which I lived when I was yet in the world was of his Order [5] ; and also because he had been a sinner—for I used to find great comfort in those Saints whom, after they had sinned, our Lord converted to Himself. I thought they would help me, and that, as our Lord had forgiven them, so also He would forgive me. One thing, however, there was that troubled me—I have spoken of it before [6]—our Lord had called them but once, and they never relapsed ; while my relapses were now so many. This it was that vexed me. But calling to mind the love that He bore me, I took courage again. Of His mercy I never doubted once, but I did very often of myself.

9. O my God, I am amazed at the hardness of my heart amidst so many succours from Thee. I am filled with dread when I see how little I could do with myself, and how I was clogged, so that I could not resolve to give myself entirely to God. When I began to read the *Confessions*, I thought I saw myself there described, and began to recommend myself greatly to this glorious Saint. When I came to his conversion, and read how he heard that voice in the garden,[7] it seemed to me

[5] Ch. ii. 8. The *Confessions* of St. Augustine were first translated into Spanish by Sebastian Toscano, a Portuguese Augustinian, who wrote Spanish very badly. They appeared at Salamanca in 1554. This is the edition used by Saint Teresa.

[6] In the Prologue.

[7] St. Augustine, being in great trouble, heard a voice from the house next door, as of boys and girls singing : "Take and read, take and read." Believing these words to be a supernatural answer to his questionings, he took a volume of the Epistles, and, opening it at random, his eyes fell on the words : "Let us walk honestly as in the day : not in rioting and drunkenness, not in chambering and impurities, not in contention and envy : But put ye on the Lord Jesus Christ, and make not provision for the flesh in its concupiscences " (Rom. xiii. 13, 14). This proved the turning-point in his life. *Confess.* bk. viii. chap. xii., § 29.

nothing less than that our Lord had uttered it for me :
I felt so in my heart.   I remained for some time lost in
tears, in great inward affliction and distress.   O my
God, what a soul has to suffer because it has lost the
liberty it had of being mistress over itself !   And what
torments it has to endure !   I wonder now how I could
live in torments so great :   God be praised Who gave
me life, so that I might escape from so fatal a death !
I believe that my soul obtained great strength from
His Divine Majesty, and that He must have heard my
cry, and had compassion upon so many tears.

10. A desire to spend more time with Him began to
grow within me, and also to withdraw from the occasions of sin :   for as soon as I had done so, I turned
lovingly to His Majesty at once.   I understood clearly,
as I thought, that I loved Him ; but I did not understand, as I ought to have understood it, wherein the
true love of God consists.   I do not think I had yet
perfectly disposed myself to seek His service when His
Majesty turned towards me with His consolations.
What others strive after with great labour, our Lord
seems to have looked out for a way to make me willing
to accept—that is, in these later years to give me joy
and comfort.   But as for asking our Lord to give me
either these things or sweetness in devotion, I never
dared to do it ; the only thing I prayed Him to give me
was the grace never to offend Him ; together with the
forgiveness of my great sins.   When I saw that my
sins were so great, I never ventured deliberately to
ask for consolation or for sweetness.   He had compassion enough upon me, I think—and, in truth, He
dealt with me according to His great mercy—when He
allowed me to stand before Him, and when He drew
me into His presence ; for I saw that, if He had not
drawn me, I should not have come at all.

11. Once only in my life do I remember asking for
consolation, being at the time in great aridities.   When
I considered what I had done, I was so confounded,

that the very distress I suffered from seeing how little humility I had, brought me that which I had been so bold as to ask for. I knew well that it was lawful to pray for it ; but it seemed to me that it is lawful only for those who are in good dispositions, who have sought with all their might to attain to true devotion—that is, not to offend God, and to be disposed and resolved for all goodness. I looked upon those tears of mine as womanish and weak, seeing that I did not obtain my desires by them ; nevertheless, I believe that they did me some service ; for, specially after those two occasions of great compunction and sorrow of heart,[8] accompanied by tears, of which I am speaking, I began in an especial way to give myself more to prayer, and to occupy myself less with those things which did me harm—though I did not give them up altogether. But God Himself, as I have just said, came to my aid, and helped me to turn away from them. As His Majesty was only waiting for some preparation on my part, the spiritual graces grew in me as I shall now explain. It is not the custom of our Lord to give these graces to any but to those who keep their consciences in greater pureness.[9]

CHAPTER X.

THE GRACES SHE RECEIVED IN PRAYER. WHAT WE CAN DO OURSELVES. THE GREAT IMPORTANCE OF UN-DERSTANDING WHAT OUR LORD IS DOING FOR US. SHE DESIRES HER CONFESSORS TO KEEP HER WRIT-INGS SECRET, BECAUSE OF THE SPECIAL GRACES OF OUR LORD TO HER, WHICH THEY HAD COM-MANDED HER TO DESCRIBE.

She begins to explain the graces God gave her in prayer, and how much we can do for ourselves, and of the im-

[8] § 1.   [9] Ch. iv. 11.

portance of understanding God's mercies towards us.
She requests those to whom this is to be sent to keep the
remainder (of this book) secret, since they have com-
manded her to go into so many details about the graces
God has shown her.

1. I USED to have at times, as I have said,[1] though it
used to pass quickly away—certain commencements
of that which I am going now to describe. When I
formed those pictures within myself of throwing myself
at the feet of Christ, as I said before,[2] and sometimes
even when I was reading, a feeling of the presence of
God would come over me unexpectedly, so that I could
in no wise doubt either that He was within me, or that
I was wholly absorbed in Him. It was not by way of
vision ; I believe it was what is called mystical theology. The soul is suspended in such a way that it
seems to be utterly beside itself. The will loves ; the
memory, so it seems to me, is as it were lost ; and the
understanding, so I think, makes no reflections—yet
is not lost : as I have just said, it is not at work, but
it stands as if amazed at the greatness of the things that
it understands ; for God wills it to understand that it
understands nothing whatever of that which His
Majesty places before it.

2. Before this, I had a certain tenderness of soul
which was very abiding, partially attainable, I believe,
in some measure, by our own efforts : a consolation
which is not wholly in the senses, nor yet altogether in
the spirit, but is all of it the gift of God. However, I
think we can contribute much towards the attaining of
it by considering our vileness and our ingratitude towards God—the great things He has done for us—His
Passion, with its grievous pains—and His life, so full
of sorrows ; also, by rejoicing in the contemplation of

---

[1] The Saint interrupts her history here to enter on the difficult questions
of mystical theology, and resumes it in ch. xxiii.
[2] Ch. ix. 4.

His works, of His greatness, and of the love that He bears us. Many other considerations there are which he who really desires to make progress will often stumble on, though he may not be very much on the watch for them. If with this there be a little love, the soul is comforted, the heart is softened, and tears flow. Sometimes it seems that we do violence to ourselves and weep ; at other times, our Lord seems to do so, so that we have no power to resist Him. His Majesty seems to reward this slight carefulness of ours with so grand a gift as is this consolation which He ministers to the soul of seeing itself weeping for so great a Lord. I am not surprised ; for the soul has reason enough, and more than enough, for its joy. Here it comforts itself—here it rejoices.

3. The comparison which now presents itself seems to me to be good. These joys in prayer are like what those of heaven must be. As the vision of the saints, which is measured by their merits here, reaches no further than our Lord wills, and as the blessed see how little merit they had, every one of them is satisfied with the place assigned him : there being the very greatest difference between one joy and another in heaven, and much greater than between one spiritual joy and another on earth—which is, however, very great. And in truth, in the beginning, a soul in which God works this grace thinks that now it has scarcely anything more to desire, and counts itself abundantly rewarded for all the service it has rendered Him. And there is reason for this : for one of those tears—which, as I have just said, are almost in our own power, though without God nothing can be done—cannot, in my opinion, be purchased with all the labours of the world, because of the great gain it brings us. And what greater gain can we have than some testimony of our having pleased God ? Let him, then, who shall have attained to this, give praise unto God—acknowledge himself to be one of His greatest debtors ; because it seems to be His

will to take him into His house, having chosen him for His kingdom, if he does not turn back.

4. Let him not regard certain kinds of humility which exist, and of which I mean to speak.[3] Some think it humility not to believe that God is bestowing His gifts upon them. Let us clearly understand this, and that it is perfectly clear God bestows His gifts without any merit whatever on our part ; and let us be grateful to His Majesty for them ; for if we do not recognize the gifts received at His hands, we shall never be moved to love Him. It is a most certain truth, that the richer we see ourselves to be, confessing at the same time our poverty, the greater will be our progress, and the more real our humility.

5. An opposite course tends to take away all courage ; for we shall think ourselves incapable of great blessings, if we begin to frighten ourselves with the dread of vain-glory when our Lord begins to show His mercy upon us.[4] Let us believe that He Who gives these gifts will also, when the devil begins to tempt us herein, give us the grace to detect him, and the strength to resist him.—that is, He will do so if we walk in simplicity before God, aiming at pleasing Him only, and not men. It is a most evident truth, that our love for a person is greater, the more distinctly we remember the good he has done us.

6. If, then, it is lawful, and so meritorious, always to remember that we have our being from God, that He has created us out of nothing, that He preserves us, and also to remember all the benefits of His death and Passion, which He suffered long before He made us, for every one of us now alive—why should it not be lawful for me to discern, confess, and consider often that I was once accustomed to speak of vanities, and that now our Lord has given me the grace to speak only of Himself ?

7. Here, then, is a precious pearl, which, when we remember that it is given us, and that we have it in

[3] Ch. xxx. 10 and 11.　　　　[4] See ch. xiii. 5.

possession, powerfully invites us to love. All this is
the fruit of prayer founded on humility. What, then,
will it be when we shall find ourselves in possession of
other pearls of greater price, such as contempt of the
world and of self, which some servants of God have
already received ? It is clear that such souls must
consider themselves greater debtors—under greater
obligations to serve Him : we must acknowledge that
we have nothing of ourselves, and confess the munificence of our Lord, Who, on a soul so wretched and poor,
and so utterly undeserving, as mine is,—for whom the
first of these pearls was enough, and more than enough,
—would bestow greater riches than I could desire.

8. We must renew our strength to serve Him, and
strive not to be ungrateful, because it is on this condition that our Lord dispenses His treasures ; for if we
do not make a good use of them, and of the high estate
to which He raises us, He will return and take them from
us, and we shall be poorer than ever. His Majesty
will give the pearls to him who shall bring them
forth and employ them usefully for himself and others.
For how shall he be useful, and how shall he spend
liberally, who does not know that he is rich ? It
is not possible, I think, our nature being what it is,
that he can have the courage necessary for great
things who does not know that God is on his side ; for
so miserable are we, so inclined to the things of this
world, that he can hardly have any real abhorrence of,
with great detachment from, all earthly things, who
does not see that he holds some pledges for those things
that are above. It is by these gifts that our Lord gives
us that strength which we through our sins have lost.

9. A man will hardly wish to be held in contempt
and abhorrence, nor will he seek after the other great
virtues to which the perfect attain, if he has not some
pledges of the love which God bears him, together with
a living faith. Our nature is so dead, that we go after
that which we see immediately before us ; and it is

these graces, therefore, that quicken and strengthen our faith. It may well be that I, who am so wicked, measure others by myself, and that others require nothing more than the verities of the faith, in order to render their works most perfect ; while I, wretched that I am ! have need of everything.

10. Others will explain this. I speak from my own experience, as I have been commanded ; and if what I say be not correct, let him [5] to whom I send it destroy it ; for he knows better than I do what is wrong in it. I entreat him, for the love of our Lord, to publish abroad what I have thus far said of my wretched life, and of my sins. I give him leave to do so ; and to all my confessors also—of whom he is one—to whom this is to be sent, if it be their pleasure, even during my life, so that I may no longer deceive people who think there must be some good in me.[6] Certainly, I speak in all sincerity, so far as I understand myself. Such publication will give me great comfort.

11. But as to that which I am now going to say, I give no such leave ; nor, if it be shown to any one, do I consent to its being said who the person is whose experience it describes, nor who wrote it. This is why I mention neither my own name, nor that of any other person whatever. I have written it in the best way I could, in order not to be known ; and this I beg of them for the love of God. Persons so learned and grave as they are[7] have authority enough to approve of whatever right things I may say, should our Lord give me the grace to do so ; and if I should say anything of the kind, it will be His, and not mine—because I am neither learned nor of good life, and I have no person of learning or any other to teach me ; for they only who ordered me to write know that I am writing, and at this moment they are not here. I have, as it were, to steal

[5] F. Pedro Ibañez, of the Order of St. Dominic, of the monastery of San Esteban at Salamanca, but for some years reader of divinity at Santo Tomás at Avila.

[6] See ch. xxxi. 17.   [7] See ch. xv. 12.

the time, and that with difficulty, because my writing
hinders me from spinning.   I am living in a house that
is poor, and have many things to do.[8]   If, indeed, our
Lord had given me greater abilities and a better
memory, I might then profit by what I have seen and
read ; but my abilities are very slight.   If, then, I
should say anything that is right, our Lord will have it
said for some good purpose ; that which may be wrong
will be mine, and your reverence will strike it out.

12. In neither case will it be of any use to publish
my name : during my life, it is clear that no good I
may have done ought to be told ; after death, there is
no reason against it, except that it will lose all authority
and credit, because related of a person so vile and so
wicked as I am.   And because I think your reverence
and the others who may see this writing will do this
that I ask of you, for the love of our Lord, I write with
freedom.   If it were not so, I should have great scruples
except in declaring my sins : and in that matter I
should have none at all.   For the rest, it is enough that
I am a woman to make my sails droop ; how much
more, then, when I am a woman, and a wicked one ?

13. So, then, everything here beyond the simple
story of my life your reverence must take upon yourself—since you have so pressed me to give some
account of the graces which our Lord bestowed upon
me in prayer—if it be consistent with the truths of our
holy Catholic faith ; if it be not, your reverence must
burn it at once—for I give my consent.   I will recount
my experience, in order that, if it be consistent with
those truths, your reverence may make some use of it ;
if not, you will deliver my soul from delusion, so that
Satan may gain nothing there where I seemed to be
gaining myself.   Our Lord knows well that I, as I
shall show hereafter,[9] have always laboured to find out
those who could give me light.

14. How clear soever I may wish to make my

[8] See ch. xiv. 12.   [9] See ch. xxiv. 5.

account of that which relates to prayer, it will be obscure enough for those who are without experience. I shall speak of certain hindrances, which, as I understand it, keep men from advancing on this road—and of other things which are dangerous, as our Lord has taught me by experience. I have also discussed the matter with men of great learning, with persons who for many years had lived spiritual lives, who admit that in the twenty-seven years only during which I have given myself to prayer—though I walked so ill, and stumbled so often on the road—His Majesty granted me that experience which others attain to in seven-and-thirty, or seven-and-forty, years ; and they, too, being persons who ever advanced in the way of penance and of virtue.

15. Blessed be God for all, and may His infinite Majesty make use of me ! Our Lord knoweth well that I have no other end in this than that He may be praised and magnified a little, when men shall see that on a dunghill so foul and rank He has made a garden of flowers so sweet. May it please His Majesty that I may not by my own fault root them out, and become again what I was before. And I entreat your reverence, for the love of our Lord, to beg this of Him for me, seeing that you have a clearer knowledge of what I am than you have allowed me to give of myself here.

CHAPTER XI.

WHY MEN DO NOT ATTAIN QUICKLY TO THE PERFECT LOVE OF GOD. OF FOUR DEGREES OF PRAYER. OF THE FIRST DEGREE. THE DOCTRINE PROFITABLE FOR BEGINNERS, AND FOR THOSE WHO HAVE NO SENSIBLE SWEETNESS.

In which she sets forth how it is that we do not love God perfectly in a short time. She begins by expounding

*by means of a comparison four degrees of prayer, of the
first of which she treats here ; this is most profitable for
beginners and for those who find no taste in prayer.*

1. I SPEAK now of those who begin to be the servants
of love ; that seems to me to be nothing else but to
resolve to follow Him in the way of prayer, who has
loved us so much. It is a dignity so great that I have
a strange joy in thinking of it ; for servile fear vanishes
at once, if we are, as we ought to be, in the first degree.
O Lord of my soul, and my good, how is it that, when
a soul is determined to love Thee—doing all it can, by
forsaking all things, in order that it may the better
occupy itself with the love of God—it is not Thy will it
should have the joy of ascending at once to the possession of perfect love ? I have spoken amiss ; I ought
to have said, and my complaint should have been, why
is it we do not ? for the fault is wholly our own that
we do not rejoice at once in a dignity so great, seeing
that the attaining to the perfect possession of this true
love brings all blessings with it.

2. We think so much of ourselves, and are so
dilatory in giving ourselves wholly to God, that, as His
Majesty will not let us have the fruition of that which
is so precious but at a great cost, so neither do we
perfectly prepare ourselves for it. I see plainly that
there is nothing by which so great a good can be procured in this world. If, however, we did what we
could, not clinging to anything upon earth, but having
all our thoughts and conversation in Heaven, I believe
that this blessing would quickly be given us, provided
we perfectly prepared ourselves for it at once, as some
of the saints have done. We think we are giving all to
God ; but, in fact, we are offering only the revenue or
the produce, while we retain the fee-simple of the land
in our own possession.

3. We resolve to become poor, and it is a resolution
of great merit ; but we very often take great care not

to be in want, not simply of what is necessary, but of
what is superfluous : yea, and to make for ourselves
friends who may supply us ; and in this way we take
more pains, and perhaps expose ourselves to greater
danger, in order that we may want nothing, than we
did formerly, when we had our own possessions in our
own power.

4. We thought, also, that we gave up all desire of
honour when we became religious, or when we began
the spiritual life, and followed after perfection ; and
yet, when we are touched on the point of honour, we
do not then remember that we had given it up to God.
We would seize it again, and take it, as they say, out
of His hands, even after we had made Him, to all
appearance, the Lord of our own will. So is it in everything else.

5. A pleasant way this of seeking the love of God !
we retain our own affections, and yet will have that
love, as they say, by handfuls. We make no efforts to
bring our desires to good effect, or to raise them
resolutely above the earth ; and yet, with all this, we
must have many spiritual consolations. This is not
well, and we are seeking things that are incompatible
one with the other. So, because we do not give ourselves up wholly and at once, this treasure is not given
wholly and at once to us. May it be the good pleasure
of our Lord to give it us drop by drop, though it may
cost us all the trials in the world.

6. He showeth great mercy unto him to whom He
gives the grace and resolution to strive for this blessing
with all his might ; for God withholds Himself from
no one who perseveres. He will by little and little
strengthen that soul, so that it may come forth victorious. I say resolution, because of the multitude of
those things which Satan puts before it at first ; to keep
it back from beginning to travel on this road ; for he
knoweth what harm will befall him thereby—he will
lose not only that soul, but many others also. If he

who enters on this road does violence to himself, with the help of God, so as to reach the summit of perfection, such a one, I believe, will never go alone to Heaven ; he will always take many with him : God gives to him, as to a good captain, those who shall be of his company.

7. Thus, then, the dangers and difficulties which Satan puts before them are so many, that they have need, not of a little, but of a very great, resolution, and great grace from God, to save them from falling away.

8. Speaking, then, of their beginnings who are determined to follow after this good, and to succeed in their enterprise—what I began to say [1] of mystical theology—I believe they call it by that name—I shall proceed with hereafter—I have to say that the labour is greatest at first ; for it is they who toil, our Lord, indeed, giving them strength. In the other degrees of prayer, there is more of fruition ; although they who are in the beginning, the middle, and the end, have their crosses to carry : the crosses, however, are different. They who would follow Christ, if they do not wish to be lost, must walk in the way He walked Himself. Blessed labours ! even here, in this life, so superabundantly rewarded !

9. I shall have to make use of a comparison ; I should like to avoid it, because I am a woman, and write simply what I have been commanded. But this language of spirituality is so difficult of utterance for those who are not learned, and such am I. I have therefore to seek for some means to make the matter plain. It may be that the comparison will very rarely be to the purpose—your reverence will be amused when you see my stupidity. I think, now, I have either read or heard of this comparison ; but as my memory is bad, I know not where, nor on what occasion ; however, I am satisfied with it for my present purpose.

10. A beginner must look upon himself as making

[1] Ch. x. 1.

a garden, wherein our Lord may take His delight, but in a soil unfruitful, and abounding in weeds. His Majesty roots up the weeds, and has to plant good herbs. Let us, then, take for granted that this is already done when a soul is determined to give itself to prayer, and has begun the practice of it. We have, then, as good gardeners, by the help of God, to see that the plants grow, to water them carefully, that they may not die, but produce blossoms, which shall send forth much fragrance, refreshing to our Lord, so that He may come often for His pleasure into this garden, and delight Himself in the midst of these virtues.

11. Let us now see how this garden is to be watered, that we may understand what we have to do : how much trouble it will cost us, whether the gain be greater than the trouble, or how long a time it will take us. It seems to me that the garden may be watered in four ways : by water taken out of a well, which is very laborious ; or with water raised by means of an engine and buckets, drawn by a windlass—I have drawn it this way sometimes—it is a less troublesome way than the first, and gives more water [2] ; or by a stream or brook, whereby the garden is watered in a much better way—for the soil is more thoroughly saturated, and there is no necessity to water it so often, and the labour of the gardener is much less ; or by showers of rain, when our Lord Himself waters it, without labour on our part—and this way is incomparably better than all the others of which I have spoken.

12. Now, then, for the application of these four ways of irrigation by which the garden is to be maintained ; for without water it must fail. The comparison is to my purpose, and it seems to me that by the help of it I shall be able to explain, in some measure, the four degrees of prayer to which our Lord, of His goodness, has occasionally raised my soul. May He graciously

---

[2] This is the appliance called *noria*, still in use in almost every farm-yard in Castile.

grant that I may so speak as to be of some service to one of those who has commanded me to write, whom our Lord has raised in four months to a greater height than I have reached in seventeen years![3] He prepared himself better than I did, and therefore is his garden, without labour on his part, irrigated by these four waters—though the last of them is only drop by drop ; but it is growing in such a way, that soon, by the help of our Lord, he will be swallowed up therein, and it will be a pleasure to me, if he finds my explanation absurd, that he should laugh at it.

13. Of those who are beginners in prayer, we may say, that they are those who draw the water up out of the well—a process which, as I have said, is very laborious ; for they must be wearied in keeping the senses recollected, and this is a great labour, because the senses have been hitherto accustomed to distractions. It is necessary for beginners to accustom themselves to disregard what they hear or see, and to put it away from them during the time of prayer ; they must be alone, and in retirement think over their past life. Though all must do this many times, beginners as well as those more advanced, all, however, must not do so equally, as I shall show hereafter.[4] Beginners at first suffer much, because they are not convinced that they are penitent for their sins ; and yet they are, because they are so sincerely resolved on serving God. They must strive to meditate on the life of Christ, and the understanding is wearied thereby. Thus far we can advance of ourselves—that is, by the grace of God—for without that, as every one knows, we never can have one good thought.

14. This is beginning to draw water up out of the well. God grant there may be water in it ! That, however, does not depend on us ; we are drawing it,

---

[3] Probably the same who is spoken of in ch. xxxiv. 8, *i.e.* Fray Garcia de Toledo.
[4] Ch. xiii. 23.

and doing what we can towards watering the flowers. So good is God, that when, for reasons known to His Majesty—perhaps for our greater good—it is His will the well should be dry, He Himself preserves the flowers without water—we, like good gardeners, doing what lies in our power—and makes our virtues grow. By water here I mean tears, and if there be none, then tenderness and an inward feeling of devotion.

15. What, then, will he do here who sees that, for many days, he is conscious only of aridity, disgust, dislike, and so great an unwillingness to go to the well for water, that he would give it up altogether, if he did not remember that he has to please and serve the Lord of the garden ; if he did not trust that his service was not in vain, and did not hope for some gain by a labour so great as that of lowering the bucket into the well so often, and drawing it up without water in it ? It will happen that he is often unable to move his arms for that purpose or to have one good thought : working with the understanding is drawing water out of the well.

16. What, then, once more, will the gardener do now ? He must rejoice and take comfort, and consider it as the greatest favour to labour in the garden of so great an Emperor ; and as he knows that he is pleasing Him in the matter—and his purpose must not be to please himself, but Him—let him praise Him greatly for the trust He has in him—for He sees that, without any recompense, he is taking so much care of that which has been confided to him ; let him help Him to carry the Cross, and let him think how He carried it all His life long ; let him not seek his kingdom here, nor ever intermit his prayer ; and so let him resolve, if this aridity should last even his whole life long, never to let Christ fall down beneath the Cross.[5]

17. The time will come when he shall be paid once for all. Let him have no fear that his labour is in

[5] See ch. xv. 17.

vain : he serves a good Master, Whose eyes are upon him. Let him make no account of evil thoughts, but remember that Satan suggested them to St. Jerome also in the desert.[6] These labours have their reward, I know it ; for I am one who underwent them for many years. When I drew but one drop of water out of this blessed well, I considered it was a mercy of God. I know these labours are very great, and require, I think, greater courage than many others in this world ; but I have seen clearly that God does not leave them without a great recompense, even in this life ; for it is very certain that in one hour, during which our Lord gave me to taste His sweetness, all the anxieties which I had to bear when persevering in prayer seem to me ever afterwards perfectly rewarded.

18. I believe that it is our Lord's good pleasure frequently in the beginning, and at times in the end, to send these torments, and many other incidental temptations, to try those who love Him, and to ascertain if they will drink the chalice,[7] and help Him to carry the Cross, before He entrusts them with His great treasures. I believe it to be for our good that His Majesty should lead us by this way, so that we may perfectly understand how worthless we are ; for the graces which He gives afterwards are of a dignity so great, that He will have us by experience know our wretchedness before He grants them, that it may not be with us as it was with Lucifer.

19. What canst Thou do, O my Lord, that is not for the greater good of that soul which Thou knowest to be already Thine, and which gives itself up to Thee to

---

[6] Epist. 22, *ad Eustochium* : " O quoties ego ipse in eremo constitutus, et in illa vasta solitudine quæ exusta solis ardoribus horridum monachis præstat habitaculum putabam me Romanis interesse deliciis. Sedebam solus. . . . Horrebant sacco membra deformia. . . . Ille igitur ego, qui ob Gehennæ metum tali me carcere damnaveram, scorpionum tantum socius et ferarum, sæpe choris intereram puellarum ; pallebant ora jejuniis, et mens desideriis æstuabat in frigido corpore, et ante hominem sua jam carne præmortuum sola libidinum incendia bulliebant."

[7] St. Matt. xx. 22 : " Potestis bibere calicem ? " *Rel.* v. 13.

follow Thee whithersoever Thou goest, even to the death of the Cross ; and which is determined to help Thee to carry that Cross, and not to leave Thee alone with it ? He who shall discern this resolution in himself has nothing to fear : no, no ; spiritual people have nothing to fear. There is no reason why he should be distressed who is already raised to so high a degree as this is of wishing to converse in solitude with God, and to abandon the amusements of the world. The greater part of the work is done ; give praise to His Majesty for it, and trust in His goodness Who has never failed those who love Him. Close the eyes of your imagination, and do not ask why He gives devotion to this person in so short a time, and none to me after so many years. Let us believe that all is for our greater good ; let His Majesty guide us whithersoever He will ; we are not our own, but His. He shows us mercy enough when it is His pleasure we should be willing to dig in His garden, and to be so near the Lord of it : He certainly is near to us. If it be His will that these plants and flowers should grow—some of them when He gives water we may draw from the well, others when He gives none—what is that to me ? Do Thou, O Lord, accomplish Thy will ; let me never offend Thee, nor let my virtues perish ; if Thou hast given me any, it is out of Thy mere goodness. I wish to suffer, because Thou, O Lord, hast suffered ; do Thou in every way fulfil Thy will in me, and may it never be the pleasure of Thy Majesty that a gift of so high a price as that of Thy love, be given to people who serve Thee only because of the sweetness they find thereby.

20. It is much to be observed, and I say so because I know by experience, that the soul which begins to walk in the way of mental prayer with resolution, and is determined not to care much, neither to rejoice nor to be greatly afflicted, whether sweetness and tenderness fail it, or our Lord grants them, has already travelled a great part of the road. Let that soul, then,

have no fear that it is going back, though it may
frequently stumble ; for the building is begun on a firm
foundation. It is certain that the love of God does not
consist in tears, nor in this sweetness and tenderness
which we for the most part desire, and with which we
console ourselves ; but rather in serving Him in justice,
fortitude, and humility. That seems to me to be a
receiving rather than a giving of anything on our
part.

21. As for poor women, such as I am, weak and
infirm of purpose, it seems to me to be necessary that I
should be led on through consolations, as God is doing
now, so that I might be able to endure certain afflictions which it has pleased His Majesty I should have.
But when the servants of God, who are men of weight,
learning, and sense, make so much account, as I see
they do, whether God gives them sweetness in devotion
or not, I am disgusted when I listen to them. I do not
say that they ought not to accept it, and make much
of it, when God gives it—because, when He gives it,
His Majesty sees it to be necessary for them—but I do
say that they ought not to grow weary when they have
it not. They should then understand that they have
no need of it, and be masters of themselves, when His
Majesty does not give it. Let them be convinced of
this, there is a fault here ; I have had experience of it,
and know it to be so. Let them believe it as an
imperfection : they are not advancing in liberty
of spirit, but shrinking like cowards from the
assault.

22. It is not so much to beginners that I say this—
though I do insist upon it, because it is of great importance to them that they should begin with this
liberty and resolution—as to others, of whom there
are many, who make a beginning, but never come to
the end ; and that is owing, I believe, in great measure,
to their not having embraced the Cross from the first.
They are distressed, thinking they are doing nothing ;

the understanding ceases from its acts, and they cannot bear it. Yet, perhaps, at that very time, the will is feeding and gathering strength, and they know it not.

23. We must suppose that our Lord does not regard these things ; for though they seem to us to be faults, yet they are not. His Majesty knoweth our misery and natural vileness better than we do ourselves. He knoweth that these souls long to be always thinking of Him and loving Him. It is this resolution that He seeks in us ; the other anxieties which we inflict upon ourselves serve to no other end but to disquiet the soul —which, if it be unable to derive any profit in one hour, will by them be disabled for four. This comes most frequently from bodily indisposition—I have had very great experience in the matter, and I know it is true ; for I have carefully observed it and discussed it afterwards with spiritual persons—for we are so wretched, that this poor prisoner of a soul shares in the miseries of the body. The changes of the seasons, and the alterations of the humours, very often compel it, without fault of its own, not to do what it would, but rather to suffer in every way. Meanwhile, the more we force the soul on these occasions, the greater the mischief, and the longer it lasts. Some discretion must be used, in order to ascertain whether ill-health be the occasion or not. The poor soul must not be stifled. Let those who thus suffer understand that they are ill ; a change should be made in the hour of prayer, and oftentimes that change should be continued for some days. Let souls pass out of this desert as they can, for it is very often the misery of one that loves God to see itself living in such wretchedness, unable to do what it would, because it has to keep so evil a guest as the body.

24. I spoke of discretion, because sometimes the devil will do the same work ; and so it is not always right to omit prayer when the understanding is greatly

distracted and disturbed, nor to torment the soul to the doing of that which is out of its power. There are other things then to be done—exterior works, as of charity and spiritual reading—though at times the soul will not be able to do them. Take care, then, of the body, for the love of God, because at many other times the body must serve the soul; and let recourse be had to some recreations—holy ones—such as conversation, or going out into the fields, as the confessor shall advise. Altogether, experience is a great matter, and it makes us understand what is convenient for us. Let God be served in all things—His yoke is sweet[8]; and it is of great importance that the soul should not be dragged, as they say, but carried gently, that it may make greater progress.

25. So, then, I come back to what I advised before[9] —and though I repeat it often, it matters not; it is of great importance that no one should distress himself on account of aridities, or because his thoughts are restless and distracted; neither should he be afflicted thereat, if he would attain to liberty of spirit, and not be always in trouble. Let him begin by not being afraid of the Cross, and he will see how our Lord will help him to carry it, how joyfully he will advance, and what profit he will derive from it all. It is now clear, if there is no water in the well, that we at least can put none into it. It is true we must not be careless about drawing it when there is any in it, because at that time it is the will of God to multiply our virtues by means thereof.

[8] St. Matt. xi. 30: " Jugum enim meum suave est."
[9] § 18.

CHAPTER XII.

WHAT WE CAN OURSELVES DO.   THE EVIL OF DESIRING TO ATTAIN TO SUPERNATURAL STATES BEFORE OUR LORD CALLS US.

Continuation of the first state.   She declares how far, with the grace of God, we can proceed by ourselves, and speaks of the danger of seeking supernatural and extraordinary experiences before God lifts up the soul.

1. My aim in the foregoing chapter—though I digressed to many other matters, because they seemed to me very necessary—was to explain how much we may attain to of ourselves ; and how, in these beginnings of devotion, we are able in some degree to help ourselves : because thinking of, and pondering on, the sufferings of our Lord for our sakes moves us to compassion, and the sorrow and tears which result therefrom are sweet. The thought of the blessedness we hope for, of the love our Lord bore us, and of His resurrection, kindles within us a joy which is neither wholly spiritual nor wholly sensual ; but the joy is virtuous, and the sorrow is most meritorious.

2. Of this kind are all those things which produce a devotion acquired in part by means of the understanding, though it can neither be merited nor had, if God grants it not. It is best for a soul which God has not raised to a higher state than this not to try to rise of itself. Let this be well considered, because all the soul will gain in that way will be a loss. In this state it can make many acts of good resolutions to do much for God, and enkindle its love ; other acts also, which may help the growth of virtues, according to that which is written in a book called *The Art of Serving God,*[1] a most excellent work, and profitable

---

[1] *Arte para servir á Dios*, by the Franciscan Alonso de Madrid, was published at Sevilla in 1521. By the time Saint Teresa came to know this work

for those who are in this state, because the under-standing is active now.

3. The soul may also place itself in the presence of Christ, and accustom itself to many acts of love directed to His sacred Humanity, and remain in His presence continually, and speak to Him, pray to Him in its necessities, and complain to Him of its troubles ; be merry with Him in its joys, and yet not forget Him because of its joys. All this it may do without set prayers, but rather with words befitting its desires and its needs.

4. This is an excellent way whereby to advance, and that very quickly. He that will strive to have this precious companionship, and will make much of it, and will sincerely love our Lord, to whom we owe so much, is one, in my opinion, who has made some progress. There is therefore no reason why we should trouble ourselves because we have no sensible devo-tion, as I said before.[2] But let us rather give thanks to our Lord, Who allows us to have a desire to please Him, though our works be poor. This practice of the presence of Christ is profitable in all states of prayer, and is a most safe way of advancing in the first state, and of attaining quickly to the second ; and as for the last states, it secures us against those risks which the devil may occasion.

5. This, then, is what we can do. He who would pass out of this state, and upraise his spirit, in order to taste consolations denied him, will, in my opinion, lose both the one and the other.[3] These consolations being supernatural, and the understanding inactive, the soul is then left desolate and in great aridity. As

---

it had already passed through six editions, and many more followed in the course of the sixteenth and seventeenth centuries. It was also translated into French.

[2] Ch. xi. 20, 25.

[3] That is, he will lose the prayer of acquired quiet, because he voluntarily abandons it before the time ; and will not attain to the prayer of infused quiet, because he attempts to rise into it before he is called (Francis a Sancto Thoma, *Medulla Mystica*, tr. iv. ch. xi. n. 69).

the foundation of the whole building is humility, the nearer we draw unto God the more this virtue should grow ; if it does not, everything is lost. It seems to be a kind of pride when we seek to ascend higher, seeing that God descends so low, when He allows us, being what we are, to draw near unto Him.

6. It must not be supposed that I am now speaking of raising our thoughts to the consideration of the high things of heaven and of its glory, or unto God and His great wisdom. I never did this myself, because I had not the capacity for it—as I said before [4] ; and I was so worthless, that, as to thinking even of the things of earth, God gave me grace to understand this truth : that in me it was no slight boldness to do so. How much more, then, the thinking of heavenly things ? Others, however, will profit in that way, particularly those who are learned ; for learning, in my opinion, is a great treasury in the matter of this exercise, if it be accompanied with humility. I observed this a few days ago in some learned men who had shortly before made a beginning, and had made great progress. This is the reason why I am so very anxious that many learned men may become spiritual. I shall speak of this by and by.[5]

7. What I am saying—namely, let them not rise if God does not raise them—is the language of spirituality. He will understand me who has had any experience ; and I know not how to explain it, if what I have said does not make it plain.

8. In mystical theology—of which I spoke before [6] —the understanding ceases from its acts, because God suspends it—as I shall explain by and by, if I can [7] ; and God give me the grace to do so. We must neither imagine nor think that we can of ourselves bring about this suspension. That is what I say must not be done ; nor must we allow the understanding to cease

---

[4] Ch. iv. 10.   [5] Ch. xi. 12 and xxxiv. 9.
[6] Ch. x. 1.   [7] Ch. xvi. 4.

from its acts ; for in that case we shall be stupid and cold, and the result will be neither the one nor the other. For when our Lord suspends the understanding, and makes it cease from its acts, He puts before it that which astonishes and occupies it : so that, without making any reflections, it shall comprehend in a moment[8] more than we could comprehend in many years with all the efforts in the world.

9. To have the powers of the mind occupied, and to think that you can keep them at the same time quiet, is folly. I repeat it, though it be not so understood, there is no great humility in this ; and, if it be blameless, it is not left unpunished—it is labour thrown away, and the soul is a little disgusted : it feels like a man about to take a leap, and is held back. Such a one seems to have used up his strength already, and finds himself unable to do that which he wished to have done : so here, in the scanty gain that remains, he who will consider the matter will trace that slight want of humility of which I have spoken[9] ; for that virtue has this excellence : there is no good work attended by humility that leaves the soul disgusted. It seems to me that I have made this clear enough ; yet, after all, perhaps only for myself. May our Lord open their eyes who read this, by giving them experience ; and then, however slight that experience may be, they will immediately understand it.

10. For many years I read much, and understood nothing ; and for a long time, too, though God gave me understanding herein, I never could utter a word by which I might explain it to others. This was no little trouble to me. When His Majesty pleases, He teaches everything in a moment, so that I am lost in wonder. One thing I can truly say : though I conversed with many spiritual persons, who sought to make me understand what our Lord was giving me, in order that I might be able to speak of it, the fact is,

[8] "En un credo."   [9] § 5.

that my dulness was so great, that I derived no
advantage whatever, much or little, from their teaching.

11. Or it may be, as His Majesty has always been
my Master—may He be blessed for ever! for I am
ashamed of myself that I can say so with truth—
that it was His good pleasure I should meet with no
one to whom I should be indebted in this matter. So,
without my wishing or asking it—I never was careful
about this, for that would have been a virtue in me,
but only about vanity—God gave me to understand
with all distinctness in a moment, and also enabled me
to express myself, so that my confessors were astonished; but I more than they, because I knew my own
dulness better. It is not long since this happened.
And so that which our Lord has not taught me, I seek
not to know it, unless it be a matter that touches my
conscience.

12. Again I repeat my advice : it is of great
moment not to raise our spirit ourselves, if our Lord
does not raise it for us ; and if He does, there can be
no mistaking it. For women, it is specially wrong,
because the devil can delude them—though I am
certain our Lord will never allow him to hurt any one
who labours to draw near unto God in humility. On
the contrary, such a one will derive more profit and
advantage out of that attack by which Satan intended
to hurt him.

13. I have dwelt so long upon this matter because
this way of prayer is the most common with beginners,
and because the advice I have given is very important.
It will be found much better given elsewhere : that I
admit ; and I admit, also, that in writing it I am
ashamed of myself, and covered with confusion—
though not so much so as I ought to be. Blessed for
ever be our Lord, of whose will and pleasure it is that
I am allowed, being what I am, to speak of things
which are His, of such a nature, and so deep.

CHAPTER XIII.

OF CERTAIN TEMPTATIONS OF SATAN.   INSTRUCTIONS RELATING THERETO.

She continues to treat of the first degree and gives advice with respect to certain temptations sometimes sent by Satan. This is most profitable.

1. I HAVE thought it right to speak of certain temptations I have observed to which beginners are liable—some of them I have had myself—and to give some advice about certain things which to me seem necessary. In the beginning, then, we should strive to be cheerful and unconstrained ; for there are people who think it is all over with devotion if they relax themselves ever so little. It is right to be afraid of self ; so that, having no confidence in ourselves, much or little, we may not place ourselves in those circumstances wherein men usually sin against God ; for it is a most necessary fear, till we become very perfect in virtue. And there are not many who are so perfect as to be able to relax themselves on those occasions which offer temptations to their natural temper ; for always while we live, were it only to preserve humility, it is well we should know our own miserable nature ; but there are many occasions on which it is permitted us—as I said just now [1]—to take some recreation, in order that we may with more vigour resume our prayer.

2. Discretion is necessary throughout. We must have great confidence ; because it is very necessary for us not to contract our desires, but put our trust in God ; for, if we do violence to ourselves by little and little, we shall, though not at once, reach that height which many Saints by His grace have reached. If

[1] Ch. xi. 24.

they had never resolved to desire, and had never by little and little acted upon that resolve, they never could have ascended to so high a state.

3. His Majesty seeks and loves courageous souls; but they must be humble in their ways, and have no confidence in themselves. I never saw one of those lag behind on the road; and never a cowardly soul, though aided by humility, make that progress in many years which the former makes in a few. I am astonished at the great things done on this road by encouraging oneself to undertake great things, though we may not have the strength for them at once; the soul takes a flight upwards and ascends high, though, like a little bird whose wings are weak, it grows weary and rests.

4. At one time I used often to think of those words of St. Paul: "That all things are possible in God." [2] I saw clearly that of myself I could do nothing. This was of great service to me. So also was the saying of St. Augustine: "Give me, O Lord, what Thou commandest, and command what Thou wilt." [3] I was often thinking how St. Peter lost nothing by throwing himself into the sea, though he was afterwards afraid. [4] These first resolutions are a great matter—although it is necessary in the beginning that we should be very reserved, controlled by the discretion and authority of a director; but we must take care that he be one who does not teach us to crawl like toads, nor one who may be satisfied when the soul shows itself fit only to catch lizards. Humility must always go before: so that we may know that this strength can come out of no strength of our own.

5. But it is necessary we should understand what manner of humility this should be, because Satan, I believe, does great harm; for he hinders those who

---

[2] Philipp. iv. 13: "Omnia possum in Eo."
[3] *Confess*. bk. x. ch. 29: "Da quod jubes, et jube quod vis."
[4] St. Matt. xiv. 30: "Videns vero ventum validum, timuit."

begin to pray from going onwards, by suggesting to
them false notions of humility. He makes them think
it is pride to have large desires, to wish to imitate the
Saints, and to long for martyrdom. He tells us forthwith, or he makes us think, that the actions of the
Saints are to be admired, not to be imitated, by us
who are sinners. I, too, say the same thing ; but we
must see what those actions are which we are to admire,
and what those are which we are to imitate ; for it
would be wrong in a person who is weak and sickly to
undertake much fasting and sharp penances, to retire
into the desert, where he could not sleep, nor find
anything to eat ; or, indeed, to undertake any austerities of this kind.

6. But we ought to think that we can force ourselves, by the grace of God, to hold the world in profound contempt—to make light of honour, and be
detached from our possessions. Our hearts, however,
are so mean that we think the earth would fail us
under our feet, if we were to cease to care even for a
moment for the body, and give ourselves up to spirituality. Then we think that to have all we require
contributes to recollection, because anxieties disturb
prayer. It is painful to me that our confidence in
God is so scanty, and our self-love so strong, as that
any anxiety about our own necessities should disturb
us. But so it is ; for when our spiritual progress is
so slight, a mere nothing will give us as much trouble
as great and important matters will give to others.
And we think ourselves spiritual !

7. Now, to me, this way of going on seems to
betray a disposition to reconcile soul and body together, in order that we may not miss our ease in this
world, and yet have the fruition of God in the next ;
and so it will be if we walk according to justice, clinging
to virtue ; but it is the pace of a hen—it will never
bring us to liberty of spirit. It is a course of proceeding, as it seems to me, most excellent for those who are

in the married state, and who must live according to their vocation ; but for the other state, I by no means wish for such a method of progress, neither can I be made to believe it to be sound ; for I have tried it, and I should have remained in that way, if our Lord in His goodness had not taught me another and a shorter road.

8. Though, in the matter of desires, I always had generous ones ; but I laboured, as I said before,[5] to make my prayer, and, at the same time, to live at my ease. If there had been any one to rouse me to a higher flight, he might have brought me, so I think, to a state in which these desires might have had their effects ; but, for our sins, so few and so rare are they whose discretion in that matter is not excessive. That, I believe, is reason enough why those who begin do not attain more quickly to great perfection ; for our Lord never fails us, and it is not His fault ; the fault and the wretchedness of this being all our own.

9. We may also imitate the Saints by striving after solitude and silence, and many other virtues that will not kill these wretched bodies of ours, which insist on being treated so orderly, that they may disorder the soul ; and Satan, too, helps much to make them unmanageable. When he sees us a little anxious about them, he wants nothing more to convince us that our way of life must kill us, and destroy our health ; even if we weep, he makes us afraid of blindness. I have passed through this, and therefore I know it ; but I know no better sight or better health that we can desire, than the loss of both in such a cause. Being myself so sickly, I was always under constraint, and good for nothing, till I resolved to make no account of my body nor of my health ; even now I am worthless enough.

10. But when it pleased God to let me find out this device of Satan, I used to say to the latter, when

5 Ch. vii. 27, 31.

he suggested to me that I was ruining my health,
that my death was of no consequence ; when he suggested rest, I replied that I did not want rest, but
the Cross. His other suggestions I treated in the
same way. I saw clearly that in most things, though
I was really very sickly, it was either a temptation
of Satan, or a weakness on my part. My health has
been much better since I have ceased to look after my
ease and comforts. It is of great importance not to
let our own thoughts frighten us in the beginning,
when we set ourselves to pray. Believe me in this,
for I know it by experience. As a warning to others,
it may be that this story of my failures may be useful.

11. There is another temptation, which is very
common ; when people begin to have pleasure in the
rest and the fruit of prayer, they will have everybody else be very spiritual also. Now, to desire this is
not wrong, but to try to bring it about may not be
right, except with great discretion and with much
reserve, without any appearance of teaching. He who
would do any good in this matter ought to be endowed
with solid virtues, that he may not put temptation in
the way of others. It happened to me—that is how I
know it—when, as I said before,[6] I made others apply
themselves to prayer, to be a source of temptation and
disorder ; for, on the one hand, they heard me say
great things of the blessedness of prayer, and, on the
other, saw how poor I was in virtue, notwithstanding
my prayer. They had good reasons on their side, and
afterwards they told me of it ; for they knew not how
these things could be compatible one with the other.
This it was that made them not to regard that as evil
which was really so in itself, namely, that they saw
me do it myself, now and then, during the time that
they thought well of me in some measure.

12. This is Satan's work : he seems to take ad-

---

[6] Ch. vii. 16. Her father was one of the three persons who, she says
(§ 12), profited by her advice.

vantage of the virtues we may have, for the purpose
of giving a sanction, so far as he can, to the evil he
aims at ; how slight soever that evil may be, his gain
must be great, if it prevail in a religious house.   How
much, then, must his gain have been, when the evil
I did was so very great !   And thus, during many
years, only three persons were the better for what I
said to them ; but now that our Lord has made me
stronger in virtue, in the course of two or three years
many persons have profited, as I shall show hereafter.[7]

13. There is another great inconvenience in addition to this : the loss to our own soul ; for the utmost
we have to do in the beginning is to take care of our
own soul only, and consider that in the whole world
there is only God and our soul.   This is a point of
great importance.

14. There is another temptation—we ought to be
aware of it, and be cautious in our conduct : persons
are carried away by a zeal for virtue, through the
pain which the sight of the sins and failings of others
occasions them.   Satan tells them that this pain arises
only out of their desire that God may not be offended,
and out of their anxiety about His honour ; so they
immediately seek to remedy the evil./ This so disturbs them, that they cannot pray.   The greatest evil
of all is their thinking this an act of virtue, of perfection,
and of a great zeal for God.   I am not speaking of
the pain which public sins occasion, if they be habitual
in any community, nor of wrongs done to the Church,
nor of heresies by which so many souls are visibly lost ;
for this pain is most wholesome, and being wholesome
is no source of disquiet.   The security, therefore, of
that soul which would apply itself to prayer lies in
casting away from itself all anxiety about persons and
things, in taking care of itself, and in pleasing God.
This is the most profitable course.

15. If I were to speak of the mistakes which I

[7] See chs. xxxi. 7, xxxviii. 4, and xxxix. 14.

have seen people make, in reliance on their own good
intentions, I should never come to an end. Let us
labour, therefore, always to consider the virtues and
the good qualities which we discern in others, and
with our own great sins cover our eyes, so that we may
see none of their failings. This is one way of doing our
work ; and though we may not be perfect in it at
once, we shall acquire one great virtue—we shall look
upon all men as better than ourselves ; and we begin
to acquire that virtue in this way, by the grace of God,
which is necessary in all things—for when we have it
not, all our endeavours are in vain—and by imploring
Him to give us this virtue ; for He never fails us, if
we do what we can.

16. This advice, also, they must take into their
consideration who make much use of their understanding, eliciting from one subject many thoughts and
conceptions. As to those who, like myself, cannot do
it, I have no advice to give, except that they are to
have patience, until our Lord shall send them both
matter and light ; for they can do so little of themselves, that their understanding is a hindrance to them
rather than a help.

17. To those, then, who can make use of their
understanding, I say that they are not to spend the
whole time in that way ; for though it be most meritorious, yet they must not, when prayer is sweet, suppose that there never will be a Sunday or a time when
no work ought to be done. They think it lost time to
do otherwise ; but I think that loss is their greatest
gain. Let them, rather, as I have said,[8] place themselves in the presence of Christ, and, without fatiguing
the understanding, converse with Him, and in Him
rejoice, without wearying themselves in searching out
reasons ; but let them rather lay their necessities before Him, and the just reasons there are why He should
not suffer us in His presence : at one time this, at

[8] Ch. xii. 3.

another time that, lest the soul should be wearied by always eating of the same food. These meats are most savoury and wholesome, if the palate be accustomed to them ; they will furnish a great support for the life of the soul, and they have many other advantages also.

18. I will explain myself further ; for the doctrine of prayer is difficult, and, without a director, very hard to understand. Though I would willingly be concise, and though a mere hint is enough for his clear intellect who has commanded me to write on the subject of prayer, yet so it is, my dulness does not allow me to say or explain in a few words that which it is so important to explain well. I, who have gone through so much, am sorry for those who begin only with books ; for there is a strange difference between that which we learn by reading and that which we learn by experience.

19. Going back, then, to what I was saying. We set ourselves to meditate upon some mystery of the Passion : let us say, our Lord at the pillar. The understanding goeth about seeking for the sources out of which came the great dolours and the bitter anguish which His Majesty endured in that desolation. It considers that mystery in many lights, which the intellect, if it be skilled in its work, or furnished with learning, may there obtain. This is a method of prayer which should be to every one the beginning, the middle, and the end : a most excellent and safe way, until our Lord shall guide them to other supernatural ways.

20. I say to all, because there are many souls who make greater progress by meditation on other subjects than on the Sacred Passion ; for as there are many mansions in heaven, so there are also many roads leading thither. Some persons advance by considering themselves in hell, others in heaven—and these are distressed by meditations on hell. Others meditate on death ; some persons, if tender-hearted, are greatly fatigued by continual meditations on the Passion ; but

are consoled and make progress when they meditate on the power and greatness of God in His creatures, and on His love visible in all things. This is an admirable method—not omitting, however, from time to time, the Passion and Life of Christ, the Source of all good that ever came, and that ever shall come.

21. He who begins is in need of instruction, whereby he may ascertain what profits him most. For this end it is very necessary he should have a director, who ought to be a person of experience ; for if he be not, he will make many mistakes, and direct a soul without understanding its ways, or suffering it to understand them itself ; for such a soul, knowing that obedience to a director is highly meritorious, dares not transgress the commandments it receives. I have met with souls cramped and tormented, because he who directed them had no experience : that made me sorry for them. Some of them knew not what to do with themselves ; for directors who do not understand the spirit of their penitents afflict them soul and body, and hinder their progress.[9]

22. One person I had to do with had been kept by her director for eight years, as it were, in prison ; he would not allow her to quit the subject of self-knowledge ; and yet our Lord had already raised her to the prayer of quiet ; so she had much to suffer.

23. Although this matter of self-knowledge must never be put aside—for there is no soul so great a giant on this road but has frequent need to turn back, and be again an infant at the breast ; and this must never be forgotten. I shall repeat it,[10] perhaps, many times, because of its great importance—for among all the states of prayer, however high they may be, there is not one in which it is not often necessary to go back to the beginning. The knowledge of our sins, and of our own selves, is the bread which we have to eat with all

---

[9] See St. John of the Cross, *Living Flame*, iii. 31, 56–67
[10] See ch. xv. 20.

the meats, however delicate they may be, in the way of prayer ; without this bread, life cannot be sustained, though it must be taken by measure. When a soul beholds itself resigned, and clearly understands that there is no goodness in it—when it feels itself abashed in the presence of so great a King, and sees how little it pays of the great debt it owes Him—why should it be necessary for it to waste its time on this subject ? Why should it not rather proceed to other matters which our Lord places before it, and for neglecting which there is no reason ? His Majesty surely knows better than we do what kind of food is proper for us.

24. So, then, it is of great consequence that the director should be prudent—I mean, of sound understanding—and a man of experience. If, in addition to this, he is a learned man, it is a very great matter. But if these three qualities cannot be had together, the first two are the most important, because learned men may be found with whom we can communicate when it is necessary. I mean, that for beginners learned men are of little use, if they are not men of prayer. I do not say that they are to have nothing to do with learned men, because a spirituality, the foundations of which are not resting on the truth, I would rather were not accompanied with prayer. Learning is a great thing, for it teaches us who know so little, and enlightens us ; so when we have come to the knowledge of the truths contained in the holy writings, we do what we ought to do. From silly devotions, God deliver us !

25. I will explain myself further, for I am meddling, I believe, with too many matters. It has always been my failing that I could never make myself understood —as I said before [11] —but at the cost of many words. A nun begins to practise prayer ; if her director be silly, and if he should take it into his head, he will make her feel that it is better for her to obey him than

[11] § 18.

her own superior.   He will do all this without any evil
purpose, thinking that he is doing right.   For if he be
not a religious himself, he will think this right enough.
If his penitent be a married woman, he will tell her that
it is better for her to give herself unto prayer, when she
ought to attend to her house, although she may thereby displease her husband.   And so it is, he knows not
how to make arrangements for time and business, so
that everything may be done as it ought to be done ;
he has no light himself, and can therefore give none to
others, however much he may wish to do so.

26. Though learning does not seem necessary for
discretion, my opinion has always been, and will be,
that every Christian should continue to be guided by a
learned director if he can, and the more learned the
better.   They who walk in the way of prayer have the
greater need of learning ; and the more spiritual they
are, the greater is that need.   Let them not say that
learned men not given to prayer are not fit counsellors
for those who pray : that is a delusion.   I have conversed with many ; and now for some years I have
sought them the more, because of my greater need of
them.   I have always been fond of them ; for though
some of them have no experience, they do not dislike
spirituality, neither are they ignorant of what it is,
because in the sacred writings with which they are
familiar they always find the truth about spirituality.
I am certain myself that a person given to prayer, who
treats of these matters with learned men, unless he is
deceived with his own consent, will never be carried
away by any illusions of the devil.   I believe that the
evil spirits are exceedingly afraid of learned men who
are humble and virtuous, knowing that they will be
found out and defeated by them.

27. I have said this because there are opinions held
to the effect that learned men, if they are not spiritual,
are not suited for persons given to prayer.   I have just
said that a spiritual director is necessary ; but if he be

not a learned man, he is a great hindrance. It will help us much if we consult those who are learned, provided they be virtuous ; even if they be not spiritual, they will be of service to me, and God will enable them to understand what they should teach ; He will even make them spiritual, in order that they may help us on. I do not say this without having had experience of it ; and I have met with more than two.

28. I say, then, that a person who shall resign his soul to be wholly subject to one director will make a great mistake, if he is in religion, unless he finds a director of this kind, because of the obedience due to his own superior. His director may be deficient in the three requisites I speak of,[12] and that will be no slight cross, without voluntarily subjecting the understanding to one whose understanding is none of the best. At least I have never been able to bring myself to do it, neither does it seem to me to be right.

29. But if he be a person living in the world, let him praise God for the power he has of choosing whom he will obey, and let him not lose so excellent a liberty ; yea, rather let him be without a director till he finds him—for our Lord will give him one, if he is really humble, and has a desire to meet with the right person. I praise God greatly—we women, and those who are unlearned, ought always to render Him unceasing thanks—because there are persons who, by labours so great, have attained to the truth, of which we unlearned people are ignorant. I often wonder at learned men—particularly those who are in religion—when I think of the trouble they have had in acquiring that which they communicate to me for my good, and that without any more trouble to me than the asking for it. And yet there are people who will not take advantage of their learning : God grant it may not be so !

30. I see them undergo the poverty of the religious life, which is great, together with its penances, its

---

[12] Prudence, experience, and learning ; see § 24.

meagre food, the yoke of obedience, which makes me
ashamed of myself at times ; and with all this, interrupted sleep, trials everywhere, everywhere the Cross,
I think it would be a great evil for any one to lose so
great a good by his own fault. It may be some of
us, who are exempted from these burdens—who have
our food put into our mouths, as they say, and live
at our ease—may think, because we give ourselves
a little more to prayer, that we are raised above the
necessity of such great hardships. Blessed be Thou,
O Lord, who hast made me so incapable and so useless ; but I bless Thee still more for this—that Thou
quickenest so many to quicken us. Our prayer must
therefore be very earnest for those who give us light.
What should we be without them in the midst of these
violent storms which now disturb the Church ? If
some have fallen, the good will shine more and more.[13]
May it please our Lord to hold them in His hand, and
help them, that they may help us.

31. I have gone far away from the subject I began
to speak of ; but all is to the purpose for those who are
beginners, that they may begin a journey which is so
high in such a way as that they shall go on by the right
road. Coming back, then, to what I spoke of before,[14]
the meditation on Christ bound to the pillar, it is well
we should make reflections for a time, and consider the
sufferings He there endured, for whom He endured
them, who He is who endured them, and the love with
which He bore them. But a person should not always
fatigue himself in making these reflections, but rather
let him remain there with Christ, in the silence of the
understanding.

32. If he is able, let him employ himself in looking
upon Christ, who is looking upon him ; let him accom-
pany Him, and make his petitions to Him ; let him

---

[13] Dan. xii. 3. "Qui autem docti fuerint, fulgebunt quasi splendor
firmamenti."
[14] § 19

humble himself, and delight himself in Christ, and keep
in mind that he never deserved to be there.   When he
shall be able to do this, though it may be in the
beginning of his prayer, he will find great advantage ;
and this way of prayer brings great advantages with
it—at least so my soul has found it.   I do not know
whether I am describing it aright ; you, my father,
will see to it.   May our Lord grant me to please Him
rightly for ever !   Amen.

CHAPTER XIV.

THE SECOND STATE OF PRAYER.   ITS SUPERNATURAL
CHARACTER.

*She begins to explain the second degree of prayer, in
which God already gives the soul special consolations,
which she shows here to be supernatural. This is most
noteworthy.*

1. HAVING spoken of the toilsome efforts and of the
strength required for watering the garden when we
have to draw the water out of the well, let us now
speak of the second manner of drawing the water,
which the Lord of the vineyard has ordained ; of the
machine of wheel and buckets whereby the gardener
may draw more water with less labour, and be able to
take some rest without being continually at work.
This, then, is what I am now going to describe ; and
I apply it to the prayer called the prayer of quiet.

2. Herein the soul begins to be recollected ; it is
now touching on the supernatural—for it never could
by any efforts of its own attain to this.   True, it seems
at times to have been wearied at the wheel, labouring
with the understanding, and filling the buckets ; but
in this second degree the water is higher, and accord-

ingly the labour is much less than it was when the water had to be drawn up out of the well ; I mean, that the water is nearer to it, for grace reveals itself more distinctly to the soul.

3. This is a gathering together of the faculties of the soul within itself, in order that it may have the fruition of that contentment in greater sweetness ; but the faculties are not lost, neither are they asleep ; the will alone is occupied in such a way that, without knowing how it has become a captive, it gives a simple consent to become the prisoner of God ; for it knows well what it is to be the captive of Him it loves. O my Jesus and my Lord, how pressing now is Thy love ! [1] It binds our love in bonds so straitly, that it is not in its power at this moment to love anything else but Thee.

4. The other two faculties help the will, that it may render itself capable of the fruition of so great a good ; nevertheless, it occasionally happens, even when the will is in union, that they hinder it very much ; but then it should never heed them at all, simply abiding in its fruition and quiet.[2] For if it tried to make them recollected, it would miss its way together with them, because they are at this time like doves which are not satisfied with the food the master of the dovecote gives them without any labouring for it on their part, and which go forth in quest of it elsewhere, and so hardly find it that they come back. And so the memory and the understanding come and go, seeking whether the will is going to give them that into the fruition of which it has entered itself.

5. If it be our Lord's pleasure to throw them any food, they stop ; if not, they go again to seek it. They must be thinking that they are of some service to the will ; and now and then the memory or the imagination, seeking to represent to it that of which

---

[1] 2 Cor. v. 14 : " Caritas enim Christi urget nos."
[2] See ch. xvii. 12 ; *Way of Perfection*, ch. xxxi. 6, 7.

it has the fruition, does it harm. The will, therefore, should be careful to deal with them as I shall explain. Everything that takes place now in this state brings the very greatest consolation ; and the labour is so slight, that prayer, even if persevered in for some time, is never wearisome. The reason is, that the understanding is now working very gently, and is drawing very much more water than it drew out of the well. The tears, which God now sends, flow with joy ; though we feel them, they are not the result of any efforts of our own.

6. This water of grand blessings and graces, which our Lord now supplies, makes the virtues thrive much more, beyond all comparison, than they did in the previous state of prayer ; for the soul is already ascending out of its wretched state, and some little knowledge of the blissfulness of glory is communicated to it. This, I believe, is it that makes the virtues grow the more, and also to draw nearer to essential virtue, God Himself, from Whom all virtues proceed ; for His Majesty has begun to communicate Himself to this soul, and will have it feel how He is communicating Himself.

7. As soon as the soul has arrived thus far, it begins to lose the desire of earthly things,[3] and no wonder ; for it sees clearly that, even for a moment, this joy is not to be had on earth ; that there are no riches, no dominion, no honours, no delights that can for one instant, even for the twinkling of an eye, minister such a joy ; for it is a true satisfaction, and the soul sees that it really does satisfy. Now, we who are on earth, as it seems to me, scarcely ever understand wherein our satisfaction lies, for it is always liable to disappointment ; but in this, at that time, there is none ; the disappointment cometh afterwards, when the soul sees that all is over, and that it has no power to recover it, neither does it know how ; for if

[3] See *Relation* i. 12.

it cut itself in pieces by penance and prayer, and every other kind of austerities, all would be of little use, if our Lord did not grant it. God, in His great mercy, will have the soul comprehend that His Majesty is so near to it, that it need not send messengers to Him, but may speak to Him itself, and not with a loud crying, because so near is He already, that He understands even the movements of its lips.

8. It seems absurd to say this, seeing that we know that God understands us always, and is present with us. It is so, and there can be no doubt of it ; but our Emperor and Lord will have us now understand that He understands us ; and also have us understand what His presence bringeth about, and that He means in a special way to begin a work in the soul, which is manifested in the great joy, inward and outward, which He communicates, and in the difference there is, as I said just now, between this joy and delight and all the joys of earth ; for He seems to be filling up the void in our souls occasioned by our sins.

9. This satisfaction lies in the innermost part of the soul, and the soul knows not whence, nor how, it came, very often it knows not what to do, or wish, or pray for. It seems to find all this at once, and knoweth not what it hath found ; nor do I know how to explain it, because learning is necessary for many things. Here, indeed, learning would be very much to the purpose, in order to explain the general and particular helps of grace ; for there are many who know nothing about them. Learning would serve to show how our Lord now will have the soul to see, as it were, with the naked eye, as men speak, this particular help of grace, and be also useful in many other ways wherein I am likely to go astray. But as what I write is to be seen by those who have the learning to discover whether I make mistakes or not, I go on without anxiety ; for I know I need have none whatever about either the letter or the spirit, because it is in their power to whom

it is to be sent to do with it as they will : they will understand it, and blot out whatever may be amiss.

10. I should like them to explain this, because it is a principal point, and because a soul, when our Lord begins to bestow these graces upon it, does not understand them, and does not know what to do with itself ; for if God leads it by the way of fear, as He led me, its trial will be heavy, if there be no one who understands the state it is in ; and to see itself as in a picture is a great comfort ; and then it sees clearly that it is travelling on that road. The knowledge of what it has to do is a great blessing for it, so that it may advance forwards in every one of these degrees of prayer ; for I have suffered greatly, and lost much time, because I did not know what to do ; and I am very sorry for those souls who find themselves alone when they come to this state ; for though I read many spiritual books, wherein this very matter is discussed, they threw very little light upon it. And if it be not a soul much exercised in prayer, it will find it enough to understand its state, be the books ever so clear.

11. I wish much that our Lord would help me to describe the effects on the soul of these things, now that they begin to be supernatural, so that men might know by these effects whether they come from the Spirit of God. I mean, known as things are known here below—though it is always well to live in fear, and on our guard ; for even if they do come from God, now and then the devil will be able to transform himself into an angel of light [4] ; and the soul, if not experienced herein, will not understand the matter ; and it must have so much experience for the understanding thereof, that it is necessary it should have attained to the highest perfection of prayer.

12. The little time I have helps me but little, and it is therefore necessary His Majesty should under-

[4] 2 Cor. xi. 14 : " Ipse enim Satanas transfigurat se in angelum lucis."

take it Himself ; for I have to live in community, and have very many things to employ me, as I am in a house which is newly founded—as will appear here-after [5] ; and so I am writing, with very many interruptions, by little and little at a time. I wish I had leisure ; for when our Lord gives the spirit, it is more easily and better done ; it is then as with a person working embroidery with the pattern before her ; but if the spirit be wanting, there is no more meaning in the words than in gibberish, so to speak, though many years may have been spent in prayer. And thus I think it a very great advantage to be in this state of prayer when I am writing this ; for I see clearly that it is not I who speak, nor is it I who with her understanding has arranged it ; and afterwards I do not know how I came to speak so accurately.[6] It has often happened to me thus.

13. Let us now return to our orchard, or flower-garden, and behold now how the trees begin to fill with sap for the bringing forth of the blossoms, and then of the fruit—the flowers and the plants, also, their fragrance. This illustration pleases me ; for very often, when I was beginning—and our Lord grant that I have really begun to serve His Majesty—I mean, begun in relation to what I have to say of my life,—it was to me a great joy to consider my soul as a garden, and our Lord as walking in it. I used to beseech Him to increase the fragrance of the little flowers of virtues —which were beginning, as it seemed, to bud—and preserve them, that they might be to His glory ; for I desired nothing for myself. I prayed Him to cut

---

[5] See ch. x. 11, xxxvi. 23.

[6] See ch. xvi. 2, 9 ; xviii. 10.   In the second Report of the Rota, p. 477— quoted by Benedict XIV., *De Canoniz.* iii. 26, n. 12, and by the Bollandists in the *Acta*, 1315—we have these words, and they throw great light on the text : " Sunt et alii testes de visu affirmantes quod quando beata Theresia scribebat libros, facies ejus resplendebat."   In the information taken in Granada, the Mother Anne of the Incarnation says she saw the Saint one night, while writing one of her books, with her face shining ; and Mary of St. Francis deposes to the same effect in the informations taken in Medina.

those He liked, because I already knew that they would grow the better.

14. I say cut ; for there are times in which the soul has no recollection of this garden—everything seems parched, and there is no water to be had for preserving it—and in which it seems as if the soul had never possessed any virtue at all. This is the season of heavy trials ; for our Lord will have the poor gardener suppose all the trouble he took in maintaining and watering the garden to have been taken to no purpose. Then is the time really for weeding and rooting out every plant, however small it may be, that is worthless, in the knowledge that no efforts of ours are sufficient, if God withholds from us the waters of His grace ; and in despising ourselves as being nothing, and even less than nothing. In this way we gain great humility—the flowers grow afresh.

15. O my Lord, and my God ! I cannot utter these words without tears, and rejoicing in my soul ; for Thou wilt be thus with us, and art with us, in the Sacrament. We may believe so most truly ; for so it is, and the comparison I make is a great truth ; and, if our sins stand not in the way, we may rejoice in Thee, because Thou rejoicest in us ; for Thou hast told us that Thy delight is to be with the children of men.[7] O my Lord, what does it mean ? Whenever I hear these words, they always give me great consolation, and did so even when I was most wicked.

16. Is it possible, O Lord, that there can be a soul which, after attaining to this state wherein Thou bestowest upon it the like graces and consolations, and wherein it understands that Thou delightest to be with it, can yet fall back and offend Thee after so many favours, and such great demonstrations of the love Thou bearest it, and of which there cannot be any doubt, because the effect of it is so visible ? Such a soul there certainly is ; for I have done so, not once,

[7] Prov. viii. 31 : " Deliciæ meæ esse cum filiis hominum."

but often. May it please Thy goodness, O Lord, that I may be alone in my ingratitude—the only one who has committed so great an iniquity, and whose ingratitude has been so immeasurable! But even out of my ingratitude Thine infinite goodness has brought forth some good ; and the greater my wickedness, the greater the splendour of the great mercy of Thy compassions. Oh, what reasons have I to magnify them for ever!

17. May it be so, I beseech Thee, O my God, and may I sing of them for ever, now that Thou hast been pleased to show mercies so great unto me that they who see them are astonished, mercies which draw me out of myself continually, that I may praise Thee more and more! for, remaining in myself, without Thee, I could do nothing, O my Lord, but be as the withered flowers of the garden ; so that this miserable earth of mine becomes a heap of refuse, as it was before. Let it not be so, O Lord!—let not a soul which Thou hast purchased with so many labours be lost, one which Thou hast so often ransomed anew and delivered from between the teeth of the hideous dragon!

18. You, my father, must forgive me for wandering from the subject ; and, as I am speaking to the purpose I have in view, you must not be surprised. What I write is what my soul has understood ; and it is very often hard enough to abstain from the praises of God when, in the course of writing, the great debt I owe Him presents itself before me. Nor do I think that it can be disagreeable to you ; because both of us, I believe, may sing the same song, though in a different way ; for my debt is much the greater, seeing that God has forgiven me more, as you, my father, know.[8]

[8] See note to ch. xi. 12.

CHAPTER XV.

INSTRUCTIONS FOR THOSE WHO HAVE ATTAINED TO
THE PRAYER OF QUIET. MANY ADVANCE SO FAR,
BUT FEW GO FARTHER.

Continuing the same subject, she gives certain advice how one should behave in the prayer of quiet. She shows that many souls advance so far, but that few go beyond. The matters treated of in this chapter are very necessary and profitable.

1. LET us now go back to the subject. This quiet and recollection of the soul makes itself in great measure felt in the satisfaction and peace, attended with very great joy and repose of the faculties, and most sweet delight, wherein the soul is established.[1] It thinks, because it has not gone beyond it, that there is nothing further to wish for but that its abode might be there, and it would willingly say so with St. Peter.[2] It dares not move nor stir, because it thinks that this blessing it has received must then escape out of its hands ; now and then, it could wish it did not even breathe.[3] The poor little soul is not aware that, as of itself it could do nothing to draw down this blessing on itself, it is still less able to retain it a moment longer than our Lord wills it should remain.

2. I have already said that, in the prior recollection and quiet,[4] there is no failure of the powers of the soul ; but the soul is so satisfied in God that, although two of its powers be distracted, yet, while the recollection lasts, as the will abides in union with God, so its peace and quiet are not disturbed ; on the contrary, the will by degrees brings the understanding and the memory back again ; for though the will is not yet altogether absorbed, it continues still occupied

---

[1] See *Way of Perfection*, ch. xxxi. 1, 2.
[2] St. Matt. xvii. 4 : " Bonum est nos hic esse."
[3] See ch. xvii. 6   [4] Ch. x. 1.

without knowing how, so that, notwithstanding all the efforts of the memory and the understanding, they cannot rob it of its delight and joy [5]—yea, rather, it helps without any labour at all to keep this little spark of the love of God from being quenched.

3. Oh, that His Majesty would be gracious unto me, and enable me to give a clear account of the matter ; for many are the souls who attain to this state, and few are they who go farther : and I know not who is in fault ; most certainly it is not God ; for when His Majesty shows mercy unto a soul, so that it advances so far, I believe that He will not fail to be more merciful still, if there be no shortcomings on our part.

4. And it is of great importance for the soul that has advanced so far as this to understand the great dignity of its state, the great grace given it by our Lord, and how in all reason it should not belong to earth ; because He, of His goodness, seems to make it here a denizen of heaven, unless it be itself in fault. And miserable will that soul be if it turns back ; it will go down, I think so, even to the abyss, as I was going myself, if the mercy of our Lord had not brought me back ; because, for the most part, it must be the effect of grave faults—that is my opinion : nor is it possible to forsake so great a good otherwise than through the blindness occasioned by much evil.

5. Therefore, for the love of our Lord, I implore those souls to whom His Majesty has given so great a grace—the attainment of this state—to know and make much of themselves, with a humble and holy presumption, in order that they may never return to the flesh-pots of Egypt. And if through weakness and wickedness, and a mean and wretched nature, they should fall, as I did, let them always keep in mind the good they have lost ; let them suspect and fear— they have reason to do so—that, if they do not resume

[5] Ch. xiv. 3, 4.

their prayer, they may go on from bad to worse. I
call that a real fall which makes us hate the way by
which so great a good was obtained. I address myself to those souls ; but I am not saying that they will
never offend God, nor fall into sin,—though there are
good reasons why those who have received these
graces should keep themselves carefully from sin ; but
we are miserable creatures. What I earnestly advise
is this: let there be no giving up of prayer ; it is by
prayer they will understand what they are doing, and
obtain from our Lord the grace to repent, and strength
to rise again ; they must believe and believe again
that, if they cease from praying, they run—so I think
—into danger. I know not if I understand what I
am saying ; for, as I said before, I measure others by
myself.[6]

6. The prayer of quiet, then, is a little spark of
the true love of Himself, which our Lord begins to
enkindle in the soul ; and His will is, that the soul
should understand what this love is by the joy it brings.
This quiet and recollection and little spark, if it is the
work of the Spirit of God, and not a sweetness supplied by Satan, or brought about by ourselves, produces
great results. A person of experience, however, cannot possibly fail to understand at once that it is not a
thing that can be acquired, were it not that our
nature is so greedy of sweetness, that it seeks for it in
every way. But it becomes cold very soon ; for,
however much we try to make the fire burn, in order
to obtain this sweetness, it does not appear that we
do anything else but throw water on it, to put it out.
This spark, then, given of God, however slight it may
be, causes a great crackling ; and if men do not quench
it by their faults, it is the beginning of the great fire,
which sends forth—I shall speak of it in the proper
place [7]—the flames of that most vehement love of God
which His Majesty will have perfect souls to possess.

[6] Ch. x. 9.   [7] Ch. xviii. 4, and ch. xxi. 9.

7. This little spark is a sign or pledge which God gives to a soul, in token of His having chosen it for great things, if it will prepare to receive them. It is a great gift, much too great for me to be able to speak of it. It is a great sorrow to me ; because, as I said before, I know that many souls come thus far, and that those who go farther, as they ought to go, are so few, that I am ashamed to say it. I do not mean that they are absolutely few : there must be many, because God is patient with us, for some reasons ; I speak of what I have seen.

8. I should like much to recommend these souls to take care that they do not hide their talent ; for it may be that God has chosen them to be the edification of many others, especially in these days, when the friends of God should be strong, in order that they may support the weak. Those who discern in themselves this grace, must look upon themselves as such friends, if they would fulfil the law which even the honourable friendship of the world respects ; if not, as I said just now, let them fear and tremble, lest they should be doing mischief to themselves—and God grant it be to themselves only !

9. What the soul has to do at those seasons wherein it is raised to the prayer of quiet is nothing more than to be gentle and without noise. By noise, I mean going about with the understanding in search of words and reflections whereby to give God thanks for this grace, and heaping up its sins and imperfections together to show that it does not deserve it. All this commotion takes place now, and the understanding comes forward, and the memory is restless, and certainly to me these powers bring much weariness at times ; for, though my memory is not strong, I cannot control it. Let the will quietly and wisely understand that it is not by dint of labour on our part that we can converse to any good purpose with God, and

⁸ § 3.   ⁹ § 5.

that our own efforts are only great logs of wood, laid on without discretion to quench this little spark ; and let it confess this, and in humility say, O Lord, what can I do here ? what has the servant to do with her Lord, and earth with heaven ? or words of love that suggest themselves now, firmly grounded in the conviction that what it says is truth ; and let it make no account of the understanding, which is simply tiresome.

10. And if the will wishes to communicate to the understanding any portion of that the fruition of which itself has entered on, or if it labours to make the understanding recollected, it shall not succeed ; for it will often happen that the will is in union and at rest, while the understanding is in extreme disorder. It is better for it to leave it alone, and not to run after it—I am speaking of the will ; for the will should abide in the fruition of that grace, recollected itself, like the prudent bee ; for if no bees entered the hive, and each of them wandered abroad in search of the rest, the honey would hardly be made. In the same way, the soul will lose much if it be not careful now, especially if the understanding be acute ; for when it begins to make reflections and search for reasons, it will think at once that it is doing something if its reasons and reflections are good.

11. The only reason that ought to be admitted now is to understand clearly that there is no reason whatever, except His mere goodness, why God should grant us so great a grace, and to be aware that we are so near Him, and to pray to His Majesty for mercies, to make intercession for the Church, for those who had been recommended to us, and for the souls in purgatory,—not, however, with noise of words, but with a heartfelt desire to be heard. This is a prayer that contains much, and by it more is obtained than by many reflections of the understanding. Let the will stir up some of those reasons, which proceed from reason

itself, to quicken its love, such as the fact of its being in a better state, and let it make certain acts of love, as what it will do for Him to whom it owes so much, —and that, as I said just now, without any noise of the understanding, in the search after profound reflections.   A little straw,—and it will be less than straw, if we bring it ourselves,—laid on with humility, will be more effectual here, and will help to kindle a fire more than many fagots of most learned reasons, which, in my opinion, will put it out in a moment.[10] .

12. This is good for those learned men who have commanded me to write,[11] and who all, by the goodness of God, have come to this state ; for it may be that they spend the time in making applications of passages of the Scriptures.   And though learning could not fail to be of great use to them, both before and after prayer, still, in the very time of prayer itself, there is little necessity for it, in my opinion, unless it be for the purpose of making the will tepid ; for the understanding then, because of its nearness to the light, is itself illuminated ; so that even I, who am what I am, seem to be a different person.   And so it is ; for it has happened to me, who scarcely understand a word of what I read in Latin, and specially in the Psalms, when in the prayer of quiet, not only to understand the Latin as if it were Spanish, but, still more, to take a delight in dwelling on the meaning of that I knew through the Spanish.   We must make an exception : if these learned men have to preach or to teach, they will do well to take advantage of their learning, that they may help poor people of little learning, of whom I am one.   Charity is a great thing ; and so always is ministering unto souls, when done simply for God.

13. So, then, when the soul is in the prayer of quiet, let it repose in its rest—let learning be put on one side.   The time will come when they may make use of it

---

[10] Ch. xxx. 25 ; xxxi. 25.   [11] Ch. x. 1.

in the service of our Lord—when they that possess it will appreciate it so highly as to be glad that they had not neglected it even for all the treasures of the world, simply because it enables them to serve His Majesty ; for it is a great help. But in the eyes of Infinite Wisdom, believe me, a little striving after humility, and a single act thereof, are worth more than all the science in the world. This is not the time for discussing, but for understanding plainly what we are, and presenting ourselves in simplicity before God, who will have the soul make itself as a fool—as, indeed, it is—in His presence, seeing that His Majesty so humbles Himself as to suffer it to be near Him, we being what we are.

14. Moreover, the understanding bestirs itself to make its thanksgiving in phrases well arranged ; but the will, in peace, not daring to lift up its eyes with the publican,[12] makes perhaps a better act of thanksgiving than the understanding, with all the tropes of its rhetoric. In a word, mental prayer is not to be abandoned altogether now, nor even vocal prayer, if at any time we wish, or care, to make use of either of them ; for if the state of quiet be profound, it becomes difficult to speak, and it can be done only with great pain.

15. I believe myself that we know whether this proceeds from the Spirit of God, or is brought about by endeavours of our own, in the commencement of devotion which God gives ; and we seek of ourselves, as I said before,[13] to pass onwards to this quiet of the will. Then, no effect whatever is produced ; it is quickly over, and aridity is the result. If it comes from Satan, the practised soul, in my opinion, will detect it, because it leaves trouble behind, and scant humility and poor dispositions for those effects which are wrought if it comes from God ; it leaves neither

---

[12] St. Luke xviii. 13 : " Nolebat nec oculos ad cœlum levare."
[13] Ch. xii. 5.

light in the understanding nor steadiness in the truth.[14]

16. Here Satan can do little or no harm, if the soul directs unto God the joy and sweetness it then feels ; and if it fixes the thoughts and desires on Him according to the advice already given, the devil can gain nothing whatever—on the contrary, by the permission of God, he will lose much by that very joy which he causes in the soul, because that joy will help the soul, inasmuch as it thinks the joy comes from God, to betake itself often to prayer in its desire for it. And if the soul is humble, indifferent to, and detached from, all joy, however spiritual, and if it loves the cross, it will make no account of the sweetness which Satan sends. But it cannot so deal with that which comes from the Spirit of God ; of that it will make much. Now, when Satan sends it, as he is nothing but a lie, and when he sees that the soul humbles itself through that joy and sweetness—and here, in all things relating to prayer and sweetness, we must be very careful to endeavour to make ourselves humble—Satan will not often repeat his work, when he sees that he loses by it.

17. For this and for many other reasons, when I was speaking of the first degree of prayer, and of the first method of drawing the water,[15] I insisted upon it that the great affair of souls is when they begin to pray, to begin also to detach themselves from every kind of joy, and to enter on it resolved only on helping to carry the cross of Christ like good soldiers, willing to serve their King without present pay, because they are sure of it at last, having their eyes directed to the

[14] " Firmeza en la verdad." Franciscus a St. Thoma, in his *Medulla Mystica*, p. 204, quoting this passage, has, " firmeza en la voluntad." Philip a SS. Trinitate, *Theolog. Mystic.* p. 354, and his Abbreviator, Anton. a Spiritu Sancto, *Direct. Mystic.* tr. iv. disp. i. § 11, n. 94, seem also to have preferred " voluntad " to " verdad " ; for the words they use are, " nec intellectui lux nec voluntati firmitas " ; and, " defectus lucis in intellectu, et firmitatis in voluntate."

[15] Ch. xi. 16.

true and everlasting kingdom at the conquest of which we are aiming.

18. It is a very great matter to have this always before our eyes, especially in the beginning ; afterwards, it becomes so clear, that it is rather a matter of necessity to forget it, in order to live on. Now, labouring to keep in mind that all things here below are of short duration, that they are all nothing, that the rest we have here is to be accounted as none,—all this, I say, seems to be exceedingly low ; and so indeed, it is,—because those who have gone on to greater perfection would look upon it as a reproach, and be ashamed of themselves if they thought that they were giving up the goods of this world because they are perishable, or that they would not be glad to give them up for God—even if they were to last for ever. The greater the perfection of these persons, the greater their joy, and the greater also would that joy be if the duration of these worldly goods were greater.

19. In these persons, thus far advanced, love is already grown, and love is that which does this work. But as to beginners, to them it is of the utmost importance, and they must not regard this consideration as unbecoming, for the blessings to be gained are great —and that is why I recommend it so much to them ; for they will have need of it—even those who have attained to great heights of prayer—at certain times, when God will try them, and when His Majesty seems to have forsaken them.

20. I have said as much already, and I would not have it forgotten,[16] in this our life on earth, the growth of the soul is not like that of the body. We, however, so speak of it—and, in truth, it does grow. A youth that is grown up, whose body is formed, and who is become a man, does not ungrow, nor does his body lessen in size ; but as to the soul, it is so by our Lord's

[16] Ch. xiii. 23.

will, so far as I have seen it in my own experience,
—but I know nothing of it in any other way.[17] It
must be in order to humble us for our greater good,
and to keep us from being careless during our exile ;
seeing that he who has ascended the higher has the
more reason to be afraid, and to be less confident in
himself. A time may come when they whose will is
so wrapt up in the will of God—and who, rather than
fall into a single imperfection, would undergo torture
and suffer a thousand deaths—will find it necessary,
if they would be delivered from offending God, and
from the commission of sin, to make use of the first
armour of prayer, to call to mind how everything is
coming to an end, that there is a heaven and a hell,
and to make use of other reflections of that nature,
when they find themselves assailed by temptations
and persecutions.

21. Let us go back to what I was saying. The
great source of our deliverance from the cunning devices and the sweetness which Satan sends is to begin
with a resolution to walk in the way of the Cross from
the very first, and not to desire any sweetness at all,
seeing that our Lord Himself has pointed out to us
the way of perfection, saying, " Take up thy cross and
follow Me." [18] He is our example ; and whosoever
follows His counsels only to please Him has nothing
to fear. In the improvement which they detect in
themselves, they who do so will see that this is no
work of Satan ; and if they fall, they have a sign of the
presence of our Lord in their rising again at once.
They have other signs, also, of which I am going to
speak.

22. When it is the work of the Spirit of God, there
is no necessity for going about searching for reasons,
on the strength of which we may elicit acts of humility
and of shame, because our Lord Himself supplies them

---

[17] St. John of the Cross, *Ascent of Mount Carmel*, bk. ii. ch. xv. 1.
[18] St. Matt. xvi. 24 ; " Tollat crucem suam et sequatur Me."

in a way very different from that by which we could acquire them by our own poor reflections, which are as nothing in comparison with that real humility arising out of the light which our Lord here gives us, and which begets a confusion of face that undoes us. The knowledge with which God supplies us, in order that we may know that of ourselves we have no good in us, is perfectly apprehended—and the more perfectly, the greater the graces. It fills us with a great desire of advancing in prayer, and of never giving it up, whatever troubles may arise. The soul offers to suffer everything. A certain security, joined with humility and fear concerning our salvation, casts out servile fear at once from the soul, and in its place plants a loyal fear [19] of more perfect growth. [20] There is a visible beginning of a love of God, utterly divested of all self-interest, together with a longing after seasons of solitude, in order to obtain a greater fruition of this good.

23. In short, not to weary myself, it is the beginning of all good : the flowers have so thriven, that they are on the point of budding. And this the soul sees most clearly, and it is impossible to persuade it now that God was not with it, till it turns back upon itself, and beholds its own failings and imperfections. Then it fears for everything ; and it is well it should do so—though there are souls whom the certain conviction that God is with them benefits more than all the fear they may ever have. If a soul love greatly, and is thankful naturally, the remembrance of the mercies of God makes it turn to Him more effectually than all the chastisements of hell it can ever picture to itself— at least, it was so with me, though I am so wicked.

24. As I shall speak at greater length of the signs of a good spirit [21]—it has cost me much labour to be clear about them—I do not treat of them here. I

---

[19] " Fiel temor."   In the previous editions it was *filial.*
[20] Ch. xi. 1.   [21] See ch. xxv

believe, too, that, with the help of God, I shall be able
to speak somewhat to the point, because—setting
aside the experience I have had, and by which I
learned much—I have had the help of some most learned
men and persons of great holiness, whom we may
reasonably believe in the matter. Souls, therefore,
are not to weary themselves so much as I did, when,
by the goodness of our Lord, they may have come to
this state.

CHAPTER XVI.

THE THIRD STATE OF PRAYER. DEEP MATTERS. WHAT THE SOUL CAN DO THAT HAS REACHED IT. EFFECTS OF THE GREAT GRACES OF OUR LORD.

*On the third degree of prayer she declares things of
an elevated nature ; what the soul that has come so far
can do, and the effect of such great graces of God. This
is calculated greatly to animate the spirit to the praise
of God, and contains advice for those who have reached
this point.*

1. LET us now speak of the third water wherewith this
garden is watered,—water running from a river or
from a brook,—whereby the garden is watered with very
much less trouble, although there is some in directing
the water.[1] In this state our Lord will help the gardener, and in such a way as to be, as it were, the Gardener Himself, doing all the work. It is a sleep of the
powers of the soul, which are not wholly lost, nor yet
understanding how they are at work. The pleasure,
sweetness, and delight are incomparably greater than

[1] " The third degree, or third water, of the Saint, must begin, I think,
with the prayer of infused recollection, include that of infused quiet, and end
in that of inebriation ; because it is not in our power to draw this water—
all we can do is to direct the stream " (Francis. a St. Thoma, *Medulla Mystica*,
tr. iv. ch. xii. p. 208).

in the former state of prayer ; and the reason is, that the waters of grace have risen up to the neck of the soul, so that it can neither advance nor retreat—nor does it know how to do so ; it seeks only the fruition of exceeding bliss. It is like a dying man with the candle in his hand, on the point of dying the death desired. It is rejoicing in this agony with unutterable joy ; to me it seems to be nothing else but a death, as it were, to all the things of this world, and a fruition of God. I know of no other words whereby to describe it or to explain it ; neither does the soul then know what to do;—for it knows not whether to speak or be silent, whether it should laugh or weep. It is a glorious folly, a heavenly madness, wherein true wisdom is acquired ; and to the soul a kind of fruition most full of delight.[2]

2. It is now some five or six years, I believe, since our Lord raised me to this state of prayer, in its fulness, and that more than once,—and I never understood it, and never could explain it ;[3] and so I was resolved, when I should come thus far in my story, to say very little or nothing at all. I knew well enough that it was not altogether the union of all the faculties, and yet most certainly it was higher than the previous state of prayer ; but I confess that I could not determine and understand the difference.

3. The humility of your reverence, willing to be helped by a simplicity so great as mine, has been the cause, I believe, why our Lord, to-day, after Communion, admitted me to this state of prayer, without the power of going further, and suggested to me these comparisons, and taught me how to speak of it, and of what the soul must do therein. Certainly, I was amazed, and in a moment understood it all. I have often been thus, as it were, beside myself, drunk with love, and yet never could understand how it was. I

[2] See St. John of the Cross, *Spiritual Canticle*, stanza xvii. 7.
[3] Ch. xiv. 12 ; xviii. 10.

knew well that it was the work of God, but I never was able to understand the manner of His working here ; for, in fact, the faculties are almost all completely in union, yet not so absorbed that they do not act. I have been singularly delighted in that I have been able to comprehend the matter at last. Blessed be our Lord, who has thus consoled me !

4. The faculties of the soul now retain only the power of occupying themselves wholly with God ; not one of them ventures to stir, neither can we move one of them without making great efforts to distract ourselves—and, indeed, I do not think we can do it at all at this time. Many words are then uttered in praise of God—but disorderly, unless it be that our Lord orders them Himself. At least, the understanding is utterly powerless here ; the soul longs to send forth words of praise, but it has no control over itself,—it is in a state of sweet restlessness. The flowers are already opening ; they are beginning to send forth their fragrance.

5. The soul in this state would have all men behold it, and know of its bliss, to the praise of God, and help it to praise Him. It would have them to be partakers of its joy ; for its joy is greater than it can bear. It seems to me that it is like the woman in the Gospel, who would, or used to, call in her neighbours.[4] The admirable spirit of David, the royal prophet, must have felt in the same way, so it seems to me, when he played on the harp, singing the praises of God. I have a very great devotion to this glorious king [5] ; and I wish all had it, particularly those who are sinners like myself.

6. O my God, what must that soul be when it is in this state ? It wishes it were all tongue, in order that it may praise our Lord. It utters a thousand

---

[4] St. Luke xv. 9 : " Convocat amicas et vicinas."

[5] *Foundations*, ch. xxix. 9. The feast of King David appears first in the Calendar of the Order revised by the General Chapter of 1564.

holy follies, striving continually to please Him by whom it is thus possessed. I know one [6] who, though she was no poet, yet composed, without any preparation, certain stanzas, full of feeling, most expressive of her pain : they were not the work of her own understanding ; but, in order to have a greater fruition of that bliss which so sweet a pain occasioned her, she complained of it in that way to God. She was willing to be cut in pieces, soul and body, to show the delight she felt in that pain. To what torments could she be then exposed, that would not be delicious to endure for her Lord ? She sees clearly that the martyrs did little or nothing, so far as they were concerned, when they endured their tortures, because the soul is well aware that its strength is derived from another source.

7. But what will be its sufferings when it returns to the use of the senses, to live in the world, and go back to the anxieties and the fashions thereof ? I do not think that I have exaggerated in any way, but rather have fallen short, in speaking of that joy, which our Lord, of His good pleasure, gives to the soul in this its exile. Blessed for ever be Thou, O Lord ! and may all created things praise Thee for ever !

8. O my King, seeing that I am now, while writing this, still under the power of this heavenly madness, an effect of Thy mercy and goodness,—and it is a mercy I never deserved,—grant, I beseech Thee, that all those with whom I may have to converse may become mad through Thy love, or let me converse with none, or so order it that I may have nothing to do in the world, or take me away from it. This Thy servant, O my God, is no longer able to endure sufferings so great as those are which she must bear when she sees herself without Thee : if she must live, she seeks no repose in this life,—and do Thou give her none. This my soul longs to be free—eating is killing it, and

---

[6] The Saint herself. *Rel.* viii. 3.

sleep is wearisome ; it sees itself wasting the time of
this life in comforts, and that there is no comfort for
it now but in Thee ; it seems to be living contrary
to nature—for now, it desires to live not in itself, but
in Thee.

9. O my true Lord and my happiness! what a
cross hast Thou prepared for those who attain to this
state!—light and most heavy at the same time : light,
because sweet ; heavy, because now and then there
is no patience left to endure it—and yet the soul never
wishes to be delivered from it, unless it be that it may
come to Thee.   When the soul remembers that it has
never served Thee at all, and that by living on it may
do Thee some service, it longs for a still heavier cross,
and never to die before the end of the world.   Its own
repose it counts as nothing in comparison with doing
a slight service to Thee.   It knows not what to desire ;
but it clearly understands that it desires nothing else
but Thee.

10. O my son,[7] so humble is he to whom this
writing is directed and who has commanded me to
write, that he suffers himself to be thus addressed,—
you, my father, only must see these things, in which
I seem to have transgressed all bounds ; for no reason
can keep me reasonable when our Lord draws me out
of myself.   Since my communion this morning,[8] I do
not believe that I am the person who is speaking ; I
seem to be dreaming the things I see, and I wish I
might never see any but people ill, as I am now.   I
beseech you, my father, let us all be mad, for the love
of Him who for our sakes suffered men to say of Him
that He was mad.[9]

11. You, my father, say that you wish me well.
I wish you would prove it by disposing yourself so

---

[7] This was either F. Ibañez or more probably F. Garcia de Toledo.   F.
Dominic Bañes struck out " son," and wrote " father " in its place, omitting
the words, " so humble is he."

[8] See § 3, above.

[9] St. John x. 20 : " Dæmonium habet et insanit."

that God may bestow this grace upon you ; for I see
very few people who have not too much sense for
everything they have to do : and it may be that I
have more than anybody else. Your reverence must
not allow it ; you are my father, for you are my confessor, and the person to whom I have trusted my
soul ; disperse my delusions by telling the truth ; for
truths of this sort are very rarely told.

12. I wish we five, who now love one another in
our Lord, had made some such arrangement as this :
as others in these times have met together in secret [10]
to plot wickedness and heresies against His Majesty,
so we might contrive to meet together now and then,
in order to undeceive one another, to tell each other
wherein we might improve ourselves, and be more
pleasing unto God ; for there is no one that knows
himself as well as he is known of others who see him,
if it be with eyes of love and the wish to do him good.
I say, in secret ; for language of this kind is no longer
in use ; even preachers go about arranging their sermons so as to displease no one.[11] They have a good
intention, and their work is good ; yet still few amend
their lives. But how is it that they are not many who,
in consequence of these sermons, abstain from public
sins ? Well, I think it is because the preachers are
highly sensible men. They are not burning with the
great fire of the love of God, as the Apostles were, casting worldly prudence aside ; and so their fire throws
out but little heat. I do not say that their fire ought

[10] The Saint refers to the secret meetings of heretics in Valladolid, under
the direction of a fallen priest, the Doctor Agustín Cazalla, whose vanity led
him to imitate Luther. Some nuns in Valladolid were imprisoned, Cazalla
strangled, and his body burnt, in 1559. It is doubtful who the five persons
alluded to in the text may have been. Fuente thinks, besides St. Teresa,
Julian de Avila, chaplain of the convent of St. Joseph at Avila, Don
Francisco de Salcedo, St. John of the Cross, and Don Lorenzo de Cepeda,
brother of the Saint. But this is impossible at the date of this part
of the " Life."   It is more probable that she meant the two Dominicans
Pedro de Ibañez and Garcia de Toledo, and perhaps Francisco de Salcedo and
Gaspar Daza. But the question remains open.

[11] Father Bañes wrote here on the margin of the Saint's MS : " Legant
prædicatores."

to burn like that of the Apostles, but 'I do wish it were a stronger fire than I see it is. Do you, my father, know wherein much of this fire consists? In the hatred of this life, in the desertion of its honours, in being utterly indifferent whether we lose or gain anything or everything, provided the truth be told and maintained for the glory of God; for he who is courageously in earnest for God, looks upon loss or gain indifferently. I do not say that I am a person of this kind, but I wish I was.

13. Oh, grand freedom, to regard it as a captivity to be obliged to live and converse with men according to the laws of the world! It is the gift of our Lord; there is not a slave who would not imperil everything that he might escape and return to his country; and as this is the true road, there is no reason why we should linger; for we shall never effectually gain a treasure so great, so long as this life is not ended. May our Lord give us His grace for that end! You, my father, if it shall seem good to you, will tear up what I have written, and consider it as a letter for yourself alone, and forgive me that I have been very bold.

CHAPTER XVII.

THE THIRD STATE OF PRAYER. THE EFFECTS THEREOF. THE HINDRANCE CAUSED BY THE IMAGINATION AND THE MEMORY.

Continues to declare matters concerning the third degree of prayer and completes the explanation of its effects. She also treats of the impediment caused by the imagination and the memory.

1. ENOUGH has been said of this manner of prayer, and of what the soul has to do, or rather, to speak more correctly, of what God is doing within it; for it is He who now takes upon Himself the gardener's work

and who will have the soul take its ease ; except that
the will is consenting to the graces, the fruition of
which it has, and that it must resign itself to all that
the True Wisdom would accomplish in it—for which
it is certain it has need of courage ; because the joy is
so great, that the soul seems now and then to be on
the very point of going forth out of the body ; and
what a blessed death that would be ! Now, I think
it is for the soul's good—as you, my father, have been
told—to abandon itself into the arms of God altogether ; if He will take it to heaven, let it go ; if to
hell, no matter, as it is going thither with its sovereign
Good.   If life is to come to an end for ever, so it wills ;
if it is to last a thousand years, it wills that also :
His Majesty may do with it as with His own property,
—the soul no longer belongs to itself, it has been given
wholly to our Lord ; let it cast all care utterly away.

2. My meaning is that, in a state of prayer so high
as this, the soul understands that God is doing His
work without any fatiguing of the understanding,
except that, as it seems to me, it is as if amazed in
beholding our Lord taking upon Himself the work of
the good gardener, refusing to let the soul undergo any
labour whatever, but that of taking its pleasure in the
flowers beginning to send forth their fragrance ; for
when God raises a soul up to this state, it can do all
this, and much more,—for these are the effects of it.

3. In one of these visits, how brief soever it may
be, the Gardener, being who He is,—in a word, the
Creator of the water,—pours the water without stint ;
and what the poor soul, with the labour, perhaps, of
twenty years in fatiguing the understanding, could
not bring about, that the heavenly Gardener accom-
plishes in an instant, causing the fruit both to grow
and ripen ; so that the soul, such being the will of our
Lord, may derive its sustenance from its garden.   But
He allows it not to divide the fruit with others, until
by eating thereof, it is strong enough not to waste it

in the mere tasting of it,—giving to Him of the produce, nor making any compensation for it to Him who supplies it,—lest it should be maintaining others, feeding them at its own cost, and itself perhaps dying of hunger.[1] The meaning of this is perfectly clear for those who have understanding enough to apply it—much more clear than I can make it ; and I am tired.

4. Finally, the virtues are now stronger than they were during the preceding prayer of quiet ; for the soul sees itself to be other than it was, and it knows not how it is beginning to do great things in the odour which the flowers send forth ; it being our Lord's will that the flowers should open, in order that the soul may believe itself to be in possession of virtue ; though it sees most clearly that it cannot, and never could, acquire them in many years, and that the heavenly Gardener has given them to it in that instant. Now, too, the humility of the soul is much greater and deeper than it was before ; because it sees more clearly that it did neither much nor little, beyond giving its consent that our Lord might work those graces in it, and then accepting them willingly.

5. This state of prayer seems to me to be a most distinct union of the whole soul with God, but for this, that His Majesty appears to give the faculties leave to be intent upon, and have the fruition of, the great work He is doing then. It happens at times, and indeed very often, that, the will being in union, the soul should be aware of it, and see that the will is a captive and in joy, that the will alone is abiding in great peace,—while, on the other hand, the under-standing and the memory are so free, that they can be employed in affairs and be occupied in works of charity. I say this, that you, my father, may see it is so, and understand the matter when it shall happen to yourself ; at least, it carried me out of myself, and that is the reason why I speak of it here.

[1] See ch xix. 4, 22.

6. It differs from the prayer of quiet, of which I have spoken,[2] though it does seem as if it were all one with it. In that prayer, the soul, which would willingly neither stir nor move, is delighting in the holy repose of Mary; but in this prayer it can be like Martha also.[3] Accordingly, the soul is, as it were, living the active and contemplative life at once, and is able to apply itself to works of charity and the affairs of its state, and to spiritual reading. Still, those who arrive at this state are not wholly masters of themselves, and are well aware that the better part of the soul is elsewhere. It is as if we were speaking to one person, and another speaking to us at the same time, while we ourselves are not perfectly attentive either to the one or the other. It is a state that is most easily ascertained, and one, when attained to, that ministers great joy and contentment, and that prepares the soul in the highest degree, by observing times of solitude, or of freedom from business, for the attainment of the most tranquil quietude. It is like the life of a man who is full, requiring no food, with his appetite satisfied, so that he will not eat of everything set before him, yet not so full either as to refuse to eat if he saw any desirable food. So the soul has no satisfaction in the world, and seeks no pleasure in it then; because it has in itself that which gives it a greater satisfaction, greater joys in God, longings for the satisfaction of its longing to have a deeper joy in being with Him—this is what the soul seeks.

7. There is another kind of union, which, though not a perfect union, is yet more so than the one of which I have just spoken; but not so much so as this spoken of as the third water. You, my father, will be delighted greatly if our Lord should bestow them all upon you, if you have them not already, to find an account of the matter in writing, and to understand

[2] Ch. xv. 1.
[3] See *Relation* viii. 6; and *Way of Perfection*, ch. xxxi. 4. See also *Concept. of the Love of God*, ch. vii. 4.

it ; for it is one grace that our Lord gives grace ; and it is another grace to understand what grace and what gift it is ; and it is another and further grace to have the power to describe and explain it to others.[4] Though it does not seem that more than the first of these—the giving of the grace—is necessary to enable the soul to advance without confusion and fear, and to walk with the greater courage in the way of our Lord, trampling under foot all the things of this world, it is a great advantage and a great grace to understand it ; for every one who has it has great reason to praise our Lord ; and so, also, has he who has it not : because His Majesty has bestowed it upon some person living who is to make us profit by it.

8. This union, of which I would now speak, frequently occurs, particularly to myself. God has very often bestowed such a grace upon me, whereby He constrains the will, and even the understanding, as it seems to me, seeing that it makes no reflections, but is occupied in the fruition of God ; like a person who looks on, and sees so many things, that he knows not where to look—one object puts another out of sight, and none of them leaves any impression behind.

9. The memory remains free, and it must be so, together with the imagination ; and so, when it finds itself alone, it is marvellous to behold what war it makes on the soul, and how it labours to throw everything into disorder. As for me, I am wearied by it, and I hate it ; and very often do I implore our Lord to deprive me of it on these occasions, if I am to be so much troubled by it. Now and then, I say to Him : O my God, when shall my soul praise Thee without distraction, not dissipated in this way, unable to control itself ! I understand now the mischief that sin has done, in that it has rendered us unable to do what we desire—to be always occupied in God.[5]

---

4 Ch. xxiii. 12.
5 See *Relation* viii. 17.

10. I say that it happens to me from time to time, —it has done so this very day, and so I remember it well,—to see my soul tear itself, in order to find itself there where the greater part of it is, and to see, at the same time, that it is impossible : because the memory and the imagination assail it with such force, that it cannot prevail against them ; yet, as the other faculties give them no assistance, they are not able to do it any harm—none whatever ; they do enough when they trouble its rest. When I say they do no harm, my meaning is, that they cannot really hurt it, because they have not strength enough, and because they are too discursive. As the understanding gives no help, neither much nor little, in the matters put before the soul, they never rest anywhere, but hurry to and fro, like nothing else but gnats at night, troublesome and unquiet : and so they go about from one subject to another.

11. This comparison seems to me to be singularly to the purpose ; for the memory and the imagination, though they have no power to do any harm, are very troublesome. I know of no remedy for it ; and, hitherto, God has told me of none. If He had, most gladly would I make use of it ; for I am, as I say, tormented very often. This shows our wretchedness, and brings out most distinctly the great power of God, seeing that the faculty which is free hurts and wearies us so much ; while the others, occupied with His Majesty, give us rest.

12. The only remedy I have found, after many years of weariness, is that I spoke of when I was describing the prayer of quiet : [6] to make no more account of it than of a madman, but let it go with its subject ; for God alone can take it from it,—in short, it is a slave here. We must bear patiently with it, as Jacob bore with Lia ; for our Lord showeth us mercy enough when we are allowed to have Rachel with us.

[6] Ch. xiv. 4.   See also *Way of Perfection*, ch. xxxi. 7.

13. I say that it remains a slave ; for, after all, let it do what it will, it cannot drag the other faculties in its train ; on the contrary, they, without taking any trouble, compel it to follow after them. Sometimes God is pleased to take pity on it, when He sees it so lost and so unquiet, through the longing it has to be united with the other faculties, and His Majesty consents to its burning itself in the flame of that divine candle by which the others are already reduced to ashes, and their nature lost, being, as it were, supernaturally in the fruition of blessings so great.

14. In all these states of prayer of which I have spoken, while explaining this last method of drawing the water out of the well, so great is the bliss and repose of the soul, that even the body most distinctly shares in its joy and delight,—and this is most plain ; and the virtues continue to grow, as I said before.[7] It seems to have been the good pleasure of our Lord to explain these states of prayer, wherein the soul finds itself, with the utmost clearness possible, I think, here on earth.

15. Do you, my father, discuss it with any spiritual person who has arrived at this state, and is learned. If he says of it, it is well, you may believe that God has spoken it, and you will give thanks to His Majesty ; for, as I said just now,[8] in the course of time you will rejoice greatly in that you have understood it. Meanwhile, if He does not allow you to understand what it is, though He does give you the possession of it, yet, with your intellect and learning, seeing that His Majesty has given you the first, you will know what it is, by the help of what I have written here. Unto Him be praise for ever and ever ! Amen.

[7] Ch. xiv. 6.   [8] § 7.

CHAPTER XVIII.

THE FOURTH STATE OF PRAYER. THE GREAT DIGNITY
OF THE SOUL RAISED TO IT BY OUR LORD. ATTAIN-
ABLE ON EARTH, NOT BY OUR MERIT, BUT BY THE
GOODNESS OF OUR LORD.

*She treats of the fourth degree of prayer and begins
to explain in an excellent manner in what high dignity
God holds a soul that has attained this state. This should
animate those who are given to prayer to make an effort
to reach so high a state, since it can be obtained in this
world, though not by merit, but only through the goodness
of God. To be read with great care, as it is explained
in a most delicate way, and contains many noteworthy
points.**

1. MAY our Lord teach me words whereby I may in
some measure describe the fourth water.[1] I have great
need of His help,—even more than I had while speaking
of the last ; for in that the soul still feels that it is not
dead altogether. We may thus speak, seeing that to
the world it is really dead. But, as I have said,[2] it
retains the sense to see that it is in the world, and to
feel its own loneliness ; and it makes use of that which
is outward for the purpose of manifesting its feelings,
at least by signs. In the whole of the prayer already
spoken of, and in all the states of it, the gardener
undergoes some labour : though in the later states the
labour is attended with so much bliss and comfort of
the soul, that the soul would never willingly pass out
of it,—and thus the labour is not felt as labour, but
as bliss.

2. In this the fourth state there is no sense of anything, only fruition, without understanding what that

---

* The two last lines are scored through in the MS.
[1] See ch. xi. 11.   [2] Ch. xvi. 7, 8.

is the fruition of which is granted. It is understood
that the fruition is of a certain good containing in
itself all good together at once ; but this good is not
comprehended. The senses are all occupied in this
fruition in such a way that not one of them is at
liberty, so as to be able to attend to anything else,
whether outward or inward.

3. The senses were permitted before, as I have said,[3]
to give some signs of the great joy they feel ; but now,
in this state, the joy of the soul is incomparably greater,
and the power of showing it is still less ; for there is no
power in the body, and the soul has none, whereby
this fruition can be made known. Everything of that
kind would be a great hindrance, a torment, and a
disturbance of its rest. And I say, if it really be a
union of all the faculties, that the soul, even if it
wished,—I mean, when it is in union,—cannot make
it known ; and if it can, then it is not union at all.

4. How this, which we call union, is effected, and
what it is, I cannot tell. Mystical theology explains
it, and I do not know the terms of that science ; nor
can I understand what the mind is, nor how it differs
from the soul or spirit either : all three seem to me
but one ; though I do know that the soul sometimes
leaps forth out of itself, like a fire that is burning and
is become a flame ; and occasionally this fire increases
violently—the flame ascends high above the fire ; but
it is not therefore a different thing : it is still the same
flame of the same fire. Your learning, my fathers, will
enable you to understand the matter ; I can go no
further.

5. What I undertake to explain is that which the
soul feels when it is in the divine union. It is plain
enough what union is—two distinct things becoming
one. O my Lord, how good Thou art ! Blessed be
Thou for ever, O my God ! Let all creatures praise
Thee, Who hast so loved us that we can truly speak

[3] Ch. xvii. 5.

of this communication which Thou hast with souls in this our exile! Yea, even if they be good souls, it is on Thy part great munificence and magnanimity,—in a word, it is Thy munificence, O my Lord, seeing that Thou givest like Thyself. O infinite Munificence! —how magnificent are Thy works! Even he whose understanding is not occupied with the things of earth is amazed that he is unable to understand these truths. Why, then, give graces so high to souls who have been such great sinners? Truly, this passeth my understanding; and when I come to think of it, I can get no further. Is there any way at all for me to go on which is not a going back? For, as to giving Thee thanks for mercies so great, I know not how to do it. Sometimes I relieve myself by giving utterance to follies. It often happens to me, either when I receive these graces, or when God is about to bestow them,—for, in the midst of them, I have already said,[4] I was able to do nothing,—that I would break out into words like these:

6. O Lord, consider what Thou art doing; forget not so soon the great evils that I have done. To forgive me, Thou must already have forgotten them; yet, in order that there may be some limit to Thy graces, I beseech thee remember them. O my Creator, pour not a liquor so precious into a vessel so broken; for Thou hast already seen how on other occasions I allowed it to run waste. Lay not up treasures like this, where the longing after the consolations of this life is not so mortified as it ought to be; for it will be utterly lost. How canst Thou commit the defence of the city and the keys of its fortress to a commander so cowardly, who at the first assault will let the enemy enter within? Oh, let not Thy love be so great, O King Eternal, as to imperil jewels so precious! O my Lord, to me it seems that it becomes a ground for undervaluing them, when Thou puttest them in the power of one so

4 § 3.

wretched, so vile, so frail, so miserable, and so worthless as I am, who, though she may labour not to lose
them, by the help of Thy grace,—and I have need of
no little grace for that end, being what I am,—is not
able to win over any one to Thee,—in short, I am a
woman, not good, but wicked. It seems to me that
the talents are not only hidden, but buried, when they
are committed to earth so vile. It is not Thy wont,
O Lord, to bestow graces and mercies like these upon
a soul, unless it be that it may edify many.

7. Thou, O my God, knowest already that I beg
this of Thee with my whole will, from the bottom of
my heart, and that I have done so more than once,
and I account it a blessing to lose the greatest blessings
which may be had on earth, if Thou wouldst but
bestow these graces upon him who will make a better
use of them to the increase of Thy glory. These, and
expressions like these, it has happened to me often
to utter. I saw afterwards my own foolishness and
want of humility ; for our Lord knoweth well what
is expedient, and that there is no strength in my soul
to be saved, if His Majesty did not give it with graces
so great.

8. I purpose also to speak of the graces and effects
which abide in the soul, and of that which the soul
itself can do, or rather, if it can do anything of itself
towards attaining to a state so high. The elevation of
the spirit, or union, comes together with heavenly
love ; but, as I understand it, union is a different thing
from elevation in union itself. To him who may not
have had any experience of the latter, it must seem
that it is not ; and, according to my view of it, even
if they are both one, the operations of our Lord therein
are different : there is a growth of the soul's detachment from creatures more abundantly still in the
flight of the spirit.[5] I have clearly seen that this is
a particular grace, though, as I say, it may be the

[5] See ch. xx. 10 ; and *Relation* viii. 10.

same, or seem to be so, with the other ; but a little fire, also, is as much fire as a great fire, and yet there is a visible difference between them. Before a small piece of iron is made red-hot in a little fire, some time must pass ; but if the fire be great, the iron very quickly, though bulky, loses its nature altogether in appearance.

9. So, it seems to me, is it with these two kinds of graces which our Lord bestows. He who has had raptures will, I am sure, understand it well ; to him who has not had that experience, it must appear folly. And, indeed, it may well be so ; for if a person like myself should speak of a matter of this kind, and give any explanation at all of that for the description of which no words ever can possibly be found, it is not to be wondered at that I may be speaking foolishly.

10. But I have this confidence in our Lord, that He will help me here ; for His Majesty knoweth that my object in writing —the first is to obey—is to inspire souls with a longing after so high a good. I will speak of nothing that I do not know by great experience : and so, when I began to describe the last kind of water, I thought it more impossible for me to speak of it at all than to speak Greek. It is a very difficult matter ; so I left it, and went to Communion. Blessed be our Lord, who is merciful to the ignorant ! Oh, virtue of obedience ! it can do everything ! God enlightened my understanding—at one time suggesting the words, at another showing me how to use them ; for, as in the preceding state of prayer, so also now. His Majesty seems to utter what I can neither speak nor understand.[6]

11. What I am saying is the simple truth ; and therefore whatever is good herein is His teaching ; what is erroneous, clearly comes out of that sea of evil—myself. If there be any—and there must be many—who, having attained to these states of prayer

[6] See ch. xiv. 12 ; xvi. 2.

whereunto our Lord in His mercy has brought me—
wretch that I am!—and who, thinking they have
missed their way, desire to treat of these matters with
me, I am sure that our Lord will help His servant to
declare the truth more plainly.

12. I am now speaking of the water which cometh
down from heaven to fill and saturate in its abundance
the whole of this garden with water. If our Lord
never ceased to pour it down whenever it was necessary, the gardener certainly would have plenty of
rest; and if there were no winter, but an ever tem-
perate season, fruits and flowers would never fail.
The gardener would have his delight therein; but
in this life that is impossible. We must always be
careful, when one water fails, to obtain another. This
water from heaven comes down very often when the
gardener least expects it.

13. The truth is that, in the beginning, this almost
always happens after much mental prayer. Our Lord
advances step by step to lay hold of the little bird, and
to lay it in the nest where it may repose. He observed
it fluttering for a long time, striving with the understanding and the will, and with all its might, to seek
God and to please Him; so now it is His pleasure to
reward it, even in this life. And what a reward!—one
moment is enough to repay all the possible trials of
this life.

14. The soul, while thus seeking after God, is conscious, with a joy excessive and sweet, that it is, as
it were, utterly fainting away in a kind of trance:
breathing, and all the bodily strength, fail it, so that
it cannot even move the hands without great pain;
the eyes close involuntarily, and if they are open, they
are as if they saw nothing; nor is reading possible,—
the very letters seem strange, and cannot be distinguished,—the letters, indeed, are visible, but, as the
understanding furnishes no help, all reading is im-
practicable, though seriously attempted. The ear

hears ; but what is heard is not comprehended. The senses are of no use whatever, except to hinder the soul's fruition ; and so they rather hurt it. It is useless to try to speak, because it is not possible to conceive a word ; nor, if it were conceived, is there strength sufficient to utter it ; for all bodily strength vanishes, and that of the soul increases, to enable it the better to have the fruition of its joy. Great and most perceptible, also, is the outward joy now felt.

15. This prayer, however long it may last, does no harm—at least, it has never done any to me ; nor do I remember, however ill I might have been when our Lord had mercy upon me in this way, that I ever felt the worse for it—on the contrary, I was always better afterwards. But so great a blessing, what harm can it do ? The outward effects are so plain as to leave no doubt possible that there must have been some great cause, seeing that it thus robs us of our bodily powers with so much joy, in order to leave them greater.

16. The truth is, it passes away so quickly in the beginning—at least, so it was with me [7]—that neither by the outward signs, nor by the failure of the senses, can it be perceived when it passes so quickly away. But it is plain, from the overflowing abundance of grace, that the brightness of the sun which had shone there must have been great, seeing that it has thus made the soul to melt away. And this is to be considered ; for, as it seems to me, the period of time, however long it may have been, during which the faculties of the soul were entranced, is very short ; if half an hour, that would be a long time. I do not think that I have ever been so long.[8] The truth of the matter is this : it is extremely difficult to know how long, because the senses are in suspense ; but I think that at any time it cannot be very long before

[7] Ch. xx. 25.
[8] See Anton. a Spiritu Sancto, *Director. Mystic.* tr. iv. § 9, n. 72.

some one of the faculties recovers itself. It is the will that persists in the work ; the other two faculties quickly begin to molest it. As the will is calm, it entrances them again ; they are quiet for another moment, and then they recover themselves once more.

17. In this way, some hours may be, and are, passed in prayer ; for when the two faculties begin to drink deep, and to perceive the taste of this divine wine, they give themselves up with great readiness, in order to be the more absorbed : they follow the will, and the three rejoice together. But this state of complete absorption, together with the utter rest of the imagination,—for I believe that even the imagination is then wholly at rest,—lasts only for a short time ; though the faculties do not so completely recover themselves as not to be for some hours afterwards as if in disorder: God, from time to time, drawing them to Himself.

18. Let us now come to that which the soul feels interiorly. Let him describe it who knows it; for as it is impossible to understand it, much more is it so to describe it. When I purposed to write this, I had just communicated, and had risen from the very prayer of which I am speaking. I am thinking of what the soul was then doing. Our Lord said to me : It undoes itself utterly, My daughter, in order that it may give itself more and more to Me : it is not itself that then lives, it is I. · As it cannot comprehend what it understands, it understands by not understanding.[9]

---

[9] Thomas a Jesu, *De Contemplatione Divina*, lib. v. c. xiii. : "Quasi dicat : Cum intellectus non possit Dei immensam illam claritatem et incomprehensibilem plenitudinem comprehendere, hoc ipsum est illam conspicere ac intelligere, intelligere se non posse intellectu cognoscere : quod quidem nihil aliud est quam Deum sub ratione incomprehensibilitatis videre ac cognoscere."

Philippus à SS. Trinitate, *Theolog. Mystic. Disc. Proem.* art. iv. p. 6 : "Cum ipsa [S. Theresia] scire vellet, quid in illa mystica unione operaretur intellectus, respondit (Christus) illi, cum non possit comprehendere quod intelligit, est non intelligere intelligendo : tum quia præ claritate nimia quodammodo offuscatur intellectus, unde præ altissima et supereminentissima Dei cognitione videtur anima potius Deum ignorare quam cognoscere."

19. He who has had experience of this will understand it in some measure, for it cannot be more clearly described, because what then takes place is so obscure. All I am able to say is, that the soul is represented as being close to God ; and that there abides a conviction thereof so certain and strong, that it cannot possibly help believing so. All the faculties fail now, and are suspended in such a way that, as I said before,[10] their operations cannot be traced. If the soul is making a meditation on any subject, the memory of it is lost at once, just as if it had never been thought of. If it reads, what is read is not remembered nor dwelt upon ; neither is it otherwise with vocal prayer. Accordingly, the restless little butterfly of the memory has its wings burnt now, and it cannot fly. The will must be fully occupied in loving, but it understands not how it loves ; the understanding, if it understands, does not understand how it understands—at least, it can comprehend nothing of that it understands : it does not understand, as it seems to me, because, as I said just now, this cannot be understood. I do not understand it at all myself.

20. In the beginning, it happened to me that I was ignorant of one thing—I did not know that God was in all things [11] : and when He seemed to me to be so near, I thought it impossible. Not to believe that He was present, was not in my power ; for it seemed to me, as it were, evident that I felt there His very presence. Some unlearned men used to say to me, that He was present only by His grace. I could not believe that, because, as I am saying, He seemed to me to be present Himself : so I was distressed. A most learned man, of the Order of the glorious St. Dominic, delivered me from this doubt ; for he told me that He was present, and

---

[10] Ch. x. 1, and ch. xviii. 16.
[11] See *Interior Castle*, M. v. ch. i. 9 ; *Rel.* ix. 17 ; xi. 8.   St. John of the Cross, *Ascent*, bk. ii. ch. v. 3 ; *Spiritual Canticle*, xi. 2.   Fr. Gracian, *Peregrinación de Anastasio* (Burgos, 1905), p. 171.

how He communed with us: this was a great comfort to me.

21. It is to be observed and understood that this water from heaven,—this greatest grace of our Lord,— always leaves in the soul the greatest fruits, as I shall now show.

CHAPTER XIX.

THE EFFECTS OF THIS FOURTH STATE OF PRAYER. EARNEST EXHORTATIONS TO THOSE WHO HAVE ATTAINED TO IT NOT TO GO BACK, NOR TO CEASE FROM PRAYER, EVEN IF THEY FALL. THE GREAT CALAMITY OF GOING BACK.

She continues the same subject, and begins to explain the effects on the soul of this degree of prayer. She earnestly exhorts not to turn back nor to give up prayer even if, after having received this favour, one should fall. She shows the damage that would result. This is most noteworthy and consoling for the weak and for sinners.

1. THERE remains in the soul, when the prayer of union is over, an exceedingly great tenderness; so much so, that it would undo itself—not from pain, but through tears of joy: it finds itself bathed therein, without being aware of it, and it knows not how or when it wept them. But to behold the violence of the fire subdued by the water, which yet makes it burn the more, gives it great delight. It seems as if I were speaking an unknown language. So it is, however.

2. It has happened to me occasionally, when this prayer was over, to be so beside myself as not to know whether I had been dreaming, or whether the bliss I felt had really been mine; and, on finding myself in a flood of tears—which had painlessly flowed, with

such violence and rapidity that it seemed as if a cloud from heaven [1] had shed them—to perceive that it was no dream.   Thus it was with me in the beginning, when it passed quickly away.   The soul remains possessed of so much courage, that if it were now hewn in pieces for God, it would be a great consolation to it.   This is the time of resolutions, of heroic determinations, of the living energy of good desires, of the beginning of hatred of the world, and of the most clear perception of its vanity.   The soul makes greater and higher progress than it ever made before in the previous states of prayer ; and grows in humility more and more, because it sees clearly that neither for obtaining nor for retaining this grace, great beyond all measure, has it ever done, or ever been able to do, anything of itself.[2]   It looks upon itself as most unworthy—for in a room into which the sunlight enters strongly, not a cobweb can be hid ; it sees its own misery ; self-conceit is so far away, that it seems as if it never could have had any—for now its own eyes behold how very little it could ever do, or rather, that it never did anything, that it hardly gave even its own consent, but that it rather seemed as if the doors of the senses were closed against its will in order that it might have more abundantly the fruition of our Lord. . It is abiding alone with Him : what has it to do but to love Him ?   It neither sees nor hears, unless on compulsion : no thanks to it.   Its past life stands before it then, together with the great mercy of God, in great distinctness ; and it is not necessary for it to go forth to hunt with the understanding, because what it has to eat and ruminate upon, it sees now ready prepared.   It sees, so far as itself is concerned, that it has deserved hell, and that its punishment is bliss.   It undoes itself in the praises of God, and I would gladly undo myself now.

---

[1] See ch. xx. 2.
[2] Ch. xx. 38, *Way of Perfection*, ch. xxxvi. 8.

3. Blessed be Thou, O my Lord, who, out of a pool so filthy as I am, bringest forth water so clean as to be meet for Thy table! Praised be Thou, O Joy of the Angels, who hast been thus pleased to exalt so vile a worm!

4. The good effects of this prayer abide in the soul for some time. Now that it clearly apprehends that the fruit is not its own, the soul can begin to share it with others, and that without any loss to itself. It begins to show signs of its being a soul that is guarding the treasures of heaven, and to be desirous of communicating them to others,[3] and to pray to God that itself may not be the only soul that is rich in them. It begins to benefit its neighbours, as it were, without being aware of it, nor doing anything consciously: its neighbours understand the matter, because the odour of the flowers has grown so strong as to make them eager to approach them. They understand that this soul is full of virtue: they see the fruit, how delicious it is, and they wish to help that soul to eat it.

5. If this ground be well dug by troubles, by persecutions, detractions, and infirmities,—they are few who ascend so high without this,—if it be well broken up by great detachment from all self-interest, it will drink in so much water that it can hardly ever be parched again. But if it be ground which is mere waste, and covered with thorns (as I was when I began); if the occasions of sin be not avoided; if it be an ungrateful soil, unfitted for so great a grace,— it will be parched up again. If the gardener become careless,—and if our Lord, out of His mere goodness, will not send down rain upon it,—the garden is ruined. Thus has it been with me more than once, so that I am amazed at it; and if I had not found it so by experience, I could not have believed it.

6. I write this for the comfort of souls which are weak, as I am, that they may never despair, nor cease

[3] See ch. xvii. 3.

to trust in the power of God ; even if they should fall after our Lord has raised them to so high a degree of prayer as this is, they must not be discouraged, unless they would lose themselves utterly. Tears gain everything, and one drop of water attracts another.

7. One of the reasons that move me, who am what I am, under obedience to write this, and give an account of my wretched life, and of the graces our Lord has wrought in me,—though I never served Him, but offended Him rather,—is what I have just given : and, certainly, I wish I was a person of great authority, that people might believe what I say. I pray to our Lord that His Majesty would be pleased to grant me this grace. I repeat it, let no one who has begun to give himself to prayer be discouraged, and say : If I fall into sin, it will be worse for me if I go on now with the practice of prayer. I think so too, if he gives up prayer, and does not correct his evil ways ; but if he does not give up prayer,[4] let him be assured of this— prayer will bring him to the haven of light.

8. In this the devil turned his batteries against me, and I suffered so much because I thought it showed but little humility if I persevered in prayer when I was so wicked, that—as I have already said[5]—I gave it up for a year and a half—at least, for a year, but I do not remember distinctly the other six months. This could not have been, neither was it, anything else but to throw myself down into hell ; there was no need of any devils to drag me thither. O my God, was there ever blindness so great as this ? How well Satan prepares his measures for his purpose, when he pursues us in this way ! The traitor knows that he has already lost that soul which perseveres in prayer, and that every fall which he can bring about helps it, by the goodness of God, to make greater progress in His service. Satan has some interest in this.

[4] § 16.
[5] Ch. vii. 17, and ch. viii. 5.

9. O my Jesus, what a sight that must be—a soul so highly exalted falling into sin, and raised up again by Thee ; who, in Thy mercy, stretchest forth Thine hand to save ! How such a soul confesses Thy greatness and compassion and its own wretchedness ! It really looks on itself as nothingness, and confesses Thy power. It dares not lift up its eyes ; it raises them, indeed, but it is to acknowledge how much it oweth unto Thee. It becomes devout to the Queen of Heaven, that she may propitiate Thee ; it invokes the Saints, who fell after Thou hadst called them, for succour. Thou seemest now to be too bountiful in Thy gifts, because it feels itself to be unworthy of the earth it treads on. It has recourse to the Sacraments, to a quickened faith, which abides in it at the contemplation of the power which Thou hast lodged in them. It praises Thee because Thou hast left us such medicines and ointment for our wounds, which not only heal them on the surface, but remove all traces whatever of them.

10. The soul is amazed at it. Who is there, O Lord of my soul, that is not amazed at compassion so great and mercy so surpassing, after treason so foul and so hateful ? I know not how it is that my heart does not break when I write this, for I am wicked. With these scanty tears which I am now weeping, but yet Thy gift,—water out of a well, so far as it is mine, so impure,—I seem to make Thee some recompense for treachery so great as mine, in that I was always doing evil, labouring to make void the graces Thou hast given me. Do Thou, O Lord, make my tears available ; purify the water which is so muddy ; at least, let me not be to others a temptation to rash judgments, as I have been to myself, when I used to think such thoughts as these : Why, O Lord, dost Thou pass by most holy persons, who have always served Thee, and who have been tried ; who have been brought up in religion, and are really religious—not such as I am,

having only the name—so as to make it plain that they are not recipients of those graces which Thou hast bestowed upon me?

11. I see clearly now, O Thou my Good, Thou hast kept the reward to give it them all at once: my weakness has need of these succours. They, being strong, serve Thee without them, and Thou dealest with them as with a strong race, free from all self-interest. But yet Thou knowest, O my Lord, that I have often cried unto Thee, making excuses for those who murmured against me; for I thought they had reason on their side. This I did then when Thou of Thy goodness hadst kept me back from offending Thee so much, and when I was departing from everything which I thought displeasing unto Thee. It was when I did this that Thou, O Lord, didst begin to lay open Thy treasures for Thy servant. It seemed as if Thou wert looking for nothing else but that I should be willing and ready to receive them; accordingly, Thou didst begin at once, not only to give them, but also to make others know that Thou wert giving them.

12. When this was known, there began to prevail a good opinion of her, of whom all had not yet clearly understood how wicked she was, though much of that wickedness was plain enough. Calumny and persecution began at once, and, as I think, with good reason; so I looked on none of them as an enemy, but made my supplications to Thee, imploring Thee to consider the grounds they had. They said that I wished to be a saint, and that I invented novelties; but I had not then attained in many things even to the observance of my rule; nor had I come near those excellent and holy nuns who were in the house, —and I do not believe I ever shall, if God of His goodness will not do that for me Himself; on the contrary, I was there only to do away with what was good, and introduce customs which were not good; at least, I did what I could to bring them in, and I was very

powerful for evil. Thus it was that they were blameless, when they blamed me. I do not mean the nuns only, but the others as well : they told me truths ; for it was Thy will.

13. I was once saying the Office,—I had had this temptation for some time,—and when I came to these words, "Justus es, Domine, et rectum judicium tuum,"[6] I began to think what a deep truth it was. Satan never was strong enough to tempt me in any way to doubt of Thy goodness, or of any article of the faith : on the contrary, it seems to me that the more these truths were above nature, the more firmly I held them, and my devotion grew ; when I thought of Thy omnipotence, I accepted all Thy wonderful works, and I say it again, I never had a doubt. Then, as I was thinking how it could be just in Thee to allow so many, who, as I said, are Thy most faithful servants, to remain without those consolations and graces which Thou hast given to me, who am what I am, Thou, O my Lord, didst answer me : Serve Thou Me, and meddle not with this.

14. This was the first word which I ever heard Thee speak to me, and it made me greatly afraid. But as I shall speak hereafter[7] of this way of hearing, and of other matters, I say nothing here ; for to do so would be to digress from my subject, and I have already made digressions enough. I scarcely know what I have said, nor can it be otherwise ; but you, my father, must bear with these interruptions ; for when I consider what God must have borne with from me, and when I see the state I am in, it is not strange that I should wander in what I am saying, and what I have still to say.

15. May it please our Lord that my wanderings may be of this kind, and may His Majesty never suffer

---

[6] Psalm cxviii. 137 : "Thou art just, O Lord, and Thy judgment is right." St. Teresa wrote : "Justus es domine y tus juyçios."
[7] See ch. xxv.

me to have strength to resist Him even in the least ;
yea, rather than that, may He destroy me this moment.
It is evidence enough of His great compassions, that
He has forgiven so much ingratitude, not once, but
often. He forgave St. Peter once ; but I have been
forgiven many times. Satan had good reasons for
tempting me : I ought never to have pretended to
a strict friendship with One, my hatred of whom I
made so public. Was there ever blindness so great
as mine ? Where could I think I should find help but
in Thee ? What folly to run away from the light,
to be for ever stumbling ! What a proud humility
was that which Satan devised for me, when I ceased
to lean upon the pillar, and threw the staff away which
supported me, in order that my fall might not be great.[8]

16. I make the sign of the cross this moment. I
do not think I ever escaped so great a danger as this
device of Satan, which he would have imposed upon
me in the disguise of humility.[9] He filled me with
such thoughts as these : How could I make my prayer,
who was so wicked, and yet had received so many
mercies ? It was enough for me to recite the Office,
as all others did ; but as I did not that much well,
how could I desire to do more ? I was not reverential
enough, and made too little of the mercies of God.
There was no harm in these thoughts and feelings
in themselves ; but to act upon them, that was an
exceedingly great wickedness. Blessed be Thou, O
Lord ; for Thou camest to my help. This seems to
me to be in principle the temptation of Judas, only
that Satan did not dare to tempt me so openly. But
he might have led me by little and little, as he led
Judas, to the same pit of destruction.

17. Let all those who give themselves to prayer,
for the love of God, look well to this. They should
know that when I was neglecting it, my life was much
worse than it had ever been ; let them reflect on the

[8] See ch. viii. 1, *supra* § 7.   [9] Ch. vii. 17.

excellent help and the pleasant humility which Satan
provided for me : it was a grave interior disquietude.
But how could my spirit be quiet ? It was going
away in its misery from its true rest. I remembered
the graces and mercies I had received, and felt that
the joys of this world were loathsome. I am astonished
that I was able to bear it. It must have been the hope
I had ; for, as well as I can remember now, it is more
than twenty-one years ago. I do not think I ever
gave up my purpose of resuming my prayer ; but I
was waiting to be very free from sin first.

18. Oh, how deluded I was in this expectation!
The devil would have held it out before me till the
Day of Judgment, that he might then take me with
him to hell. Then, when I applied myself to prayer
and to spiritual reading,—whereby I might perceive
these truths, and the evil nature of the way I was
walking in, and was often importunate with our Lord
in tears,—I was so wicked, that it availed me nothing ;
when I gave that up, and wasted my time in amusing
myself, in great danger of falling into sin, and with
scanty helps,—and I may venture to say no help at
all, unless it was a help to my ruin,—what could I
expect but that of which I have spoken ?

19. I believe that a certain Dominican friar, a
most learned man, has greatly merited in the eyes
of God ; for it was he who roused me from this slumber.
He made me—I think I said so before [10]—go to Communion once a fortnight, and be less given to evil ; I
began to be converted, though I did not cease to
offend our Lord all at once ; however, as I had not
lost my way, I walked on in it, though slowly, falling
and rising again ; and he who does not cease to
walk and press onwards, arrives at last, even if late.
To lose one's way is—so it seems to me—nothing
else but the giving up of prayer. God, of His mercy,
keeps us from this !

[10] Ch. vii. 27.

20. It is clear from this,—and for the love of God, consider it well,—that a soul, though it may receive great graces from God in prayer, must never rely on itself, because it may fall, nor expose itself in any way whatever to any risks of sin. This should be well considered, because much depends on it ; for the delusion here, wherein Satan is able to entangle us afterwards, though the grace be really from God, lies in the traitor's making use of that very grace, so far as he can, for his own purpose, and particularly against persons not grown strong in virtues, who are neither mortified nor detached ; for these are not at present strong enough—as I shall explain hereafter [11]— to expose themselves to dangerous occasions, notwithstanding the noble desires and resolutions they may have.

21. This doctrine is excellent, and not mine, but the teaching of God, and accordingly I wish ignorant people like myself knew it ; for even if a soul were in this state, it must not rely so much upon itself as to go forth to the battle, because it will have enough to do in defending itself. Defensive armour is the present necessity ; the soul is not yet strong enough to assail Satan, and to trample him under foot as those are who are in the state of which I shall speak further on.[12]

22. This is the delusion by which Satan prevails : when a soul sees itself so near unto God, when it sees the difference there is between the things of heaven and those of earth, and when it sees the love which our Lord bears it, there grows out of that love a certain trust and confidence that there is to be no falling away from that the fruition of which it then possesses. It seems to see the reward distinctly, as if it were impossible for it to abandon that which, even in this life, is so delicious and sweet, for anything so mean and

[11] Ch. xxxi. 21.
[12] Ch. xx. 33, and ch. xxv. 24.

impure as worldly joy. Through this confidence,
Satan robs it of that distrust which it ought to have
in itself ; and so, as I have just said,[13] the soul exposes
itself to dangers, and begins, in the fulness of its zeal,
to give away without discretion the fruit of its garden,
thinking that now it has no reason to be afraid for
itself. Yet this does not come out of pride ; for the
soul clearly understands that of itself it can do no
good thing ; but rather out of an excessive confidence
in God, without discretion : because the soul does
not see itself to be unfledged. It can go forth out of
its nest, and God Himself may take it out, but still
it cannot fly, because the virtues are not strong, and
itself has no experience wherewith to discern the
dangers ; nor is it aware of the evil which trusting to
itself may do it.

23. This it was that ruined me. Now, to understand this, and everything else in the spiritual life,
we have great need of a director, and of conference
with spiritual persons. I fully believe, with respect
to that soul which God raises to this state, that He
will not cease to be gracious to it, nor suffer it to be
lost, if it does not utterly forsake His Majesty. But
when that soul—as I said—falls, let it look to it again
and again, for the love of our Lord, that Satan deceive
it not by tempting it to give up prayer, as he tempted
me, through that false humility of which I have
spoken before,[14] and would gladly speak of again and
again. Let it rely on the goodness of God, which is
greater than all the evil we can do. When we, acknowledging our own vileness, desire to return into
His grace, He remembers our ingratitude no more,—
no, not even the graces He has given us, for the purpose of chastising us, because of our misuse of them ;
yea, rather, they help to procure our pardon the sooner,
as of persons who have been members of His household, and who, as they say, have eaten of His bread.

---

[13] Ch. xvii. 3, xix. 4.   [14] See § 16.

24. Let them remember His words, and behold what He hath done unto me, who grew weary of sinning before He grew weary of forgiving. He is never weary of giving, nor can His compassion be exhausted. Let us not grow weary ourselves of receiving. May He be blessed for ever, Amen ; and may all created things praise Him !

CHAPTER XX.

THE DIFFERENCE BETWEEN UNION AND RAPTURE.   WHAT
    RAPTURE IS.   THE BLESSING IT IS TO THE   SOUL.
    THE EFFECTS OF IT.

*She speaks of the difference between union and trance, and explains what a trance is. She also says something about the good a soul derives from being, through God's goodness, led so far. She speaks of the effect of union. This is most admirable.**

1. I WISH I could explain, with the help of God, wherein union differs from rapture, or from transport, or from flight of the spirit, as they speak, or from a trance, which are all one.[1] I mean, that all these are only different names for that one and the same thing, which is also called ecstasy.   It is more excellent than union,[2] the fruits of it are much greater, and its other opera-

---

* These last words are deleted in the MS.
[1] See *Interior Castle*, M. vi. ch. v. ; Philippus a SS. Trinitate, *Theolog. Mystic.* par. iii. tr. 1, disp. iii., art. 3 ; " Hæc oratio raptus superior est præcedentibus orationis gradibus, etiam oratione unionis ordinariæ, et habet effectus multo excellentiores et multas alias operationes."
[2] " She says that rapture is more excellent than union ; that is, that the soul in a rapture has a greater fruition of God, and that God takes it then more into His own hands.   That is evidently so ; because in a rapture the soul loses the use of its exterior and interior faculties.   When she says that union is the beginning, middle, and end, she means that pure union is almost always uniform ; but that there are degrees in rapture, of which some are, as it were, the beginning, some the middle, others the end.   That is the reason why it is called by different names ; some of which denote the least, others the most, perfect form of it, as it will appear hereafter."—Note in the Spanish edition of Lopez (*De la Fuente*).

tions more manifold ; for union is uniform in the
beginning, the middle, and the end, and is so also
interiorly. But as raptures have ends of a much
higher kind, they produce effects both within and
without.[3] As our Lord has explained the other
matters, so also may He explain this ; for certainly,
if He had not shown me in what way and by what
means this explanation was in some measure possible,
I should never have been able to do it.

2. Consider we now that this last water, of which I
am speaking, is so abundant that, were it not that
the ground refuses to receive it, we might suppose that
the cloud of His great Majesty is here raining down
upon us on earth. And when we are giving Him
thanks for this great mercy, drawing near to Him in
earnest, with all our might, then it is our Lord draws
up the soul, as the clouds, so to speak, gather the
mists from the face of the earth, and carries it away
out of itself,—I have heard it said that the clouds,
or the sun, draw the mists together,[4]—and as a cloud,
rising up to heaven, takes the soul with Him, and
begins to show it the treasures of the kingdom which
He has prepared for it. I know not whether the
comparison be accurate or not ; but the fact is, that
is the way in which it is brought about. During
rapture, the soul does not seem to animate the body,
the natural heat of which is perceptibly lessened ;
the coldness increases, though accompanied with
exceeding joy and sweetness.[5]

[3] Anton. a Spiritu Sancto, *Direct. Mystic.* tr. 4, d. i. n. 95 : " Licet oratio
raptus idem sit apud mysticos ac oratio volatus, seu elevationis spiritus seu
extasis ; reipsa tamen raptus aliquid addit super extasim ; nam extasis
importat simplicem excessum mentis in seipso secundum quem aliquis extra
suam cognitionem ponitur. Raptus vero super hoc addit violentiam quan-
dam ab aliquo extrinseco."

[4] The words between the dashes are in the handwriting of the Saint—not
however, in the text, but on the margin.

[5] See *Interior Castle*, M. vi. ch. v. " Primus effectus orationis ecstaticæ est
in corpore, quod ita remanet, ac si per animam non informaretur, infrigidatur
enim calore naturali deficiente, clauduntur suaviter oculi, et alii sensus
amittuntur : contingit tamen quod corpus infirmum in hac oratione sanitatem
recuperat." Anton. a Spiritu Sancto, *Direct. Mystic.* tr. iv. d. 2, § 4, n. 150.

3. A rapture is absolutely irresistible, whilst union, inasmuch as we are then on our own ground, may be hindered, though that resistance be painful and violent ; it is, however, almost always impossible. But rapture, for the most part, is irresistible. It comes, in general, as a shock, quick and sharp, before you can collect your thoughts, or help yourself in any way, and you see and feel it as a cloud, or a strong eagle rising upwards, and carrying you away on its wings.

4. I repeat it : you feel and see yourself carried away, you know not whither. For though we feel how delicious it is, yet the weakness of our nature makes us afraid at first, and we require a much more resolute and courageous spirit than in the previous states, in order to risk everything, come what may, and to abandon ourselves into the hands of God, and go willingly whither we are carried, seeing that we must be carried away, however painful it may be ; and so trying is it, that I would very often resist, and exert all my strength, particularly at those times when the rapture was coming on me in public. I did so, too, very often when I was alone, because I was afraid of delusions. Occasionally I was able, by great efforts, to make a slight resistance ; but afterwards I was worn out, like a person who had been contending with a strong giant ; at other times it was impossible to resist at all : my soul was carried away, and almost always my head with it,—I had no power over it,—and now and then the whole body as well, so that it was lifted up from the ground.

5. This has not happened to me often : once, however, it took place when we were all together in choir, and I, on my knees, on the point of communicating. It was a very sore distress to me ; for I thought it a most extraordinary thing, and was afraid it would occasion much talk ; so I commanded the nuns—for it happened after I was made Prioress—

never to speak of it.⁶   But at other times, the moment
I felt that our Lord was about to repeat the act, and
once, in particular, during a sermon,—it was the feast
of our house, some great ladies being present,—I threw
myself on the ground ; then the nuns came around
me to hold me ; but still the rapture was observed.

6. I made many supplications to our Lord, that
He would be pleased to give me no more of those
graces which were outwardly visible ; for I was
weary of living under such great restraint, and because His Majesty could not bestow such graces on
me without their becoming known.   It seems that,
of His goodness, He has been pleased to hear my
prayer ; for I have never been enraptured since.
It is true that it was not long ago.

7. It seemed to me, when I tried to make some resistance, as if a great force beneath my feet lifted me up.
I know of nothing with which to compare it ; but it was
much more violent than the other spiritual visitations,
and I was therefore as one ground to pieces ; for it is a
great struggle, and, in short, of little use, whenever our
Lord so wills it.   There is no power against His power.

8. At other times He is pleased to be satisfied when
He makes us see that He is ready to give us this grace,
and that it is not He that withholds it.   Then, when
we resist it out of humility, He produces those very
effects which would have resulted if we had fully consented to it.

⁶ This incident has been described by several witnesses.   It occurred on
the feast of St. Joseph, March 19, 1564 or 1565.   Yepes says the Bishop of
Avila was saying mass, and as he approached the little opening in the grating
through which Holy Communion used to be administered, saw St. Teresa
lifted into the air in an ecstasy.   A niece of the Saint, Mary of St. Jerome, nun
at St. Joseph's, reports that Teresa, feeling what was about to happen, clung
with both hands to the iron grating.   She always disliked such a thing
to happen in presence of the community, but when outsiders were present
she was inconsolable.   She would then attribute it to her weak heart, and
ask for a drop of water or some food so as to make it appear that physical
suffering was the cause of it.

Another religious, Mary Baptiste, says that each time St. Teresa communicated, or heard mass, or listened to a sermon, or engaged in prayer, or merely
heard a word reminding her of God, her soul seemed to be raised above the senses.

9. The effects of rapture are great : one is that the mighty power of our Lord is manifested ; and as we are not strong enough, when His Majesty wills it, to control either soul or body, so neither have we any power over it ; but, whether we like it or not, we see that there is One mightier than we are, that these graces are His gifts, and that of ourselves we can do nothing whatever ; and humility is deeply imprinted in us. And further, I confess that it threw me into great fear, very great indeed at first ; for when I saw my body thus lifted up from the earth, how could I help it ? Though the spirit draws it upwards after itself, and that with great sweetness, if unresisted, the senses are not lost ; at least, I was so much myself as to be able to see that I was being lifted up. The majesty of Him who can effect this so manifests itself, that the hairs of my head stand upright,[7] and a great fear comes upon me of offending God, Who is so mighty. This fear is bound up in exceedingly great love, which is acquired anew, and directed to Him, Who, we see, bears so great a love to a worm so vile, and Who seems not to be satisfied with attracting the soul to Himself in so real a way, but Who will have the body also, though it be mortal and of earth so foul, such as it is through our sins, which are so great.

10. Rapture leaves behind a certain strange detachment also, which I shall never be able to describe ; I think I can say that it is in some respects different from—yea, higher than—the other graces, which are simply spiritual ; for though these effect a complete detachment in spirit from all things, it seems that in this of rapture our Lord would have the body itself to be detached also : and thus a certain singular estrangement from the things of earth is wrought, which makes life much more distressing. Afterwards it causes a

[7] Job iv. 15 : " Inhorruerunt pili carnis meæ." See St. John of the Cross, *Spiritual Canticle*, stanzas xiv.-xv., 23 *sqq.*

pain, which we can never inflict of ourselves, nor remove when once it has come.

11. I should like very much to explain this great pain, and I believe I shall not be able ; however, I will say something if I can. And it is to be observed that this is my present state, and one to which I have been brought very lately, after all the visions and revelations of which I shall speak, and after that time, wherein I gave myself to prayer, in which our Lord gave me so much sweetness and delight.[8] Even now I have that sweetness occasionally ; but it is the pain of which I speak that is the most frequent and the most common. It varies in its intensity. I will now speak of it when it is sharpest ; for I shall speak later on[9] of the great shocks I used to feel when our Lord would throw me into those trances, and which are, in my opinion, as different from this pain as the most corporeal thing is from the most spiritual ; and I believe that I am not exaggerating much. For though the soul feels that pain, it is in company with the body[10] ; both soul and body apparently share it, and it is not attended with that extremity of abandonment which belongs to this.

12. As I said before,[11] we have no part in causing this pain ; but very often there springs up a desire unexpectedly,—I know not how it comes,—and because of this desire, which pierces the soul in a moment, the soul begins to be wearied, so much so that it rises upwards above itself, and above all created things. God then so strips it of everything, that, do what it may, there is nothing on earth that can be its companion. Neither, indeed, would it wish to have any ; it would rather die in that loneliness. If people spoke to it, and if itself made every effort possible to speak, it would be of little use : the spirit, notwithstanding all it may do, cannot be withdrawn from that loneliness ; and though God seems, as it were, far away from

---

[8] See ch. xxix.   [9] See ch. xx. 21.   [10] § 9, *supra*.   [11] § 10.

the soul at that moment, yet He reveals His grandeurs at times in the strangest way conceivable. That way is indescribable; I do not think any one can believe or comprehend it who has not previously had experience of it. It is a communication made, not to console, but to show the reason why the soul must be weary: because it is far away from the Good which in itself comprehends all good.

13. In this communication the desire grows, so also does the bitterness of that loneliness wherein the soul beholds itself, suffering a pain so sharp and piercing that, in that very loneliness in which it dwells, it may literally say of itself,—and perhaps the royal prophet said so, being in that very loneliness himself, except that our Lord may have granted to him, being a saint, to feel it more deeply,—" Vigilavi, et factus sum sicut passer solitarius in tecto." [12]   These words presented themselves to me in such a way that I thought I saw them fulfilled in myself. It was a comfort to know that others had felt this extreme loneliness; how much greater my comfort, when these persons were such as David was! The soul is then—so I think—not in itself, but on the house-top, or on the roof, above itself, and above all created things; for it seems to me to have its dwelling higher than even in the highest part of itself.

14. On other occasions, the soul seems to be, as it were, in the utmost extremity of need, asking itself, and saying, " Where is thy God? " [13]   And it is to be remembered, that I did not know how to express in Spanish the meaning of those words. Afterwards, when I understood what it was, I used to console myself with the thought, that our Lord, without any effort of mine, had made me remember them. At other times, I used to recollect a saying of St. Paul's,

---

[12] Psalm ci. 8: " I have watched, and become as a sparrow alone on the house-top." St. Teresa wrote: " Vigilavi ed fatus sun sicud passer solitarius yn tecto."
[13] Psalm xli. 4: " Ubi est Deus tuus ? "

to the effect that he was crucified to the world.[14] I do not mean that this is true of me : I know it is not ; but I think it is the state of the enraptured soul. No consolation reaches it from heaven, and it is not there itself ; it wishes for none from earth, and it is not there either ; but it is, as it were, crucified between heaven and earth, enduring its passion : receiving no succour from either.

15. Now, the succour it receives from heaven— which, as I have said,[15] is a most marvellous know- ledge of God, above all that we can desire—brings with it greater pain ; for the desire then so grows, that, in my opinion, its intense painfulness now and then robs the soul of all sensation ; only, it lasts but for a short time after the senses are suspended. It seems as if it were at the point of death ; only, the agony carries with it so great a joy, that I know of nothing where- with to compare it. It is a sharp martyrdom, full of sweetness ; for if any earthly thing be then offered to the soul, even though it may be that which it habitu- ally found most sweet, the soul will have none of it ; yea, it seems to throw it away at once. The soul sees distinctly that it seeks nothing but God ; yet its love dwells not on any attribute of Him in particular ; it seeks Him as He is, and knows not what it seeks. I say that it knows not, because the imagination forms no representation whatever ; and, indeed, as I think, during much of that time the faculties are at rest. Pain suspends them then, as joy suspends them in union and in a trance.

16. O Jesus! oh, that some one would clearly explain this to you, my father, were it only that you may tell me what it means, because this is the habitual state of my soul ! Generally, when I am not par- ticularly occupied, I fall into these agonies of death,

[14] Galat. vi. 14 : "In cruce Jesu Christi : per quem mihi mundus cruci- fixus est, et ego mundo."
[15] §§ 9 and 12.

and I tremble when I feel them coming on, because they are not unto death. But when I am in them, I then wish to spend therein all the rest of my life, though the pain be so very great, that I can scarcely endure it. Sometimes my pulse, ceases, as it were, to beat at all,—so the sisters say, who sometimes approach me, and who now understand the matter better,— my bones are racked, and my hands become so rigid, that I cannot always join them. Even on the following day I have a pain in my wrists, and over my whole body, as if my bones were out of joint.[16]   Well, I think sometimes, if it continues as at present, that it will end, in the good pleasure of our Lord, by putting an end to my life ; for the pain seems to me sharp enough to cause death ; only, I do not deserve it.

17. All my anxiety at these times is that I should die : I do not think of purgatory, nor of the great sins I have committed, and by which I have deserved hell. I forget everything in my eagerness to see God ; and this abandonment and loneliness seem preferable to any company in the world. If anything can be a consolation in this state, it is to speak to one who has passed through this trial, seeing that, though the soul may complain of it, no one seems disposed to believe in it.

18. The soul is tormented also because the pain has increased so much, that it seeks solitude no longer, as it did before, nor companionship, unless it be that of those to whom it may make its complaint. It is now like a person who, having a rope around his neck, and being strangled, tries to breathe. This desire of companionship seems to me to proceed from our weakness ; for, as pain brings with it the risk of death,—which it certainly does ; for I have been occasionally in danger of death, in my great sickness and infirmities, as I have said before,[17] and I think I may say that this pain is as

---

[16] Daniel x. 16 : " In visione tua dissolutæ sunt compages meæ." See St. John of the Cross, *Spiritual Canticle*, st. xiv. 26 ; and also *Relation* viii. 13, where this is repeated.
[17] Ch. v. 18.

great as any,—so the desire not to be parted, which
possesses soul and body, is that which raises the cry
for succour in order to breathe, and by speaking of
it, by complaining, and distracting itself, causes the
soul to seek means of living very much against the
will of the spirit, or the higher part of the soul, which
would not wish to be delivered from this pain.

19. I am not sure that I am correct in what I say,
nor do I know how to express myself, but to the best
of my knowledge it comes to pass in this way. See,
my father, what rest I can have in this life, now that
what I once had in prayer and loneliness—therein our
Lord used to comfort me—has become in general a
torment of this kind ; while, at the same time, it is
so full of sweetness, that the soul, discerning its inestimable worth, prefers it to all those consolations
which it formerly had. It seems also to be a safer
state, because it is the way of the cross ; and involves,
in my opinion, a joy of exceeding worth, because the
state of the body in it is only pain. It is the soul that
suffers and exults alone in that joy and contentment
which suffering supplies.

20. I know not how this can be, but so it is ; it
comes from the hand of our Lord, and, as I said before,[18]
is not anything that I have acquired myself, because
it is exceedingly supernatural, and I think I would
not barter it for all the graces of which I shall speak
further on : I do not say for all of them together,
but for any one of them separately. And it must not
be forgotten that, as I have just said, these impetuosities came upon me after I had received those graces
from our Lord[19] which I am speaking of now, and all
those described in this book, and it is in this state our
Lord keeps me at this moment.[20]

21. In the beginning I was afraid—it happens to

[18] § 12.
[19] The words from " I have just said " to " our Lord " are in the margin
of the text, but in the handwriting of the Saint.
[20] See § 11.

me to be almost always so when our Lord leads me by a new way, until His Majesty reassures me as I proceed—and so our Lord bade me not to fear, but to esteem this grace more than all the others He had given me ; for the soul was purified by this pain—burnished, or refined as gold in the crucible, so that it might be the better enamelled with His gifts, and the dross burnt away in this life, which would have to be burnt away in purgatory.

22. I understood perfectly that this pain was a great grace ; but I was much more certain of it now : and my confessor tells me I did well. And though I was afraid, because I was so wicked, I never c uld believe it was anything wrong : on the other hand, the exceeding greatness of the blessing made me afraid, when I called to mind how little I had deserved it. Blessed be our Lord, who is so good ! Amen.[21]

23. I have, it seems, wandered from my subject ; for I began by speaking of raptures, and that of which I have been speaking is even more than a rapture, and the effects of it are what I have described. Now let us return to raptures, and speak of their ordinary characteristics. I have to say that, when the rapture was over, my body seemed frequently to be buoyant, as if all weight had departed from it ; so much so, that now and then I scarcely knew that my feet touched the ground. But during the rapture itself the body is very often as if it were dead, perfectly powerless. It continues in the position it was in when the rapture

[21] Isabelle of St. Dominic, who entered the convent of St. Joseph, Avila. in October, 1563, says that St. Teresa's desire to be freed from the prison of this world and to be with our Lord caused her such suffering that she seemed to be in danger of death. One day the Saint had retired to one of the small hermitages in the garden of the convent, where Isabelle found her with the hands rigid and cold as though she were dead. She represented to St. Teresa how wrong it was for her to undergo such tortures, which might cause her death and thus end a life of such value. The Saint replied : " Hold your peace, child ; do you think this depends upon myself ? " But the sister prevailed upon her to come to the choir for matins. She afterwards complained to the confessor, Father Dominic Bañez, asking him to forbid the Saint to withdraw from the community when an ecstasy was coming on.

came upon it—if sitting, sitting ; if the hands were open, or if they were shut, they will remain open or shut.[22] For though the senses fail but rarely, it has happened to me occasionally to lose them wholly— seldom, however, and then only for a short time. But in general they are in disorder ; and though they have no power whatever to deal with outward things, there remains the power of hearing and seeing ; but it is as if the things heard and seen were at a great distance, far away.

24. I do not say that the soul sees and hears when the rapture is at the highest,—I mean by at the highest, when the faculties are lost, because profoundly united with God,--for then it neither sees, nor hears, nor perceives, as I believe ; but, as I said of the previous prayer of union,[23] this utter transformation of the soul in God continues only for an instant ; yet while it continues no faculty of the soul is aware of it, or knows what is passing there. Nor can it be understood while we are living on the earth—at least, God will not have us understand it, because we must be incapable of understanding it. I know it by experience.

25. You, my father, will ask me : How comes it, then, that a rapture occasionally lasts so many hours ? What has often happened to me is this,--I spoke of it before, when writing of the previous state of prayer,[24] —the rapture is not continuous, the soul is frequently absorbed, or, to speak more correctly, our Lord absorbs it in Himself ; and when He has held it thus for a moment, the will alone remains in union with Him. The movements of the two other faculties seem to me to be like those of the needle of sun-dials, which is never at rest ; yet when the Sun of Justice will have it so, He can hold it still.

26. This I speak of lasts but a moment ; yet, as

---

[22] See *Relation* viii. 8 ; *Way of Perfection*, ch. xxxii. 17 ; *Interior Castle*, M. vi. ch. iv. 16.
[23] Ch. xviii. 16.   [24] Ch. xviii. 17.

the impulse and the upraising of the spirit were vehement, and though the other faculties bestir themselves again, the will continues absorbed, and causes this operation in the body, as if it were the absolute mistress ; for now that the two other faculties are restless, and attempt to disturb it, it takes care—for if it is to have enemies, the fewer the better—that the senses also shall not trouble it : and thus it comes to pass that the senses are suspended ; for so our Lord wills it. And for the most part the eyes are closed, though we may not wish to close them ; and if occasionally they remain open, as I said just now, the soul neither discerns nor considers what it sees.

27. What the body then can do here is still less, in order that, when the faculties come together again, there may not be so much to do. Let him, therefore, to whom our Lord has granted this grace, be not discouraged when he finds himself in this state—the body under constraint for many hours, the understanding and the memory occasionally astray. The truth is that, in general, they are inebriated with the praises of God, or with searching to comprehend or understand that which has passed over them. And yet even for this they are not thoroughly awake, but are rather like one who has slept long, and dreamed, and is hardly yet awake.

28. I dwell so long on this point because I know that there are persons now, even in this place,[25] to whom our Lord is granting these graces ; and if their directors have had no experience in the matter, they will think, perhaps, that they must be as dead persons during the trance--and they will think so the more if they have no learning. It is piteous to see what those confessors who do not understand this make people suffer. I shall speak of it by and by.[26] Perhaps I do not know what I am saying. You, my father, will understand it, if I am at all correct ; for our Lord has

[25] Avila.	[26] Ch. xxv. 18.

admitted you to the experience of it : yet, because that experience is not very great, it may be, perhaps, that you have not considered the matter so much as I have done.

29. So then, though I do all I can, my body has no strength to move for some time ; the soul took it all away. Very often, too, he who was before sickly and full of pain remains healthy, and even stronger ; for it is something great that is given to the soul in rapture ; and sometimes, as I have said already,[27] our Lord will have the body rejoice, because it is obedient in that which the soul requires of it. When we recover our consciousness, the faculties may remain, if the rapture has been deep, for a day or two, and even for three days, so absorbed, or as if stunned,—so much so, as to be in appearance no longer themselves.

30. Here comes the pain of returning to this life ; here it is the wings of the soul grew, to enable it to fly so high : the weak feathers are fallen off. Now the standard of Christ is raised up aloft, which seems to be nothing else but the going up, or the carrying up, of the Captain of the fort to the highest tower of it, there to raise up the standard of God. The soul, as in a place of safety, looks down on those below ; it fears no dangers now—yea, rather, it courts them, as one assured beforehand of victory. It sees most clearly how lightly are the things of this world to be esteemed, and the nothingness thereof. The soul now seeks not, and possesses not, any other will but that of doing our Lord's will,[28] and so it prays Him to let it be so ; it gives to Him the keys of its own will. Lo, the gardener is now become the commander of a fortress ! The soul will do nothing but the will

[27] § 9.
[28] St. Teresa wrote : " Ni tener libre alvedrio aun querria " (would prefer not even to have the freedom of her will), which words Bañez (followed by nearly all editors and translators) changed into : " Ni tener otra voluntàd sino hacer la de Nuestro Señor " as above, the original version being somewhat subject to misunderstanding.

of our Lord ; it will not act as the owner even of itself,
nor of anything, not even of a single apple in the orchard ; only, if there be any good thing in the garden,
it is at His Majesty's disposal ; for from henceforth the
soul will have nothing of its own,—all it seeks is to do
everything for His glory, and according to His will.

31. This is really the way in which these things
come to pass ; if the raptures be true raptures, the
fruits and advantages spoken of abide in the soul ;
but if they did not, I should have great doubts about
their being from God—yea, rather, I should be afraid
they were those frenzies of which St. Vincent speaks.[29]
I have seen it myself, and I know it by experience,
that the soul in rapture is mistress of everything,
and acquires such freedom in one hour, and even in
less, as to be unable to recognize itself. It sees distinctly that all this does not belong to it, neither knows
it how it came to possess so great a good ; but it
clearly perceives the very great blessing which every
one of these raptures always brings. No one will believe this who has not had experience of it, and so they
do not believe the poor soul ; they saw it lately so
wicked, and now they see it pretend to things of so
high an order ; for it is not satisfied with serving our
Lord in the common way,—it must do so forthwith in
the highest way it can. They consider this a temptation and a folly ; yet they would not be astonished,
if they knew that it comes not from the soul, but
from our Lord, to whom it has given up the keys of
its will.

32. For my part, I believe that a soul which has
reached this state neither speaks nor acts of itself, but

---

[29] St. Vincent Ferrer, *Instruct. de Vit. Spirit.* c. xiv. p. 14 : "Si dicerent
tibi aliquid quod sit contra fidem, et contra Scripturam Sacram, aut contra
bonos mores, abhorreas earum visionem et judicia, tanquam stultas demen-
tias, et earum raptus, sicut rabiamenta "—which word the Saint translates
by "rabiamentos." The play on words—arrobamiento (rapture) and
rabiamiento (frenzy) is lost in the translation. Elsewhere St. Vincent says :
" Major pars raptuum imo rabierum nuntiorum Antichristi venit per istum
modum " (*loc. cit.* c. xii.). See also *Interior Castle*, M. iv. ch. iii. 11.

rather that the supreme King takes care of all it has
to do. O my God, how clear is the meaning of those
words, and what good reason the Psalmist had, and all
the world will ever have, to pray for the wings of a
dove ! [30] It is plain that this is the flight of the spirit
rising upwards above all created things, and chiefly
above itself : but it is a sweet flight, a delicious flight
—a flight without noise.

33. Oh, what power that soul possesses which our
Lord raises to this state ! how it looks down upon
everything, entangled by nothing ! how ashamed it is
of the time when it was entangled ! how it is amazed
at its own blindness ! how it pities those who are still
in darkness, especially if they are men of prayer, and
have received consolations from God ! It would like
to cry out to them, that they might be made to see
the delusions they are in : and, indeed, it does so now
and then ; and then a thousand persecutions fall
upon it as a shower. People consider it wanting in
humility, and think it means to teach those from whom
it should learn, particularly if it be a woman. Hence
its condemnation ; and not without reason ; because
they know not how strong the influence is that moves
it. The soul at times cannot help itself ; nor can it
refrain from undeceiving those it loves, and whom
it longs to see delivered out of the prison of this life ;
for that state in which the soul itself had been before
neither is, nor seems to be, anything else but a prison.

34. The soul is weary of the days during which it
respected points of honour, and the delusion which led
it to believe that to be honour which the world calls
by that name ; now it sees it to be the greatest lie,
and that we are all walking therein. It understands
that true honour is not delusive, but real, esteeming
that which is worthy of esteem, and despising that
which is despicable ; for everything is nothing, and
less than nothing, whatever passeth away, and is not

[30] Psalm liv. 7 : " Quis dabit mihi pennas sicut columbæ ? "—*Rel.* viii. 11.

pleasing unto God. The soul laughs at itself when it thinks of the time in which it regarded money, and desired to possess it,—though, as to this, I verily believe that I never had to confess such a fault ; it was fault enough to have regarded money at all. If I could purchase with money the blessings which I possess, I should make much of it ; but it is plain that these blessings are gained by abandoning all things.

35. What is there that is procurable by this money which we desire ? Is it anything of worth, and anything lasting ? Why, then, do we desire it ? A dismal resting-place it provides, which costs so dear ! Very often it obtains for us hell itself, fire everlasting, and torments without end. Oh, if all men would but regard it as profitless dross, how peaceful the world would be ! how free from bargaining ! How friendly all men would be one with another, if no regard were paid to honour and money ! I believe it would be a remedy for everything.

36. The soul sees how blind men are to the nature of pleasure—how by means of it they provide for themselves trouble and disquietude even in this life. What restlessness ! how little satisfaction ! what labour in vain ! It sees, too, not only the cobwebs that cover it, and its great faults, but also the specks of dirt, however slight they may be ; for the sun shines most clearly ; and thus, however much the soul may have laboured at its own perfection, it sees itself to be very unclean, if the rays of the sun fall really upon it. The soul is like water in a vessel, which appears pellucid when the sun does not shine through it ; but if it does, the water then is found to be full of motes.

37. This comparison is literally correct. Before the soul fell into the trance, it thought itself to be careful about not offending God, and that it did what it could in proportion to its strength ; but now that it has attained to this state, in which the Sun of Justice

shines upon it, and makes it open its eyes, it beholds so many motes, that it would gladly close them again. It is not so truly the child of the noble eagle, that it can gaze upon the sun ; but, for the few instants it can keep them open, it beholds itself wholly unclean. It remembers the words : " Who shall be just in Thy presence ? " [31] When it looks on this Divine Sun, the brightness thereof dazzles it,—when it looks on itself, its eyes are blinded by the dust : the little dove is blind. So it happens very often : the soul is utterly blinded, absorbed, amazed, dizzy at the vision of so much grandeur.

38. It is in rapture that true humility is acquired— humility that will never say any good of self, nor suffer others to do so. The Lord of the garden, not the soul, distributes the fruit thereof, and so none remains in its hands ; all the good it has, it refers to God ; if it says anything about itself, it is for His glory.[32] It knows that it possesses nothing here ; and even if it wished, it cannot continue ignorant of that. It sees this, as it were, with the naked eye ; for, whether it will or not, its eyes are shut against the things of this world, and open to see the truth.

CHAPTER XXI.

CONCLUSION OF THE SUBJECT. PAIN OF THE AWAKENING. LIGHT AGAINST DELUSIONS.

She continues and concludes this last degree of prayer and says what a soul, having reached it, feels when obliged to turn back and live in the world, and speaks of the lights God gives concerning the deceits (of the world). This is good doctrine.

1. To bring this matter to an end, I say that it is not

---

[31] Job iv. 17 : " Numquid homo Dei comparatione justificabitur ? "
[32] Ch. xix. 2 ; *Way of Perfection*, xxxvi. 8, 9.

necessary for the soul to give its consent here ; it is already given : the soul knows that it has given up its will into His hands,[1] and that it cannot deceive Him, because He knoweth all things. It is not here as it is in the world, where all life is full of deceit and double-dealing. When you think you have gained one man's good will, because of the outward show he makes, you afterwards learn that all was a lie. No one can live in the midst of so much scheming, particularly if there be any interests at stake.

2. Blessed, then, is that soul which our Lord draws on to the understanding of the truth ! Oh, what a state for kings ! How much better it would be for them if they strove for this, rather than for great dominions ! How justice would prevail under their rule ! What evils would be prevented, and might have been prevented already ! Here no man fears to lose life or honour for the love of God. What a grand thing this would be to him who is more bound than those beneath him to regard the honour of our Lord ! —for it is kings whom the crowd must follow. To make one step in the propagation of the faith, and to give one ray of light to heretics, I would forfeit a thousand kingdoms. And with good reason : for it is another thing altogether to gain a kingdom that shall never end, because one drop of the water of that kingdom, if the soul but tastes it, renders the things of this world utterly loathsome.

3. If, then, the soul should be wholly engulfed, what then ? O Lord, if Thou wert to give me the right to publish this abroad, people would not believe me—as they do not believe many who are able to speak of it in a way very different from mine ; but I should satisfy myself, at least. I believe I should count my life as nothing,if I might make others understand but one of these truths. I know not what I shall do afterwards, for I cannot trust myself ; though I

[1] Ch. xx. 30.

am what I am, I have a violent desire, which is wasting
me, to say this to those who are in authority. And
now that I can do no more, I betake myself to
Thee, O my Lord, to implore a remedy for all. Thou
knowest well that I would gladly divest myself of all
the graces which Thou hast given me,—provided I
remained in a condition never to offend Thee,—and
give them up to those who are kings; for I know
it would then be impossible for them to allow what
they allow now, or fail to receive the very greatest
blessings.

4. O my God, make kings to understand how far
their obligations reach! Thou hast been pleased to
distinguish them on earth in such a way that—so I
have heard—Thou showest signs in the heavens when
Thou takest any of them away. Certainly, when I
think of this, my devotion is stirred, because Thou
wilt have them learn, O my King, even from this,
that they must imitate Thee in their lives, seeing that,
when they die, signs are visible in the heavens, as it
was when Thou wert dying Thyself.

5. I am very bold; if it be wrong, you, my father,
will tear this out: only believe that I should speak
much more to the purpose in the presence of kings,—
if I might, or thought they would listen to me,—for I
recommend them greatly to God, and I wish I might
be of service to them. All this makes one risk life;
for I long frequently to lose mine,—and that would
be to lose a little for the chance of gaining much; for
surely it is not possible to live, when we see with our
eyes the great delusion wherein we are walking, and
the blindness in which we are living.

6. A soul that has attained to this is not limited to
the desires it has to serve God; for His Majesty gives
it strength to bring those desires to good effect. Nothing can be put before it into which it will not throw
itself, if only it thinks that God may be served thereby: and yet it is doing nothing, because, as I said

before,[2] it sees clearly that all is nothing, except pleasing God. The trial is, that those who are so worthless as I am, have no trial of the kind. May it be Thy good pleasure, O my God, that the time may come in which I may be able to pay one farthing at least of the heavy debt I owe Thee! Do Thou, O Lord, so dispose matters according to Thy will, that this Thy servant may do Thee some service. Other women there have been who did heroic deeds for Thee ; I am good only to talk ; and so it has not been Thy pleasure, O my God, that I should do anything : all ends in talk and desires—that is all my service. And yet even in this I am not free, because it is possible I might fail altogether.

7. Strengthen Thou my soul, and prepare it, O Good of all good ; and, my Jesus, then ordain Thou the means whereby I may do something for Thee so that there may be not even one who can bear to receive so much, and make no payment in return. Cost what it may, O Lord, let me not come before Thee with hands so empty,[3] seeing that the reward of every one will be according to his works.[4] Behold my life, behold my good name and my will ; I have given them all to Thee ; I am Thine ; dispose of me according to Thy will. I see well enough, O Lord, how little I can do ; but now, having drawn near to Thee,—having ascended to this watch-tower, from which the truth may be seen,—and while Thou departest not from me, I can do all things ; but if Thou departest from me, were it but for a moment, I shall go thither where I was once—that is, to hell.[5]

8. Oh, what it is for a soul in this state to have to return to the commerce of the world, to see and look on the farce of this life,[6] so ill-ordered ; to waste its

---

[2] Ch. xx. 34.
[3] Exod. xxiii. 15 : " Non apparebis in conspectu meo vacuus."
[4] Apoc. ii. 23 : " Dabo unicuique vestrum secundum opera sua."
[5] See ch. xxxii. 1.
[6] " Farsa de esta vida tan mal concertada."

time in attending to the body by sleeping and eating ! [7]
All is wearisome ; it cannot run away,—it sees itself
chained and imprisoned ; it feels then most keenly the
captivity into which the body has brought us, and the
wretchedness of this life.   It understands the reason
why St. Paul prayed to God to deliver him from it.
The soul cries with the Apostle, and calls upon God to
deliver it, as I said on another occasion.[9]   But here it
often cries with so much violence, that it seems as if
it would go out of the body in search of its freedom,
now that they do not take it away.   It is as a slave
sold into a strange land ; and what distresses it most
is, that it cannot find many who make the same complaint and the same prayer : the desire of life is more
common.

9. Oh, if we were utterly detached,—if we never
placed our happiness in anything of this world,—how
the pain, caused by living always away from God,
would temper the fear of death with the desire of en-
joying the true life ! Sometimes, I consider, if a person
like myself—because our Lord has given this light to
me, whose love is so cold, and whose true rest is so
uncertain, for I have not deserved it by my works—
frequently feels her banishment so much, what the
feelings of the Saints must have been.   What must
St. Paul and the Magdalene, and others like them,
have suffered, in whom the fire of the love of God has
grown so strong ?   Their life must have been a continual martyrdom.   It seems to me that they who
bring me any comfort, and whose conversation is any
relief, are those persons in whom I find these desires—
I mean, desires with acts.   I say with acts, for there
are people who think themselves detached, and who
say so of themselves,—and it must be so, for their
vocation demands it, as well as the many years that
are passed since some of them began to walk in the

[7] *Interior Castle*, M. iv. ch. i. 11.
[8] Rom. vii. 24 : '' Quis me liberabit de corpore mortis hujus ? ''
[9] Ch. xvi. 7.

way of perfection,—but my soul distinguishes clearly, and afar off, between those who are detached in words, and those who make good those words by deeds. The little progress of the former, and the great progress of the latter, make it plain. This is a matter which a person of any experience can see into most clearly.

10. So far, then, of the effects of those raptures which come from the Spirit of God. The truth is, that these are greater or less. I say less, because in the beginning, though the effects are wrought, they are not tested by works, and so it cannot be clear that a person has them ; and perfection, too, is a thing of growth, and of labouring after freedom from the cobwebs of memory ; and this requires some time. Meanwhile, the greater the growth of love and humility in the soul, the stronger the perfume of the flowers of virtues is for itself and for others. The truth is, that our Lord can so work in the soul in an instant during these raptures, that but little remains for the soul to do in order to attain to perfection. No one, who has not had experience of it, will ever be able to believe what our Lord now bestows on the soul. No effort of ours—so I think—can ever reach so far.

11. However, I do not mean to say that those persons who during many years make use of the method prescribed by writers on prayer,—who discuss the principles thereof, and the means whereby it may be acquired,—will not, by the help of our Lord, attain to perfection and great detachment, with much labour ; but they will not attain to it so rapidly as by the way of raptures, in which our Lord works independently of us, draws the soul utterly away from earth, and gives it dominion over all things here below, though the merits of that soul may not be greater than mine were : I cannot use stronger language, for my merits are as nothing. Why His Majesty doeth this is, because it is His pleasure, and He doeth it according to His pleasure ; even if the soul be without the fitting disposition, He

disposes it for the reception of that blessing which He is giving to it. Although it be most certain that He never fails to comfort those who do well, and strive to be detached, still He does not always give these effects because they have deserved them at His hands by cultivating the garden, but because it is His will to show His greatness at times in a soul which is most worthless, as I have just said, and to prepare it for all good : and all this in such a way that it seems as if the soul was now, in a manner, unable to go back and live in sin against God, as it did before.

12. The mind is now so inured to the comprehension of that which is truth indeed, that everything else seems to it to be but child's play. It laughs to itself, at times, when it sees grave men—men given to prayer, men of religion—make much of points of honour, which itself is trampling beneath its feet. They say that discretion, and the dignity of their callings, require it of them as a means to do more good ; but that soul knows perfectly well that they would do more good in one day by preferring the love of God to this their dignity, than they will do in ten years by considering it.[10]

13. The life of this soul is a life of trouble : the cross is always there, but the progress it makes is great. When those who have to do with it think it has arrived at the summit of perfection, within a little while they see it much more advanced ; for God is ever giving it grace upon grace. God is the soul of that soul now ; it is He who has the charge of it ; and so He enlightens it ; for He seems to be watching over it, always attentive to it, that it may not offend Him,—giving it grace, and stirring it up in His service. When my soul reached this state, in which God showed me mercy so great, my wretchedness came to an end, and our Lord gave me strength to rise above it. The former occasions of sin, as well as the persons with whom I was

[10] See *Way of Perfection*, ch. xxxvi. 2.

accustomed to distract myself, did me no more harm than if they had never existed [11] ; on the contrary, that which ordinarily did me harm, helped me on. Everything contributed to make me know God more, and to love Him ; to make me see how much I owed Him, as well as to be sorry for being what I had been.

14. I saw clearly that this did not come from myself, that I had not brought it about by any efforts of my own, and that there was not time enough for it. His Majesty, of His mere goodness, had given me strength for it. From the time our Lord began to give me the grace of raptures, until now, this strength has gone on increasing. He, of His goodness, hath held me by the hand, that I might not go back. I do not think that I am doing anything myself—certainly I do not ; for I see distinctly that all this is the work of our Lord. For this reason, it seems to me that the soul in which our Lord worketh these graces,—if it walks in humility and fear, always acknowledging the work of our Lord, and that we ourselves can do, as it were, nothing,—may be thrown among any companions, and, however distracted and wicked these may be, will neither be hurt nor disturbed in any way ; on the contrary, as I have just said, that will help it on, and be a means unto it whereby it may derive much greater profit.

15. Those souls are strong which are chosen by our Lord to do good to others ; still, this their strength is not their own. When our Lord brings a soul on to this state, He communicates to it of His greatest secrets by degrees. True revelations—the great gifts and visions—come by ecstasies, all tending to make the soul humble and strong, to make it despise the things of this world, and have a clearer knowledge of the greatness of the reward which our Lord has prepared for those who serve Him.[12]

[11] Ch. vii. 10.
[12] 1 Cor. ii. 9 : " Quæ præparavit Deus iis qui diligunt Illum."

16. May it please His Majesty that the great muni-ficence with which He hath dealt with me, miserable sinner that I am, may have some weight with those who shall read this, so that they may be strong and courageous enough to give up everything utterly for God. If His Majesty repays us so abundantly, that even in this life the reward and gain of those who serve Him, become visible, what will it be in the next?

CHAPTER XXII.

THE SECURITY OF CONTEMPLATIVES LIES IN THEIR NOT ASCENDING TO HIGH THINGS IF OUR LORD DOES NOT RAISE THEM. THE SACRED HUMANITY MUST BE THE ROAD TO THE HIGHEST CONTEMPLATION. A DE-LUSION IN WHICH THE SAINT WAS ONCE ENTANGLED.

In which she shows that the safest way for contem-plation is not to lift up the spirit to high things, but to wait for God to lift it up. How the sacred Humanity of Christ is the medium for the most exalted contempla-tion. She mentions an error under which she laboured for some time. This chapter is most profitable.

1. THERE is one thing I should like to say—I think it important : and if you, my father, approve, it will serve for a lesson that possibly may be necessary ; for in some books on prayer the writers say that the soul, though it cannot in its own strength attain to this state,—because it is altogether a supernatural work wrought in it by our Lord,—may nevertheless succeed, by lifting up the spirit above all created things, and raising it upwards in humility, after some years spent in a purgative life, and advancing in the illuminative. I do not very well know what they mean by illumi-native : I understand it to mean the life of those who

are making progress. And they advise us much to withdraw from all bodily imagination, and draw near to the contemplation of the Divinity ; for they say that those who have advanced so far would be embarrassed or hindered in their way to the highest contemplation, if they regarded even the Sacred Humanity itself.[1] They defend their opinion [2] by bringing forward the words [3] of our Lord to the Apostles, concerning the coming of the Holy Ghost ; I mean that coming which was after the Ascension. If the Apostles had believed, as they believed after the coming of the Holy Ghost, that He is both God and Man, His bodily Presence would, in my opinion, have been no hindrance ; for those words were not said to the Mother of God, though she loved Him more than all.[4] They think that, as this work of contemplation is wholly spiritual, any bodily object whatever can disturb or hinder it. They say that the contemplative should regard himself as being within a definite space, God everywhere around, and himself absorbed in Him. This is what we should aim at.

2. This seems to me right enough now and then ; but to withdraw altogether from Christ, and to compare His Divine Body with our miseries or with any created thing whatever is what I cannot endure. May God help me to explain myself ! I am not contradicting them on this point, for they are learned and spiritual persons, understanding what they say : God, too, is guiding souls by many ways and methods, as He has guided mine. It is of my own soul that I wish

---

[1] See *Interior Castle*, M. vi. ch. vii. 6.

[2] This opinion is supposed to be justified by the words of St. Thomas, 3 Sent. dist. 22, qu. 3, art. 1, *ad quintum.* " Corporalis præsentia Christi in duobus poterat esse nociva. Primo, quantum ad fidem, quia videntes Eum in forma in qua erat minor Patre, non ita de facili crederent Eum æqualem Patri, ut dicit glossa super Joannem. Secundo, quantum ad dilectionem, quia Eum non solum spiritualiter, sed etiam carnaliter diligeremus, conversantes cum Ipso corporaliter, et hoc est de imperfectione dilectionis."

[3] St. John xvi. 7 : " Expedit vobis ut Ego vadam ; si enim non abiero, Paracletus non veniet ad vos."

[4] This sentence is in the margin of the original MS., not in the text, but in the handwriting of the Saint.

to speak now,—I do not intermeddle with others,—and of the danger I was in because I would comply with the directions I was reading. I can well believe that he who has attained to union, and advances no further,—that is, to raptures, visions, and other graces of God given to souls,—will consider that opinion to be best, as I did myself : and if I had continued in it, I believe I should never have reached the state I am in now. I hold it to be a delusion : still, it may be that it is I who am deluded. But I will tell you what happened to me.

3. As I had no director, I used to read these books, where, by little and little, I thought I might understand something. I found out afterwards that, if our Lord had not shown me the way, I should have learned but little from books ; for I understood really nothing till His Majesty made me learn by experience : neither did I know what I was doing. So, in the beginning, when I attained to some degree of supernatural prayer, —I speak of the prayer of quiet,—I laboured to remove from myself every thought of bodily objects ; but I did not dare to lift up my soul, for that I saw would be presumption in me, who was always so wicked. I thought, however, that I had a sense of the presence of God : this was true, and I contrived to be in a state of recollection before Him. This method of prayer is full of sweetness, if God helps us in it, and the joy of it is great. And so, because I was conscious of the profit and delight which this way furnished me, no one could have brought me back to the contemplation of the Sacred Humanity ; for that seemed to me to be a real hindrance to prayer.

4. O Lord of my soul, and my Good ! Jesus Christ crucified ! I never think of this opinion, which I then held, without pain ; I believe it was an act of high treason, though done in ignorance. Hitherto, I had been all my life long so devout to the Sacred Humanity —for this happened but lately ; I mean by lately, that

it was before our Lord gave me the grace of raptures and visions.[5] I did not continue long in this error, and so I returned to my habit of delighting in our Lord, particularly at Communion. I wish I could have His picture and image always before my eyes, since I cannot have Him graven in my soul as deeply as I wish.

5. Is it possible, O my Lord, that I could have had the thought, if only for an hour, that Thou couldst be a hindrance to my greatest good ? Whence are all my blessings ? are they not from Thee ? I will not think that I was blamable, for I was very sorry for it, and it was certainly done in ignorance. And so it pleased Thee, in Thy goodness, to succour me, by sending me one who has delivered me from this delusion [6] ; and afterwards by showing Thyself to me so many times, as I shall relate hereafter, that I might clearly perceive how great my delusion was, and also tell it to many persons ; which I have done, as well as describe it as I am doing now. I believe myself that this is the reason why so many souls, after advancing to the prayer of union, make no further progress, and do not attain to very great liberty of spirit.

6. It seems to me, that there are two considerations on which I may ground this opinion. Perhaps I am saying nothing to the purpose, yet what I say is the result of experience ; for my soul was in a very evil plight, till our Lord enlightened it : all its joys were but sips ; and when it had come forth therefrom, it never found itself in that company which afterwards it had in trials and temptations.

7. The first consideration is this : there is a little absence of humility—so secret and so hidden, that we do not observe it. Who is there so proud and wretched as I, that, even after labouring all his life in penances

---

[5] " I mean by lately . . . and visions " is in the margin of the MS., but in the handwriting of the Saint.

[6] Probably Fr. Juan de Pradanos : see ch. xxiii. 18 ; *cf.* ch. xxviii. 4.

and prayers and persecutions, can possibly imagine himself not to be exceedingly rich, most abundantly rewarded, when our Lord permits him to stand with St. John at the foot of the cross? I know not into whose head it could have entered to be not satisfied with this, unless it be mine, which has gone wrong in every way where it should have gone right onwards.

8. Then, if our constitution,—or perhaps sickness—will not permit us always to think of His Passion, because it is so painful, who is to hinder us from thinking of Him risen from the grave, seeing that we have Him so near us in the Sacrament, where He is glorified, and where we shall not see Him in His great weariness—scourged, streaming with blood, faint by the way, persecuted by those to whom He had done good, and not believed in by the Apostles? Certainly it is not always that one can bear to meditate on sufferings so great as were those He underwent. Behold Him here, before His ascension into heaven, without pain, all-glorious, giving strength to some and courage to others. In the most Holy Sacrament, He is our companion, as if it was not in His power to withdraw Himself for a moment from us. And yet it was in my power to withdraw from Thee, O my Lord, that I might serve Thee better! It may be that I knew Thee not when I sinned against Thee; but how could I, having once known Thee, ever think I should gain more in this way? O Lord, what an evil way I took! and I was going out of the way, if Thou hadst not brought me back to it. When I see Thee near me, I see all good things together. No trial befalls me that is not easy to bear, when I think of Thee standing before those who judged Thee.

9. With so good a Friend and Captain ever present, Himself the first to suffer, everything can be borne. He helps, He strengthens, He never fails, He is the true Friend. I see clearly, and since then have always seen, that if we are to please God, and if He is to give

us His great graces, everything must pass through the
hands of His most Sacred Humanity, in whom His
Majesty said that He is well pleased.[7] I know this by
repeated experience : our Lord has told it me. I have
seen clearly that this is the door[8] by which we are to
enter, if we would have His supreme Majesty reveal to
us His great secrets.

10. So, then, I would have your reverence[9] seek no
other way, even if you were arrived at the highest contemplation. This way is safe. Our Lord is He by
whom all good things come to us ; He will teach you.
Consider His life ; that is the best example. What
more can we want than so good a Friend at our side,
Who will not forsake us when we are in trouble and
distress, as they do who belong to the world ! Blessed
is he who truly loves Him, and who always has Him
near him ! Let us consider the glorious St. Paul, who
seems as if Jesus was never absent from his lips, as if
he had Him deep down in his heart. After I had
heard this of some great Saints given to contemplation, I considered the matter carefully ; and I see
that they walked in no other way. St. Francis with
the stigmata proves it, St. Antony of Padua with the
Infant Jesus ; St. Bernard rejoiced in the Sacred
Humanity ; so did St. Catherine of Siena, and many
others, as your reverence knows better than I do.

11. This withdrawing from bodily objects must no
doubt be good, seeing that it is recommended by
persons who are so spiritual ; but, in my opinion, it
ought to be done only when the soul has made very
great progress ; for until then it is clear that the
Creator must be sought for through His creatures. All
this depends on the grace which our Lord distributes

[7] St. Matt. iii. 17 : " Hic est Filius Meus dilectus, in quo Mihi complacui."
[8] St. John x. 7, 9 : "Ego sum ostium."
[9] V^a Merced, Señor. In writing to the Bishop of Avila (July 6, 1567) St.
Teresa speaks of Garcia de Toledo : " El señor fray Garcia." There can be
little doubt that the religious whom in the *Life* she addresses V. Merced, Señor,
is this same Garcia.

to every soul. I do not intermeddle here. What I would say is, that the most Sacred Humanity of Christ is not to be counted among the objects from which we have to withdraw. Let this be clearly understood. I wish I knew how to explain it.[10]

12. When God suspends all the powers of the soul,— as we see He does in the states of prayer already described,—it is clear that, whether we wish it or not, this presence is withdrawn. Be it so, then. The loss is a blessed one, because it takes place in order that we may have a deeper fruition of what we seem to have lost ; for at that moment the whole soul is occupied in loving Him whom the understanding has toiled to know ; and it loves what it has not comprehended, and rejoices in what it could not have rejoiced in so well, if it had not lost itself, in order, as I am saying, to gain itself the more. But that we should carefully and laboriously accustom ourselves not to strive with all our might to have always—and please God it be always !—the most Sacred Humanity before our eyes,—this, I say, is what seems to me not to be right : it is making the soul, as they say, to walk in the air ; for it has nothing to rest on, how full soever of God it may think itself to be.

13. It is a great matter for us to have our Lord before us as Man while we are living and in the flesh. This is that other inconvenience which I say must be met with. The first—I have already begun to describe it—is a little failure in humility, in that the soul desires to rise of itself before our Lord raises it, and is not satisfied with meditation on so excellent a subject,— seeking to be Mary before it has laboured with Martha. If our Lord will have a soul to be Mary, even on the first day, there is nothing to be afraid of ; but we must not be self-invited guests, as I think I said on another occasion.[11] This little mote of want of humility,

---

[10] See St. John of the Cross, *Ascent of Mount Carmel*, bk. iii. ch. i. 12.
[11] Ch. xii. 5, 7.

though in appearance a mere nothing, does a great deal of harm to those who wish to advance in contemplation.

14. I now come back to the second consideration. We are not angels, for we have a body ; to seek to make ourselves angels while we are on the earth, and so much on the earth as I was, is an act of folly. In general, our thoughts must have something to rest on, though the soul may go forth out of itself now and then, or it may be very often so full of God as to be in need of no created thing by the help of which it may recollect itself. But this is not so common a case ; for when we have many things to do, when we are persecuted and in trouble, when we cannot have much rest, and when we have our seasons of dryness, Christ is our best Friend ; for we regard Him as Man, and behold Him faint and in trouble, and He is our Companion ; and when we shall have accustomed ourselves in this way, it is very easy to find Him near us, although there will be occasions from time to time when we can do neither the one nor the other.

15. For this end, that is useful which I spoke of before [12] : we must not show ourselves as labouring after spiritual consolations ; come what may, to embrace the cross is the great thing. The Lord of all consolation was Himself forsaken : they left Him alone in His sorrows. Do not let us forsake Him ; for His hand will help us to rise more than any efforts we can make ; and He will withdraw Himself when He sees it to be expedient for us, and when He pleaseth will also draw the soul forth out of itself, as I said before.[13]

16. God is greatly pleased when He beholds a soul in its humility making His Son a Mediator between itself and Him, and yet loving Him so much as to confess its own unworthiness, even when He would raise it up to the highest contemplation, and saying

[12] Ch. xv. 21.   [13] Ch. xx. 2.

with St. Peter [14] : "Go Thou away from me, O Lord, for I am a sinful man." I know this by experience : it was thus that God directed my soul. Others may walk, as I said before,[15] by another and a shorter road. What I have understood of the matter is this : that the whole foundation of prayer must be laid in humility, and that the more a soul humbles itself in prayer, the more God lifts it up. I do not remember that He ever showed me any of those marvellous mercies of which I shall speak hereafter,[16] at any other time than when I was as one brought to nothing,[17] by seeing how wicked I was. Moreover, His Majesty contrived to make me understand matters that helped me to know myself, but which I could never have even imagined of myself.

17. I believe myself that if a soul makes any effort of its own to further itself in the way of the prayer of union, and though it may seem to make immediate progress, it will quickly fall back, because the foundations were not duly laid. I fear, too, that such a soul will never attain to true poverty of spirit, which consists in seeking consolation or sweetness, not in prayer, —the consolations of the earth are already abandoned, —but rather in sorrows, for the love of Him who always lived in sorrows Himself [18] ; and in being calm in the midst of sorrows and aridities. Though the soul may feel it in some measure, there is no disquiet, nor any of that pain which some persons suffer, who, if they are not always labouring with the understanding and with a sense of devotion, think everything lost,—as if their efforts merited so great a blessing !

18. I am not saying that men should not seek to be devout, nor that they should not stand with great reverence in the presence of God, but only that they are not to vex themselves if they cannot find even one

---

[14] St. Luke v. 8 : " Exi a me, quia homo peccator sum, Domine."
[15] Ch. xii. 6.
[16] Ch. xxviii.
[17] Psalm lxxii. 22 : " Et ego ad nihilum redactus sum, et nescivi."
[18] Isaias liii. 3 : " Virum dolorum, et scientem infirmitatem."

good thought, as I said in another place [19] ; for we are unprofitable servants.[20]   What do we think we can do ?   Our Lord grant that we understand this, and that we may be those little asses who drive the windlass I spoke of [21] : these, though their eyes are bandaged, and they do not understand what they are doing, yet draw up more water than the gardener can draw with all his efforts. We must walk in liberty on this road, committing ourselves into the hands of God. If it be His Majesty's good pleasure to raise us and place us among His chamberlains and secret councillors, we must go willingly ; if not, we must serve Him in the lower offices of His house, and not sit down on the upper seats.[22]   As I have sometimes said,[23] God is more careful of us than we are ourselves, and knows what each one of us is fit for.

19. What use is there in governing oneself by oneself, when the whole will has been given up to God ? I think this less endurable now than in the first state of prayer, and it does much greater harm ; for these blessings are supernatural. If a man has a bad voice, let him force himself ever so much to sing, he will never improve it ; but if God gives him a good voice, he has no need to try it twice. Let us, then, pray Him always to show His mercy upon us, with a submissive spirit, yet trusting in the goodness of God. And now that the soul is permitted to sit at the feet of Christ, let it contrive not to quit its place, but keep it anyhow. Let it follow the example of the Magdalene ; and when it shall be strong enough, God will lead it into the wilderness.[24]

20. You, then, my father, must be content with this until you meet with some one of more experience

[19] Ch. xi. 15.
[20] St. Luke xvii. 10 : " Servi inutiles sumus."
[21] Ch. xi. 11.
[22] St. Luke xiv. 8 : " Non discumbas in primo loco."   See *Way of Perfection*, ch. xvii. 1.
[23] Ch. xi. 23, ch. xviii. 6.
[24] Os. ii. 14 : " Ducam eam in solitudinem."

and better knowledge than I am. If you see people who are beginning to taste of God, do not trust them if they think that they advance more, and have a deeper fruition of God, when they make efforts of their own. Oh, when God wills it, how He discovers Himself without these little efforts of ours! We may do what we like, but He throws the spirit into a trance as easily as a giant takes up a straw; no resistance is possible. What a thing to believe, that God will wait till the toad shall fly of itself, when He has already willed it should do so! Well, it seems to me still more difficult and hard for our spirit to rise upwards, if God does not raise it, seeing that it is burdened with earth, and hindered in a thousand ways. Its willingness to rise is of no service to it; for, though an aptness for flying be more natural to it than to a toad, yet is it so sunk in the mire as to have lost it by its own fault.

21. I come, then, to this conclusion: whenever we think of Christ, we should remind ourselves of the love that made Him bestow so many graces upon us, and also how great that love is which our Lord God has shown us, in giving us such a pledge of the love He bears us; for love draws forth love. And though we are only at the very beginning, and exceedingly wicked, yet let us always labour to keep this in view, and stir ourselves up to love; for if once our Lord grants us this grace, of having this love imprinted in our hearts, everything will be easy, and we shall do great things in a very short time, and with very little labour. May His Majesty give us that love,—He knows the great need we have of it,—for the sake of that love which He bore us, and of His glorious Son, to whom it cost so much to make it known to us! Amen.

22. There is one thing I should like to ask you, my father. How is it that, when our Lord begins to bestow upon a soul a grace so great as this of perfect contemplation, it is not, as it ought to be, perfect at once? Certainly, it seems it should be so; for he

who receives a grace so great ought never more to seek consolations on earth. How is it, I ask, that a soul which has ecstasies, and so far is more accustomed to receive graces, should yet seem to bring forth fruits still higher and higher,—and the more so, the more it is detached,—when our Lord might have sanctified it at once, the moment He came near it? How is it, I ask again, that the same Lord brings it to the perfection of virtue only in the course of time? I should be glad to learn the reason, for I know it not. I do know, however, that in the beginning, when a trance lasts only the twinkling of an eye, and is almost imperceptible but for the effects it produces, the degree of strength which God then gives is very different from that which He gives when this grace is a trance of longer duration.

23. Very often, when thinking of this, have I imagined the reason might be, that the soul does not despise itself all at once, till our Lord instructs it by degrees, and makes it resolute, and gives it the strength of manhood, so that it may trample utterly upon everything. He gave this strength to the Magdalene in a moment. He gives the same grace to others, according to the measure of their abandonment of themselves into the hands of His Majesty, that He may do with them as He will. We never thoroughly believe that God rewards a hundredfold even in this life.[25]

24. I also thought of this comparison: supposing the grace given to those who are far advanced to be the same with that given to those who are but beginners, we may then liken it to a certain food of which many persons partake: they who eat a little retain the savour of it for a moment, they who eat more are nourished by it, but those who eat much receive life and strength. Now, the soul may eat so frequently and so abundantly of this food of life as

[25] St. Matt. xix. 29 : " Qui reliquerit domum, ... centuplum accipiet."

to have no pleasure in eating any other food, because it sees how much good it derives from it. Its taste is now so formed upon it, that it would rather not live than have to eat any other food ; for all food but this has no other effect than to take away the sweet savour which this good food leaves behind.

25. Further, the conversation of good people does not profit us in one day as much as it does in many ; and we may converse with them long enough to become like them, by the grace of God. In short, the whole matter is as His Majesty wills. He gives His grace to whom He pleases ; but much depends on this : he who begins to receive this grace must make a firm resolution to detach himself from all things, and esteem this grace according to reason.

26. It seems also to me as if His Majesty were going about to try those who love Him,—now one, now another,—revealing Himself in supreme joy, so as to quicken our belief, if it should be dead, in what He will give us, saying, Behold ! this is but a drop of the immense sea of blessings ; for He leaves nothing undone for those He loves ;. and as He sees them receive it, so He gives, and He gives Himself. He loves those who love Him. Oh, how dear He is !—how good a friend ! O my soul's Lord, who can find words to describe what Thou givest to those who trust in Thee, and what they lose who come to this state, and yet dwell in themselves ! Oh, let not this be so, O my Lord ! for Thou doest more than this when Thou comest to a lodging so mean as mine. Blessed be Thou for ever and ever !

27. I now humbly ask you, my father, if you mean to discuss what I have written on prayer with spiritual persons, to see that they are so really ; for if they be persons who know only one way, or who have stood still midway, they will not be able to understand the matter. There are also some whom God leads at once by the highest way ; these think that others might

advance in the same manner—quiet the understanding, and make bodily objects none of their means ; but these people will remain dry as a stick.   Others, also, there are who, having for a moment attained to the prayer of quiet, think forthwith that, as they have had the one, so they may have the other.   These, instead of advancing, go back, as I said before.[26]   So, throughout, experience and discretion are necessary. May our Lord, of His goodness, bestow them on us !

CHAPTER XXIII.

THE SAINT RESUMES THE HISTORY OF HER LIFE.   AIMING AT PERFECTION.   MEANS WHEREBY IT MAY BE GAINED.   INSTRUCTIONS FOR CONFESSORS.

She returns to the history of her life, how she began to practise greater perfection.   This is profitable for those who have to direct souls practising prayer that they may know how to deal with beginners, and she speaks of the profit she derived from such knowledge.

1. I SHALL now return to that point in my life where I broke off,[1] having made, I believe, a longer digression than I need have made, in order that what is still to come may be more clearly understood.   Henceforth, it is another and a new book,—I mean, another and a new life.   Hitherto, my life was my own ; my life since I began to explain these methods of prayer, is the life which God lived in me,—so it seems to me ; for I feel it to be impossible that I should have escaped in so short a time from ways and works that were so wicked.   May our Lord be praised, who has delivered me from myself !

[26] Ch. xii. 5.
[1] At the end of ch. ix.   The thirteen chapters interposed between that and this—the twenty-third—are a treatise on mystical theology.

2. When, then, I began to avoid the occasions of sin, and to give myself more unto prayer, our Lord also began to bestow His graces upon me, as one who desired, so it seemed, that I too should be willing to receive them. His Majesty began to give me most frequently the grace of the prayer of quiet, and very often that of union, which lasted some time. But as in these days, women have fallen into great delusions and deceits of Satan,[2] I began to be afraid, because the joy and sweetness which I felt were so great, and very often beyond my power to avoid. On the other hand, I felt in myself a very deep conviction that God was with me, especially when I was in prayer. I saw, too, that I grew better and stronger thereby.

3. But if I was a little distracted, I began to be afraid, and to imagine that perhaps it was Satan that suspended my understanding, making me think it to be good, in order to withdraw me from mental prayer, hinder my meditation on the Passion, and debar me the use of my understanding : this seemed to me, who did not comprehend the matter, to be a grievous loss ; but, as His Majesty was pleased to give me light to offend Him no more, and to understand how much I owed Him, this fear so grew upon me, that it made me seek diligently for spiritual persons with whom I might treat of my state. I had already heard of some ; for the Fathers of the Society of Jesus had come hither[3] ;

---

[2] She refers to a Franciscan nun of Cordoba, called Magdalene of the Cross, who, by her revelations, prophecies, and raptures, had acquired renown throughout Spain, and was consulted by high and low as an oracle. She had been elected abbess, and governed her convent for nine years ; but at length it transpired that, from the age of five, she had been subject to delusions, and had knowingly and wilfully deceived many persons. She was degraded by the Inquisition, and condemned to death (1541). She made a full confession of her crimes, and submitted with Christian resignation to her punishment.

[3] The Jesuit College of St. Giles at Avila was founded in 1554, but some of the Fathers, among whom St. Francis Borja, had come thither from time to time since 1550, and their sanctity as well as their eloquence left a lasting impression upon the citizens. The bishop, Don Diego de Alava y Esquivel, welcomed the new foundation, which received substantial support from a young ecclesiastic who joined the Society, Fernando Alvarez del Aguila, and later on became one of St. Teresa's confessors.

and I, though I knew none of them, was greatly
attracted by them, merely because I had heard of
their way of life and of prayer ; but I did not think
myself fit to speak to them, or strong enough to obey
them ; and this made me still more afraid ; for to
converse with them, and remain what I was, seemed
to me somewhat rude.

4. I spent some time in this state, till, after much
inward contention and fear, I determined to confer
with some spiritual person, to ask him to tell me what
that method of prayer was which I was using, and to
show me whether I was in error.   I was also resolved
to do everything I could not to offend God ; for the
want of courage of which I was conscious, as I said
before,[4] made me so timid.   Was there ever delusion
so great as mine, O my God, when I withdrew from
good in order to become good !   The devil must lay
much stress on this in the beginning of a course of
virtue ; for I could not overcome my repugnance.   He
knows that the whole relief of the soul consists in con-
ferring with the friends of God.   Hence it was that no
time was fixed in which I should resolve to do this.   I
waited to grow better first, as I did before when I
ceased to pray,[5]—and perhaps I never should have
become better ; for I had now sunk so deeply into the
petty ways of an evil habit,—I could not convince
myself that they were wrong,—that I needed the help
of others, who should hold out a hand to raise me up.
Blessed be Thou, O Lord !—for the first hand out-
stretched to me was Thine.

5. When I saw that my fear was going so far, it
struck me—because I was making progress in prayer
—that this must be a great blessing, or a very great
evil ; for I understood perfectly that what had happened was something supernatural, because at times
I was unable to withstand it ; to have it when I would
was also impossible.   I thought to myself that there

<hr />

[4] Ch. vii. 37.   [5] Ch. xix. 7, 8.

was no help for it, but in keeping my conscience pure, avoiding every occasion even of venial sins ; for if it was the work of the Spirit of God, the gain was clear ; and if the work of Satan, so long as I strove to please, and did not offend, our Lord, Satan could do me little harm ; on the contrary, he must lose in the struggle. Determined on this course, and always praying God to help me, striving also after purity of conscience for some days, I saw that my soul had not strength to go forth alone to a perfection so great. I had certain attachments to trifles, which, though not very wrong in themselves, were yet enough to ruin all.

6. I was told of a learned ecclesiastic,[6] dwelling in this city, whose goodness and pious life our Lord was beginning to make known to the world. I contrived to make his acquaintance through a saintly nobleman [7] living in the same place. This latter is a married man ; but his life is so edifying and virtuous, so given to prayer, and so full of charity, that the goodness and perfection of it shine forth in all he does : and most justly so ; for many souls have been greatly blessed through him, because of his great gifts, which, though his condition of a layman be a hindrance to him, never lie idle. He is a man of great sense, and very gentle with all people ; his conversation is never wearisome, but so sweet and gracious, as well as upright and holy, that he pleases everybody very much with whom he has any relations. He directs it all to the great good

---

[6] Gaspar Daza had formed a society of priests in Avila, and was a very laborious and holy man. It was he who said the first Mass in the convent of St. Joseph, founded by St. Teresa, whom he survived, dying Nov. 24, 1592. He committed the direction of his priests to F. Baltasar Alvarez. His body, as well as those of his mother and sister, was interred in the chapel of the Nativity in the convent of St. Joseph.

[7] Don Francisco de Salcedo. After the death of his wife he became a priest, and was chaplain and confessor of the Carmelite nuns of St. Joseph. For twenty years of his married life he attended regularly the theological lectures of the Dominicans, in the convent of St. Thomas. His death took place Sept. 12, 1580, when he had been a priest for ten years. He was buried in the chapel of St. Paul (commonly, but erroneously, called the Primitive Chapel of St. Joseph's convent), which he had built.

of those souls with whom he converses ; and he seems
to have no other end in view but to do all he may be
permitted to do for all men, and make them content.

7. This blessed and holy man, then, seems to me, by
the pains he took, to have been the beginning of salvation to my soul. His humility in his relations with
me makes me wonder ; for he had spent, I believe,
nearly forty years in prayer,—it may be two or three
years less,—and all his life was ordered with that perfection which his state admitted. His wife is so great
a servant of God, and so full of charity, that nothing
is lost to him on her account,[8]—in short, she was the
chosen wife of one who God knew would serve Him
so well. Some of their kindred are married to some of
mine. Besides, I had also much communication with
another great servant of God, married to one of my
first cousins.

8. It was thus I contrived that the ecclesiastic I
speak of, who was so great a servant of God, and his
great friend, should come to speak to me, intending to
confess to him, and to take him for my director. When
he had brought him to speak to me, I, in the greatest
confusion at finding myself in the presence of so holy
a man, revealed to him the state of my soul, and my
way of prayer. He would not be my confessor ; he
said that he was very much occupied : and so, indeed,
he was. He began with a holy resolution to direct
me as if I was strong,—I ought to have been strong,
according to the method of prayer which he saw I
used,—so that I should in nothing offend God. When
I saw that he was resolved to make me break off at
once with the petty ways I spoke of before,[9] and that
I had not the courage to go forth at once in the perfection he required of me, I was distressed ; and when
I perceived that he ordered the affairs of my soul as if

---

[8] Doña Mencia del Aguila, wife of Don Francisco de Salcedo, was probably
related to Doña Catalina del Aguila, wife of Don Pedro de Cepeda, St. Teresa's
uncle.   [9] § 4.

I ought to be perfect at once, I saw that much more care was necessary in my case.   In a word, I felt that the means he would have employed were not those by which my soul could be helped onwards ; for they were fitted for a soul more perfect than mine ; and though the graces I had received from God were very many, I was still at the very beginning in the matter of virtue and of mortification.

9. I believe, certainly, if I had only had this ecclesiastic to confer with, that my soul would have made no progress ; for the pain it gave me to see that I was not doing—and, as I thought, could not do—what he told me, was enough to destroy all hope, and make me abandon the matter altogether.   I wonder at times how it was that he, being one who had a particular grace for the direction of beginners in the way of God, was not permitted to understand my case, or to undertake the care of my soul.   I see it was all for my greater good, in order that I might know and converse with persons so holy as the members of the Society of Jesus.

10. After this, I arranged with that saintly nobleman that he should come and see me now and then.   It shows how deep his humility was ; for he consented to converse with a person so wicked as I was.   He began his visits, he encouraged me, and told me that I ought not to suppose I could give up everything in one day ; God would bring it about by degrees : he himself had for some years been unable to free himself from some very slight imperfections.   O humility ! what great blessings thou bringest to those in whom thou dwellest, and to them who draw near to those who possess thee ! This holy man—for I think I may justly call him so— told me of weaknesses of his own, in order to help me. He, in his humility, thought them weaknesses ; but, if we consider his state, they were neither faults nor imperfections ; yet, in my state, it was a very great fault to be subject to them.

11. I am not saying this without a meaning, though

I seem to be enlarging on trifles ; but these trifles contribute so much towards the beginning of the soul's
progress and its flight upwards, though it has no wings,
as they say ; and yet no one will believe it who has
not had experience of it ; but, as I hope in God that
your reverence will help many a soul, I speak of it
here. My whole salvation depended on his knowing
how to treat me, on his humility, on the charity with
which he conversed with me, and on his patient endurance of me when he saw that I did not mend my
ways at once. He went on discreetly, by degrees
showing me how to overcome Satan. My affection
for him so grew upon me, that I never was more at
ease than on the day I used to see him. I saw him,
however, very rarely. When he was long in coming,
I used to be very much distressed, thinking that he
would not see me because I was so wicked.

12. When he found out my great imperfections,—
they might well have been sins, though since I conversed with him I am somewhat improved,—and when
I recounted to him, in order to obtain light from him,
the great graces which God had bestowed upon me, he
told me that these things were inconsistent one with
another ; that these consolations were given to people
who had made great progress, and led mortified lives ;
that he could not help being very much afraid—he
thought that the evil spirit might have something to
do in my case ; he would not decide that question,
however, but he would have me carefully consider my
whole method of prayer, and then tell him of it. That
was the difficulty : I did not understand it myself,
and so I could tell him nothing of my prayer ; for the
grace to understand it—and, understanding it, to
describe it—has only lately been given me of God.
This saying of his, together with the fear I was in,
distressed me exceedingly, and I cried ; for certainly
I was anxious to please God, and I could not persuade
myself that Satan had anything to do with it. But

I was afraid, on account of my great sins, that God
might leave me blind, so that I should understand
nothing.

13. Looking into books to see if I could find anything there by which I might recognise the prayer I
practised, I found in one of them, called the *Ascent of
Mount Sion*,[10] and in that part of it which relates to
the union of the soul with God, all those marks which
I had in myself, in that I could not think of anything.
This is what I most dwell on—that I could think of
nothing when I was in prayer. I marked that passage, and gave him the book, that he, and the ecclesiastic mentioned before,[11] saint and servant of God,
might consider it, and tell me what I should do. If
they thought it right, I would give up that method of
prayer altogether ; for why should I expose myself
to danger, when, at the end of nearly twenty years,
during which I had used it, I had gained nothing,
but had fallen into a delusion of the devil ? It was
better for me to give it up. And yet this seemed to
me hard ; for I had already discovered what my soul
would become without prayer. Everything seemed
full of trouble. I was like a person in the middle of
a river, who, in whatever direction he may turn, fears
a still greater danger, and is well-nigh drowned. This
is a very great trial, and I have gone through many
like it, as I shall show hereafter [12] ; and though it does
not seem to be of any importance, it will perhaps be
advantageous to understand how the spirit is to be
tried.

14. And certainly the affliction to be borne is
great, and caution is necessary, particularly in the
case of women,—for our weakness is great,—and
much evil may be the result of telling them very distinctly that the devil is busy with them ; yea, rather,

---

[10] *Subida del Monte Sion*, by a Franciscan lay brother Bernardino de Laredo
(1482-1540 ; originally physician to the King of Portugal). It appeared
anonymously at Sevilla, 1533, and again at Medina del Campo in 1542.

[11] § 6.   [12] See ch. xxv. 18.

the matter should be very carefully considered, and they should be removed out of reach of the dangers that may arise. They should be advised to keep things secret ; and it is necessary, also, that their secret should be kept. I am speaking of this as one to whom it has been a sore trouble ; for some of those with whom I spoke of my prayer did not keep my secret, but, making inquiries, one of another for a good purpose, did me much harm ; for they made things known which might well have remained secret, because not intended for every one : and it seemed as if I had made them public myself.[13]

15. I believe that our Lord permitted [14] this to be done without sin on their part, in order that I might suffer. I do not say that they revealed anything I discussed with them in confession ; still, as they were persons to whom, in my fears, I gave a full account of myself, in order that they might give me light, I thought they ought to have been silent. Nevertheless, I never dared to conceal anything from such persons. My meaning, then, is, that women should be directed with much discretion ; their directors should encourage them, and bide the time when our Lord will help them, as He has helped me. If He had not, the greatest harm would have befallen me, for I was in great fear and dread ; and as I suffered from disease of the heart,[15] I am astonished that all this did not do me a great deal of harm.

16. Then, when I had given him the book, and told the story of my life and of my sins, the best way I could in general,—for I was not in confession, because he was a layman ; yet I gave him clearly to understand how wicked I was,—those two servants of God, with great charity and affection, considered what was best for me. When they had made up their minds what to say,—I was waiting for it in great dread, having

---

[13] See ch. xxviii. 18.   [14] See *Relation* vii. 17.

[15] See ch. iv. 6.

begged many persons to pray to God for me, and I too had prayed much during those days,—the nobleman came to me in great distress, and said that, in the opinion of both, I was deluded by an evil spirit ; that the best thing for me to do was to apply to a certain father of the Society of Jesus, who would come to me if I sent for him, saying I had need of him ; that I ought, in a general confession, to give him an account of my whole life, and of the state I was in,—and all with great clearness : God would, in virtue of the Sacrament of Confession, give him more light concerning me ; for those fathers were very experienced men in matters of spirituality. Further, I was not to swerve in a single point from the counsels of that father ; for I was in great danger, if I had no one to direct me.

17. This answer so alarmed and distressed me, that I knew not what to do—I did nothing but cry. Being in an oratory in great affliction, not knowing what would become of me, I read in a book—it seemed as if our Lord had put it into my hands—that St. Paul said, God is faithful [16] ; that He will never permit Satan to deceive those who love Him. This gave me great consolation. I began to prepare for my general confession, and to write out all the evil and all the good : a history of my life, as clearly as I understood it, and knew how to make it, omitting nothing whatever. I remember, when I saw I had written so much evil, and scarcely anything that was good, that I was exceedingly distressed and sorrowful. It pained me, also, that the nuns of the community should see me converse with such holy persons as those of the Society of Jesus ; for I was afraid of my own wickedness, and I thought I should be obliged to cease from it, and give up my amusements ; and that if I did not do so, I should grow worse : so I persuaded the sacristan and the

---

[16] I Cor. x. 13 : " Fidelis autem Deus est, qui non patietur vos tentari supra id quod potestis."

portress to tell no one of it. This was of little use,
after all ; for when I was called down there was one
at the door, as it happened, who told it to the whole
convent. But what difficulties and what terrors Satan
troubles them with who would draw near unto God !
    18. I communicated the whole state of my soul to
that servant of God,[17] and he was a great servant of
His, and very prudent. He understood all I told him,
explained it to me, and encouraged me greatly. He
said that all was very evidently the work of the Spirit
of God ; only it was necessary for me to go back again
to my prayer, because I was not well grounded, and
had not begun to understand what mortification
meant,—that was true, for I do not think I knew it
even by name,—that I was by no means to give up
prayer ; on the contrary, I was to do violence to myself in order to practise it, because God had bestowed
on me such special graces as made it impossible to
say whether it was, or was not, the will of our Lord to
do good to many through me. He went further, for
he seems to have prophesied of that which our Lord
afterwards did with me, and said that I should be very
much to blame if I did not correspond with the graces
which God bestowed upon me. It seems to me that
the Holy Ghost was speaking by his mouth in order
to heal my soul, so deep was the impression he made.
He made me very much ashamed of myself, and
directed me by a way which seemed to change me
altogether. What a grand thing it is to understand
a soul ! He told me to make my prayer every day
on some mystery of the Passion, and that I should
profit by it, and to fix my thoughts on the Sacred
Humanity only, resisting to the utmost of my power

[17] F. Juan de Padranos, or Pradanos, whom St. Francis de Borja had sent
in 1555, with F. Fernando Alvarez del Aguila, to found the house of the Society
in Avila. Ribera, i. 5, says he heard that F. Juan de Padranos gave in part
the exercises of St. Ignatius to the Saint. He spent many years at Valladolid,
where he proved a faithful friend of the Carmelite nuns during a time of trouble
(Letter of St. Teresa of Nov. 2, 1576). He also died there.

those recollections and delights, to which I was not to yield in any way till he gave me further directions in the matter.

19. He left me consoled and fortified : our Lord came to my succour and to his, so that he might understand the state I was in, and how he was to direct me. I made a firm resolution not to swerve from anything he might command me, and to this day I have kept it. Our Lord be praised, who has given me grace to be obedient to my confessors,[18] however imperfectly !—and they have almost always been those blessed men of the Society of Jesus ; though, as I said, I have but imperfectly obeyed them. My soul began to improve visibly, as I am now going to say.

CHAPTER XXIV.

PROGRESS   UNDER   OBEDIENCE.   HER   INABILITY   TO
     RESIST   THE   GRACES   OF   GOD.   GOD   MULTIPLIES   HIS
     GRACES.

She continues the same subject and tells how her soul improved since she began to practise obedience, and how little she was able to resist God's graces, and how His Majesty continued to give them more and more abundantly.

1. AFTER this my confession, my soul was so docile that, as it seems to me, there was nothing in the world I was not prepared to undertake. I began at once to make a change in many things, though my confessor never pressed me—on the contrary, he seemed to make light of it all. I was the more influenced by this, because ʼhe led me on by the way of the love of God ;

18 See *Relation* i. 9.

he left me free, and did not press me, unless I did so myself, out of love. I continued thus nearly two months, doing all I could to resist the sweetness and graces that God sent. As to my outward life, the change was visible ; for our Lord gave me courage to go through with certain things, of which those who knew me—and even those in the community—said that they seemed to them extreme ; and, indeed, compared with what I had been accustomed to do, they were extreme : people, therefore, had reason to say so. Yet, in those things which were of obligation, considering the habit I wore, and the profession I had made, I was still deficient. By resisting the sweetness and joys which God sent me, I gained this, that His Majesty taught me Himself ; for, previously, I used to think that, in order to obtain sweetness in prayer, it was necessary for me to hide myself in secret places, and so I scarcely dared to stir. Afterwards, I saw how little that was to the purpose ; for the more I tried to distract myself, the more our Lord poured over me that sweetness and joy which seemed to me to be flowing around me, so that I could not in any way escape from it : and so it was. I was so careful about this resistance, that it was a pain to me. But our Lord was more careful to show His mercies, and during those two months to reveal Himself more than before, so that I might the better comprehend that it was no longer in my power to resist Him.

2. I began with a renewed love of the most Sacred Humanity ; my prayer began to be solid, like a house, the foundations of which are strong ; and I was inclined to practise greater penance, having been negligent in this matter hitherto because of my great infirmities. The holy man who heard my confession told me that certain penances would not hurt me, and that God perhaps sent me so much sickness because I did no penance ; His Majesty would therefore impose it Himself. He ordered me to practise certain

acts of mortification not very pleasant for me.[1] I did so, because I felt that our Lord was enjoining it all, and giving him grace to command me in such a way as to make me obedient unto him.

3. My soul was now sensitive to every offence I committed against God, however slight it might be ; so much so, that if I had any superfluity about me, I could not recollect myself in prayer till I had got rid of it. I prayed earnestly that our Lord would hold me by the hand, and not suffer me to fall again, now that I was under the direction of His servants. I thought that would be a great evil, and that they would lose their credit through me.

4. At this time, Father Francis, who was Duke of Gandia,[2] came here ; he had left all he possessed some years before, and had entered the Society of Jesus. My confessor, and the nobleman of whom I spoke before,[3] contrived that he should visit me, in order that I might speak to him, and give him an account of my way of prayer ; for they knew him to be greatly favoured and comforted of God : he had given up much, and was rewarded for it even in this life. When he had heard me, he said to me that it was the work of the Spirit of God,[4] and that he thought it was not right now to prolong that resistance ; that hitherto it had been safe enough,—only, I should always begin my prayer by meditating on some part of the Passion ; and that if our Lord should then raise up my spirit, I should make no resistance, but suffer His Majesty to raise it upwards, I myself not seeking it. He gave both medicine and advice, as one who had made great

---

[1] The Saint now treated her body with extreme severity, disciplining herself even unto blood (*Reforma*, vol. i. lib. i. cap. xx. § 4).

[2] St. Francis de Borja, Duke of Gandía, born in 1510, married in 1529 Doña Eleonora de Castro, by whom he had eight children. Having become a widower and divested himself of his estates and dignities, he entered the Society of Jesus, and was nominated Superior of the Spanish Jesuits. As such he repeatedly visited Avila, and made the acquaintance of St. Teresa in 1557. He was elected General in 1567, and died in Rome, October 1, 1572.

[3] Ch. xxiii. 6.   [4] See *Relation* viii. 6.

progress himself ; for experience is very important in these matters. I was exceedingly consoled ; so, too, was the nobleman, who rejoiced greatly when he was told that it was the work of God. He always helped me and gave me advice according to his power,—and that power was great.

5. At this time they changed my confessor's residence. I felt it very much, for I thought I should go back to my wickedness, and that it was not possible to find another such as he. My soul was, as it were, in a desert, most sorrowful and afraid. I knew not what to do with myself. One of my kinswomen contrived to get me into her house, and I contrived at once to find another confessor,⁵ in the Society of Jesus. It pleased our Lord that I should commence a friendship with a noble lady,⁶ a widow, much given to prayer, who had much to do with the fathers. She made her own confessor hear me, and I remained in her house some days. She lived near, and I delighted in the many conferences I had with the fathers ; for merely by observing the holiness of their way of life, I felt that my soul profited exceedingly.

6. This father began by putting me in the way of greater perfection. He used to say to me, that I ought to leave nothing undone that I might be wholly pleasing unto God. He was, however, very prudent and very gentle at the same time ; for my soul was not at all strong, but rather very weak, especially as to giving up certain friendships, though I did not offend God by them : there was much natural affection in them, and I thought it would be an act of ingratitude

---

⁵ F. Baltasar Alvarez, born in 1533, belonged to the College of St. Giles at Avila since 1557. He remained her confessor for six years, and Bouix says that in this paragraph the Saint passes rapidly over the events of a whole year. Father Juan de Pradanos was removed from Avila at the time of the visit of St. Francis de Borja in the spring of 1557, while Father Baltasar Alvarez, later on the Saint's confessor, was only ordained in 1558. In the meantime she had for a confessor Fr. Fernando Alvarez del Aguila, and perhaps occasionally some other priests of the Society.
⁶ Doña Guiomar de Ulloa. See below, ch. xxxii. 13.

if I broke them off. And, so as I did not offend God, I asked him if I must be ungrateful. He told me to lay the matter before God for a few days, and recite the hymn, " Veni, Creator," that God might enlighten me as to the better course. One day, having prayed for some time, and implored our Lord to help me to please Him in all things, I began the hymn ; and as I was saying it, I fell into a trance—so suddenly, that I was, as it were, carried out of myself. I could have no doubt about it, for it was most plain.

7. This was the first time that our Lord bestowed on me the grace of ecstasy. I heard these words : " I will not have thee converse with men, but with angels." This made me wonder very much ; for the commotion of my spirit was great, and these words were uttered in the very depth of my soul. They made me afraid,— though, on the other hand, they gave me great comfort, which, when I had lost the fear,—caused, I believe, by the strangeness of the visitation,—remained with me.

8. Those words have been fulfilled ; for I have never been able to form friendship with, nor have any comfort in, nor any particular love for, any persons whatever, except those who, as I believe, love God, and who strive to serve Him. It has not been in my power to do it. It is nothing to me that they are my kindred, or my friends, if I do not know them to be lovers of God, or persons given to prayer. It is to me a painful cross to converse with any one. This is the truth, so far as I can judge.[7] From that day forth, I have had courage so great as to leave all things for God, who in one moment—and it seems to me but a moment—was pleased to change His servant into another person. Accordingly, there was no necessity for laying further commands upon me in this matter. When my confessor saw how much I clung to these friendships, he did not venture to bid me distinctly to give them up. He must have waited till our Lord

[7] See *Relation* i. 6.

did the work—as He did Himself. Nor did I think myself that I could succeed ; for I had tried before, and the pain it gave me was so great that I abandoned the attempt, on the ground that there was nothing unseemly in those attachments. Now our Lord set me at liberty, and gave me strength also to use it.

9. So I told my confessor of it, and gave up everything, according to his advice. It did a great deal of good to those with whom I used to converse, to see my determination. God be blessed for ever ! Who in one moment set me free, while I had been for many years making many efforts, and had never succeeded, very often also doing such violence to myself as injured my health ; but, as it was done by Him Who is almighty, and the true Lord of all, it gave me no pain whatever.

CHAPTER XXV.

DIVINE LOCUTIONS.   DISCUSSIONS ON THAT SUBJECT.

Of the manner in which locutions of God are perceived by the soul without being actually heard ; and of some deceits that might take place in this matter, and how one is to know which is which. This is most profitable for those who are in this degree of prayer, because it is very well explained and contains excellent doctrine.

1. IT will be as well, I think, to explain these locutions of God, and to describe what the soul feels when it receives them, in order that you, my father, may understand the matter ; for ever since that time of which I am speaking, when our Lord granted me that grace, it

has been an ordinary occurrence until now, as will appear by what I have yet to say.[1]

2. The words are very distinctly formed ; but by the bodily ear they are not heard. They are, however, much more clearly understood than they would be if they were heard by the ear. It is impossible not to understand them, whatever resistance we may offer. When we wish not to hear anything in this world, we can stop our ears, or give attention to something else : so that, even if we do hear, at least we can refuse to understand. In this locution of God addressed to the soul there is no escape, for in spite of ourselves we must listen ; and the understanding must apply itself so thoroughly to the comprehension of that which God wills we should hear that it is nothing to the purpose whether we will it or not ; for it is His will, Who can do all things. We should understand that His will must be done ; and He reveals Himself as our true Lord, having dominion over us. I know this by much experience ; for my resistance lasted nearly two years,[2] because of the great fear I was in : and even now I resist occasionally ; but it is of no use.

3. I should like to explain the delusions which may happen here, though he who has had much experience will run little or no risk, I think ; but the experience must be great. I should like to explain also how those locutions which come from the Good Spirit differ from

[1] Philippus a SS. Trinitate, *Theolog. Mystic.* par. 2. tr. iii. disc. iv. art. v. : " Tres sunt modi divinæ locutionis ; completur enim divina locutio vel verbis successivis, vel verbis formalibus, vel verbis substantialibus. Completur verbis successivis cum anima in semetipsa multum collecta quosdam discursus internos de Deo vel de aliis divina format directione ; hujusmodi quippe discursus, quamvis ab ipsa sibi formati, a Deo tamen dirigente procedunt. Completur verbis formalibus cum anima vel in se collecta, vel aliis occupata, percipit quædam verba formaliter ac distincte divinitus expressa, ad quorum formationem anima passive penitus se habet. Completur verbis substantialibus cum anima vel in se collecta, vel etiam distracta, percipit quædam verba viva et efficacia, divinitus ad se directa, quæ virtutem aut substantialem effectum per ipsa significatum fortiter ac infallibiliter causant." See also St. John of the Cross, *Ascent of Mount Carmel*, bk. ii. chs. xxviii. to xxx.

[2] From 1555 to 1557, when the Saint was advised by St. Francis de Borja to make no further resistance.

those which come from an evil spirit ; and, further,
how they may be but an apprehension of the understanding,—for that is possible,—or even words which
the mind addressed to itself. I do not know if it be
so ; but even this very day I thought it possible. I
know by experience in many ways, when these locutions come from God. I have been told things two or
three years beforehand, which have all come to pass ;
and in none of them have I been hitherto deceived.
There are also other things in which the Spirit of God
may be clearly traced, as I shall relate by and by.[3]

4. It seems to me that a person commending a
matter to God with great love and earnestness, may
think that he hears in some way or other whether his
prayer will be granted or not, and this is quite possible ;
but he who has heard the divine locution will see
clearly enough what this is, because there is a great
difference between the two. If it be anything which
the understanding has fashioned, however cunningly
it may have done so, he sees that it is the understanding
which has arranged that locution, and that it is speaking of itself. A real locution is nothing else but a
word uttered by one, and listened to by another :
but in the other case, the understanding will see that
it has not been listening only, but also forming the
words ; and the words it forms are something indistinct, fantastic, and not clear like the divine locutions.
It is in our power to turn away our attention from
these locutions of our own, just as we can be silent
when we are speaking ; but, with respect to the
former, that cannot be done.

5. There is another test more decisive still. The
words formed by the understanding effect nothing ;
but, when our Lord speaks, it is at once word and
work ; and though the words may not be meant to
stir up our devotion, but are rather words of reproof,
they dispose a soul at once, strengthen it, make it

---

[3] See ch. xxvii. 4.

tender, give it light, console and calm it ; and if it should be in dryness, or in trouble and uneasiness, all is removed, as if by the action of a hand, and even better ; for it seems as if our Lord would have the soul understand that He is all-powerful, and that His words are deeds.

6. It seems to me that there is as much difference between these two locutions as there is between speaking and listening, neither more nor less ; for when I speak, as I have just said,[4] I go on with my understanding arranging what I am saying ; but if I am spoken to by others, I do nothing else but listen, without any labour. The human locution is as something which we cannot well make out, as if we were half asleep ; but the divine locution is a voice so clear that not a syllable of its utterance is lost. It may occur, too, when the understanding and the soul are so troubled and distracted that they cannot form one sentence correctly ; and yet grand sentences, perfectly arranged, such as the soul in its most recollected state never could have formed, are uttered, and at the first word, as I said,[5] change it utterly. Still less could it have formed them if they are uttered in an ecstasy, when the faculties of the soul are suspended ; for how should the soul then comprehend anything, when it remembers nothing ?—yea, rather, how can it remember them then, when the memory can hardly do anything at all, and the imagination is, as it were, suspended ?

7. But it is to be observed, that if we see visions and hear words it never is at the time when the soul is in union in the very rapture itself,—so it seems to me. At that moment, as I have shown,—I think it was when I was speaking of the second water,[6]—all the faculties of the soul are suspended ; and, as I think,

---

[4] § 4.   [5] § 5.
[6] The doctrine here laid down is not that of the second water,—chs. xiv. and xv.,—but that of the third, ch. xvi. The Saint herself speaks doubtfully ; and as she had but little time for writing, she could not correct nor read again what she had written (*De la Fuente*).

neither vision, noi understanding, nor hearing, is possible at that time. The soul is then wholly in the power of another ; and in that instant—a very brief one, in my opinion—our Lord leaves it free for nothing whatever ; but when this instant is passed, the soul continuing still entranced, then is the time of which I am speaking ; for the faculties, though not completely suspended, are so disposed that they are scarcely active, being, as it were, absorbed, and incapable of making any reflections.

8. There are so many ways of ascertaining the nature of these locutions, that if a person be once deceived, he will not be deceived often.   I mean, that a soul accustomed to them, and on its guard, will most clearly see what they are ; for, setting other considerations aside which prove what I have said, the human locution produces no effect, neither does the soul accept it,—though it must admit the other, whether we like it or not,—nor does it believe it ; on the contrary, it is known to be a delusion of the understanding, and is therefore put away as we would put away the ravings of a lunatic.

9. But as to the divine locution, we listen to that as we do to a person of great holiness, learning, or authority, whom we know to be incapable of uttering a falsehood.   And yet this is an inadequate illustration ; for these locutions proceed occasionally in such great majesty that, without our recollecting who it is that utters them, they make us tremble if they be words of reproof, and die of love if words of love. They are also, as I have said,[7] matters of which the memory has not the least recollection ; and expressions so full are uttered so rapidly, that much time must have been spent in arranging them, if we formed them ourselves ; and so it seems to me that we cannot possibly be ignorant at the time that we have never formed them ourselves at all.

[7] § 6.

10. There is no reason, therefore, why I should dwell longer on this matter. It is a wonder to me that any experienced person, unless he deliberately chooses to do so, can fall into delusions. It has often happened to me, when I had doubts, to distrust what I had heard, and to think that it was all imagination,— but this I did afterwards : for at the moment that is impossible.—and at a later time to see the whole fulfilled ; for our Lord makes the words dwell in the memory so that they cannot be forgotten. Now, that which comes forth from our understanding is, as it were, the first movement of thought, which passes away and is forgotten ; but the divine locution is a work done ; and though some of it may be forgotten, and time have lapsed, yet is it not so wholly forgotten that the memory loses all traces of what was once spoken,—unless, indeed, after a very long time, or unless the locution were words of grace or of instruction. But as to prophetic words, they are never forgotten, in my opinion ; at least, I have never forgotten any,—and yet my memory is weak.

11. I repeat it, unless a soul be so wicked as to pretend that it has these locutions, which would be a great sin, and say that it hears divine words when it hears nothing of the kind, it cannot possibly fail to see clearly that itself arranges the words, and utters them to itself. That seems to me altogether impossible for any soul that has ever known the Spirit of God. If it has not, it may continue all its life long in this delusion, and imagine that it hears and understands, though I know not how that can be. A soul desires to hear these locutions, or it does not ; if it does not, it is distressed because it hears them, and is unwilling to listen to them, because of a thousand fears which they occasion, and for many other reasons it has for being quiet in prayer without these interruptions. How is it that the understanding has time enough to arrange these locutions ? They require time.

12. But, on the other side, the divine locutions instruct us without loss of time, and we understand matters which seem to require a month on our part to arrange. The understanding itself, and the soul, stand amazed at some of the things we understand. So it is ; and he who has any experience of it will see that what I am saying is literally true. I give God thanks that I have been able thus to explain it. I end by saying that, in my opinion, we may hear the locutions that proceed from the understanding whenever we like, and think that we hear them whenever we pray. But it is not so with the divine locutions : for many days I may desire to hear them, and I cannot ; and at other times, even when I would not, as I said before,[8] hear them, I must. It seems to me that any one disposed to deceive people by saying that he heard from God that which he has invented himself, might as easily say that he heard it with his bodily ears. It is most certainly true that I never imagined there was any other way of hearing or understanding till I had proof of it in myself ; and so, as I have said before,[9] it gave me trouble enough.

13. Locutions that come from Satan not only do not leave any good effects behind, but do leave evil effects. This has happened to me ; but not more than two or three times. Our Lord warned me at once that they came from Satan. Over and above the great aridity which remains in the soul after these evil locutions, there is also a certain disquiet, such as I have had on many other occasions, when, by our Lord's permission, I fell into great temptations and travail of soul in diverse ways ; and though I am in trouble often enough, as I shall show hereafter,[10] yet this disquiet is such that I know not whence it comes ; only the soul seems to resist, is troubled and distressed, without knowing why ; for the words of Satan are good,

[8] § 2.
[9] Ch. vii. 12.   [10] Ch. xxviii. 6, ch. xxx. 10.

and not evil. I am thinking whether this may not be so because one spirit is conscious of the presence of another.

14. The sweetness and joy which Satan gives are, in my opinion, of a very different kind. By means of these sweetnesses he may deceive any one who does not, or who never did, taste of the sweetness of God,— by which I mean a certain sweet, strong, impressive, delightsome, and calm refreshing. Those little, fervid bursts of tears, and other slight emotions,—for at the first breath of persecution these flowers wither,—I do not call devotion, though they are a good beginning, and are holy impressions ; but they are not a test to determine whether these locutions come from a good or an evil spirit. It is therefore best for us to proceed always with great caution ; for those persons who have advanced in prayer only so far as this may most easily fall into delusions, if they have visions or revelations. For myself, I never had a single vision or revelation till God had led me on to the prayer of union,—unless it be on that occasion, of which I have spoken before,[11] now many years ago, when I saw our Lord. Oh, that His Majesty had been pleased to let me then understand that it was a true vision, as I have since understood it was ! it would have been no slight blessing to me.

15. After these locutions of the evil one, the soul is never gentle, but is, as it were, terrified, and greatly disgusted.

16. I look upon it as a most certain truth, that the devil will never deceive, and that God will not suffer him to deceive, the soul which has no confidence whatever in itself ; which is strong in faith, and resolved to undergo a thousand deaths for any one article of the creed ; which in its love of the faith, infused of God once for all,—a faith living and strong,—always labours, seeking for further light on this side and on that, to mould itself on the teaching of the Church, as

[11] Ch. vii. 11.

one already deeply grounded in the truth. No imaginable revelations, not even if it saw the heavens open, could make that soul swerve in any degree from the doctrine of the Church. If, however, it should at any time find itself wavering even in thought on this point, or stopping to say to itself, If God says this to me, it may be true, as well as what He said to the Saints—the soul must not be sure of it. I do not mean that it so believes, only that Satan has taken the first step towards tempting it ; and the giving way to the first movements of a thought like this is evidently most wrong. I believe, however, that these first movements will not take place if the soul is so strong in the matter —as that soul is to whom our Lord sends these graces— that it seems as if it could crush the evil spirits in defence of the very least of the truths which the Church holds.

17. If the soul does not discern this great strength in itself, and if the particular devotion or vision help it not onwards, then it must not look upon it as safe. For though at first the soul is conscious of no harm, great harm may by degrees ensue ; because so far as I can see, and by experience understand, that which purports to come from God is received only in so far as it corresponds with the sacred writings ; but if it varies therefrom ever so little, I am incomparably more convinced that it comes from Satan than I am now convinced it comes from God, however deep that conviction may be. In this case, there is no need to ask for signs, nor from what spirit it proceeds, because this varying is so clear a sign of the devil's presence, that if all the world were to assure me that it came from God, I would not believe it. The fact is, that all good seems to be lost out of sight, and to have fled from the soul, when the devil has spoken to it ; the soul is thrown into a state of disgust, and is troubled, able to do no good thing whatever—for if it conceives good desires, they are not strong ; its humility is

fictitious, disturbed, and without sweetness. Any one who has ever tasted of the Spirit of God will, I think, understand it.

18. Nevertheless, Satan has many devices ; and so there is nothing more certain than that it is safer to be afraid, and always on our guard, under a learned director, from whom nothing is concealed. If we do this, no harm can befall us, though much has befallen me through the excessive fears which possessed some people. For instance, it happened so once to me, when many persons in whom I had great confidence, and with good reason, had assembled together,—five or six in number, I think,—and all very great servants of God. It is true, my relations were with one of them only ; but by his orders I made my state known to the others. They had many conferences together about my necessities; for they had a great affection for me, and were afraid I was under a delusion. I, too, was very much afraid whenever I was not occupied in prayer ; but when I prayed, and our Lord bestowed His graces upon me, I was instantly reassured. My confessor told me they were all of opinion that I was deceived by Satan ; that I must communicate less frequently, and contrive to distract myself in such a way as to be less alone.

19. I was in great fear myself, as I have just said, and my disease of the heart [12] contributed thereto, so that very often I did not dare to remain alone in my cell during the day. When I found so many maintain this, and myself unable to believe them, I had at once a most grievous scruple ; for it seemed to me that I had very little humility, especially as they all led lives incomparably better than mine : they were also learned men. Why should I not believe them ? I did all I could to believe them. I reflected on my wicked life, and therefore what they said to me must be true.

[12] Ch. iv. 6, ch. v. 14.

20. In this distress, I quitted the church,[13] and entered an oratory. I had not been to Communion for many days, nor had I been alone, which was all my comfort. I had no one to speak to, for every one was against me. Some, I thought, made a mock of me when I spoke to them of my prayer, as if I were a person under delusions of the imagination ; others warned my confessor to be on his guard against me ; and some said it was clear the whole was an operation of Satan. My confessor, though he agreed with them for the sake of trying me, as I understood afterwards, always comforted me : and he alone did so. He told me that, if I did not offend God, my prayer, even if it was the work of Satan, could do me no harm ; that I should be delivered from it. He bade me pray much to God : he himself, and all his penitents, and many others did so earnestly ; I, too, with all my might, and as many as I knew to be servants of God, prayed that His Majesty would be pleased to lead me by another way. This lasted, I think, about two years ; and this was the subject of my continual prayer to our Lord.

21. But there was no comfort for me when I thought of the possibility that Satan could speak to me so often. Now that I was never alone for prayer, our Lord made me recollected even during conversation : He spoke what He pleased,—I could not avoid it ; and, though it distressed me, I was forced to listen. I was by myself, having no one in whom I could find any comfort ; unable to pray or read, like a person stunned by heavy trials, and by the dread that the evil one had deluded me ; utterly disquieted and wearied, not knowing what would become of me. I have been occasionally—yea, very often—in distress, but never before in distress so great. I was in this state for four or five hours ; there was no comfort for me, either

---

[13] It was the church of the Jesuits. It is not known who the confessor was who treated her so harshly. F. Baltasar Alvarez, indeed, deprived her once of Communion for twenty days, but the events spoken of in this paragraph appear to have taken place before he undertook her direction.

from heaven or on earth—only our Lord left me to suffer, afraid of a thousand dangers.

22. O my Lord, how true a friend art Thou ! how powerful ! Thou showest Thy power when Thou wilt ; and Thou doest will it always, if only we will it also. Let the whole creation praise Thee, O Thou Lord of the world ! Oh, that a voice might go forth over all the earth, proclaiming Thy faithfulness to those who love Thee ! All things fail ; but Thou, Lord of all, never failest ! They who love Thee, oh, how little they have to suffer ! oh, how gently, how tenderly, how sweetly Thou, O my Lord, dealest with them ! Oh, that no one had ever been occupied with any other love than Thine ! It seems as if Thou didst subject those who love Thee to a severe trial : but it is in order that they may learn, in the depths of that trial, the depths of Thy love. O my God, oh, that I had understanding and learning, and a new language, in order to magnify Thy works, according to the knowledge of them which my soul possesses ! Everything fails me, O my Lord ; but if Thou wilt not abandon me, I will never fail Thee. Let all the learned rise up against me,—let the whole creation persecute me,—let the evil spirits torment me,—but do Thou, O Lord, fail me not ; for I know by exerpience now the blessedness of that deliverance which Thou doest effect for those who trust only in Thee. In this distress,—for then I had never had a single vision,—these Thy words alone were enough to remove it, and give me perfect peace : " Be not afraid, my daughter : it is I ; and I will not abandon thee. Fear not." [14]

23. It seems to me that, in the state I was in then, many hours would have been necessary to calm me, and that no one could have done it. Yet I found myself, through these words alone, tranquil and strong, courageous and confident, at rest and enlightened ; in

[14] See *Interior Castle*, M. vi. ch. iii. 8 ; *Rel.* vii. 22. St. John of the Cross, *Ascent of Mount Carmel*, bk. ii. ch. xxxi. 1.

a moment, my soul seemed changed, and I felt I could maintain against all the world that my prayer was the work of God. Oh, how good is God! how good is our Lord, and how powerful! He gives not counsel only, but relief as well. His words are deeds. O my God! as He strengthens our faith, love grows. So it is, in truth; for I used frequently to recollect how our Lord, when the tempest arose, commanded the winds to be still over the sea.[15] So I said to myself: Who is He, that all my faculties should thus obey Him? Who is He, that gives light in such darkness in a moment; who softens a heart that seemed to be made of stone; who gives the waters of sweet tears, where for a long time great dryness seems to have prevailed; who inspires these desires; who bestows this courage? What have I been thinking of? what am I afraid of? what is it? I desire to serve this my Lord; I aim at nothing else but His pleasure; I seek no joy, no rest, no other good than that of doing His will. I was so confident that I had no other desire, that I could safely assert it.

24. Seeing, then, that our Lord is so powerful,—as I see and know He is,—and that the evil spirits are His slaves, of which there can be no doubt, because it is of faith,—and I am a servant of this our Lord and King,— what harm can Satan do unto me? Why have I not strength enough to fight against all hell? I took up the cross in my hand,—I was changed in a moment into another person, and it seemed as if God had really given me courage enough not to be afraid of encountering all the evil spirits. It seemed to me that I could, with the cross, easily defeat them altogether. So I cried out, Come on, all of you; I am the servant of our Lord: I should like to see what you can do against me.

25. And certainly they seemed to be afraid of me,

---

[15] St. Matt. viii. 26; "Imperavit ventis et mari, et facta est tranquillitas magna."

for I was left in peace : I feared them so little, that the terrors, which until now oppressed me, quitted me altogether ; and though I saw them occasionally,—I shall speak of this by and by,[16]—I was never again afraid of them—on the contrary, they seemed to be afraid of me.[17] I found myself endowed with a certain authority over them, given me by the Lord of all, so that I cared no more for them than for flies. They seem to be such cowards ; for their strength fails them at the sight of any one who despises them. These enemies have not the courage to assail any but those whom they see ready to give in to them, or when God permits them to do so, for the greater good of His servants, whom they may try and torment.

26. May it please His Majesty that we fear Him whom we ought to fear,[18] and understand that one venial sin can do us more harm than all hell together ; for that is the truth. The evil spirits keep us in terror, because we expose ourselves to the assaults of terror by our attachments to honours, possessions, and pleasures. For then the evil spirits, uniting themselves with us,— we become our own enemies when we love and seek what we ought to hate,—do us great harm. We ourselves put weapons into their hands, that they may assail us ; those very weapons with which we should defend ourselves. It is a great pity. But if, for the love of God, we hated all this, and embraced the cross, and set about His service in earnest, Satan would fly away before such realities, as from the plague. He is the friend of lies, and a lie himself.[19] He will have nothing to do with those who walk in the truth. When he sees the understanding of any one obscured he simply helps to pluck out his eyes ; if he sees any one already blind, seeking peace in vanities,—for all the

[16] Ch. xxxi. 2.

[17] St. John of the Cross, *Spiritual Canticle*, st. xxiv. 5.

[18] St. Matt. x. 26, 28 ; " Ne ergo timueritis eos, . . . sed potius timete Eum."

[19] St. John viii. 44 : " Mendax est, et pater ejus."

things of this world are so utterly vanity, that they seem to be but the playthings of a child,—he sees at once that such a one is a child ; he treats him as a child, and ventures to wrestle with him—not once, but often.

27. May it please our Lord that I be not one of these ; and may His Majesty give me grace to take that for peace which is really peace, that for honour which is really honour, and that for delight which is really a delight. Let me never mistake one thing for another—and then I snap my fingers at all the devils, for they shall be afraid of me. I do not understand those terrors which make us cry out, Satan, Satan ! when we may say, God, God ! and make Satan tremble. Do we not know that he cannot stir without the permission of God ? What does it mean ? I am really much more afraid of those people who have so great a fear of the devil, than I am of the devil himself. Satan can do me no harm whatever, but they can trouble me very much, particularly if they be confessors. I have spent some years of such great anxiety, that even now I am amazed that I was able to bear it. Blessed be our Lord, who has so effectually helped me !

CHAPTER XXVI.

HOW THE FEARS OF THE SAINT VANISHED. HOW SHE WAS ASSURED THAT HER PRAYER WAS THE WORK OF THE HOLY SPIRIT.

She continues the same subject ; explains and tells things that have happened to her which caused her to lose fear and convinced her that the spirit which spoke to her was a good one.

1. I LOOK upon the courage which our Lord has implanted in me against evil spirits as one of the greatest

mercies which He has bestowed upon me; for a cowardly soul, afraid of anything but sin against God, is a very unseemly thing, when we have on our side the King omnipotent, our Lord most high Who can do all things, and subjects all things to Himself. There is nothing to be afraid of if we walk, as I said before,[1] in the truth, in the sight of His Majesty, with a pure conscience. And for this end, as I said in the same place, I would have myself all fears, that I may not for one instant offend Him who in that instant is able to destroy us. If His Majesty is pleased with us, whoever resists us—be he who he may—will be utterly disappointed.

2. It may be so, you will say; but then, where is that soul so just as to please Him in everything?— and that is the reason why we are afraid. Certainly it is not my soul, which is most wretched, unprofitable, and full of misery. God is not like man in His ways; He knows our weakness. But the soul perceives, by the help of certain great signs, whether it loves God of a truth; for the love of those souls who have come to this state is not hidden, as it was at first, but is full of high impulses, and of longings for the vision of God, as I shall show hereafter—or rather, as I have shown already.[2] Everything wearies, everything distresses, everything torments the soul, unless it be suffered with God, or for God. There is no rest which is not a weariness, because the soul knows itself to be away from its true rest; and so love is made most manifest, and, as I have just said, impossible to hide.

3. It happened to me, on another occasion, to be grievously tried, and much spoken against on account of a certain affair,—of which I shall speak hereafter,[3]— by almost everybody in the place where I am living, and by the members of my Order. When I was in this distress, and afflicted by many occasions of dis-

---

[1] Ch. xxv. 26.   [2] Ch. xv. 6.
[3] The foundation of the house of St. Joseph; ch. xxxiii.

quiet wherein I was placed, our Lord spoke to me,
saying : " What art thou afraid of ? knowest thou not
that I am almighty ?   I will do what I have promised
thee." And so, afterwards, was it done.   I found
myself at once so strong, that I could have undertaken
anything, so it seemed, immediately, even if I had to
endure greater trials for His service, and had to enter
on a new state of suffering. These locutions are so
frequent, that I cannot count them ; many of them
are reproaches, and He sends them when I fall into
imperfections. They are enough to destroy a soul.
They correct me, however ; for His Majesty—as I said
before [4]—gives both counsel and relief. There are
others which bring my former sins into remembrance,
—particularly when He is about to bestow upon me
some special grace,—in such a way that the soul beholds itself as being really judged ; for those reproaches
of God put the truth before it so distinctly, that it
knows not what to do with itself. Some are warnings
against certain dangers to myself or others ; many of
them are prophecies of future things, three or four years
beforehand ; and all of them have been fulfilled [5] : some
of them I could mention. Here, then, are so many
reasons for believing that they come from God, as make
it impossible, I believe, for anybody to mistake them.

4. The safest course in these things is to declare,
without fail, the whole state of the soul, together with
the graces our Lord gives me, to a confessor who is
learned, and obey him. I do so ; and if I did not, I
should have no peace. Nor is it right that we women,
who are unlearned, should have any : there can be no
danger in this, but rather great profit. This is what
our Lord has often commanded me to do, and it is
what I have often done. I had a confessor [6] who

---

[4] Ch. xxv. 23.   [5] See *Relation* ii. 17.

[6] The Bollandists, n. 185, attribute some of the severity with which her
confessor treated the Saint to the spirit of desolation with which he was then
tried himself ; and, in proof of it, refer to the account which F. Baltasar
Alvarez gave of his own prayer to the General of the Society.

mortified me greatly, and now and then distressed
me : he tried me heavily, for he disquieted me exceedingly ; and yet he was the one who, I believe, did me
the most good.   Though I had a great affection for
him, I was occasionally tempted to leave him ; I
thought that the pain he inflicted on me disturbed my
prayer.   Whenever I was resolved on leaving him, I
used to feel instantly that I ought not to do so ; and
one reproach of our Lord would press more heavily
upon me than all that my confessor did.   Now and
then, I was worn out—torture on the one hand, reproaches on the other.   I required it all, for my will
was but little subdued.   Our Lord said to me once
that there was no obedience where there was no resolution to suffer ; that I was to think of His sufferings,
and then everything would be easy.

   5. One of my confessors, to whom I went in the beginning, advised me once, now that my spiritual state
was known to be the work of God, to keep silence, and
not to speak of these things to any one, on the ground
that it was safer to keep these graces secret.   To me,
the advice seemed good, because I felt it so much whenever I had to speak of them to my confessor[7] ; I was
also so ashamed of myself, that I felt it more keenly at
times to speak of them than I should have done in confessing grave sins, particularly when the graces I had
to reveal were great.   I thought they did not believe
me, and that they were laughing at me.   I felt it so
much,—for I look on this as an irreverent treatment of
the marvels of God,—that I was glad to be silent.   I
learned then that I had been ill-advised by that confessor, because I ought never to hide anything from
my confessor ; for I should find great security if I told
everything ; and if I did otherwise, I might at any
time fall into delusions.[8]

   6. Whenever our Lord commanded me to do one

---

[7] See *Relation* vii. 7.
[8] St. John of the Cross, *Ascent of Mount Carmel*, bk. ii. ch. xxii. 14.

thing in prayer, and if my confessor forbade it, our Lord
Himself told me to obey my confessor. His Majesty
afterwards would change the mind of that confessor, so
that he would have me do what he had forbidden
before. When we were deprived of many books
written in Spanish, and forbidden to read them,—I
felt it deeply, for some of these books were a great
comfort to me, and I could not read them in Latin,—
our Lord said to me, " Be not troubled ; I will give
thee a living book." I could not understand why this
was said to me, for at that time I had never had a
vision.[9] But, a very few days afterwards, I understood it well enough ; for I had so much to think of,
and such reasons for self-recollection in what I saw
before me, and our Lord dealt so lovingly with me, in
teaching me in so many ways, that I had little or no
need whatever of books. His Majesty has been to me
a veritable Book, in which I saw all truth. Blessed be
such a Book, which leaves behind an impression of
what is read therein, and in such a way that it cannot
be forgotten !

7. Who can look upon our Lord, covered with
wounds, and bowed down under persecutions, without
accepting, loving, and longing for them ? Who can
behold but a part of that glory which He will give to
those who serve Him without confessing that all he
may do, and all he may suffer, is altogether as nothing,
when we may hope for such a reward ? Who can look
at the torments of lost souls without acknowledging
the torments of this life to be joyous delights in comparison, and confessing how much they owe to our
Lord in having saved them so often from the place of

---

[9] See ch iv. 12. The Grand Inquisitor, D. Fernando de Valdes, published
in 1559 an Index, in which he forbade not only many heretical works, but also
a very large number of books of devotion in Spanish, to which no exception
could possibly be taken unless that they were written for the uneducated
laity and might be misunderstood by them. Even Luis de Granada, one of
the greatest writers on subjects of devotion, was hit by this sweeping condemnation.

torments ? [10]   But as, by the help of God, I shall speak
more at large of certain things, I wish now to go on
with the story of my life.   Our Lord grant that I have
been clear enough in what I have hitherto said !   I
feel assured that he will understand me who has had
experience herein, and that he will see I have partially
succeeded ; but as to him who has had no such experience, I should not be surprised if he regarded it all
as folly.   It is enough for him that it is I who say it,
in order to be free from blame ; neither will I blame
any one who shall so speak of it.   Our Lord grant that
I may never fail to do His will !   Amen.

CHAPTER XXVII.

THE SAINT PRAYS TO BE DIRECTED BY A DIFFERENT WAY. INTELLECTUAL VISIONS.

*Of another way in which God teaches a soul, and
without speaking, makes His will known in an admirable
manner. She goes on to explain a vision, though not
an imaginary one, and a great grace with which God
favoured her. This chapter is noteworthy.*

1. I NOW resume the story of my life.   I was in great
pain and distress ; and many prayers, as I said,[1] were
made on my behalf, that our Lord would lead me by
another and a safer way ; for this, they told me, was
so suspicious.   The truth is, that though I was praying
to God for this, and wished I had a desire for another
way, yet, when I saw the progress I was making, I
was unable really to desire a change,—though I always
prayed for it,—excepting on those occasions when I
was extremely cast down by what people said to me,
and by the fears with which they filled me.

[10] St. Luke xvi. 28 : " Ne et ipsi veniant in hunc locum tormentorum."
[1] Ch. xxv. 20.

2. I felt that I was wholly changed ; I could do nothing but put myself in the hands of God : He knew what was expedient for me ; let Him do with me according to His will in all things. I saw that by this way I was directed heavenwards, and that formerly I was going down to hell. I could not force myself to desire a change, nor believe that I was under the influence of Satan. Though I was doing all I could to believe the one and to desire the other, it was not in my power to do so. I offered up all my actions, if there should be any good in them, for this end ; I had recourse to the Saints for whom I had a devotion, that they might deliver me from the evil one ; I made novenas ; I commended myself to St. Hilarion, to the Angel St. Michael, to whom I had recently become devout, for this purpose ; and many other Saints I importuned, that our Lord might show me the way,— I mean, that they might obtain this for me from His Majesty.

3. At the end of two years spent in prayer by myself and others for this end, namely, that our Lord would either lead me by another way, or show the truth of this,—for now the locutions of our Lord were extremely frequent,—this happened to me. I was in prayer one day,—it was the feast of the glorious St. Peter,[2] when I saw Christ close by me, or, to speak more correctly, felt Him ; for I saw nothing with the eyes of the body, nothing with the eyes of the soul. He seemed to me to be close beside me ; and I saw, too, as I believe, that it was He who was speaking to me. As I was utterly ignorant that such a vision was possible,[3] I was extremely afraid at first, and did nothing but weep ; however, when He spoke to me but one word to reassure me, I recovered myself, and was, as usual, calm and comforted, without any fear whatever.

[2] See ch. xxviii. 5, and ch. xxix. 1. The vision took place on June 29, 1557. See ch. xxix. 6.
[3] See ch. vii. 12 ; xxviii. 1

Jesus Christ seemed to be by my side continually, and, as the vision was not imaginary, I saw no form ; but I had a most distinct feeling that He was always on my right hand, a witness of all I did ; and never at any time, if I was but slightly recollected, or not too much distracted, could I be ignorant of His near presence.[4]

4. I went at once to my confessor,[5] in great distress, to tell him of it. He asked in what form I saw our Lord. I told him I saw no form. He then said : " How did you know that it was Christ ? " I replied, that I did not know how I knew it ; but I could not help knowing that He was close beside me,—that I saw Him distinctly, and felt His presence,—that the recollectedness of my soul was very deep, as in the prayer of quiet, and more continuous,—that the effects thereof were very different from what I had hitherto experienced,—and that it was most certain. I could only make comparisons in order to explain myself ; and certainly there are no comparisons, in my opinion, by which visions of this kind can be described. Afterwards I learnt from Friar Peter of Alcantara, a holy man of great spirituality,—of whom I shall speak by and by,[6]—and from others of great learning, that this vision was of the highest order, and one with which Satan can least interfere ; and therefore there are no words whereby to explain,—at least, none for us women, who know so little : learned men can explain it better.

5. For if I say that I see Him neither with the eyes of the body, nor with those of the soul,—because it was not an imaginary vision,—how is it that I can understand and maintain that He stands beside me, and be more certain of it than if I saw Him ? If it be supposed that it is as if a person were blind, or in the dark, and therefore unable to see another who is close to

---

[4] See Anton. a Spiritu Sancto, *Direct. Mystic.* tr. iii. disp. v. § 3.
[5] Her confessor was then Fr. Juan de Pradanos. See *Interior Castle*, M. vi. ch. viii. 3 ; St. John of the Cross, *Dark Night of the Soul*, bk. ii. ch. xxiii. 9.
[6] § 17, *infra*.

him, the comparison is not exact. There is a certain likelihood about it, however, but not much, because the other senses tell him who is blind of that presence : he hears the other speak or move, or he touches him ; but in these visions there is nothing like this. The darkness is not felt ; only He renders Himself present to the soul by a certain knowledge of Himself which is more clear than the sun.[7] I do not mean that we now see either a sun or any brightness, only that there is a light not seen, which illumines the understanding so that the soul may have the fruition of so great a good. This vision brings with it great blessings.

6. It is not like that presence of God which is frequently felt, particularly by those who have attained to the prayer of union and of quiet, when we seem, at the very commencement of our prayer, to find Him with whom we would converse, and when we seem to feel that He hears us by the effects and the spiritual impressions of great love and faith of which we are then conscious, as well as by the good resolutions, accompanied by sweetness, which we then make. This is a great grace from God ; and let him to whom He has given it esteem it much, because it is a very high degree of prayer ; but it is not vision. God is understood to be present there by the effects He works in the soul : that is the way His Majesty makes His presence felt ; but here, in this vision, it is seen clearly that Jesus Christ is present, the Son of the Virgin. In the prayer of union and of quiet, certain inflowings of the Godhead are present ; but in the vision, the Sacred Humanity also, together with them, is pleased to make Himself felt as our companion and to do us good.

7. My confessor next asked me, who told me it was Jesus Christ.[8] I replied that He often told me

[7] See *Relation* vii. 26.
[8] *Interior Castle*, M. vi. ch. viii. 3.

so Himself ; but, even before He told me so, there
was an impression on my understanding that it was
He ; and before this He used to tell me so, and I saw
Him not. If a person whom I had never seen, but of
whom I had heard, came to speak to me, and I were
blind or in the dark, and he told me who he was, I
should believe him ; but I could not so confidently
affirm that he was that person, as I might do if I had
seen him. But in this vision I could do so, because
so clear a knowledge is impressed on the soul that all
doubt seems impossible, though He is not seen. Our
Lord wills that this knowledge be so graven on the
understanding, that we can no more question His
presence than we can question that which we see with
our eyes : not so much even ; for very often there
arises a suspicion that we have imagined things we
think we see ; but here, though there may be a suspicion in the first instant, there remains a certainty
so great, that the doubt has no force whatever. So
also is it when God teaches the soul in another way,
and speaks to it without speaking, in the way I have
described.

8. There is so much of heaven in this language,
that it cannot well be understood on earth, though
we may desire ever so much to explain it, if our Lord
will not teach it experimentally. Our Lord impresses
in the innermost soul that which He wills that soul
to understand ; and He manifests it there without
images or formal words, after the manner of the vision
I am speaking of. Consider well this way in which
God works, in order that the soul may understand
what He means—His great truths and mysteries ;
for very often what I understand, when our Lord
explains to me the vision, which it is His Majesty's
pleasure to set before me, is after this manner ; and
it seems to me that this is a state with which the devil
can least interfere, for these reasons ; but if these
reasons are not good, I must be under a delusion. The

vision and the language are matters of such pure spirituality, that there is no turmoil of the faculties, or of the senses, out of which—so it seems to me—the devil can derive any advantage.

9. It is only at intervals, and for an instant, that this occurs ; for generally—so I think—the senses are not taken away, and the faculties are not suspended : they preserve their ordinary state. It is not always so in contemplation ; on the contrary, it is very rarely so ; but when it is so, I say that we do nothing whatever ourselves : no work of ours is then possible ; all that is done is apparently the work of our Lord. It is as if food had been received into the stomach which had not first been eaten, and without our knowing how it entered ; but we do know well that it is there, though we know not its nature, nor who it was that placed it there. In this vision, I know who placed it ; but I do not know how He did it. I neither saw it, nor felt it ; I never had any inclination to desire it, and I never knew before that such a thing was possible.

10. In the locutions of which I spoke before,[9] God makes the understanding attentive, though it may be painful to understand what is said ; then the soul seems to have other ears wherewith it hears ; and He forces it to listen, and will not let it be distracted. The soul is like a person whose hearing was good, and who is not suffered to stop his ears, while people standing close beside him speak to him with a loud voice. He may be unwilling to hear, yet hear he must. Such a person contributes something of his own ; for he attends to what is said to him ; but here there is nothing of the kind : even that little, which is nothing more than the bare act of listening, which is granted to it in the other case, is now out of its power. It finds its food prepared and eaten ; it has nothing more to do but to enjoy it. It is as if one without ever learn-

[9] Ch. xxv. 1.

ing, without taking the pains even to learn to read, and without studying any subject whatever, should find himself in possession of all knowledge, not knowing how or whence it came to him, seeing that he had never taken the trouble even to learn the alphabet. This last comparison seems to me to throw some light on this heavenly gift ; for the soul finds itself learned in a moment, and the mystery of the most Holy Trinity so clearly revealed to it, together with other most deep doctrines, that there is no theologian in the world with whom it would hesitate to dispute for the truth of these matters.

11. It is impossible to describe the surprise of the soul when it finds that one of these graces is enough to change it utterly, and make it love nothing but Him who, without waiting for anything itself might do, renders it fit for blessings so high, communicates to it His secrets, and treats it with so much affection and love. Some of the graces He bestows are liable to suspicion because they are so marvellous, and given to one who has deserved them so little—incredible, too, without a most lively faith. I intend, therefore, to mention very few of those graces which our Lord has wrought in me, if I should not be ordered otherwise ; but there are certain visions of which I shall speak, an account of which may be of some service. In doing so, I shall either dispel his fears to whom our Lord sends them, and who, as I used to do, thinks them impossible, or I shall explain the way or the road by which our Lord has led me ; and that is what I have been commanded to describe.

12. Now, going back to speak of this way of understanding, what it is seems to me to be this : it is our Lord's will in every way that the soul should have some knowledge of what passes in heaven ; and I think that, as the blessed there without speech understand one another,—I never knew this for certain till our Lord of His goodness made me see it ; He showed it to me in a

trance,—so is it here : God and the soul understand one another, merely because His Majesty so wills it, without the help of other means, to express the love there is between them both. In the same way on earth, two persons of sound sense, if they love each other much, can even, without any signs, understand one another only by their looks. It must be so here, though we do not see how, as these two lovers earnestly regard each the other : the bridegroom says so to the bride in the Canticle, so I believe, and I have heard that it is spoken of there.[10]

13. Oh, marvellous goodness of God, in that Thou permittest eyes which have looked upon so much evil as those of my soul to look upon Thee ! May they never accustom themselves, after looking on Thee, to look upon vile things again ! and may they have pleasure in nothing but in Thee, O Lord ! Oh, ingratitude of men, how far will it go ! I know by experience that what I am saying is true, and that all we can say is exceedingly little, when we consider what Thou doest to the soul which Thou hast led to such a state as this. O souls, you who have begun to pray, and you who possess the true faith, what can you be in search of even in this life, let alone that which is for ever, that is comparable to the least of these graces ? Consider, and it is true, that God gives Himself to those who give up everything for Him. God is not an accepter of persons.[11] He loves all ; there is no excuse for any one, however wicked he may be, seeing that He hath thus dealt with me, raising me to the state I am in. Consider, that what I am saying is not even an iota of what may be said ; I say only that which is necessary to show the kind of the vision and of the grace which God bestows on the soul ; for that cannot be told which it feels when

---

[10] Cant. vi. 4 : " Averte oculos tuos a me, quia ipsi me avolare fecerunt."
St. John of the Cross, *Ascent of Mount Carmel*, bk. ii. ch. xxix. 6.
[11] Acts x. 34 : " Non est personarum acceptor Deus."

our Lord admits it to the understanding of His secrets
and of His mighty works. The joy of this is so far
above all conceivable joys, that it may well make us
loathe all the joys of earth ; for they are all but dross ;
and it is an odious thing to make them enter into the
comparison, even if we might have them for ever.
Those which our Lord gives, what are they ? One
drop only of the waters of the overflowing river which
He is reserving for us.

14. It is a shame ! And, in truth, I am ashamed
of myself ; if shame could have a place in heaven, I
should certainly be the most ashamed there. Why do
we seek blessings and joys so great, bliss without end,
and all at the cost of our good Jesus ? Shall we not
at least weep with the daughters of Jerusalem,[12] if we
do not help to carry His cross with the Cyrenean ? [13]
Is it by pleasure and idle amusements that we can
attain to the fruition of what He purchased with so
much blood ? It is impossible. Can we think that
we can, by preserving our honour, which is vanity,
recompense Him for the sufferings He endured, that
we might reign with Him for ever ? This is not the
way ; we are going by the wrong road utterly, and we
shall never arrive there. You, my father, must lift up
your voice, and utter these truths aloud, seeing that
God has taken from me the power of doing it. I
should like to utter them to myself for ever. I listened
to them myself, and came to the knowledge of God so
late, as will appear by what I have written, that I am
ashamed of myself when I speak of this ; and so I
should like to be silent.[14]

15. Of one thing, however, I will speak, and I think
of it now and then,—may it be the good pleasure of our
Lord to bring me on, so that I may have the fruition of
it !—what will be the accidental glory and the joy of

[12] St. Luke xxiii. 28 : " Filiæ Jerusalem, nolite flere super Me, sed super
vos ipsas flete."
[13] St. Matt. xxvii. 32 : " Hunc angariaverunt ut tolleret crucem Ejus."
[14] *Interior Castle*, M. iv. ch. iii. 3.

the blessed who have entered on it, when they see that, though they were late, yet they left nothing undone which it was possible for them to do for God, who kept nothing back they could give Him, and who gave what they gave in every way they could, according to their strength and their measure,—they who had more gave more. How rich will he be who gave up all his riches for Christ! How honourable will he be who, for His sake, sought no honours whatever, but rather took pleasure in seeing himself abased! How wise he will be who rejoiced when men accounted him as mad!— they did so of Wisdom Itself! [15] How few there are of this kind now, because of our sins! Now, indeed, they are all gone whom people regarded as mad,[16] because they saw them perform heroic acts, as true lovers of Christ.

16. O world, world! how thou art gaining credit because they are few who know thee! But do we suppose that God is better pleased when men account us wise and discreet persons? We think forthwith that there is but little edification given when people do not go about, every one in his degree, with great gravity, in a dignified way. Even in the friar, the ecclesiastic, and the nun, if they wear old and patched garments, we think it a novelty, and a scandal to the weak; and even if they are very recollected and given to prayer. Such is the state of the world, and so for- gotten are matters of perfection, and those grand impetuosities of the Saints. More mischief, I think, is done in this way, than by any scandal that might arise if the religious showed in their actions, as they proclaim it in words, that the world is to be held in contempt. Out of scandals such as this, our Lord obtains great fruit. If some people took scandal, others are filled with remorse : anyhow, we should have before us some likeness of that which our Lord and His

[15] St. John x. 20 : " Dæmonium habet et insanit : quid Eum auditis ? "
[16] Sap. v. 4 : " Nos insensati vitam illorum æstimabamus insaniam."

apostles endured ; for we have need of it now more than ever.

17. And what an excellent likeness in the person of that blessed friar, Peter of Alcantara, God has just taken from us ! [17] The world cannot bear such perfection now ; it is said that men's health is grown feebler, and that we are not now in those former times. But this holy man lived in our day ; he had a spirit strong as those of another age, and so he trampled on the world. If men do not go about barefooted, nor undergo sharp penances, as he did, there are many ways, as I have said before,[18] of trampling on the world ; and our Lord teaches them when He finds the necessary courage. How great was the courage with which His Majesty filled the Saint I am speaking of ! He did penance—oh, how sharp it was !—for seven-and-forty years, as all men know. I should like to speak of it, for I know it to be all true.

18. He spoke of it to me and to another person,[19] from whom he kept few or no secrets. As for me, it was the affection he bore me that led him to speak ; for it was our Lord's will that he should undertake my defence, and encourage me, at a time when I was in great straits, as I said before, and shall speak of again.[20] He told me, I think, that for forty years he slept but an hour and a half out of the twenty-four, and that the most laborious penance he underwent, when he began, was this of overcoming sleep. For that purpose, he was always either kneeling or standing. When he slept he sat down, his head resting against a piece of wood driven into the wall. Lie down he could not, if he wished it ; for his cell, as every one knows, was only

[17] Oct. 18, 1562. Born in 1499 at Alcantara, Estramadura, he took the Franciscan habit at the age of sixteen, and began his reform in 1540.

[18] Ch. xiv. 7.

[19] Probably the Ven. Maria Diaz, of whom St. Teresa speaks in her letters (September 1568 and January 1582). She died Nov. 17, 1572. St. Peter used to say that Avila possessed three holy women—Mother Teresa, Maria Diaz, and Doña Catalina Davila.

[20] Ch. xxvi. 3 ; ch. xxxii. 16.

four feet and a half in length. In all these years, he never covered his head with his hood, even when the sun was hottest, or the rain heaviest. He never covered his feet : the only garment he wore was made of sackcloth, and that was as tight as it could be, with nothing between it and his flesh ; over this, he wore a cloak of the same stuff. He told me that, in the severe cold, he used to take off his cloak, and open the door and the window of his cell, in order that when he put his cloak on again, after shutting the door and the window, he might give some satisfaction to his body in the pleasure it might have in the increased warmth. His ordinary practice was to eat but once in three days. He said to me, " Why are you astonished at it ? it is very possible for any one who is used to it."   One of his companions told me that he would be occasionally eight days without eating : that must have been when he was in prayer ; for he was subject to trances, and to the impetuosities of the love of God, of which I was once a witness myself.[21]

19. His poverty was extreme ; and his mortification, from his youth, was such,—so he told me,—that he was three years in one of the houses of his Order without knowing how to distinguish one friar from another, otherwise than by his voice ; for he never raised his eyes : and so, when he was obliged to go from one part of the house to the other, he never knew the way, unless he followed the friars. His journeys, also, were made in the same way. For many years, he never saw a woman's face. He told me that it was nothing to him then whether he saw it or not : but he was an aged man when I made his acquaintance[22] ; and his weakness was so great, that he seemed like nothing else but the roots of trees. With all his sanctity, he was very agreeable ; though his words

[21] Probably in 1561, when St. Peter, having come to Avila on business, visited St. Teresa at the convent of the Incarnation. She offered him some food, but he, in presence of several persons, went into an ecstasy.

[22] At their first meeting in August 1558 he was less than sixty years old.

were few, unless when he was asked questions, he was very pleasant to speak to, for he had a most clear understanding.

20. Many other things I should like to say of him, if I were not afraid, my father, that you will say, Why does she meddle here? and it is in that fear I have written this. So I leave the subject, only saying that his last end was like his life—preaching to, and exhorting, his brethren. When he saw that the end was come, he repeated the Psalm,[23] "Lætatus sum in his quæ dicta sunt mihi"; and then, kneeling down, he died.

21. Since then, it has pleased our Lord that I should find more help from him than during his life. He advises me in many matters. I have often seen him in great glory. The first time he appeared to me, he said: "O blessed penance, which has merited so great a reward!" with other things. A year before his death he appeared to me, being then far away. I knew he was about to die, and so I sent him word to that effect, when he was some leagues from here. When he died, he appeared to me, and said that he was going to his rest. I did not believe it. I spoke of it to some persons, and within eight days came the news that he was dead—or, to speak more correctly, he had begun to live for evermore.[24]

22. Behold here, then, how that life of sharp penance is perfected in such glory: and now he is a greater comfort to me, I do believe, than he was on earth. Our Lord said to me on one occasion, that persons could not ask Him anything in his name, and He not hear them. I have recommended many things

---

[23] Psalm cxxi. The words in the MS. are : " Letatun sun yn is que dita sun miqui."

[24] See ch. xxx. 2. In autumn 1561, when St. Teresa was preparing the foundation of the convent of St. Joseph, she received a Brief from Rome, in which one of the most essential clauses was wanting. She was in great trouble about it, until St. Peter of Alcantara appeared to her, giving her practical advice how to bring the matter to a successful issue.

to him that he was to ask of our Lord, and I have seen my petitions granted. God be blessed for ever! Amen.

23. But how I have been talking in order to stir you up never to esteem anything in this life!—as if you did not know this, or as if you were not resolved to leave everything, and had already done it! I see so much going wrong in the world, that though my speaking of it is of no other use than to weary me by writing it, it is some relief to me that all I am saying makes against myself. Our Lord forgive me all that I do amiss herein; and you too, my father, for wearying you to no purpose. It seems as if I would make you do penance for my sins herein.

CHAPTER XXVIII.

VISIONS OF THE SACRED HUMANITY, AND OF THE GLORIFIED BODIES. IMAGINARY VISIONS. GREAT FRUITS THEREOF WHEN THEY COME FROM GOD.

She treats of the great favours our Lord showed her, and how He appeared to her for the first time; she explains what an imaginary vision is, and speaks of the powerful effects it leaves, and the signs whether it is from God. This chapter is most profitable and noteworthy.

1. I NOW resume our subject. I spent some days, not many, with that vision [1] continually before me. It did me so much good, that I never ceased to pray. Even when I did cease, I contrived that it should be in such a way as that I should not displease Him Whom I saw so clearly present, an eye-witness of my acts. And though I was occasionally afraid, because so much was

[1] Ch. xxvii. 3.

said to me about delusions, that fear lasted not long, because our Lord reassured me.

2. It pleased our Lord, one day that I was in prayer, to show me His Hands, and His Hands only. The beauty of them was so great, that no language can describe it. This put me in great fear ; for everything that is strange, in the beginning of any new grace from God, makes me very much afraid. A few days later, I saw His divine Face, and I was utterly entranced. I could not understand why our Lord showed Himself in this way, seeing that, afterwards, He granted me the grace of seeing His whole Person. Later on, I understood that His Majesty was dealing with me according to the weakness of my nature. May He be blessed for ever ! A glory so great was more than one so base and wicked could bear ; and our merciful Lord, knowing this, ordered it in this way.

3. You will think, my father, that it required no great courage to look upon Hands and Face so beautiful. But so beautiful are glorified bodies, that the glory which surrounds them renders those who see that which is so supernatural and beautiful beside themselves. It was so with me : I was in such great fear, trouble, and perplexity at the sight. Afterwards there ensued a sense of safety and certainty, together with other results, so that all fear passed immediately away.[2]

4. On one of the feasts of St. Paul,[3] when I was at Mass, there stood before me the most Sacred Hu-

---

[2] Philippus a SS. Trinitate, *Theolog. Mystic.* par. 2, tr. 3, disc. iv., art. 8 : " Quamvis in principio visiones a dæmone fictæ aliquam habeant pacem ac dulcedinem, in fine tamen confusionem et amaritudinem in anima relinquunt ; cujus contrarium est in divinis visionibus, quæ sæpe turbant in principio, sed semper in fine pacem animæ relinquunt." St. John of the Cross, *Spiritual Canticle,* xiv.-xv. 25 : " In the spiritual passage from the sleep of natural ignorance to the wakefulness of the supernatural understanding, which is the beginning of trance or ecstasy, the spiritual vision then revealed makes the soul fear and tremble."

[3] See ch. xxix. 4. This vision took place on the feast of the Conversion of St. Paul, January 25, 1558 ; her confessor was then F. Fernando Alvarez del Aguila. Already before this date she had had the vision mentioned in ch. xxvii. 3, and the one of which she has given an account in the two preceding paragraphs.

manity,[4] as painters represent Him after the resurrection, in great beauty and majesty, as I particularly described it to you, my father, when you had insisted on it. It was painful enough to have to write about it, for I could not describe it without doing great violence to myself. But I described it as well as I could, and there is no reason why I should now recur to it. One thing, however, I have to say : if in heaven itself there were nothing else to delight our eyes but the great beauty of glorified bodies, that would be an excessive bliss, particularly the vision of the Humanity of Jesus Christ our Lord. If here below, where His Majesty shows Himself to us according to the measure which our wretchedness can bear, it is so great, what must it be there, where the fruition of it is complete !

5. This vision, though imaginary, I never saw with my bodily eyes, nor, indeed, any other, but only with the eyes of the soul. Those who understand these things better than I do, say that the intellectual vision is more perfect than this ; and this, the imaginary vision, much more perfect than those visions which are seen by the bodily eyes. The latter kind of visions, they say, is the lowest ; and it is by these that the devil can most delude us.[5] I did not know it then ; for I wished, when this grace had been granted me, that it had been so in such a way that I could see it with my bodily eyes, in order that my confessor might not say to me that I indulged in fancies.

6. After the vision was over, it happened that I too imagined—the thought came at once—I had

[4] " The holy Mother, Teresa of Jesus, had these imaginary visions for many years, seeing our Lord continually present before her in great beauty, risen from the dead, with His wounds and the crown of thorns. She had a picture made of Him, which she gave to me, and which I gave to Don Fernando de Toledo, Duke of Alva " (Jerome Gratian, *Union del Alma*, cap 5. Madrid, 1616).

[5] Anton. a Spiritu Sancto, *Direct. Mystic.* tr. iii. disp. 5, § 1, n. 315 : " Visio corporea est infima, visio imaginaria est media, visio intellectualis est suprema." N. 322 : " Apparitio visibilis, cum sit omnium infima, est magis exposita illusioni diaboli, nisi forte huic visioni corporali visio intellectualis adjungatur, ut in apparitione S. Gabrielis archangeli facta Beatæ Virgini."

fancied these things; so I was distressed, because I
had spoken of them to my confessor, thinking that I
might have been deceiving him.   There was another
lamentation : I went to my confessor, and told him of
my doubts.   He would ask me whether I told him the
truth so far as I knew it ; or, if not, had I intended to
deceive him ?   I would reply, that I told the truth ;
for, to the best of my belief, I did not lie, nor did I
mean anything of the kind ; neither would I tell a lie
for the whole world.[6]   This he knew well enough ;
and, accordingly, he contrived to quiet me ; and I
felt so much the going to him with these doubts, that
I cannot tell how Satan could have put it into my
head that I invented those things for the purpose of
tormenting myself.

7. But our Lord made such haste to bestow this
grace upon me, and to declare the reality of it, that all
doubts of the vision being a fancy on my part were
quickly taken away, and ever since I see most clearly
how silly I was.   For if I were to spend many years in
devising how to picture to myself anything so beautiful,
I should never be able, nor even know how, to do it ;
for it is beyond the reach of any possible imagination
here below ; the whiteness and brilliancy alone are
inconceivable.   It is not a brilliancy which dazzles,
but a delicate whiteness and a brilliancy infused, furnishing the most excessive delight to the eyes, never
wearied thereby, nor by the visible brightness which
enables us to see a beauty so divine.   It is a light so
different from any light here below that the very
brightness of the sun we see, in comparison with the
brightness and light before our eyes, seems to be
something so obscure, that no one would ever wish to
open his eyes again.

8. It is like most pellucid water running in a bed of
crystal, reflecting the rays of the sun, compared with
most muddy water on a cloudy day, flowing on the

---

[6] See ch. xxx. 18.

surface of the earth. Not that there is anything like
the sun present here, nor is the light like that of the
sun : this light seems to be natural ; and, in comparison with it, every other light is something artificial.
It is a light which knows no night ; but rather, as it is
always light, nothing ever disturbs it. In short, it is
such that no man, however gifted he may be, can ever,
in the whole course of his life, arrive at any imagination of what it is. God puts it before us so instan-
taneously, that we could not open our eyes in time to
see it, if it were necessary for us to open them at all.
But whether our eyes be open or shut, it makes no
difference whatever ; for when our Lord wills, we must
see it, whether we will or not. No distraction can shut
it out, no power can resist it, nor can we attain to it by
any diligence or efforts of our own. I know this by
experience well, as I shall show you.

9. That which I wish now to speak of is the manner
in which our Lord manifests Himself in these visions.
I do not mean that I am going to explain how it is that
a light so strong can enter the interior sense, or so distinct an image the understanding, so as to seem to be
really there ; for this must be work for learned men.
Our Lord has not been pleased to let me understand
how it is. I am so ignorant myself, and so dull of
understanding, that, although people have very much
wished to explain it to me, I have never been able to
understand how it can be.

10. This is the truth : though you, my father, may
think that I have a quick understanding, it is not so ;
for I have found out, in many ways, that my understanding can take in only, as they say, what is given
to it to eat. Sometimes my confessor used to be
amazed at my ignorance : and he never explained to
me,—nor, inded, did I desire to understand—how God
did this, nor how it could be. Nor did I ever ask ;
though, as I have said,[7] I had converse for many years

[7] Ch. xxv. 18.

with men of great learning. But I did ask them if this
or that were a sin or not : as for anything else, the
thought that God did it all was enough for me. I saw
there was no reason to be afraid, but great reason to
praise Him. On the other hand, difficulties increase
my devotion ; and the greater the difficulty the greater
the increase.

11. I will therefore relate what my experience has
shown me ; but how our Lord brought it about, you,
my father, will explain better than I can, and make
clear all that is obscure, and beyond my skill to explain. Now and then it seemed to me that what I saw
was an image ; but most frequently it was not so. I
thought it was Christ Himself, judging by the brightness in which He was pleased to show Himself. Sometimes the vision was so indistinct, that I thought it
was an image ; but still not like a picture, however
well painted—and I have seen many good pictures. It
would be absurd to suppose that the one bears any
resemblance whatever to the other, for they differ as a
living person differs from his portrait, which, however
well drawn, cannot be lifelike, for it is plain that it is a
dead thing. But let this pass, though to the purpose,
and literally true.

12. I do not say this by way of comparison, for
comparisons are never exact, but because it is the
truth itself, as there is the same difference here that
there is between a living subject and the portrait
thereof, neither more nor less : for if what I saw was
an image, it was a living image,—not a dead man, but
the living Christ : and He makes me see that He is
God and man,—not as He was in the sepulchre, but as
He was when He had gone forth from it, risen from the
dead. He comes at times in•majesty so great that no
one can have any doubt that it is our Lord Himself,
especially after Communion : we know that He is then
present, for faith says so. He shows Himself so clearly
to be the Lord of that little dwelling-place, that the

soul seems to be dissolved and lost in Christ. O my Jesus, who can describe the majesty wherein Thou showest Thyself! How utterly Thou art the Lord of the whole world, and of heaven, and of a thousand other and innumerable worlds and heavens, the creation of which is possible to Thee! The soul understands by that majesty wherein Thou showest Thyself that it is nothing for Thee to be Lord of all this.

13. Here it is plain, O my Jesus, how slight is the power of all the devils in comparison with Thine, and how he who is pleasing unto Thee is able to tread all hell under his feet. Here we see why the devils trembled when Thou didst go down to Limbus, and why they might have longed for a thousand hells still lower, that they might escape from Thy terrible Majesty. I see that it is Thy will the soul should feel the greatness of Thy Majesty, and the power of Thy most Sacred Humanity, united with Thy Divinity. Here, too, we see what the day of judgment will be, when we shall behold the King in His Majesty, and in the rigour of His justice against the wicked. Here we learn true humility, imprinted in the soul by the sight of its own wretchedness, of which now it cannot be ignorant. Here, also, is confusion of face, and true repentance for sins ; for though the soul sees that our Lord shows how He loves it, yet it knows not where to go, and so is utterly dissolved.

14. My meaning is, that so exceedingly great is the power of this vision, when our Lord shows the soul much of His grandeur and majesty, that it is impossible, in my opinion, for any soul to endure it, if our Lord did not succour it in a most supernatural way, by throwing it into a trance or ecstasy, whereby the vision of the divine presence is lost in the fruition thereof. It is true that afterwards the vision is forgotten ; but there remains so deep an impression of the majesty and beauty of God, that it is impossible

to forget it, except when our Lord is pleased that the soul should suffer from aridity and desolation, of which I shall speak hereafter[8] ; for then it seems to forget God Himself. The soul is itself no longer, it is always inebriated ; it seems as if a living love of God, of the highest kind, made a new beginning within it ; for though the former vision, which I said represented God without any likeness of Him,[9] is of a higher kind, yet because of our weakness, in order that the remembrance of the vision may last, and that our thoughts may be well occupied, it is a great matter that a presence so divine should remain and abide in our imagination. These two kinds of visions come almost always together, and they do so come ; for we behold the excellency and beauty and glory of the most Holy Humanity with the eyes of the soul. And in the other way I have spoken of,—that of intellectual vision,—we learn how He is God, is mighty, can do all things, commands all things, governs all things, and fills all things with His love.

15. This vision is to be esteemed very highly ; nor is there, in my opinion, any risk in it, because the fruits of it show that the devil has no power here. I think he tried three or four times to represent our Lord to me, in this way, by a false image of Him. He takes the appearance of flesh, but he cannot counterfeit the glory which it has when the vision is from God. Satan makes his representations in order to undo the true vision which the soul has had : but the soul resists instinctively, is troubled, disgusted, and restless ; it loses that devotion and joy it previously had, and cannot pray at all. In the beginning, it so happened to me three or four times. These satanic visions are very different things ; and even he who shall have attained to the prayer of quiet only will, I believe, detect them by those results of them which

[8] Ch. xxx. 9, 10. See St. John of the Cross, *Dark Night*, bk. ii. ch. vii.
[9] Ch. xxvii. 3.

I described when I was speaking of locutions.[10]   They are most easily recognised ; and if a soul consents not to its own delusion, I do not think that Satan will be able to deceive it, provided it walks in humility and singleness of heart.   He who shall have had the true vision, coming from God, detects the false visions at once ; for, though they begin with a certain sweetness and joy, the soul rejects them of itself ; and the joy which Satan ministers must be, I think, very different—it shows no traces of pure and holy love : Satan very quickly betrays himself.

16. Thus, then, as I believe, Satan can do no harm to any one who has had experience of these things ; for it is the most impossible of all impossible things that all this may be the work of the imagination. There is no ground whatever for the supposition ; for the very beauty and whiteness of one of our Lord's Hands [11] are beyond our imagination altogether.   How is it that we see present before us, in a moment, what we do not remember, what we have never thought of, and, moreover, what, in a long space of time, the imagination could not compass, because, as I have just said,[12] it far transcends anything we can comprehend in this life ? This, then, is not possible. Whether we have any power in the matter or not will appear by what I am now going to say.

17. If the vision were the work of a man's own understanding,—setting aside that such a vision would not accomplish the great results of the true one, nor, indeed, any at all,—it would be as the act of one who tries to go to sleep, and yet continues awake, because sleep has not come.   He longs for it, because of some necessity or weakness in his head : and so he lulls himself to sleep, and makes efforts to procure it, and now and then thinks he has succeeded ; but, if the sleep be not real, it will not support him, nor supply strength to his head : on the contrary, his

[10] Ch. xxv. 8.   [11] See § 2.   [12] § 7, supra.

head will very often be the worse for it. So will it be here, in a measure ; the soul will be dissipated, neither sustained nor strengthened ; on the contrary, it will be wearied and disgusted. But, in the true vision, the riches which abide in the soul cannot be described ; even the body receives health and comfort.

18. I urged this argument, among others, when they told me that my visions came from the evil one, and that I imagined them myself,—and it was very often,—and made use of certain illustrations, as well as I could, and as our Lord suggested to me. But all was to little purpose ; for as there were most holy persons in the place,—in comparison with whom I was a mass of perdition,—whom God did not lead by this way, they were at once filled with fear ; they thought it all came through my sins. And so my state was talked about, and came to the knowledge of many ; though I had spoken of it to no one, except my confessor, or to those to whom he commanded [13] me to speak of it.

19. I said to them once, If they who thus speak of my state were to tell me that a person with whom I had just conversed, and whom I knew well, was not that person, but that I was deluding myself, and that they knew it, I should certainly trust them rather than my own eyes. But if that person left with me certain jewels,—and if, possessing none previously, I held the jewels in my hand as pledges of a great love,— and if I were now rich, instead of poor as before,— I should not be able to believe this that they said, though I might wish it. These jewels I could now show them, for all who knew me saw clearly that my soul was changed,—and so my confessor said ; for the difference was very great in every way—not a pretence, but such as all might most clearly observe. As I was formerly so wicked, I said, I could not believe that Satan, if he wished to deceive me and take me

[13] See ch. xxiii. 14.

down to hell, would have recourse to means so adverse to his purpose as this of rooting out my faults, implanting virtues and spiritual strength ; for I saw clearly that I had become at once another person through the instrumentality of these visions.

20. My confessor, who was, as I said before,[14] one of the fathers of the Society of Jesus, and a really holy man, answered them in the same way,—so I learnt afterwards. He was a most discreet man, and of great humility ; but this great humility of his brought me into serious trouble : for, though he was a man much given to prayer, and learned, he never trusted his own judgment, because our Lord was not leading him by this way. He had, therefore, much to suffer on my account, in many ways. I knew they used to say to him that he must be on his guard against me, lest Satan should delude him through a belief in anything I might say to him. They gave instances of others who were deluded.[15] All this distressed me. I began to be afraid I should find no one to hear my confession,[16] and that all would avoid me. I did nothing but weep.

21. It was a providence of God that he was willing to stand by me and hear my confession. But he was so great a servant of God, that he would have exposed himself to anything for His sake. So he told me that if I did not offend God, nor swerve from the instructions he gave me, there was no fear I should be deserted by him. He encouraged me always, and quieted me. He bade me never to conceal anything from him ; and I never did.[17] He used to say that, so long as I

---

[14] Ch. xxiv. 5. Father Baltasar Alvarez, who had only just been ordained, and therefore with no previous experience except that of his own scruples, found himself called upon to direct a soul arrived at the summit of mysticism. He was, moreover, under the guidance of his own rector, F. Dionisio Vasquez, a man of notorious severity.

[15] There were in Spain, and elsewhere, many women who were hypocrites, or deluded. Among others was the prioress of Lisbon, afterwards notorious, who deceived Luis of Granada (De la Fuente).

[16] Interior Castle, M. vi. ch. i. 6.

[17] Ch. xxvi. 5 ; Interior Castle, M. vi. ch. ix. 10.

did this, the devil, if it were the devil, could not hurt me ; on the contrary, out of that evil which Satan wished to do me, our Lord would bring forth good. He laboured with all his might to make me perfect. As I was very much afraid myself, I obeyed him in everything, though imperfectly. He had much to suffer on my account during three years of trouble and more, because he heard my confession all that time ; for in the great persecutions that fell upon me, and the many harsh judgments of me which our Lord permitted,—many of which I did not deserve,—everything was carried to him, and he was found fault with because of me,—he being all the while utterly blameless.

22. If he had not been so holy a man, and if our Lord had not been with him, it would have been impossible for him to bear so much ; for he had to answer those who regarded me as one going to destruction ; and they would not believe what he said to them. On the other hand, he had to quiet me, and relieve me of my fears ; when my fears increased, he had again to reassure me ; for, after every vision which was strange to me, our Lord permitted me to remain in great fear. All this was the result of my being then, and of having been, a sinner. He used to console me out of his great compassion ; and, if he had trusted to his own convictions, I should not have had so much to suffer ; for God revealed the whole truth to him. I believe that he received this light from the Blessed Sacrament.

23. Those servants of God who were not satisfied had many conversations with me.[18] As I spoke to them carelessly, so they misunderstood my meaning in many things. I had a great regard for one of them ; for my soul owed him more than I can tell. He was a most holy man, and I felt it most acutely when I saw that he did not understand me. He had a great

[18] See ch. xxv. 18.

desire for my improvement, and hoped our Lord would enlighten me. So, then, because I spoke, as I was saying, without careful consideration, they looked upon me as deficient in humility ; and when they detected any of my faults—they might have detected many—they condemned me at once. They used to put certain questions to me, which I answered simply and carelessly. Then they concluded forthwith that I wished to teach them, and that I considered myself to be a learned woman. All this was carried to my confessor—for certainly they desired my amendment—and so he would reprimand me. This lasted some time, and I was distressed on many sides ; but, with the graces which our Lord gave me, I bore it all.

24. I relate this in order that people may see what a great trial it is not to find any one who knows this way of the spirit by experience. If our Lord had not dealt so favourably with me, I know not what would have become of me. There were some things that were enough to take away my reason ; and now and then I was reduced to such straits that I could do nothing but lift up my eyes to our Lord.[19] The contradiction of good people, which a wretched woman, weak, wicked, and timid as I am, must bear with, seems to be nothing when thus described ; but I, who in the course of my life passed through very great trials, found this one of the heaviest.[20]

25. May our Lord grant that I may have pleased His Majesty a little herein ; for I am sure that they pleased Him who condemned and rebuked me, and that it was all for my great good.

---

[19] 2 Paralip. xx. 12 : " Sed cum ignoremus quid agere debeamus, hoc solum habemus residui, ut oculos nostros dirigamus ad Te."
[20] See ch. xxx. 6.

CHAPTER XXIX.

OF VISIONS.   THE GRACES OUR LORD BESTOWED ON THE
   SAINT.   THE ANSWERS OUR LORD GAVE HER FOR
   THOSE WHO TRIED HER.

*She continues, and tells of some great mercies God
showed her, and what His Majesty said to her in order
to reassure her, and taught her how to answer contra-
dictors.*

1. I HAVE wandered far from the subject ; for I
undertook to give reasons why the vision was no work
of the imagination.   For how can we, by any efforts
of ours, picture to ourselves the Humanity of Christ,
and imagine His great beauty ?   No little time is
necessary, if our conception is in any way to resemble
it.   Certainly, the imagination may be able to picture
it, and a person may for a time contemplate that
picture,—the form and the brightness of it,—and
gradually make it more perfect, and so lay up that
image in his memory.   Who can hinder this, seeing
that it could be fashioned by the understanding ?
But as to the vision of which I am speaking, there
are no means of bringing it about ;   only we must
behold it when our Lord is pleased to present it before
us, as He wills and what He wills ;   and there is no
possibility of taking anything away from it, or of
adding anything to it ; nor is there there way of effecting
it, whatever we may do, nor of seeing it when we like,
nor of abstaining from seeing ;   if we try to gaze
upon it—part of the vision in particular—the vision
of Christ is lost at once.

2. For two years and a half God granted me this
grace very frequently ;   but it is now more than three
years since He has taken away from me its continual
presence, through another of a higher nature, as I

shall perhaps explain hereafter.[1] And though I saw Him speaking to me, and though I was contemplating His great beauty, and the sweetness with which those words of His came forth from His divine mouth,—they were sometimes uttered with severity,—and though I was extremely desirous to behold the colour of His eyes, or His stature,[2] so that I might be able to describe them, yet I never attained to the sight of them, and I could do nothing for that end ; on the contrary, I lost the vision altogether. And though I see that He looks upon me at times with great tenderness, yet so strong is His gaze, that my soul cannot endure it ; I fall into a trance so deep, that I lose the beautiful vision, in order to have a greater fruition of it all.

3. Accordingly, willing or not willing, the vision has nothing to do with it. Our Lord clearly regards nothing but humility and confusion of face, the acceptance of what He wishes to give, and the praise of Himself, the Giver. This is true of all visions without exception : we can contribute nothing towards them—we cannot add to them, nor can we take from them ; our own efforts can neither make nor unmake them. Our Lord would have us see most clearly that it is no work of ours, but of His Divine Majesty : we are therefore the less able to be proud of it : on the contrary, it makes us humble and afraid ; for we see that, as our Lord can take from us the power of seeing what we would see, so also can He take from us these mercies and His grace, and we may be lost for ever. We must therefore walk in His fear while we are living in this our exile.

---

[1] Ch. xxxviii. 22, 23 and ch. xl. St. Teresa wrote this portion of her life about January 1565, or a little earlier, so that the cessation of visions must be placed in the second half of 1561.

[2] All the former editions say " or the form of them," but a close inspection of the MS. shows that the " form " refers, not to the eyes alone, but to the whole body of our Lord. The " two years and a half " during which visions were frequent would cover 1559 as well as 1560, and the end of 1558 and the beginning of 1561.

4. Our Lord showed Himself to me almost always as He is after His resurrection. It was the same in the Host ; only at those times when I was in trouble, and when it was His will to strengthen me, did He show His wounds. Sometimes I saw Him on the cross, in the Garden, crowned with thorns,—but that was rarely ; sometimes also carrying His cross because of my necessities,—I may say so,—or those of others ; but always in His glorified body. Many reproaches and many vexations have I borne while telling this— many suspicions and much persecution also. So certain were they to whom I spoke that I had an evil spirit, that some would have me exorcised. I did not care much for this ; but I felt it bitterly when I saw that my confessors were afraid to hear me, or when I knew that they were told of anything about me.

5. Notwithstanding all this, I never could be sorry that I had had these heavenly visions ; nor would I exchange even one of them for all the wealth and all the pleasures of the world. I always regarded them as a great mercy from our Lord ; and to me they were the very greatest treasure,—of this our Lord assured me often. I used to go to Him to complain of all these hardships ; and I came away from prayer consoled, and with renewed strength. I did not dare to contradict those who were trying me ; for I saw that it made matters worse, because they looked on my doing so as a failure in humility. I spoke of it to my confessor ; he always consoled me greatly when he saw me in distress.

6. As my visions grew in frequency, one of those who used to help me before—it was to him I confessed when the father-minister [3] could not hear me—began to say that I was certainly under the influence of Satan. He bade me, now that I had no power of

---

[3] Baltasar Alvarez was father-minister of the house of St. Giles, Avila, in whose absence she had recourse to another father of that house, namely, F. Fernando Alvarez del Aguila.

resisting, always to make the sign of the cross when I had a vision, to point my finger at it by way of scorn,[4] and be firmly persuaded of its diabolic nature. If I did this, the vision would not recur. I was to be without fear on the point ; God would watch over me, and take the vision away.[5] This was a great hardship for me ; for, as I could not believe that the vision did not come from God, it was a fearful thing for me to do ; and I could not wish, as I said before, that the visions should be withheld. However, I did at last as I was bidden. I prayed much to our Lord that He would deliver me from delusions. I was always praying to that effect, and with many tears. I had recourse also to St. Peter and St. Paul ; for our Lord had said to me—it was on their feast that He had appeared to me the first time[6]—that they would preserve me from delusion. I used to see them frequently most distinctly on my left hand ; but that vision was not imaginary. These glorious Saints were my very good lords.

7. It was to me a most painful thing to make a show of contempt whenever I saw our Lord in a vision ; for when I saw Him before me, if I were to be cut in pieces, I could not believe it was Satan. This was to me, therefore, a heavy kind of penance ; and accordingly, that I might not be so continually crossing myself, I used to hold a crucifix in my hand. This I did almost always ; but I did not always make

---

[4] Y diese higas. " Higa es una manera de menosprecio que hacemos cerrando el puño, y mostrando el dedo pulgár por entre el dedo indice y el medio " (Cobarruvias, in voce). At the convent of Medina del Campo a small object is preserved which, it appears, was used by St. Teresa to make this " sign of scorn." It is like a little horn of flint, about an inch and a half in length, mounted in silver. Being approached to the temples it would represent one of the horns with the possession of which Satan is popularly credited, this gesture, addressed to the vision, meaning : " I know you are but Satan in disguise."

[5] See Book of the Foundations, ch. viii. 3, where the Saint refers to this advice, and to the better advice given her later by F. Dominic Bañes, one of her confessors. See also Interior Castle, M. vi. ch. ix. 11.

[6] See ch. xxvii. 3, and ch. xxviii. 4.

signs of contempt, because I felt that too much. It reminded me of the insults which the Jews heaped upon Him ; and so I prayed Him to forgive me, seeing that I did so in obedience to him who stood in His stead, and not to lay the blame on me, seeing that he was one of those whom He had placed as His ministers in His Church. He said to me that I was not to distress myself—that I did well to obey ; but He would make them see the truth of the matter. He seemed to me to be angry when they made me give up my prayer.[7] He told me to say to them that this was tyranny. He gave me reasons for believing that the vision was not satanic ; some of them I mean to repeat by and by.

8. On one occasion, when I was holding in my hand the cross of my rosary, He took it from me into His own hand. He returned it ; but it was then four large stones incomparably more precious than diamonds ; for nothing can be compared with what is supernatural. Diamonds seem counterfeits and imperfect when compared with these precious stones. The five wounds were delineated on them with most admirable art. He said to me that for the future that cross would appear so to me always ; and so it did. I never saw the wood of which it was made, but only the precious stones. They were seen, how-ever, by no one else,—only by myself.[8]

9. When they had begun to insist on my putting my visions to a test like this, and resisting them, the graces I received were multiplied more and more. I tried to distract myself ; I never ceased to be in prayer : even during sleep my prayer seemed to be continual ; for now my love grew, I made piteous

---

[7] Ch. xxv. 18.

[8] The cross was made of ebony. It is not known where that cross is now. The Saint gave it to her sister, Doña Juana de Ahumada, who begged it of her. Some say that the Carmelites of Madrid possess it ; and others, those of Valladolid ; the latter convent possesses three decades of St. Teresa's rosary, but nothing is known there of the cross.

complaints to our Lord, and told Him I could not bear it. Neither was it in my power—though I desired, and, more than that, even strove—to give up thinking of Him. Nevertheless, I obeyed to the utmost of my power ; but my power was little or nothing in the matter ; and our Lord never released me from that obedience ; but though He bade me obey my confessor, He reassured me in another way, and taught me what I was to say. He has continued to do so until now ; and He gave me reasons so sufficient, that I felt myself perfectly safe.

10. Not long afterwards His Majesty began, according to His promise, to make it clear that it was He Himself who appeared, by the growth in me of the love of God so strong, that I knew not who could have infused it ; for it was most supernatural, and I had not attained to it by any efforts of my own. I saw myself dying with a desire to see God, and I knew not how to seek that life otherwise than by dying. Certain great impetuosities [9] of love, though not so intolerable as those of which I have spoken before,[10] nor yet of so great worth, overwhelmed me. I knew not what to do ; for nothing gave me pleasure, and I had no control over myself. It seemed as if my soul were really torn away from myself. Oh, supreme artifice of our Lord ! how tenderly didst Thou deal with Thy miserable slave ! Thou didst hide Thyself from me, and didst yet constrain me with Thy love, with a death so sweet, that my soul would never wish it over.

11. It is not possible for any one to understand these impetuosities if he has not experienced them himself. They are not an upheaving of the breast, nor those devotional sensations, not uncommon, which seem on the point of causing suffocation, and are beyond control. That prayer is of a much lower order ; and those agitations should be avoided by

[9] See *Relation* i. 3.   [10] Ch. xx. 11.

gently endeavouring to be recollected ; and the soul should be kept in quiet.   This prayer is like the sobbing of little children, who seem on the point of choking, and whose disordered senses are soothed by giving them to drink.   So here reason should draw in the reins, because nature itself may be contributing to it ; and we should consider with fear that all this may not be perfect, and that much sensuality may be involved in it.   The infant soul should be soothed by the caresses of love, which shall draw forth its love in a gentle way, and not, as they say, by force of blows. This love should be inwardly under control, and not as a caldron, fiercely boiling because too much fuel has been applied to it, and out of which everything is lost.   The source of the fire must be kept under control, and the flame must be quenched in sweet tears, and not with those painful tears which come out of these emotions, and which do so much harm.

12. In the beginning, I had tears of this kind. They left me with a disordered head and a wearied spirit, and for a day or two afterwards unable to resume my prayer.   Great discretion, therefore, is necessary at first, in order that everything may proceed gently, and that the operations of the spirit may be within ;   all outward manifestations should be carefully avoided.

13. These other impetuosities are very different. It is not we who apply the fuel ; the fire is already kindled, and we are thrown into it in a moment to be consumed.   It is by no efforts of the soul that it sorrows over the wound which the absence of our Lord has inflicted on it ;   it is far otherwise ;   for an arrow is driven into the entrails to the very quick,[11] and into the heart at times, so that the soul knows not what is the matter with it, nor what it wishes for. It understands clearly enough that it wishes for

[11] *Interior Castle,* M. vi. ch. ii. per totum.   St. John of the Cross, *Spiritual Canticle,* st. i. 22 *sqq.*

God, and that the arrow seems tempered with some herb which makes the soul hate itself for the love of our Lord, and willingly lose its life for Him. It is impossible to describe or explain the way in which God wounds the soul, or the very grievous pain inflicted, which deprives it of all self-consciousness ; yet this pain is so sweet, that there is no joy in the world which gives greater delight. As I have just said,[12] the soul would wish to be always dying of this wound.

14. This pain and bliss together carried me out of myself, and I never could understand how it was. Oh, what a sight a wounded soul is !—a soul, I mean, so conscious of it as to be able to say of itself that it is wounded for so good a cause ; and seeing distinctly that it never did anything whereby this love should come to it, and that it does come from that exceeding love which our Lord bears it. A spark seems to have fallen suddenly upon it, that has set it all on fire. Oh, how often do I remember, when in this state, those words of David : " Quemadmodun desiderad çervus a fontes aguarun " ![13] They seem to me to be literally true of myself.

15. When these impetuosities are not very violent they seem to admit of a little mitigation—at least, the soul seeks some relief, because it knows not what to do—through certain penances ; the painfulness of which, and even the shedding of its blood, are no more felt than if the body were dead. The soul seeks for ways and means to do something that may be felt, for the love of God ; but the first pain is so great, that no bodily torture I know of can take it away. As relief is not to be had here, these medicines are too mean for so high a disease. Some slight mitigation

---

[12] § 10.
[13] Psalm xli. 2 : " As the longing of the hart for the fountains of waters, so is the longing of my soul for Thee, O my God." St. Teresa's spelling of Latin words is distinctly phonetic.

may be had, and the pain may pass away a little, by praying God to relieve its sufferings : but the soul sees no relief except in death, by which it thinks to attain completely to the fruition of its good. At other times, these impetuosities are so violent that the soul can do neither this nor anything else ; the whole body is contracted, and neither hand nor foot can be moved : if the body be upright at the time, it falls down, as a thing that has no control over itself. It cannot even breathe ; all it does is to moan—not loudly, because it cannot : its moaning, however, comes from a keen sense of pain.

16. Our Lord was pleased that I should have at times a vision of this kind : I saw an angel close by me, on my left side, in bodily form. This I am not accustomed to see, unless very rarely. Though I have visions of angels frequently, yet I see them only by an intellectual vision, such as I have spoken of before.[14] It was our Lord's will that in this vision I should see the angel in this wise. He was not large, but small of stature, and most beautiful—his face burning, as if he were one of the highest angels, who seem to be all of fire : they must be those whom we call cherubim.[15] Their names they never tell me ; but I see very well that there is in heaven so great a difference between one angel and another, and between these and the others, that I cannot explain it.

17. I saw in his hand a long spear of gold, and at the iron's point there seemed to be a little fire. He appeared to me to be thrusting it at times into my heart,[16] and to pierce my very entrails ; when he drew it out, he seemed to draw them out also, and to leave me all on fire with a great love of God. The

---

[14] Ch. xxvii. 3.
[15] In the MS. of the Saint preserved in the Escorial, the word is " cherubines " ; but Bañez wrote in the margin : " It seems rather those that are called seraphims," and all subsequent editors and translators until Bouix and Fuente adopted this latter term.
[16] See *Relation* viii. 16.

pain was so great that it made me moan ; and yet so surpassing was the sweetness of this excessive pain that I could not wish to be rid of it. The soul is satisfied now with nothing less than God. The pain is not bodily, but spiritual ; though the body has its share in it, even a large one. It is a caressing of love so sweet which now takes place between the soul and God, that I pray God of His goodness to make him experience it who may think that I am lying.[17]

18. During the days that this lasted I went about as if beside myself. I wished to see or speak with no one, but only to cherish my pain, which was to me a greater bliss than all created things could give me.[18]

[17] There is some uncertainty as to the date on which this phenomenon took place. It is generally assigned to the year 1559, the day being not further known except that it somewhat preceded the feast of St. Augustine (August 28). But the vision seems to have been repeated several times, for St. Teresa says *algunas veces*. The cell occupied by St. Teresa previous to her removal to the convent of St. Joseph has been converted into a large chapel of the Transverberation, on the gospel side of the conventual church, and an inscription on the floor reminds the visitor that he is treading sacred ground. But according to the tradition of the convent of the Incarnation the vision took place again during St. Teresa's priorship (1571–1574, after the completion of the Life), and the little oratory attached to the apartment of the prioress (on the first floor) is pointed out as the place where her heart was pierced by an angel. On one of the walls may be seen stains of blood, due either to her excessive mortifications or to the blood vomited by her after her heart had been wounded. The hymn which she composed on that occasion was discovered at Seville in 1700 (" En las internas entrañas "). The Saint's heart, severed from the body previous to the removal of the latter to Avila (October 25, 1585), is preserved at the convent of Carmelite nuns at Alba de Tormes, where the present writer had ample opportunity of examining it with the help of powerful magnesium light. It is of brown-greyish colour, of full natural length, but rather shrunk in width. The chief wound, distinctly visible, is horizontal, about an inch and a half in length ; it looks as if it had been inflicted with a knife, but formerly distinct traces of burning could be seen. There are several minor wounds in different parts. Until some years ago there was a kind of growth in the reliquary resembling thorns, of which about twenty could be distinguished, the theory being that whenever the Church passed through some acute crisis a new thorn was formed ; but the bishop of Salamanca, Don Tomás Camara, discovering that they consisted of remainders of the feather brush with which the reliquary (through some openings) used to be dusted, and round which small particles of the heart had gathered, caused them to be removed.

[18] Brev. Rom. in festo S. Theresiæ, Oct. 15, Lect. v. : " Tanto autem divini amoris incendio cor ejus conflagravit, ut merito viderit Angelum ignito jaculo sibi præcordia transverberantem." The Carmelites keep the feast of this piercing of the Saint's heart on August 27.

19. I was in this state from time to time, whenever it was our Lord's pleasure to throw me into those deep trances, which I could not prevent even when I was in the company of others, and which, to my deep vexation, came to be publicly known. Since then I do not feel that pain so much, but only that which I spoke of before,—I do not remember the chapter,[19]—which is in many ways very different from it, and of greater worth. On the other hand, when this pain, of which I am now speaking, begins, our Lord seems to lay hold of the soul, and to throw it into a trance, so that there is no time for me to have any sense of pain or suffering, because fruition ensues at once. May He be blessed for ever, Who hath bestowed such great graces on one who has responded so ill to blessings so great !

CHAPTER XXX.

ST. PETER OF ALCANTARA COMFORTS THE SAINT.   GREAT TEMPTATIONS AND INTERIOR TRIALS.

She continues the history of her life, and tells how God sent her a remedy for all her anxieties by calling the holy friar Fray Pedro de Alcantara, of the Order of the Glorious St. Francis, to the place where she lived. She mentions some great temptations and interior trials through which she sometimes had to pass.

1. WHEN I saw that I was able to do little or nothing towards avoiding these great impetuosities, I began also to be afraid of them, because I could not understand how this pain and joy could subsist together. I knew it was possible enough for bodily pain and spiritual joy to dwell together ; but the co-existence

[19] Ch. xx. 11.

of a spiritual pain so excessive as this, and of joy so deep, troubled my understanding. Still, I tried to continue my resistance ; but I was so little able that I was now and then wearied. I used to take up the cross for protection, and try to defend myself against Him who, by the cross, is the Protector of us all. I saw that no one understood me. I saw it very clearly myself, but I did not dare to say so to any one except my confessor ; for that would have been a real admission that I had no humility.

2. Our Lord was pleased to succour me in a great measure.—and, for the moment, altogether,—by bringing to the place where I was that blessed friar, Peter of Alcantara. Of him I spoke before, and said something of his penance.[1] Among other things, I have been assured that he wore continually, for twenty years, a girdle made of pointed wire. He is the author of certain little books, in Spanish,[2] on prayer, which are now in common use ; for, as he was much exercised therein, his writings are very profitable to those who are given to prayer. He kept the first rule of the blessed St. Francis in all its rigour, and did those things besides of which I spoke before.

3. When that widow, the servant of God and my friend, of whom I have already spoken,[3] knew that so great a man had come, she took her measures. She knew the straits I was in, for she was an eyewitness of my afflictions, and was a great comfort to me. Her faith was so strong that she could not

[1] Ch. xxvii. 17, 18, 19. The first interview took place in August, 1558.
[2] St. Peter of Alcantara wrote several treatises: namely, "Tratado de la Oración y Meditación " (an abridgment of Luis de Granada, translated into English by Giles Willoughby, and lately by George Seymour Hollings, quoted by St. Teresa in the *Interior Castle*, M. iv. ch. iii. 5) ; " Breve Introdución para los que comienzan á servir á Dios ; Tres cosas que debe hacer el que desea salvarse ; Oración devotisima, and Petición especial de Amor de Dios." They were published, together with a treatise of Savonarola on the religious vows, at Lisbon, between 1556 and 1560, and again at Medina del Campo, 1563, probably the edition known to St. Teresa.
[3] Ch. xxiv. 5. Doña Guiomar de Ulloa, who was under the direction of St. Peter of Alcantara.

help believing that what others said was the work of
the devil was really the work of the Spirit of God ;
and as she is a person of great sense and great caution,
and one to whom our Lord is very bountiful in prayer,
it pleased His Majesty to let her see what learned
men failed to discern. My confessors gave me leave
to accept relief in some things from her, because in
many ways she was able to afford it. Some of those
graces which our Lord bestowed on me fell to her
lot occasionally, together with instructions most profitable for her soul. So, then, when she knew that the
blessed man was come, without saying a word to me,
she obtained leave from the Provincial for me to
stay eight days in her house, in order that I might the
more easily confer with him. In that house, and in
one church or another, I had many conversations
with him the first time he came here ; for afterwards
I had many communications with him at diverse
times.

4. I gave him an account, as briefly as I could,
of my life, and of my way of prayer, with the utmost
clearness in my power. I have always held to this,
to be perfectly frank and exact with those to whom
I make known the state of my soul.[4] Even my first
impulses I wish them to know ; and as for doubtful
and suspicious matters, I used to make the most of
them by arguing against myself. Thus, then, without
equivocation or concealment, I laid before him the
state of my soul. I saw almost at once that he understood me, by reason of his own experience. That was
all I required ; for at that time I did not know myself
as I do now, so as to give an account of my state.
It was at a later time that God enabled me to
understand myself, and describe the graces which
His Majesty bestows upon me. It was necessary,
then, that he who would clearly understand and

---

[4] Ch. xxvi. 5. The interviews between the two Saints took place chiefly
in the chapel called Mosén Rubí and in the parish church of Santo Tomás.

explain my state should have had experience of it himself.

5. The light he threw on the matter was of the clearest ; for as to these visions, at least, which were not imaginary, I could not understand how they could be. And it seemed that I could not understand, too, how those could be which I saw with the eyes of the soul ; for, as I said before,[5] those visions only seemed to me to be of consequence which were seen with the bodily eyes : and of these I had none. The holy man enlightened me on the whole question, explained it to me, and bade me not to be distressed, but to praise God, and to abide in the full conviction that this was the work of the Spirit of God ; for, saving the faith, nothing could be more true, and there was nothing on which I could more firmly rely. He was greatly comforted in me, was most kind and service-able, and ever afterwards took great care of me, and told me of his own affairs and labours ; and when he saw that I had those very desires which in himself were fulfilled already,—for our Lord had given me very strong desires,—and also how great my resolution was, he delighted in conversing with me.

6. To a person whom our Lord has raised to this state there is no pleasure or comfort equal to that of meeting with another whom our Lord has begun to raise in the same way. At that time, however, it must have been only a beginning with me, as I believe ; and God grant I may not have gone back now. He was extremely sorry for me. He told me that one of the greatest trials in this world was that which I had borne,—namely, the contradiction of good people,[6] —and that more was in reserve for me : I had need, therefore, of some one—and there was no one in this city—who understood me ; but he would speak to my confessor, and to that married nobleman, already spoken of,[7] who was one of those who tormented me

<hr/>

[5] Ch. vii. 12.   [6] See ch. xxviii. 24.   [7] Ch. xxiii. 7.

most, and who, because of his great affection for me, was the cause of all these attacks. He was a holy but timid man, and could not feel safe about me, because he had seen how wicked I was, and that not long before. The holy man did so; he spoke to them both, explained the mattter, and gave them reasons why they should reassure themselves, and disturb me no more. My confessor was easily satisfied,—not so the nobleman; for though they were not enough to keep him quiet, yet they kept him in some measure from frightening me so much as he used to do.

7. We made an agreement that I should write to him and tell him how it fared with me, for the future, and that we should pray much for each other. Such was his humility that he held to the prayers of a wretch like me. It made me very much ashamed of myself. He left me in the greatest consolation and joy, bidding me continue my prayer with confidence and without any doubt that it was the work of God. If I should have any doubts, for my greater security, I was to make them known to my confessor, and, having done so, be in peace. Nevertheless, I was not able at all to feel that confidence, for our Lord was leading me by the way of fear; and so, when they told me that the devil had power over me, I believed them. Thus, then, not one of them was able to inspire me with confidence on the one hand, or fear on the other, in such a way as to make me believe either of them, otherwise than as our Lord allowed me. Accordingly, though the holy friar consoled and calmed me, I did not rely so much on him as to be altogether without fear, particularly when our Lord forsook me in the afflictions of my soul, of which I will now speak. Nevertheless, as I have said, I was very much consoled.

8. I could not give thanks enough to God, and to my glorious father St. Joseph, who seemed to me

to have brought him here. He was the Commissary-General of the custody[8] of St. Joseph, to whom, and to our Lady, I used to pray much.

9. I suffered at times—and even still, though not so often—the most grievous trials, together with bodily pains and afflictions arising from violent sicknesses ; so much so that I could scarcely control myself. At other times my bodily sickness was more grievous ; and as I had no spiritual pain, I bore it with great joy : but, when both pains came upon me together, my distress was so heavy that I was reduced to sore straits.

10. I forgot all the mercies our Lord had shown me, and remembered them only as a dream, to my great distress ; for my understanding was so dull that I had a thousand doubts and suspicions whether I had ever understood matters aright, thinking that perhaps all was fancy, and that it was enough for me to have deceived myself, without also deceiving good men. I looked upon myself as so wicked as to have been the cause, by my sins, of all the evils and all the heresies that had sprung up. This is but a false humility, and Satan invented it for the purpose of disquieting me, and trying whether he could thereby drive my soul to despair. I have now had so much experience that I know this was his work[9] ; so he, seeing that I understand him, does not torment me in the same way as much as he used to do.   That it is his work is clear from the restlessness and discomfort with which it begins, and the trouble it causes in the soul while it lasts ; from the obscurity and distress, the aridity and indisposition for prayer and for every good work, which it produces. It seems to stifle the soul and trammel the body, so as to make them good for nothing.

11. Now, though the soul acknowledges itself to

[8] A " custody " is a division of the province, in the Order of St. Francis, comprising a certain number of convents.
[9] *Rel.* i. 19.

be miserable, and though it is painful to us to see
ourselves as we are, and though we have most deep
convictions of our own wickedness,—deep as those
spoken of just now,[10] and really felt,—yet true humility
is not attended with trouble; it does not disturb
the soul; it causes neither obscurity nor aridity :
on the contrary, it consoles. It is altogether different,
bringing with it calm, sweetness, and light. It is
no doubt painful ; but, on the other hand, it is consoling, because we see how great is the mercy of our
Lord in allowing the soul to have that pain, and
how well the soul is occupied. On the one hand,
the soul grieves over its offences against God ; on
the other, His compassion makes it glad. It has
light, which makes it ashamed of itself ; and it gives
thanks to His Majesty, Who has borne with it so long.
That other humility, which is the work of Satan,
furnishes no light for any good work ; it pictures
God as bringing upon everything fire and sword ;
it dwells upon His justice ; and the soul's faith in
the mercy of God—for the power of the devil does
not reach so far as to destroy faith—is of such a
nature as to give me no consolation : on the contrary,
the consideration of mercies so great helps to increase
the pain, because I look upon myself as bound to
render greater service.

12. This invention of Satan is one of the most
painful, subtle, and crafty that I have known him
to possess ; I should therefore like to warn you, my
father, of it, in order that, if Satan should tempt you
herein, you may have some light, and be aware of
his devices, if your understanding should be left at
liberty : because you must not suppose that learning
and knowledge are of any use here ; for though I
have none of them myself, yet now that I have escaped
out of his hands I see clearly that this is folly. What
I understood by it is this : that it is our Lord's pleasure

[10] § 10.

to give him leave and license, as He gave him of old
to tempt Job[11]; though in my case, because of my
wretchedness, the temptation is not so sharp.

13. It happened to me to be tempted once in this
way; and I remember it was on the day before the
vigil of Corpus Christi,—a feast to which I have great
devotion, though not so great as I ought to have.
The trial then lasted only till the day of the feast
itself. But, on other occasions, it continued one,
two, and even three weeks, and—I know not—perhaps
longer. But I was specially liable to it during the
Holy Weeks, when it was my habit to make prayer
my joy. Then the devil seizes on my understanding
in a moment; and occasionally, by means of things
so trivial that I should laugh at them at any other
time, he makes it stumble over anything he likes.
The soul, laid in fetters, loses all control over itself,
and all power of thinking of anything but the absurd-
ities he puts before it, which, being more or less un-
substantial, inconsistent, and disconnected, serve only
to stifle the soul, so that it has no power over itself;
and accordingly—so it seems to me—the devils make
a football of it, and the soul is unable to escape out
of their hands. It is impossible to describe the
sufferings of the soul in this state. It goes about in
quest of relief, and God suffers it to find none. The
light of reason, in the freedom of its will, remains,
but it is not clear; it seems to me as if its eyes were
covered with a veil. As a person who, having travelled often by a particular road, knows, though it
be night and dark, by his past experience of it, where
he may stumble, and where he ought to be on his
guard against that risk, because he has seen the place
by day, so the soul avoids offending God: it seems
to go on by habit—that is, if we put out of sight
the fact that our Lord holds it by the hand, which is
the true explanation of the matter. *Tempted*

[11] Job i.

14. Faith is then as dead, and asleep, like all the other virtues ; not lost, however,—for the soul truly believes all that the Church holds ; but its profession of the faith is hardly more than an outward profession of the mouth. And, on the other hand, temptations seem to press it down, and make it dull, so that its knowledge of God becomes to it as that of something which it hears of far away. So tepid is its love that, when it hears God spoken of, it listens and believes that He is what He is, because the Church so teaches ; but it recollects nothing of its own former experience. Vocal prayer or solitude is only a greater affliction, because the interior suffering—whence it comes, it knows not—is unendurable, and, as it seems to me, in some measure a counterpart of hell. So it is, as our Lord showed me in a vision[12] ; for the soul itself is then burning in the fire, knowing not who has kindled it, nor whence it comes, nor how to escape it, nor how to put it out : if it seeks relief from the fire by spiritual reading, it cannot find any, just as if it could not read at all. On one occasion it occurred to me to read a life of a Saint, that I might forget myself, and be refreshed with the recital of what he had suffered. Four or five times I read as many lines ; and, though they were written in Spanish, I understood them less at the end than I did when I began : so I gave it up. It so happened to me on more occasions than one, but I have a more distinct recollection of this.

15. To converse with any one is worse, for the devil then sends so offensive a spirit of bad temper that I think I could eat people up ; nor can I help myself. I feel that I do something when I keep myself under control ; or rather our Lord does so, when He holds back with His hand any one in this state from saying or doing something that may be hurtful to his neighbours and offensive to God. Then,

[12] See ch. xxxii. 1, sqq.

as to going to our confessor, that is of no use ; for the certain result is—and very often has it happened to me—what I shall now describe. Though my confessors, with whom I had to do then, and have to do still, are so holy, they spoke to me and reproved me with such harshness that they were astonished at it afterwards when I told them of it. They said that they could not help themselves ; for, though they had resolved not to use such language, and though they pitied me also very much,—yea, even had scruples on the subject, because of my grievous trials of soul and body,—and were, moreover, determined to console me, they could not refrain. They did not use unbecoming words—I mean, words offensive to God ; yet their words were the most offensive that could be borne with in confession. They must have aimed at mortifying me. At other times I used to delight in this, and was prepared to bear it ; but it was then a torment altogether. I used to think, too, that I deceived them ; so I went to them, and cautioned them very earnestly to be on their guard against me, for it might be that I deceived them. I saw well enough that I would not do so advisedly, nor tell them an untruth ;[13] but everything made me afraid. One of them, on one occasion, when he had heard me speak of this temptation, told me not to distress myself ; for, even if I wished to deceive him, he had sense enough not to be deceived. This gave me great comfort.

16. Sometimes, almost always,—at least, very frequently,—I used to find rest after Communion ; now and then, even, as I drew near to the most Holy Sacrament, all at once my soul and body would be so well, that I was amazed.[14] It seemed to be nothing else but an instantaneous dispersion of the darkness that covered my soul : when the sun rose, I saw how silly I had been.

[13] See ch. xxviii. 6.
[14] See *Way of Perfection*, ch. xxxiv. 7.

17. On other occasions, if our Lord spoke to me but one word, saying only, "Be not distressed, have no fear,"—as I said before,[15]—I was made whole at once; or, if I saw a vision, I was as if I had never been amiss. I rejoiced in God, and made my complaint to Him, because He permitted me to undergo such afflictions; yet the recompense was great; for almost always, afterwards, His mercies descended upon me in great abundance. The soul seemed to come forth as gold out of the crucible, most refined, and made glorious to behold, our Lord dwelling within it. These trials afterwards are light, though they once seemed to be unendurable; and the soul longs to undergo them again, if that be more pleasing to our Lord. And though trials and persecutions increase, yet, if we bear them without offending our Lord, rejoicing in suffering for His sake, it will be all the greater gain: I, however, do not bear them as they ought to be borne, but rather in a most imperfect way. At other times, my trials came upon me —they come still—in another form; and then it seems to me as if the very possibility of thinking a good thought, or desiring the accomplishment of it, were utterly taken from me: both soul and body are altogether useless and a heavy burden. However, when I am in this state, I do not suffer from the other temptations and disquietudes, but only from a certain loathing of I know not what, and my soul finds pleasure in nothing.

18. I used to try exterior good works, in order to occupy myself partly by violence; and I know well how weak a soul is when grace is hiding itself. It did not distress me much, because the sight of my own meanness gave me some satisfaction. On other occasions I find myself unable to pray or to fix my thoughts with any distinctness upon God, or anything that is good, though I may be alone; but

[15] Ch. xx. 21, ch. xxv. 22, ch. xxvi. 3.

I have a sense that I know Him. It is the understanding and the imagination, I believe, which hurt me here ; for it seems to me that I have a good will, disposed for all good ; but the understanding is so lost, that it seems to be nothing else but a raving lunatic, which nobody can restrain, and of which I am not mistress enough to keep it quiet for a minute.[16]

19. Sometimes I laugh at myself, and recognise my wretchedness : I watch my understanding, and leave it alone to see what it will do. Glory be to God, for a wonder, it never runs on what is wrong, but only on indifferent things, considering what is going on here, or there, or elsewhere. I see then, more and more, the exceeding great mercy of our Lord to me, when He keeps this lunatic bound in the chains of perfect contemplation. I wonder what would happen if those people who think I am good knew of my extravagance. I am very sorry when I see my soul in such bad company ; I long to see it delivered therefrom, and so I say to our Lord : When, O my God, shall I see my whole soul praising Thee, that it may have the fruition of Thee in all its faculties ? Let me be no longer, O Lord, thus torn to pieces, and every one of them, as it were, running in a different direction. This has been often the case with me, but I think that my scanty bodily health was now and then enough to bring it about.

20. I dwell much on the harm which original sin has done us ; that is, I believe, what has rendered us incapable of the fruition of so great a good. My sins, too, must be in fault ; for, if I had not committed so many, I should have been more perfect in goodness. Another great affliction which I suffered was this : all the books which I read on the subject of prayer I thought I understood thoroughly, and that I required them no longer, because our Lord had given me the gift of prayer. I therefore ceased

[16] " Un Credo."

to read those books, and applied myself to lives of Saints, thinking that this would improve me and give me courage ; for I found myself very defective in every kind of service which the Saints rendered unto God. Then it struck me that I had very little humility, when I could think that I had attained to this degree of prayer ; and so, when I could not come to any other conclusion, I was greatly distressed, until certain learned persons, and the blessed friar, Peter of Alcantara, told me not to trouble myself about the matter.

21. I see clearly enough that I have not yet begun to serve God, though He showers down upon me those very graces which He gives to many good people. I am a mass of imperfection, except in desire and in love ; for herein I see well that our Lord has been gracious to me, in order that I may please Him in some measure. I really think that I love Him ; but my conduct, and the many imperfections I discern in myself, make me sad.

22. My soul, also, is subject occasionally to a certain foolishness,—that is the right name to give it,—when I seem to be doing neither good nor evil, but following in the wake of others, as they say, without pain or pleasure, indifferent to life and death, pleasure and pain. I seem to have no feeling. The soul seems to me like a little ass, which feeds and thrives, because it accepts the food which is given it, and eats it without reflection. The soul in this state must be feeding on some great mercies of God, seeing that its miserable life is no burden to it, and that it bears it patiently ; but it is conscious of no sensible movements or results, whereby it may ascertain the state it is in.

23. It seems to me now like sailing with a very gentle wind, when one makes much way without knowing how ; for in the other states so great are the effects that the soul sees almost at once an improvement in itself, because the desires instantly are

on fire, and the soul is never satisfied.   This comes from those great impetuosities of love, spoken of before,[17] in those to whom God grants them.   It is like those little wells I have seen flowing, wherein the upheaving of the sand never ceases.   This illustration and comparison seem to me to be a true description of those souls who attain to this state ;   their love is ever active, thinking what it may do ;   it cannot contain itself, as the water remains not in the earth, but is continually welling upwards.   So is the soul, in general ;   it is not at rest, nor can it contain itself, because of the love it has :   it is so saturated therewith that it would have others drink of it, because there is more than enough for itself, in order that they might help it to praise God.

24. I call to remembrance—oh, how often !—that living water of which our Lord spoke to the Samaritan woman.   That Gospel [18] has a great attraction for me ; and, indeed, so it had even when I was a little child, though I did not understand it then as I do now.   I used to pray much to our Lord for that living water ; and I had always a picture of it, representing our Lord at the well, with this inscription, " Domine, da miqui aquan." [19]

25. This love is also like a great fire, which requires fuel continually, in order that it may not burn out. So those souls I am speaking of, however much it may cost them, will always bring fuel, in order that the fire may not be quenched.   As for me, I should be glad, considering what I am, if I had but straw even to throw upon it.   And so it is with me occasionally—and, indeed, very often.   At one time, I laugh at myself ; and at another, I am very much distressed.

[17] Ch. xxix. 11.
[18] St. John iv. 5—42 : the Gospel of Friday after the Third Sunday in Lent, where the words are, " hanc aquam."
[19] " Lord, give me this water " (St. John iv. 15).   See ch. i. 6 ; and *Way of Perfection*, ch. xix. 4.   *Foundations*, xxxi. 42 ; *Interior Castle*, M. vi. ch. xi. 5.   The well in the convent of St. Joseph at Avila still bears the name given it by St. Teresa : the fountain of the Samaritan woman.

The inward stirring of my love urges me to do something for the service of God ; and I am not able to do more than adorn images with boughs and flowers, clean or arrange an oratory, or some such trifling acts, so that I am ashamed of myself. If I undertook any penitential practice, the whole was so slight, and was done in such a way, that if our Lord did not accept my good will, I saw it was all worthless, and so I laughed at myself. The failure of bodily strength, sufficient to do something for God, is no light affliction for those souls to whom He, in His goodness, has communicated this fire of His love in its fulness. It is a very good penance ; for when souls are not strong enough to heap fuel on this fire, and die of fear that the fire may go out, it seems to me that they become fuel themselves, are reduced to ashes, or dissolved in tears, and burn away : and this is suffering enough, though it be sweet.[20]

26. Let him, then, praise our Lord exceedingly, who has attained to this state ; who has received the bodily strength requisite for penance ; who has learning, ability, and power to preach, to hear confessions, and to draw souls unto God. Such a one neither knows nor comprehends the blessing he possesses, unless he knows by experience what it is to be powerless to serve God in anything, and at the same time to be receiving much from Him. May He be blessed for ever, and may the angels glorify Him ! Amen.

27. I know not if I do well to write so much in detail. But as you, my father, bade me again not to be troubled by the minuteness of my account, nor to omit anything, I go on recounting clearly and truly all I can call to mind. But I must omit much ; for if I did not, I should have to spend more time— and, as I said before,[21] I have so little to spend, and perhaps, after all, nothing will be gained.

[20] Ch. xv. 11, xxxi. 25.   [21] Ch. xiv. 12.

CHAPTER XXXI.

OF CERTAIN OUTWARD TEMPTATIONS AND APPEARANCES
OF SATAN.   OF THE SUFFERINGS THEREBY OCCA-
SIONED.   COUNSELS FOR THOSE WHO GO ON UNTO
PERFECTION.

*She speaks of some exterior temptations and appari-
tions of Satan, and how he ill-treated her.   She mentions,
moreover, some very good things by way of advice to
persons who are walking on the way of perfection.*

1. Now that I have described certain temptations
and troubles, interior and secret, of which Satan
was the cause, I will speak of others which he wrought
almost in public, and in which his presence could not
be ignored.[1]

2. I was once in an oratory, when Satan, in an
abominable shape, appeared on my left hand. I
looked at his mouth in particular, because he spoke,
and it was horrible. A huge flame seemed to issue
out of his body, perfectly bright, without any shadow.
He spoke in a fearful way, and said to me that, though
I had escaped out of his hands, he would yet lay hold
of me again. I was in great terror, made the sign of
the cross as well as I could, and then the form vanished—but it reappeared instantly. This occurred
twice. I did not know what to do ; there was some
holy water at hand ; I took some, and threw it in
the direction of the figure, and then Satan never
returned.

3. On another occasion I was tortured for five
hours with such terrible pains, such inward and
outward sufferings, that it seemed to me as if I could
not bear them. Those who were with me were frightened ; they knew not what to do, and I could not

---

[1] 2 Cor. ii. 11 : " Non enim ignoramus cogitationes ejus."

help myself. I am in the habit, when these pains and my bodily suffering are most unendurable, to make interior acts as well as I can, imploring our Lord, if it be His will, to give me patience, and then to let me suffer on, even to the end of the world. So, when I found myself suffering so cruelly, I relieved myself by making those acts and resolutions, in order that I might be able to endure the pain. It pleased our Lord to let me understand that it was the work of Satan; for I saw close beside me a most frightful little negro, gnashing his teeth in despair at losing what he attempted to seize. When I saw him, I laughed, and had no fear; for there were some then present who were helpless, and knew of no means whereby so great a pain could be relieved. My body, head, and arms were violently shaken; I could not help myself: but the worst of all was the interior pain, for I could find no ease in any way. Nor did I dare to ask for holy water, lest those who were with me should be afraid, and find out what the matter really was.

4. I know by frequent experience that there is nothing which puts the devils to flight like holy water. They run away before the sign of the cross also, but they return immediately: great, then, must be the power of holy water. As for me, my soul is conscious of a special and most distinct consolation whenever I take it. Indeed, I feel almost always a certain refreshing, which I cannot describe, together with an inward joy, which comforts my whole soul. This is no fancy, nor a thing which has occurred once only; for it has happened very often, and I have watched it very carefully. I may compare what I feel with that which happens to a person in great heat, and very thirsty, drinking a cup of cold water—his whole being is refreshed. I consider that everything ordained by the Church is very important; and I have a joy in reflecting that the words of the

Church are so mighty, that they endow water with power, so that there shall be so great a difference between holy water and water that has never been blessed. Then, as my pains did not cease, I told them, if they would not laugh, I would ask for some holy water. They brought me some, and sprinkled me with it ; but I was no better. I then threw some myself in the direction of the negro, when he fled in a moment. All my sufferings ceased, just as if some one had taken them from me with his hand ; only I was wearied, as if I had been beaten with many blows. It was of great service to me to learn that if, by our Lord's permission, Satan can do so much evil to a soul and body not in his power, he can do much more when he has them in his possession. It gave me a renewed desire to be delivered from a fellowship so dangerous.

5. Another time, and not long ago, the same thing happened to me, though it did not last so long, and I was alone at the moment. I asked for holy water ; and they who came in after the devil had gone away,—they were two nuns, worthy of all credit, and would not tell a lie for anything,—perceived a most offensive smell, like that of brimstone. I smelt nothing myself ; but the odour lasted long enough to become sensible to them.

6. On another occasion I was in choir when, in a moment, I became profoundly recollected. I went out in order that the sisters might know nothing of it ; yet those who were near heard the sound of heavy blows where I was, and I heard voices myself, as of persons in consultation, but I did not hear what they said : I was so absorbed in prayer that I understood nothing, neither was I at all afraid. This took place almost always when our Lord was pleased that some soul or other, persuaded by me, advanced in the spiritual life. Certainly, what I am now about to describe happened to me once ; there are witnesses

to testify to it, particularly my present confessor,[2] for he saw the account in a letter. I did not tell him from whom the letter came, but he knew perfectly who the person was.

7. There came to me a person who, for two years and a half, had been living in mortal sin of the most abominable nature I ever heard. During the whole of that time he neither confessed it nor ceased from it ; and yet he said Mass. He confessed his other sins ; but of this one he used to say, How can I confess so foul a sin ? He wished to give it up, but he could not prevail on himself to do so. I was very sorry for him, and it was a great grief to me to see God offended in such a way. I promised him that I would pray to God for his amendment, and get others who were better than I to do the same. I wrote to one person, and the priest undertook to get the letter delivered. It came to pass that he made a full confession at the first opportunity ; for our Lord was pleased, on account of the prayers of those most holy persons to whom I had recommended him, to have pity on this soul. I, too, wretched as I am, did all I could for the same end.

8. He wrote to me, and said that he was so far improved that he had not for some days repeated his sin ; but he was so tormented by the temptation that it seemed to him as if he were in hell already, so great were his sufferings. He asked me to pray to God for him. I recommended him to my sisters, through whose prayers I must have obtained this mercy from our Lord ; for they took the matter greatly to heart ; and he was a person whom no one could find out. I implored His Majesty to put an end to these torments and temptations, and to let the evil spirits torment me instead, provided I did not offend our Lord. Thus it was that for one month

---

[2] Either Father Dominic Bañez or F. Garcia de Toledo, who were her confessors at St. Joseph's, Avila, between 1563 and 1565.

I was most grievously tormented ; and then it was that these two assaults of Satan, of which I have just spoken, took place.

9. Our Lord was pleased to deliver him out of this temptation, so I was informed ; for I told him what happened to myself that month. His soul gained strength, and he continued free ; he could never give thanks enough to our Lord and to me as if I had been of any service—unless it be that the belief he had that our Lord granted me such graces was of some advantage to him. He said that, when he saw himself in great straits, he would read my letters, and then the temptation left him. He was very much astonished at my sufferings, and at the manner of his own deliverance : even I myself am astonished, and I would suffer as much for many years for the deliverance of that soul. May our Lord be praised for ever ! for the prayers of those who serve Him can do great things ; and I believe the sisters of this house do serve Him. The devils must have been more angry with me only because I asked them to pray, and because our Lord permitted it on account of my sins. At that time, too, I thought the evil spirits would have suffocated me one night, and when the sisters threw much holy water about I saw a great troop of them rush away as if tumbling over a precipice. These cursed spirits have tormented me so often, and I am now so little afraid of them,— because I see they cannot stir without our Lord's permission,—that I should weary both you, my father, and myself, if I were to speak of these things in detail.

10. May this I have written be of use to the true servant of God, who ought to despise these terrors, which Satan sends only to make him afraid ! Let him understand that each time we despise these terrors, their force is lessened, and the soul gains power over them. There is always some great good

obtained ; but I will not speak of it, that I may not be too diffuse. I will speak, however, of what happened to me once on the night of All Souls. I was in an oratory, and, having said one Nocturn, was saying some very devotional prayers at the end of our Breviary, when Satan put himself on the book before me, to prevent my finishing my prayer. I made the sign of the cross, and he went away. I then returned to my prayer, and he, too, came back ; he did so, I believe, three times, and I was not able to finish the prayer without throwing holy water at him. I saw certain souls at that moment come forth out of purgatory—they must have been near their deliverance, and I thought that Satan might in this way have been trying to hinder their release. It is very rarely that I saw Satan assume a bodily form ; I know of his presence through the vision I have spoken of before,[3] the vision wherein no form is seen.

11. I wish also to relate what follows, for I was greatly alarmed at it : on Trinity Sunday, in the choir of a certain monastery, and in a trance, I saw a great fight between evil spirits and the angels. I could not make out what the vision meant. In less than a fortnight it was explained clearly enough by the dispute that took place between persons given to prayer and many who were not, which did great harm to that house ; for it was a dispute that lasted long and caused much trouble.[4] On another occasion I saw a great multitude of evil spirits round about me, and, at the same time, a great light, in which I was enveloped, which kept them from coming near me. I understood it to mean that God was watching over me, that they might not approach me so as to make me offend Him. I knew the vision was real by what I saw occasionally in myself. The fact is, I know now how little power the evil spirits have, provided I am not out of the grace of God ; I have

---

[3] Ch. xxvii. 4.   [4] See ch. xxxii. 17.

scarcely any fear of them at all, for their strength is as nothing, if they do not find the souls they assail give up the contest and become cowards ; it is in this case that they show their power.

12. Now and then, during the temptations I am speaking of, it seemed to me as if all my vanity and weakness in times past had become alive again within me ; so I had reason enough to commit myself into the hands of God. Then I was tormented by the thought that, as these things came back to my memory, I must be utterly in the power of Satan, until my confessor consoled me ; for I imagined that even the first movement towards an evil thought ought not to have come near one who had received from our Lord such great graces as I had.

13. At other times I was much tormented—and even now I am tormented—when I saw people make much of me, particularly great people, and when they spake well of me. I have suffered, and still suffer, much in this way. I think at once of the life of Christ and of the Saints, and then my life seems the reverse of theirs, for they received nothing but contempt and ill-treatment. All this makes me afraid ; I dare not lift up my head, and I wish nobody saw me at all. It is not thus with me when I am persecuted ; then my soul is so conscious of strength, though the body suffers, and though I am in other ways afflicted, that I do not know how this can be ; but so it is,—and my soul seems then to be a queen in its kingdom, having everything under its feet.

14. I had such a thought now and then—and, indeed, for many days together. I regarded it as a sign of virtue and of humility ; but I see clearly now it was nothing else but a temptation. A Dominican friar, of great learning, showed it to me very plainly. When I considered that the graces which our Lord had bestowed upon me might come to the knowledge of the public, my sufferings became so excessive as

greatly to disturb my soul. They went so far that I made up my mind, while thinking of it, that I would rather be buried alive than have these things known. And so, when I began to be profoundly recollected, or to fall into a trance, which I could not resist even in public, I was so ashamed of myself that I would not appear where people might see me.

15. Once, when I was much distressed at this, our Lord said to me, What was I afraid of ? one of two things must happen—people would either speak ill of me or give glory to Him. He made me understand by this that those who believed in the truth of what was going on in me would glorify Him ; and that those who did not would condemn me without cause : in both ways I should be the gainer, and I was therefore not to distress myself.[5] This made me quite calm, and it comforts me whenever I think of it.

16. This temptation became so excessive that I wished to leave the house, and take my dower to another monastery, where enclosure was more strictly observed than in that wherein I was at this time.[6] I had heard great things of that other house, which was of the same Order as mine ; it was also at a great distance, and it would have been a great consolation to me to live where I was not known ; but my confessor would never let me go. These fears deprived me in a great measure of all liberty of spirit ; and I understood afterwards that this was not true humility, because it disturbed me so much. And our Lord taught me this truth ; if I was convinced, and certainly persuaded, that all that was good in me came wholly and only from God, and if it did not distress me to hear the praises of others,—yea,

[5] See *Interior Castle*, M. vi. ch. iv. 21.

[6] It is not known which convent of nuns the Saint thought of joining. Some (F. Frederic of St. Anthony, whose opinion the French Carmelites seem to share) thought of a convent in the Netherlands, or the one near Nantes, founded by Blessed Frances d'Amboise, but it may have been one of the Spanish convents.

rather, if I was pleased and comforted when I saw that God was working in them,—then neither should I be distressed if He showed forth His works in me.

17. I fell, too, into another extreme. I begged of God, and made it a particular subject of prayer, that it might please His Majesty, whenever any one saw any good in me, that such a one might also become acquainted with my sins, in order that he might see that His graces were bestowed on me without any merit on my part : and I always greatly desire this. My confessor told me not to do it. But almost to this day, if I saw that any one thought well of me, I used in a roundabout way, or any how, as I could, to contrive he should know of my sins [7] : that seemed to relieve me. But they have made me very scrupulous on this point. This, it appears to me, was not an effect of humility, but oftentimes the result of temptation. It seemed to me that I was deceiving everybody—though, in truth, they deceived themselves, by thinking that there was any good in me.[8] I did not wish to deceive them, nor did I ever attempt it, only our Lord permitted it for some end ; and so, even with my confessors, I never discussed any of these matters if I did not see the necessity of it, for that would have occasioned very considerable scruples.

18. All these little fears and distresses and semblance of humility I now see clearly were mere imperfections, and the result of my unmortified life ; for a soul left in the hands of God cares nothing about evil or good report, if it clearly comprehends, when our Lord is pleased to bestow upon it His grace, that it has nothing of its own. Let it trust the Giver ; it will know hereafter why He reveals His gifts, and prepare itself for persecution, which in these times is sure to come, when it is our Lord's will that it should be known of any one that He bestows upon him graces

---

[7] *Way of Perfection*, ch. xxxvi. 8.
[8] See ch. x. 10.

such as these ; for a thousand eyes are watching that
soul, while a thousand souls of another order are
observed of none. In truth, there was no little
ground for fear, and that fear should have been mine :
I was therefore not humble, but a coward ; for a
soul which God permits to be thus seen of men may
well prepare itself to be the world's martyr—because,
if it will not die to the world voluntarily, that very
world will kill it.

19. Certainly I see nothing in the world that seems
to me good except this, that it tolerates no faults in
good people, and helps them to perfection by dint of
complaints against them. I mean, that it requires
greater courage in one not yet perfect to walk in the
way of perfection than to undergo an instant martyrdom ; for perfection is not attained to at once, unless
our Lord grant that grace by a special privilege ; yet
the world, when it sees any one beginning to travel
on that road, insists on his becoming perfect at once,
and a thousand leagues off detects in him a fault,
which after all may be a virtue. He who finds fault
is doing the very same thing,—but, in his own case,
viciously,—and he pronounces it to be so wrong in
the other. He who aims at perfection, then, must
neither eat nor sleep,- –nor, as they say, even breathe ;
and the more men respect such a one, the more do
they forget that he is still in the body ; and, though
they may consider him perfect, he is living on the
earth, subject to its miseries, however much he may
tread them under his feet. And so, as I have just
said, great courage is necessary here ; for, though
the poor soul have not yet begun to walk, the world
will have it fly ; and, though its passions be not
wholly overcome, men will have it that they must be
under restraint, even upon trying occasions, as those
of the Saints are, of whom they read, after they are
confirmed in grace.

20. All this is a reason for praising God, and also

for great sorrow of heart, because very many go backwards who, poor souls, know not how to help themselves ; and I too, I believe, would have gone back also if our Lord had not so mercifully on His part done everything for me. And until He, of His goodness, had done all, nothing was done by me, as you, my father, may have seen already, beyond falling and rising again. I wish I knew how to explain it, because many souls, I believe, delude themselves in this matter ; they would fly before God gives them wings.

21. I believe I have made this comparison on another occasion,[9] but it is to the purpose here, for I see certain souls are very greatly afflicted on that ground. When these souls begin, with great fervour, courage, and desire, to advance in virtue,—some of them at least outwardly, giving up all for God,— when they see in others, more advanced than themselves, greater fruits of virtue given them by our Lord,—for we cannot acquire these of ourselves,— when they see in all the books written on prayer and on contemplation an account of what we have to do in order to attain thereto, but which they cannot accomplish themselves,—they lose heart. For instance, they read that we must not be troubled when men speak ill of us, that we are to be then more pleased than when they speak well of us ; that we must despise our own good name, be detached from our kindred, avoid their company, which should be wearisome to us, unless they be given to prayer ; with many other things of the same kind. The disposition to practise this must be, in my opinion, the gift of God ; for it seems to me a supernatural good, contrary to our natural inclinations. Let them not distress themselves ; let them trust in our Lord : what they now desire His Majesty will enable them to attain to by prayer, and by doing what they can

[9] Ch. xiii. 3.

themselves ; for it is very necessary for our weak nature that we should have great confidence, that we should not be faint-hearted, nor suppose that, if we do our best, we shall fail to obtain the victory at last. And as my experience here is large, I will say, by way of caution to you, my father, do not think—though it may seem so—that a virtue is acquired when we have not tested it by its opposing vice : we must always be suspicious of ourselves, and never negligent while we live ; for much evil clings to us if, as I said before,[10] grace be not given to us fully to understand what everything is : and in this life there is nothing without great risks.

22. I thought a few years ago, not only that I was detached from my kindred, but that they were a burden to me ; and certainly it was so, for I could not endure their conversation. An affair of some importance had to be settled, and I had to remain with a sister of mine,[11] for whom I had always before had a great affection. The conversation we had together, though she is better than I am, did not please me ; for it could not always be on subjects I preferred, owing to the difference of our conditions— she being married. I was therefore as much alone as I could ; yet I felt that her troubles gave me more trouble than did those of my neighbours, and even some anxiety. In short, I found out that I was not so detached as I thought, and that it was necessary for me to flee from dangerous occasions, in order that the virtue which our Lord had begun to implant in me might grow ; and so, by His help, I have striven to do from that time till now.

23. If our Lord bestows any virtue upon us, we must make much of it, and by no means run the risk of losing it ; so it is in those things which concern

---

[10] Ch. xx. 38.
[11] Probably Doña Juana de Ahumada, wife of Juan de Ovalle, with whom the Saint lived for some time previous to the foundation of St. Joseph's.

our good name, and many other matters. You, my father, must believe that we are not all of us detached, though we think we are ; it is necessary for us never to be careless on this point. If any one detects in himself any tenderness about his good name, and yet wishes to advance in the spiritual life, let him believe me and throw this embarrassment behind his back, for it is a chain which no file can sever ; only the help of God, obtained by prayer and much striving on his part, can do it.[12]   It seems to me to be a hindrance on the road, and I am astonished at the harm it does. I see some persons so holy in their works, and they are so great as to fill people with wonder   O my God, why is their soul still on the earth ? Why has it not arrived at the summit of perfection ? What does it mean ? What keeps him back who does so much for God ? Oh, there it is !—self-respect ! and the worst of it is, that these persons will not admit that they have it, merely because Satan now and then convinces them that they are under an obligation to observe it.

24. Well, then, let them believe me : for the love of our Lord, let them give heed to the little ant, who speaks because it is His pleasure. If they take not this caterpillar away, though it does not hurt the whole tree, because some virtues remain, the worm will eat into every one of them. Not only is the tree not beautiful, but it also never thrives, neither does it suffer the others near it to thrive ; for the fruit of good example which it bears is not sound, and endures but a short time. I say it again and again, let our self-respect be ever so slight, it will have the same result as the missing of a note on the organ when it is played,—the whole music is out of tune. It is a thing which hurts the soul exceedingly in every way, but it is a pestilence in the way of prayer.

25. Are we striving after union with God ? and

[12] *Interior Castle*, M, i. ch, ii, 19,

do we wish to follow the counsels of Christ,—Who was
loaded with reproaches and falsely accused,—and at
the same time to keep our own reputation and credit
untouched ? We cannot succeed, for these things are
inconsistent one with another. Our Lord comes to
the soul when we do violence to ourselves, and strive
to give up our rights in many things. Some will
say, I have nothing that I can give up, nor have I
any opportunity of doing so. I believe that our
Lord will never suffer any one who has made so good
a resolution as this to miss so great a blessing. His
Majesty will make so many arrangements for him,
whereby he may acquire this virtue,—more frequently,
perhaps, than he will like. Let him put his hand
to the work. I speak of the little nothings and trifles
which I gave up when I began—or at least of some
of them : the straws which I said [13] I threw into the
fire ; for I am not able to do more. All this our
Lord accepted : may He be blessed for evermore !

26. One of my faults was this : I had a very
imperfect knowledge of my Breviary and of my
duties in choir, simply because I was careless and
given to vanities ; and I knew the other novices could
have taught me. But I never asked them, that they
might not know how little I knew. It suggested itself
to me at once that I ought to set a good example :
this is very common. Now, however, that God has
opened my eyes a little, even when I know a thing,
but yet am very slightly in doubt about it, I ask the
children. I have lost neither honour nor credit by
it—on the contrary, I believe our Lord has been
pleased to strengthen my memory. My singing of
the Office was bad, and I felt it much if I had not
learned the part entrusted to me,—not because I
made mistakes before our Lord, which would have
been a virtue, but because I made them before the
many nuns who heard me. I was so full of my own

[13] Ch. xv. 11 ; xxx. 25.

reputation that I was disturbed, and therefore did not sing what I had to sing even so well as I might have done. Afterwards I ventured, when I did not know it very well, to say so. At first I felt it very much; but afterwards I found pleasure in doing it. So, when I began to be indifferent about its being known that I could not sing well, it gave me no pain at all, and I sang much better. This miserable self-esteem took from me the power of doing that which I regarded as an honour, for every one regards as honourable that which he likes.

27. By trifles such as these, which are nothing,— and I am altogether nothing myself, seeing that this gave me pain,—by little and little, doing such actions, and by such slight performances,—they become of worth because done for God,—His Majesty helps us on towards greater things; and so it happened to me in the matter of humility. When I saw that all the nuns except myself were making great progress, —I was always myself good for nothing,—I used to fold up their mantles when they left the choir. I looked on myself as doing service to angels who had been there praising God. I did so till they—I know not how—found it out; and then I was not a little ashamed, because my virtue was not strong enough to bear that they should know of it. But the shame arose, not because I was humble, but because I was afraid they would laugh at me, the matter being so trifling.

28. O Lord, what a shame for me to lay bare so much wickedness, and to number these grains of sand, which yet I did not raise up from the ground in Thy service without mixing them with a thousand meannesses! The waters of Thy grace were not as yet flowing beneath them, so as to make them ascend upwards. O my Creator, oh, that I had anything worth recounting amid so many evil things, when I am recounting the great mercies I received at Thy

hands! So it is, O my Lord. I know not how my
heart could have borne it, nor how any one who shall
read this can help having me in abhorrence when he
sees that mercies so great had been so ill-requited,
and that I have not been ashamed to speak of these
services. Ah! they are only mine, O my Lord;
but I am ashamed I have nothing else to say of myself;
and that it is that makes me speak of these wretched
beginnings, in order that he who has begun more
nobly may have hope that our Lord, who has made
much of mine, will make more of his. May it please
His Majesty to give me this grace, that I may not
remain for ever at the beginning! Amen.

CHAPTER XXXII.

OUR LORD SHOWS ST. TERESA THE PLACE WHICH SHE
    HAD BY HER SINS DESERVED IN HELL. THE TOR-
    MENTS THERE. HOW THE MONASTERY OF ST.
    JOSEPH WAS FOUNDED.

*She narrates how it pleased God to put her in spirit
in that place of hell she had deserved by her sins. She
tells a little [una cifra = a mere nothing] compared with
what there was besides of what she saw there. She begins
to speak of the manner and way of founding the convent
of St. Joseph, where she now lives.*

1. SOME considerable time after our Lord had bestowed upon me the graces I have been describing,
and others also of a higher nature, I was one day in
prayer when I found myself in a moment, without
knowing how, plunged apparently into hell. I understood that it was our Lord's will I should see the place
which the devils kept in readiness for me, and which

I had deserved by my sins.[1] It was but a moment, but it seems to me impossible I should ever forget it, even if I were to live many years.

2. The entrance seemed to be by a long narrow pass, like a furnace, very low, dark, and close. The ground seemed to be saturated with water, mere mud, exceedingly foul, sending forth pestilential odours, and covered with loathsome vermin. At the end was a hollow place in the wall, like a closet, and in that I saw myself confined. All this was even pleasant to behold in comparison with what I felt there. There is no exaggeration in what I am saying.

3. But as to what I then felt, I do not know where to begin, if I were to describe it ; it is utterly inexplicable. I felt a fire in my soul. I cannot see how it is possible to describe it. My bodily sufferings were unendurable. I have undergone most painful sufferings in this life, and, as the physicians say, the greatest that can be borne, such as the contraction of my sinews when I was paralysed,[2] without speaking of others of different kinds, yea, even those of which I have also spoken,[3] inflicted on me by Satan ; yet all these were as nothing in comparison with what I felt then, especially when I saw that there would be no intermission, nor any end to them.

4. These sufferings were nothing in comparison with the anguish of my soul, a sense of oppression, of stifling, and of pain so keen, accompanied by so hopeless and cruel an infliction, that I know not how to speak of it. If I said that the soul is continually being torn from the body it would be nothing,—for that implies the destruction of life by the hands of another ; but here it is the soul itself that is tearing

---

[1] *Way of Perfection*, ch. xiii. 2.—As Ribera remarks, it does not follow from this passage that St. Teresa had ever committed a mortal sin—and thereby deserved hell—as there is abundant evidence even from her own words that she never had such a misfortune, but only that she would have fallen into grievous sins if she had not mended her life.

[2] See ch. v. 14 ; ch. vi. 1.   [3] Ch. xxxi. 3.

itself in pieces. I cannot describe that inward fire or that despair, surpassing all torments and all pain. I did not see who it was that tormented me, but I felt myself on fire, and torn to pieces, as it seemed to me; and, I repeat it, this inward fire and despair are the greatest torments of all.

5. Left in that pestilential place, and utterly without the power to hope for comfort, I could neither sit nor lie down : there was no room. I was placed as it were in a hole in the wall ; and those walls, terrible to look on of themselves, hemmed me in on every side. I could not breathe. There was no light, but all was thick darkness. I do not understand how it is ; though there was no light, yet everything that can give pain by being seen was visible.

6. Our Lord at that time would not let me see more of hell. Afterwards I had another most fearful vision, in which I saw the punishment of certain sins. They were most horrible to look at ; but, because I felt none of the pain, my terror was not so great. In the former vision our Lord made me really feel those torments, and that anguish of spirit, just as if I had been suffering them in the body there. I know not how it was, but I understood distinctly that it was a great mercy that our Lord would have me see with mine own eyes the very place from which His compassion saved me. I have listened to people speaking of these things, and I have at other times dwelt on the various torments of hell, though not often, because my soul made no progress by the way of fear ; and I have read of the diverse tortures, and how the devils tear the flesh with red-hot pincers. But all is as nothing before this ; it is a wholly different matter. In short, the one is a reality, the other a picture ; and all burning here in this life is as nothing in comparison with the fire that is there.

7. I was so terrified by that vision,—and that terror is on me even now while I am writing,—that

though it took place nearly six years ago,[4] the natural warmth of my body is chilled by fear even now when I think of it. And so, amid all the pain and suffering which I may have had to bear, I remember no time in which I do not think that all we have to suffer in this world is as nothing. It seems to me that we complain without reason. I repeat it, this vision was one of the grandest mercies of our Lord. It has been to me of the greatest service, because it has destroyed my fear of trouble and of the contradiction of the world, and because it has made me strong enough to bear up against them, and to give thanks to our Lord, who has been my Deliverer, as it now seems to me, from such fearful and everlasting pains.

8. Ever since that time, as I was saying, everything seems endurable in comparison with one instant of suffering such as those I had then to bear in hell. I am filled with fear when I see that, after frequently reading books which describe in some manner the pains of hell, I was not afraid of them, nor made any account of them. Where was I ? How could I possibly take any pleasure in those things which led me directly to so dreadful a place ? Blessed for ever be Thou, O my God ! and, oh, how manifest is it that Thou didst love me much more than I did love Thee ! How often, O Lord, didst Thou save me from that fearful prison ! and how I used to get back to it contrary to Thy will.

9. It was that vision that filled me with the very great distress which I feel at the sight of so many lost souls, especially of the Lutherans,—for they were once members of the Church by baptism,—and also gave me the most vehement desires for the salvation of souls ; for certainly I believe that, to save even one from those overwhelming torments, I would most

[4] Writing at the beginning of 1565, the vision must have taken place about 1559.

willingly endure many deaths. If here on earth we
see one whom we specially love in great trouble or
pain, our very nature seems to bid us compassionate
him ; and if those pains be great, we are troubled
ourselves. What, then, must it be to see a soul in
danger of pain, the most grievous of all pains, for
ever ? ; Who can endure it ? It is a thought no
heart can bear without great anguish. Here we
know that pain ends with life at last, and that there
are limits to it ; yet the sight of it moves our compassion so greatly. That other pain has no ending ;
and I know not how we can be calm, when we see
Satan carry so many souls daily away.

10. This also makes me wish that, in a matter
which concerns us so much, we did not rest satisfied
with doing less than we can do on our part,—that
we left nothing undone. May our Lord vouchsafe to
give us His grace for that end ! When I consider
that, notwithstanding my very great wickedness, I
took some pains to please God, and abstained from
certain things which I know the world makes light of,
—that, in short, I suffered grievous infirmities, and
with great patience, which our Lord gave me ; that
I was not inclined to murmur or to speak ill of anybody ; that I could not—I believe so—wish harm to
any one ; that I was not, to the best of my recollection,
either avaricious or envious, so as to be grievously
offensive in the sight of God ; and that I was free
from many other faults,—for, though so wicked, I
had lived constantly in the fear of God,—I had to
look at the very place which the devils kept ready for
me. It is true that, considering my faults, I had
deserved a still heavier chastisement ; but for all
that, I repeat it, the torment was fearful, and we
run a great risk whenever we please ourselves. No
soul should take either rest or pleasure that is liable
to fall every moment into mortal sin. Let us, then,
for the love of God, avoid all occasions of sin, and

our Lord will help us, as He has helped me. May if please His Majesty never to let me out of His hands, lest I should turn back and fall, now that I have seen the place where I must dwell if I do. I entreat our Lord, for His Majesty's sake, never to permit it. Amen.

11. When I had seen this vision, and had learned other great and hidden things which our Lord, of His goodness, was pleased to show me,—namely, the joy of the blessed and the torment of the wicked,—I longed for the way and the means of doing penance for the great evil I had done, and of meriting in some degree, so that I might gain so great a good ; and therefore I wished to avoid all society, and to withdraw myself utterly from the world. I was in spirit restless, yet my restlessness was not harassing, but rather pleasant. I saw clearly that it was the work of God, and that His Majesty had furnished my soul with fervour, so that I might be able to digest other and stronger food than I had been accustomed to eat. I tried to think what I could do for God, and thought that the first thing was to follow my vocation to a religious life, which His Majesty had given me, by keeping my rule in the greatest perfection possible.

12. Though in that house in which I then lived there were many servants of God, and God was greatly served therein, yet, because it was very poor, the nuns left it very often and went to other places, where, however, we could serve God in all honour and observances of religion. The rule also was kept, not in its original exactness, but according to the custom of the whole Order, authorised by the Bull of Mitigation.[5] There were other inconveniences also : we had too many comforts, as it seemed to me ; for the house was large and pleasant. But this inconvenience of going out, though it was I that took most advantage of it, was a very grievous one for me ; for many

[5] Bull of Eugenius IV., dated Feb. 15, 1432 (Bullar, Carmelit. i. 182).

persons, to whom my superiors could not say no, were glad to have me with them. My superiors, thus importuned, commanded me to visit these persons ; and thus it was so arranged that I could not be long together in the monastery. Satan, too, must have had a share in this, in order that I might not be in the house, where I was of great service to those of my sisters to whom I continually communicated the instructions which I received from my confessors.

13. It occurred once to a person with whom I was speaking to say to me and the others that it was possible to find means for the foundation of a monastery, if we were prepared to become nuns like those of the Barefooted Orders.[6] I, having this desire, began to discuss the matter with that widowed lady who was my companion,—I have spoken of her before,[7] —and she had the same wish that I had. She began to consider how to provide a revenue for the home. I see now that this was not the way,—only the wish we had to do so made us think it was ; but I, on the other hand, seeing that I took the greatest delight in the house in which I was then living, because it was very pleasant to me, and, in my own cell, most convenient for my purpose, still held back. Nevertheless, we agreed to commit the matter with all earnestness to God.

14. One day, after Communion, our Lord commanded me to labour with all my might for this end. He made me great promises,—that the monastery would be certainly built ; that He would take great delight therein ; that it should be called St. Joseph's ; that St. Joseph would keep guard at one door, and our Lady at the other ; that Christ would be in the midst of us ; that the monastery would be a star

---

[6] This was said by Maria de Ocampo, niece of St. Teresa, then living in the monastery of the Incarnation as a pensioner ; afterwards she became Prioress of the Carmelites at Valladolid under the name of Maria Bautista.

[7] Ch. xxiv. 5. Doña Guiomar de Ulloa

shining in great splendour ; that, though the religious
Orders were then relaxed, I was not to suppose that
He was scantily served in them,—for what would
become of the world, if there were no religious in it ?—
I was to tell my confessor what He commanded me,
and that He asked him not to oppose nor thwart me
in the matter.

15. So efficacious was the vision, and such was
the nature of the words our Lord spoke to me, that
I could not possibly doubt that they came from Him.
I suffered most keenly, because I saw in part the
great anxieties and troubles that the work would
cost me, and I was also very happy in the house I
was in then ; and though I used to speak of this
matter in past times, yet it was not with resolution
nor with any confidence that the thing could ever
be done. I saw that I was now in a great strait ;
and when I saw that I was entering on a work of
great anxiety, I hesitated ; but our Lord spoke of
it so often to me, and set before me so many reasons
and motives, which I saw could not be gainsaid,—I
saw, too, that such was His will ; so I did not dare
do otherwise than put the whole matter before my
confessor, and give him an account in writing of all
that took place.

16. My confessor did not venture definitely to
bid me abandon my purpose ; but he saw that naturally there was no way of carrying it out ; because
my friend, who was to do it, had very little or no
means available for that end. He told me to lay the
matter before my superior,[8] and do what he might

---

[8] This was not Fray Angel de Salazar, as all previous editors and biographers of the Saint have asserted, for at the General Chapter of May,
1564, he had not yet fulfilled his three years' tenure of office, as results from
the Acts of the chapter. The Provincial who in 1560 first gave his consent
to the foundation, and afterwards withdrew it, was his predecessor, Gregorio
Fernandez. He appears as simple religious of Avila in 1531 and again in
1537, as prior of the same house in 1541, as conventual in 1547, vicar 1548,
provincial 1551, 1552, and 1553, and again in 1559, 1560, and probably
during the greater part of 1561. See note to ch. xxxviii. 34.

bid me do.   I never spoke of my visions to my superior, but that lady who desired to found the monastery communicated with him.   The Provincial was very much pleased, for he loves the whole Order, gave her every help that was necessary, and promised to acknowledge the house.   Then there was a discussion about the revenues of the monastery, and for many reasons we never would allow more than thirteen sisters together.[9]   Before we began our arrangements we wrote to the holy friar, Peter of Alcantara, telling him all that was taking place ;   and he advised us not to abandon our work, and gave us his sanction on all points.

17.   As soon as the affair began to be known here there fell upon us a violent persecution, which cannot be very easily described—sharp sayings and keen jests.   People said it was folly in me, who was so well off in my convent ;   as to my friend, the persecution was so continuous that it wearied her.   I did not know what to do, and I thought that people were partly in the right.   When I was thus heavily afflicted, I commended myself to God, and His Majesty began to console and encourage me.   He told me that I could then see what the Saints had to go through who founded the religious Orders :   that I had much heavier persecutions to endure than I could imagine, but I was not to mind them.   He told me also what I was to say to my friend ;   and what surprised me most

[9] The Saint appears to have changed her mind several times about the number of sisters to be admitted into the convent.   Here, as well as in ch. xxxvi.19, they were to be thirteen, *i.e.* twelve sisters and the prioress, but in her letter to her brother, Don Lorenzo de Cepeda (December 30, 1561), she speaks of fifteen.   The General John Baptiste Rubeo, in his patent of April 27, 1567, allowed twenty-five, but in letters of Oct. 19, 1569 and Jan. 17, 1570 St. Teresa says there should be not more than thirteen nuns in each convent ;   however, on Sept. 2, 1571, the apostolic visitor, Fr. Pedro Hernandez, Dominican, ruled that the number of choir sisters in unendowed convents should not go beyond thirteen or fourteen, in endowed houses twenty ;   and on July 16, 1574, St. Teresa expresses a wish that he should also make some rule about lay sisters.   Their number was finally limited to three.

was that we were consoled at once as to the past, and resolved to withstand everybody courageously. And so it came to pass ; for among people of prayer, and indeed in the whole neighbourhood, there was hardly one who was not against us, and who did not think our work the greatest folly.

18. There was so much talking and confusion in the very convent wherein I was that the Provincial began to think it hard for him to set himself against everybody ; so he changed his mind, and would not acknowledge the new house. He said that the revenue was not certain, and too little, while the opposition was great. On the whole, it seemed that he was right ; he gave it up at last, and would have nothing to do with it. It was a very great pain to us,—for we seemed now to have received the first blow,—and in particular to me, to find the Provincial against us ; for when he approved of the plan I considered myself blameless before all. They would not give absolution to my friend if she did not abandon the project ; for they said she was bound to remove the scandal.

19. She went to a very learned man, and a very great servant of God, of the Order of St. Dominic,[10] to whom she gave an account of all this matter. This was even before the Provincial had withdrawn his consent ; for in this place we had no one who would give us advice ; and so they said that it all proceeded solely from our obstinacy. That lady gave an account of everything, and told the holy man how much she received from the property of her husband. Having a great desire that he would help us,—for he was the most learned man here, and there are few in his Order more learned than he,—I told him myself all we intended to do, and some of my motives. I never said a word of any revelation whatever, speaking only of the natural reasons which influenced me ;

[10] F. Pedro Ibañez.

for I would not have him give an opinion otherwise
than on those grounds. He asked us to give him
eight days before he answered, and also if we had
made up our minds to abide by what he might say.
I said we had ; but though I said so, and though I
thought so, I never lost a certain confidence that
the monastery would be founded. My friend had
more faith than I ; nothing they could say could
make her give it up. As for myself, though, as I
said, it seemed to me impossible that the work should
be finally abandoned, yet my belief in the truth of
the revelation went no further than in so far as it was
not against what is contained in the sacred writings,
nor against the laws of the Church, which we are
bound to keep. Though the revelation seemed to
me to have come really from God, yet, if that learned
man had told me that we could not go on without
offending God and going against our conscience, I
believe I should have given it up, and looked out for
some other way ; but our Lord showed me no other
way than this.

20. The servant of God told me afterwards that
he had made up his mind to insist on the abandonment of our project, for he had already heard the
popular cry : moreover, he, as everybody did, thought
it folly ; and a certain nobleman also, as soon as he
knew that we had gone to him, had sent him word
to consider well what he was doing, and to give us
no help ; that when he began to consider the answer
he should make us, and to ponder on the matter, the
object we had in view, our manner of life, and the
Order, he became convinced that it was greatly for
the service of God, and that we must not give it up.
Accordingly, his answer was that we should make
haste to settle the matter. He told us how and in
what way it was to be done ; and if our means were
scanty, we must trust somewhat in God. If any one
made any objections, they were to go to him—he

would answer them ; and in this way he always helped us, as I shall show by and by.[11]

21. This answer was a great comfort to us ; so also was the conduct of certain holy persons who were usually against us : they were now pacified, and some of them even helped us. One of them was the saintly nobleman [11] of whom I spoke before [13] ; he looked on it—so, indeed, it was—as a means of great perfection, because the whole foundation was laid in prayer. He saw also very many difficulties before us, and no way out of them,—yet he gave up his own opinion, and admitted that the work might be of God. Our Lord Himself must have touched his heart, as He also did that of the doctor, the priest and servant of God, to whom, as I said before,[14] I first spoke, who is an example to the whole city,— being one whom God maintains there for the relief and progress of many souls ; he, too, came now to give us his assistance.

22. When matters had come to this state, and always with the help of many prayers, we purchased a house in a convenient spot ; and though it was small, I cared not at all for that, for our Lord had told me to go into it as well as I could,—that I should see afterwards what He would do ; and how well I have seen it ! I saw, too, how scanty were our means ; and yet I believed our Lord would order these things by other ways, and be gracious unto us.

[11] Ch. xxxiii. 8.
[13] Ch. xxiii. 6.
[12] Don Francis de Salcedo.
[14] Gaspar Daza. See ch. xxiii. 6.

CHAPTER XXXIII.

THE FOUNDATION OF THE MONASTERY HINDERED.
OUR LORD CONSOLES THE SAINT.

She continues the subject of the foundation of the glorious St. Joseph. How she was commanded to have nothing further to do with it, how she abandoned it; also the troubles it brought her, and how God consoled her in all this.

1. WHEN the matter was in this state—so near its conclusion, that on the very next day the papers were to be signed—then it was that the Father Provincial changed his mind. I believe that the change was divinely ordered—so it appeared afterwards ; for while so many prayers were made, our Lord was perfecting His work and arranging its execution in another way. When the Provincial refused us, my confessor bade me forthwith to think no more of it, notwithstanding the great trouble and distress which our Lord knows it cost me to bring it to this state. When the work was given up and abandoned, people were the more convinced that it was altogether the foolishness of women ; and the complaints against me were multiplied, although I had until then this commandment of my Provincial to justify me.

2. I was now very much disliked throughout the whole convent, because I wished to found another with stricter enclosure. It was said I insulted my sisters ; that I could serve God among them as well as elsewhere, for there were many among them much better than I ; that I did not love the house, and that it would have been better if I had procured greater resources for it than for another. Some said I ought to be put in prison [1] ; others—but they were

---

[1] The prison of the convent of the Incarnation is still to be seen. It is a small cell on the top story.

not many—defended me in some degree. I saw well enough that they were for the most part right, and now and then I made excuses for myself ; though, as I could not tell them the chief reason, which was the commandment of our Lord, I knew not what to do, and so was silent.

3. In other respects God was most merciful unto me, for all this caused me no uneasiness ; and I gave up our design with much readiness and joy, as if it cost me nothing. No one could believe it, not even those men of prayer with whom I conversed ; for they thought I was exceedingly pained and sorry : even my confessor himself could hardly believe it. I had done, as it seemed to me, all that was in my power. I thought myself obliged to do no more than I had done to fulfil our Lord's commandment, and so I remained in the house where I was, exceedingly happy and joyful ; though, at the same time, I was never able to give up my conviction that the work would be done. I had now no means of doing it, nor did I know how or when it would be done ; but I firmly believed in its accomplishment.

4. I was much distressed at one time by a letter which my confessor wrote to me, as if I had done anything in the matter contrary to his will. Our Lord also must have meant that suffering should not fail me there where I should feel it most ; and so, amid the multitude of my persecutions, when, as it seemed to me, consolations should have come from my confessor, he told me that I ought to recognise in the result that all was a dream ; that I ought to lead a new life by ceasing to have anything to do for the future with it, or even to speak of it any more, seeing the scandal it had occasioned. He made some further remarks, all of them very painful. This was a greater affliction to me than all the others together. I considered whether I had done anything myself, and whether I was to blame for anything that was

an offence unto God; whether all my visions were illusions, all my prayers a delusion, and I, therefore, deeply deluded and lost. This pressed so heavily upon me that I was altogether disturbed and most grievously distressed. But our Lord, who never failed me in all the trials I speak of, so frequently consoled and strengthened me that I need not speak of it here. He told me then not to distress myself; that I had pleased God greatly, and had not sinned against Him throughout the whole affair; that I was to do what my confessors required of me, and be silent on the subject till the time came to resume it. I was so comforted and so happy that the persecution which had befallen me seemed to be as nothing at all.

5. Our Lord now showed me what an exceedingly great blessing it is to be tried and persecuted for His sake; for the growth of the love of God in my soul, which I now discerned, as well as of many other virtues, was such as to fill me with wonder. It made me unable to abstain from desiring trials, and yet those about me thought I was exceedingly disheartened; and I must have been so if our Lord in that extremity had not succoured me with His great compassion. Now was the beginning of those more violent impetuosities of the love of God of which I have spoken before,[2] as well as of those profounder trances. I kept silence, however, and never spoke of those graces to any one. The saintly Dominican[3] was as confident as I was that the work would be done; and as I would not speak of it, in order that nothing might take place contrary to the obedience I owed my confessor, he communicated with my companion, and they wrote letters to Rome and made their preparations.

6. Satan also contrived now that persons should hear one from another that I had had a revelation in

---

[2] Ch. xxi. 6; ch. xxix. 10, 11.
[3] Pedro Ibañez. See ch. xxxviii. 15.

the matter ; and people came to me in great terror, saying that the times were dangerous, that something might be laid to my charge, and that I might be taken before the Inquisitors. I heard this with pleasure, and it made me laugh, because I never was afraid of them ; for I knew well enough that in matters of faith I would not break the least ceremony of the Church, that I would expose myself to die a thousand times rather than that any one should see me go against it or against any truth of Holy Writ. So I told them I was not afraid of that, for my soul must be in a very bad state if there was anything the matter with it of such a nature as to make me fear the Inquisition ; I would go myself and give myself up if I thought there was anything amiss ; and if I should be denounced, our Lord would deliver me, and I should gain much.

7. I had recourse to my Dominican father ; for I could rely upon him, because he was a learned man. I told him all about my visions, my way of prayer, the great graces our Lord had given me, as clearly as I could, and I begged him to consider the matter well, and tell me if there was anything therein at variance with the Holy Writings, and give me his opinion on the whole matter. He reassured me much, and, I think, profited himself ; for though he was exceedingly good, yet, from this time forth, he gave himself more and more to prayer, and retired to a monastery of his Order which was very lonely, that he might apply himself more effectually to prayer, where he remained more than two years. He was dragged out of his solitude by obedience, to his great sorrow : his superiors required his services ; for he was a man of great ability. I, too, on my part, felt his retirement very much, because it was a great loss to me, though I did not disturb him. But I knew it was a gain to him ; for when I was so much distressed at his departure, our Lord bade me be comforted,

not to take it to heart, for he was gone under good guidance.

8. So, when he came back, his soul had made such great progress, and he was so advanced in the ways of the spirit, that he told me on his return he would not have missed that journey for anything in the world. And I, too, could say the same thing ; for where he reassured and consoled me formerly by his mere learning, he did so now through that spiritual experience he had gained of supernatural things. And God, too, brought him here in time ; for He saw that His help would be required in the foundation of the monastery which His Majesty willed should be laid.

9. I remained quiet after this for five or six months, neither thinking nor speaking of the matter ; nor did our Lord once speak to me about it. I know not why, but I could never rid myself of the thought that the monastery would be founded. At the end of that time the then Rector [4] of the Society of Jesus having gone away, His Majesty brought into his place another [5] of great spirituality, high courage, strong understanding, and profound learning, at the very time when I was in great straits. As he who then heard my confession had a superior over him—the fathers of the Society are extremely strict about the virtue of obedience, and never stir but in conformity with the will of their superiors,—so he would not dare,

[4] Dionisio Vasquez. Of him the Bollandists say that he was very austere and harsh to his subjects, notwithstanding his great learning : " homini egregie docto ac rebus gestis claro, sed in subditos, ut ex historia Societatis Jesu liquet, valde immiti " (n. 309). He had joined the Society in 1550, and was for several years the companion and confessor of St. Francis Borja. At a later period he endeavoured to subtract the Spanish houses of the Jesuits from the authority of the General, but failed, and underwent punishment for his intrigues. He died a holy death at Toledo in 1589.

[5] Gaspar Salazar, native of Toledo, entered the Society in 1552 at Alcalá. He remained only nine months at Avila, being relieved of his office on account of a quarrel with the bishop Don Alvaro de Mendoza, the friend and protector of St. Teresa. But he remained a faithful supporter of the latter, and at one time thought even of joining the Discalced Carmelites (letter of Feb. 10, 1578), not altogether to the delight of the Saint. He died at Alcalá, Sept. 27, 1593, aged sixty-four.

though he perfectly understood my spirit, and desired the accomplishment of my purpose, to come to any resolution ; and he had many reasons to justify his conduct. I was at the same time subject to such great impetuosities of spirit that I felt my chains extremely heavy ; nevertheless, I never swerved from the commandment he gave me.

10. One day, when in great distress, because I thought my confessor did not trust me, our Lord said to me, Be not troubled ; this suffering will soon be over. I was very much delighted, thinking I should die shortly ; and I was very happy whenever I recalled those words to remembrance. Afterwards I saw clearly that they referred to the coming of the rector of whom I am speaking, for never again had I any reason to be distressed. The rector that came never interfered with the father-minister who was my confessor. On the contrary, he told him to console me,—that there was nothing to be afraid of,—and not to direct me along a road so narrow, but to leave the operations of the Spirit of God alone ; for now and then it seemed as if these great impetuosities of the spirit took away the very breath of the soul.

11. The rector came to see me, and my confessor bade me speak to him in all freedom and openness. I used to feel the very greatest repugnance to speak of this matter ; but so it was, when I went into the confessional, I felt in my soul something, I know not what. I do not remember to have felt so either before or after towards any one. I cannot tell what it was, nor do I know of anything with which I could compare it. It was a spiritual joy, and a conviction in my soul that his soul must understand mine, that it was in unison with it, and yet, as I have said, I knew not how. If I had ever spoken to him, or had heard great things of him, it would have been nothing out of the way that I should rejoice in the conviction that he would understand me ; but he had never

spoken to me before, nor I to him, and, indeed, he was a person of whom I had no previous knowledge whatever.

12. Afterwards I saw clearly that my spirit was not deceived; for my relations with him were in every way of the utmost service to me and my soul, because his method of direction is proper for those persons whom our Lord seems to have led far on the way, seeing that He makes them run, and not to crawl step by step. His plan is to render them thoroughly detached and mortified, and our Lord has endowed him with the highest gifts herein as well as in many other things beside. As soon as I began to have to do with him, I knew his method at once, and saw that he had a pure and holy soul, with a special grace of our Lord for the discernment of spirits. He gave me great consolation. Shortly after I had begun to speak to him our Lord began to constrain me to return to the affair of the monastery, and to lay before my confessor and the father-rector many reasons and considerations why they should not stand in my way. Some of these reasons made them afraid, for the father-rector never had a doubt of its being the work of the Spirit of God, because he regarded the fruits of it with great care and attention. At last, after much consideration, they did not dare to hinder me.[6]

13. My confessor gave me leave to prosecute the work with all my might. I saw well enough the trouble I exposed myself to, for I was utterly alone, and able to do so very little. We agreed that it should be carried on with the utmost secrecy; and so I contrived that one of my sisters,[7] who lived out of the town, should buy a house, and prepare it as

---

[6] St. Teresa was commanded by our Lord to ask Father Baltasar Alvarez to make a meditation on Psalm xci. 6: "Quam magnificata sunt opera Tua." The Saint obeyed, and the meditation was made. From that moment, as F. Alvarez afterwards told Father de Ribera (*Life of S. Teresa*, bk. i. ch. vii.), there was no further hesitation on the part of the Saint's confessor.

[7] Doña Juana de Ahumada, wife of Juan de Ovalle.

if for herself, with money which our Lord provided for us.[8] I made it a great point to do nothing against obedience ; but I knew that if I spoke of it to my superiors all was lost, as on the former occasion, and worse even might happen. In holding the money, in finding the house, in treating for it, in putting it in order, I had so much to suffer ; and, for the most part, I had to suffer alone, though my friend did what she could : she could do but little, and that was almost nothing. Beyond giving her name and her countenance, the whole of the trouble was mine ; and that fell upon me in so many ways that I am astonished now how I could have borne it.[9] Sometimes, in my affliction, I used to say : O my Lord, how is it that Thou commandest me to do that which seems impossible ?—for, though I am a woman, yet, if I were free, it might be done ; but when I am tied in so many ways, without money, or the means of procuring it, either for the purpose of the Brief or for any other,—what, O Lord, can I do ?

14. Once when I was in one of my difficulties, not knowing what to do, unable to pay the workmen, St. Joseph, my true father and lord, appeared to me, and gave me to understand that money would not be wanting, and I must hire the workmen. So I did, though I was penniless ; and our Lord, in a way that filled those who heard of it with wonder, provided for me. The house offered me was too small,—so much so, that it seemed as if it could never be made into a monastery,—and I wished to buy another, but had not the means, and there was neither way nor

---

[8] The money was a present from her brother, Don Lorenzo de Cepeda, at that time royal treasurer at Quito ; and the Saint acknowledges the receipt of it, and confesses the use made of it, in a letter to her brother, written in Avila, Dec. 30, 1561.

[9] One day she went with her sister—she was staying in her house—to hear a sermon in the church of Santo Tomás. The zealous preacher denounced visions and revelations ; and his observations were so much to the point that there was no need of his saying that they were directed against St. Teresa, who was present. Her sister was greatly hurt, and persuaded the Saint to return to the monastery at once (*Reforma*, bk. i. ch. xlii. 1).

means to do so. I knew not what to do. There was
another little house close to the one we had, which
might have formed a small church. One day, after
Communion, our Lord said to me, I have already
bidden thee to go in anyhow. And then, as if ex-
claiming, said : Oh, covetousness of the human race,
thinking that even the whole earth is too little for
it ! how often have I slept in the open air, because
I had no place to shelter Me ? [10] I was alarmed, and
saw that He had good reasons to complain. I went
to the little house, arranged the divisions of it, and
found that it would make a sufficient, though small
monastery. I did not care now to add to the site by
purchase, and so I did nothing but contrive to have
it prepared in such a way that it could be lived in.
Everything was coarse, and nothing more was done
to it than to render it not ·hurtful to health—and
that must be done everywhere.

15. As I was going to Communion on her feast,
St. Clare appeared to me in great beauty, and bade
me take courage, and go on with what I had begun ;
she would help me. I began to have a great devotion
to St. Clare ; and she has so truly kept her word,
that a monastery of nuns of her Order in our neighbourhood helped us to live ; and, what is of more
importance, by little and little she so perfectly fulfilled
my desire that the poverty which the blessed Saint
observes in her own house is observed in this, and
we are living on alms. It cost me no small labour
to have this matter settled by the plenary sanction
and authority of the Holy Father,[11] so that it shall

[10] St. Luke ix. 58 : " Filius autem hominis non habet ubi caput reclinet."
[11] The first brief of Feb. 7, 1562 (*Bullar. Carmel.* ii. 120) said that the
nuns were to have their revenues in common, for St. Teresa had not yet
resolved upon absolute poverty. Animated by the advice of St. Peter of
Alcantara, she applied once more to the Holy See, and obtained a rescript
of the penitentiary, dated Dec. 5, 1562 (*ibid.* 123), granting the necessary
authorisation. A final brief of July 17, 1565, confirmed the foundation of
the convent of St. Joseph at Avila with Teresa of Jesus as " abbess, or, as
she may be called, Mother " (*ibid.* 135).

never be otherwise, and we possess no revenues. Our Lord is doing more for us – perhaps we owe it to the prayers of this blessed Saint ; for, without our asking anybody, His Majesty supplies most abundantly all our wants.   May He be blessed for ever !   Amen.

16. On one of these days—it was the Feast of the Assumption of our Lady—I was in the church of the monastery of the Order of the glorious St. Dominic, thinking of the events of my wretched life, and of the many sins which in times past I had confessed in that house.   I fell into so profound a trance that I was, as it were, beside myself.   I sat down, and it seemed as if I could neither see the Elevation nor hear Mass.   This afterwards became a scruple to me.   I thought then, when I was in that state, that I saw myself clothed with a garment of excessive whiteness and splendour.   At first I did not see who was putting it on me.   Afterwards I saw our Lady on my right hand, and my father St. Joseph on my left, clothing me with that garment.   I was given to understand that I was then cleansed from my sins. When I had been thus clad—I was filled with the utmost delight and joy—our Lady seemed at once to take me by both hands.   She said that I pleased her very much by being devout to the glorious St. Joseph ; that I might rely on it my desires about the monastery were accomplished, and that our Lord and they too would be greatly honoured in it ; that I was to be afraid of no failure whatever, though the obedience under which it would be placed might not be according to my mind, because they would watch over us, and because her Son had promised to be with us [12]—and, as a proof of this, she would give me that jewel.   She then seemed to throw around my neck a most splendid necklace of gold, from which hung a cross of great value.   The stones and gold were so different from any in this world that there is nothing wherewith to

[12] Ch. xxxii. 14.

compare them.   The beauty of them is such as can
be conceived by no imagination,—and no understanding can find out the materials of the robe, nor
picture to itself the splendours which our Lord revealed,
in comparison with which all the splendours of earth,
so to say, are a daubing of soot.   This beauty, which
I saw in our Lady, was exceedingly grand, though I
did not trace it in any particular feature, but rather
in the whole form of her face.   She was clothed in
white, and her garments shone with excessive lustre,
that was not dazzling but soft.   I did not see St.
Joseph so distinctly, though I saw clearly that he was
there, as in the visions of which I spoke before,[13] in
which nothing is seen.   Our Lady seemed to be very
young.

17. When they had been with me for a while,—I,
too, in the greatest delight and joy, greater than I
had ever had before, as I think, and with which I
wished never to part,—I saw them, so it seemed,
ascend up to heaven, attended by a great multitude
of angels.   I was left in great loneliness, though so
comforted and raised up, so recollected in prayer and
softened, that I was for some time unable to move
or speak—being, as it were, beside myself.   I was
now possessed by a strong desire to be consumed
for the love of God, and by other affections of the
same kind.   Everything took place in such a way
that I could never have a doubt—though I often
tried—that the vision came from God.   It left me in
the greatest consolation and peace.

18. As to that which the Queen of the Angels spoke
about obedience, it is this : it was painful to me not
to subject the monastery to the Order, and our Lord
had told me that it was inexpedient to do so.   He
told me the reasons why it was in no wise convenient
that I should do it, but I must send to Rome in a
certain way, which He also explained ; He would

[13] See ch. xxvii. 7.

take care that I found help there : and so I did. I
sent to Rome, as our Lord directed me,—for we should
never have succeeded otherwise,—and most favourable
was the result.

19. And as to subsequent events, it was very
convenient to be under the Bishop,[14] but at that
time I did not know him, nor did I know what kind
of a superior he might be. It pleased our Lord that
he should be as good and favourable to this house
as it was necessary he should be on account of the
great opposition it met with at the beginning, as I
shall show hereafter,[15] and also for the sake of bringing
it to the condition it is now in. Blessed be He Who
has done it all! Amen.

CHAPTER XXXIV.

THE SAINT LEAVES HER MONASTERY OF THE INCARNATION FOR A TIME, AT THE COMMAND OF HER SUPERIOR. CONSOLES AN AFFLICTED WIDOW.

She shows how at that time it happened that she absented herself from this place, and how her superior commanded her to go away at the request of a very noble lady who was in great affliction. She begins to tell what happened to her there, and the great grace God bestowed upon her, in determining, through her instrumentality, a person of distinction to serve Him truly ; and how that person found favour and help in her (St. Teresa). This is noteworthy.

1. Now, though I was very careful that no one should

[14] Don Alvaro de Mendoza, Bishop of Avila, afterwards of Palencia, where he died, April 19, 1586. His greatest desire, to be buried near St. Teresa (for which purpose he had built a chapel in the conventual church of St. Joseph's, Avila), was not destined to be fulfilled, for St. Teresa's body rests at Alba de Tormes.

[15] See ch. xxxvi. 15 ; *Way of Perfection*, ch. v. 4 ; *Foundations*, ch. xxxi. 1.

know what we were doing, all this work could not
be carried on so secretly as not to come to the knowledge of divers persons ; some believed in it, others
did not.   I was in great fear lest the Provincial should
be spoken to about it when he came, and find himself
compelled to order me to give it up ; and if he did
so, it would have been abandoned at once.   Our
Lord provided against it in this way.   In a large
city, more than twenty leagues distant, was a lady
in great distress on account of her husband's death.[1]
She was in such extreme affliction that fears were
entertained about her life.   She had heard of me, a
poor sinner,—for our Lord had provided that,—and
men spoke well to her of me, for the sake of other
good works which resulted from it.   This lady knew
the Provincial [2] well ; and as she was a person of some
consideration, and knew that I lived in a monastery
the nuns of which were permitted to go out, our
Lord made her desire much to see me.   She thought
that my presence would be a consolation to her,
and that she could not be comforted otherwise.   She
therefore strove by all the means in her power to
get me into her house, sending messages to the Provincial, who was at a distance far away.

2. The Provincial sent me an order, charging me
in virtue of my obedience to go immediately, with

[1] Doña Luisa de la Cerda, sister of the Duke of Medina-Cœli, was now
the widow of Arias Pardo, Marshal of Castile, Lord of Malagon and Para-
cuellos.   Don Arias was nephew of Cardinal Tabera, Archbishop of Toledo.

[2] The Provincial of whom St. Teresa henceforth speaks is not Gregorio
Fernandez, whom she mentioned in ch. xxxii. 16 and 18, but Angel de Salazar,
who, having made his profession at Sevilla, in the province of Andalucia,
was transterred to that of Castile, and became prior of Toledo in 1555 and
of Avila in 1559.   His election to the provincialship must have taken place
in 1561.   In April 1563 he was sent by the Vicar-General (Rubeo) to Portugal on affairs of the Order.   He assisted at the General Chapter, 1564, in
Rome, during which he was promoted to the degree of Master in Divinity
(June 10).   His term of office was prolonged till after the General's canonical
visitation in Castile (April, 1567), when he became Prior of Avila.   He
held the provincialship again from 1570 to 1576 ; in 1579 he was prior of
Valladolid and Vicar-General from 1580 to 1583 Provincial ; on April 26,
1586, he was nominated Vicar-General, and in 1592 he was again Provincial.
The date and place of his death are not on record.

one companion. I knew of it on Christmas night.[3] It caused me some trouble and much suffering to see that they sent for me because they thought there was some good in me ; I, knowing myself to be so wicked, could not bear it. I commended myself earnestly to God, and during Matins, or the greater part of them, was lost in a profound trance. Our Lord told me I must go without fail, and give no heed to the opinions of people, for they were few who would not be rash in their counsel ; and though I should have troubles, yet God would be served greatly : as to the convent, it was expedient I should be absent till the Brief came, because Satan had contrived a great plot against the coming of the Provincial ; that I was to have no fear,—He would help me. I repeated this to the rector, and he told me that I must go by all means, though others were saying I ought not to go, that it was a trick of Satan to bring some evil upon me there, and that I ought to send word to the Provincial.

3. I obeyed the rector, and went without fear, because of what I had understood in prayer, though in the greatest confusion when I thought of the reasons why they sent for me, and how very much they were deceived. It made me more and more importunate with our Lord that He would not abandon me. It was a great comfort that there was a house of the Society of Jesus there [4] whither I was going, and so I thought I should be in some degree safe under the direction of those fathers, as I had been here.

4. It was the good pleasure of our Lord that the lady who sent for me should be so much consoled, that a visible improvement was the immediate result : she was comforted every day more and more. This

---

[3] In the letter to her brother of Dec. 30, 1561, written from Avila, she makes no mention of the impending journey.

[4] Founded in 1558, the rector being F. Pedro Domenech, who became a great friend of the Saint.

was very remarkable, because, as I said before, her suffering had reduced her to great straits. Our Lord must have done this in answer to the many prayers which the good people of my acquaintance made for me, that I might prosper in my work. She had a profound fear of God, and was so good that her great devotion supplied my deficiencies. She conceived a great affection for me—I, too, for her, because of her goodness ; but all was as it were a cross for me ; for the comforts of her house were a great torment, and her making so much of me made me afraid. I kept my soul continually recollected—I did not dare to be careless : nor was our Lord careless of me ; for while I was there [5] He bestowed the greatest graces upon me, and those graces made me so free, and filled me with such contempt for all I saw,—and the more I saw the greater my contempt,—that I never failed to treat those ladies, whom to serve would have been a great honour for me, with as much freedom as if I had been their equal.

5. I derived very great advantages from this, and I said so. I saw that she was a woman, and as much liable to passion and weakness as I was ; that rank is of little worth, and the higher it is the greater the anxiety and trouble it brings. People must be careful of the dignity of their state, which will not suffer them to live at ease ; they must eat at fixed hours and by rule, for everything must be according to their state, and not according to their constitutions ; and they have frequently to take food fitted more for their state than for their liking.

6. So it was that I came to hate the very wish to be a great lady. God deliver me from this wicked, artificial life !—though I believe that this lady, notwithstanding that she was one of the chief personages of the realm, was a woman of great simplicity, and

[5] The house of Doña Luisa de la Cerda ultimately became the convent of the Carmelite nuns, who still continue to inhabit it.

that few were more humble than she was. I was very sorry for her, for I saw how often she had to submit to much that was disagreeable to her because of the requirements of her rank. Then, as to servants, though this lady had very good servants, how slight is that little trust that may be put in them! One must not be conversed with more than another; otherwise he who is so favoured is envied by the rest. This of itself is a slavery, and one of the lies of the world is that it calls such persons masters, who, in my eyes, are nothing else but slaves in a thousand ways.

7. It was our Lord's pleasure that the household of that lady improved in the service of His Majesty during my stay there, though I was not exempted from some trials and some jealousies on the part of some of its members, because of the great affection their mistress had for me. They perhaps must have thought I had some personal interest to serve. Our Lord must have permitted such matters, and others of the same kind, to give me trouble, in order that I might not be absorbed in the comforts which otherwise I had there; and He was pleased to deliver me out of it all with great profit to my soul.

8. When I was there a religious person of great consideration, and with whom I had conversed occasionally some years ago,[6] happened to arrive. When I was at Mass, in a monastery of his Order, near the house in which I was staying, I felt a longing to know the state of his soul,—for I wished him to be a great servant of God—and I rose up in order to go and speak to him. But as I was then recollected in prayer it seemed to me a waste of time—for what had I to do in that matter?—and so I returned to my place. Three times I think I did this, and at

---

[6] Ribera, Yepez, and Bouix think this was F. Vicente Baron, of whom the Saint speaks in ch. vii. 26, but there is every reason to believe it was another Dominican, Fr. Garcia de Toledo.

last my good angel prevailed over the evil one, and I went and asked for him ; and he came to speak to me in one of the confessionals.   We began by asking one another of our past lives, for we had not seen one another for many years.   I told him that my life had been one in which my soul had had many trials. He insisted much on my telling him what those trials were.   I said that they were not to be told, and that I was not to tell them.   He replied that the Dominican father,[7] of whom I have spoken, knew them, and that, as they were great friends, he could learn them from him, and so I had better tell them without hesitation.

9. The fact is, that it was not in his power not to insist, nor in mine, I believe, to refuse to speak ; for notwithstanding all the trouble and shame I used to feel formerly, I spoke of my state to him, and to the rector whom I have referred to before,[8] without any difficulty whatever ; on the contrary, it was a great consolation to me ; and so I told him all in confession.   He seemed to me then more prudent than ever ; though I had always looked upon him as a man of great understanding.   I considered what high gifts and endowments for great services he had if he gave himself wholly unto God.   I had this feeling now for many years, so that I never saw any one who pleased me much without wishing at once he were given wholly unto God ; and sometimes I feel this so keenly, that I can hardly contain myself. Though I long to see everybody serve God, yet my desire about those who please me is very vehement, and so I importune our Lord on their behalf.

10. So it happened with respect to this religious. He asked me to pray much for him to God.   There was no necessity for his doing so, because I could not do anything else, and so I went back to my place where I was in the habit of praying alone, and began

---

[7] Fr. Pedro Ibañez.   [8] Ch. xxxiii. 11.

to pray to our Lord, being extremely recollected, in that my simple, silly way, when I speak without knowing very often what I am saying. It is love that speaks, and my soul is so beside itself that I do not regard the distance between it and God. That love which I know His Majesty has for it makes it forget itself, and think itself to be one with Him ; and so, as being one with Him, and not divided from Him, the soul speaks foolishly. When I had prayed with many tears that the soul of this religious might serve Him truly,—for, though I considered it good, it was not enough for me ; I would have it much better,—I remember I said, " O Lord, Thou must not refuse me this grace ; behold him,—he is a fit person to be our friend."

11. Oh, the great goodness and compassion of God ! How He regards not the words, but the desire and the will with which they are spoken ! How He suffered such a one as I am to speak so boldly before His Majesty ! May He be blessed for evermore !

12. I remember that during those hours of prayer on that very night I was extremely distressed by the thought whether I was in the grace of God, and that I could never know whether I was so or not,—not that I wished to know it ; I wished, however, to die, in order that I might not live a life in which I was not sure that I was not dead in sin, for there could be no death more dreadful for me than to think that I had sinned against God. I was in great straits at this thought. I implored Him not to suffer me to fall into sin, with great sweetness, dissolved in tears. Then I heard that I might console myself, and be sure [9] that I was in a state of grace, because a love of God like mine, together with the graces and feelings with which His Majesty filled my soul, was of such a

[9] All the old editors read " and trust " (confiar), but the MS. has clearly " be sure " (estar cierta). F. Bouix was the first to notice the difference, but even Fuente, in the letterpress to the autograph edition, writes thoughtlessly " confiar,"

nature as to be inconsistent with a state of mortal sin.

13. I was now confident that our Lord would grant my prayer as to that religious. He bade me repeat certain words to him. This I felt much, because I knew not how to speak to him; for this carrying messages to a third person, as I have said,[10] is what I have always felt the most, especially when I did not know how that person would take them, nor whether he would not laugh at me. This placed me in great difficulties, but at last I was so convinced I ought to do it, that I believe I made a promise to God I would not neglect that message; and because of the great shame I felt, I wrote it out, and gave it in that way. The result showed clearly enough that it was a message from God, for that religious resolved with great earnestness to give himself to prayer, though he did not do so at once. Our Lord would have Him for Himself, so He sent me to tell him certain truths which, without my understanding them, were so much to the purpose that he was astonished. Our Lord must have prepared him to receive them as from His Majesty; and though I am but a miserable sinner myself, yet I made many supplications to our Lord to convert him thoroughly, and to make him hate the pleasures and the things of this life. And so he did—blessed be God!—for every time that he spoke to me I was in a manner beside myself; and if I had not seen it, I should never have believed that our Lord would have given him in so short a time graces so matured, and filled him so full of God, that he seemed to be alive to nothing on earth.

14. May His Majesty hold him in His hand! If he will go on—and I trust in our Lord he will do so, now that he is so well grounded in the knowledge of himself—he will be one of the most distinguished servants of God, to the great profit of many souls,

[10] Ch. xxxiii. 12.

because he has in a short time had great experience in spiritual things : that is a gift of God, which He gives when He will and as He will, and it depends not on length of time nor extent of service.   I do not mean that time and service are not great helps, but very often our Lord will not give to some in twenty years the grace of contemplation, while He gives it to others in one,—His Majesty knoweth why.   We are under a delusion when we think that in the course of years we shall come to the knowledge of that which we can in no way attain to but by experience ; and thus many are in error, as I have said,[11] when they would understand spirituality without being spiritual themselves.   I do not mean that a man who is not spiritual, if he is learned, may not direct one that is spiritual ; but it must be understood that in outward and inward things, in the order of nature, the direction must be an act of reason ; and in supernatural things, according to the teaching of the sacred writings.   In other matters, let him not distress himself, nor think that he can understand that which he understandeth not ; neither let him quench the Spirit [12] ; for now another Master, greater than he, is directing these souls, so that they are not left without authority over them.

15. He must not be astonished at this, nor think it impossible : all things are possible to our Lord [13] ; he must strive rather to strengthen his faith, and humble himself, because in this matter our Lord imparts perhaps a deeper knowledge to some old woman than to him, though he may be a very learned man.   Being thus humble, he will profit souls and himself more than if he affected to be a contemplative without being so ; for, I repeat it, if he have no experience, if he have not a most profound humility,

---

[11] Ch. xiv. 10.
[12] 1 Thess. v. 19 : " Spiritum nolite extinguere."
[13] St. Matt. xix. 26 : " Apud Deum autem omnia possibilia sunt."

whereby he may see that he does not understand, and that the thing is not for that reason impossible, he will do himself but little good, and still less to his penitent. But if he is humble, let him have no fear that our Lord will allow either the one or the other to fall into delusion.

16. Now as to this father I am speaking of, as our Lord has given him light in many things, so has he laboured to find out by study that which in this matter can be by study ascertained ; for he is a very learned man, and that of which he has no experience himself he seeks to find out from those who have it, and our Lord helps him by increasing his faith, and so he has greatly benefited himself and some other souls, of whom mine is one. As our Lord knew the trials I had to undergo, His Majesty seems to have provided that, when He took away unto Himself some of those who directed me,[14] others might remain, who helped me in my great afflictions, and rendered me great services.

17. Our Lord wrought a complete change in this father, so much so that he scarcely knew himself, so to speak. He has given him bodily health, so that he may do penance, such as he never had before ; for he was sickly. He has given him courage to undertake good works, with other gifts, so that he seems to have received a most special vocation from our Lord. May He be blessed for ever !

18. All these blessings, I believe, came to him through the graces our Lord bestowed upon him in prayer ; for they are real. It has been our Lord's pleasure already to try him in certain difficulties, out of which he has come forth like one who knows the true worth of that merit which is gained by suffering persecutions. I trust in the munificence of our Lord that great good will, by his means, accrue to

---

[14] Probably an allusion to the death of St. Peter of Alcantara (Oct. 18, 1562) and F. Pedro Ibañez (Feb. 2, 1565).

some of his Order and to the Order itself. This is beginning to be understood. I have had great visions on the subject, and our Lord has told me wonderful things of him and of the Rector of the Society of Jesus, whom I am speaking of,[15] and also of two other religious of the Order of St. Dominic, particularly of one who, to his own profit, has actually learned of our Lord certain things which I had formerly understood of him. But there were greater things made known of him to whom I am now referring : one of them I will now relate.

19. I was with him once in the parlour when in my soul and spirit I felt what great love burned within him, and became as it were lost in ecstasy by considering the greatness of God, who had raised that soul in so short a time to a state so high. It made me ashamed of myself when I saw him listen with so much humility to what I was saying about certain matters of prayer, when I had so little myself that I could speak on the subject to one like him. Our Lord must have borne with me in this on account of the great desire I had to see that religious making great progress. My interview with him did me great good,—it seems as if it left a new fire in my soul, burning with desire to serve our Lord as in the begining. O my Jesus ! what is a soul on fire with Thy love ! How we ought to prize it, and implore our Lord to let it live long upon earth ! He who has this love should follow after such souls, if it be possible.

20. It is a great thing for a person ill of this disease to find another struck down by it,—it comforts him much to see that he is not alone ; they help one another greatly to suffer and to merit. They are strong with a double strength who are resolved to risk a thousand lives for God, and who long for an opportunity of losing them. They are like soldiers who, to acquire booty, and therewith enrich them-

[15] F. Gaspar de Salazar.

selves, wish for war, knowing well that they cannot
become rich without it.   This is their work—to suffer.
Oh, what a blessing it is when our Lord gives light
to understand how great is the gain of suffering for
Him ! This is never understood till we have left all
things ; for if anybody is attached to any one thing,
that is a proof that he sets some value upon it ; and
if he sets any value upon it, it is painful to be compelled to give it up.   In that case, everything is
imperfect and lost.   The saying is to the purpose
here,—he who follows what is lost, is lost himself ;
and what greater loss, what greater blindness, what
greater calamity, can there be than making much of
that which is nothing ?

21. I now return to that which I had begun to
speak of.   I was in the greatest joy, beholding that
soul.   It seemed as if our Lord would have me see
clearly the treasures He had laid up in it ; and so,
when I considered the favour our Lord had shown
me, in that I should be the means of so great a
good, I recognised my own unworthiness for such an
end.   I thought much of the graces our Lord had
given him, and held myself as indebted for them
more than if they had been given to myself.   So I
gave thanks to our Lord, when I saw that His Majesty
had fulfilled my desires and heard my petition that
He would raise up persons like him.   And now my
soul, no longer able to bear the joy that filled it, went
forth out of itself, losing itself that it might gain the
more.   It lost sight of the reflections it was making ;
and the hearing of that divine language which the
Holy Ghost seemed to speak threw me into a deep
trance, which almost deprived me of all sense, though
it did not last long.   I saw Christ, in exceeding great
majesty and glory, manifesting His joy at what was
then passing.   He told me as much, and it was His
pleasure that I should clearly see that He was always
present at similar interviews, and how much He was

pleased when people thus found their delight in speaking of Him.

22. On another occasion, when far away from this place,[16] I saw him carried by angels in great glory. I understood by that vision that his soul was making great progress : so it was ; for an evil report was spread abroad against him by one to whom he had rendered a great service, and whose reputation and whose soul he had saved. He bore it with much joy. He did also other things greatly to the honour of God, and underwent more persecutions. I do not think it expedient now to speak further on this point ; if, however, you, my father, who know all, should hereafter think otherwise, more might be said to the glory of our Lord.

23. All the prophecies spoken of before,[17] relating to this house, as well as others, of which I shall speak hereafter, relating to it and to other matters, have been accomplished. Some of them our Lord revealed to me three years before they became known, others earlier, and others later. But I always made them known to my confessor, and to the widow my friend ; for I had leave to communicate with her, as I said before.[18] She, I know, repeated them to others, and these know that I lie not. May God never permit me, in any matter whatever,—much more in things of this importance,—to say anything but the whole truth !

24. One of my brothers-in-law died [19] suddenly ; and as I was in great distress at this, because he had not cared to make his confession,[20] our Lord said to me in prayer that my sister also was to die in the same way ; that I must go to her, and make her

---

[16] Avila.   [17] Ch. xxvi. 3.
[18] Ch. xxx. 3.   Doña Guiomar de Ulloa.
[19] Don Martin de Guzman y Barrientos, husband of Doña Maria de Cepeda, the Saint's sister.
[20] Most of the older editors read " he had no opportunity of making his confession," but what St. Teresa really says is something quite different.

prepare herself for such an end. I told this to my confessor ; but as he would not let me go, I heard the same warning again ; and now, when he saw this, he told me I might go, and that I should lose nothing by going. My sister was living in the country ; and as I did not tell her why I came, I gave her what light I could in all things. I made her go frequently to confession, and look to her soul in everything. She was very good, and did as I asked her. Four or five years after she had begun this practice, and keeping a strict watch over her conscience, she died, with nobody near her, and without being able to go to confession. This was a blessing to her, for it was little more than a week since she had been to her accustomed confession. It was a great joy to me when I heard of her death. She was but a short time in purgatory.

25. I do not think it was quite eight days afterwards, when, after Communion, our Lord appeared to me, and was pleased that I should see Him receive my sister into glory. During all those years, after our Lord had spoken to me, until her death, what I then learnt with respect to her was never forgotten either by myself or by my friend, who, when my sister was thus dead, came to me in great amazement at the fulfilment of the prophecy. God be praised for ever, Who takes such care of souls that they may not be lost !

CHAPTER XXXV.

THE FOUNDATION OF THE HOUSE OF ST. JOSEPH. THE OBSERVATION OF HOLY POVERTY THEREIN. HOW THE SAINT LEFT TOLEDO.

Continuation of the foundation of this house of our glorious father St. Joseph ; in what manner our Lord ordained that holy poverty should be observed there; the reason why she left the lady with whom she had been staying, and some other things that happened.

1. WHEN I was staying with this lady,[1] already spoken of, in whose house I remained more than six months, our Lord ordained that a holy woman [2] of our Order should hear of me, who was more than seventy leagues away from the place. She happened to travel this way, and went some leagues out of her road that she might see me. Our Lord had moved her in the same year, and in the same month of the year, that He had moved me, to found another monastery of the Order; and as He had given her this desire, she sold all she possessed, and went to Rome to obtain the necessary faculties. She went on foot, and barefooted. She is a woman of great penance and prayer, and one to whom our Lord gave many graces; and our Lady appeared to her, and commanded her to undertake this work. Her progress in the service of our Lord was so much greater than mine that I was ashamed to stand in her presence. She showed me Briefs she brought from Rome, and during the fortnight she

---

[1] Doña Luisa de la Cerda.

[2] Maria of Jesus, born in 1522, was the daughter of a Reporter of Causes in the Chancery of Granada; but his name and that of his wife are not known. Maria married, but became a widow soon afterwards. She then became a novice in the Carmelite convent of the Incarnation in Granada, and during her noviciate had revelations, like those of St. Teresa, about a reform of the Order. Her confessor made light of these, and she then referred them to F. Gaspar de Salazar, a confessor of St. Teresa, who was then in Granada. He approved of them, and Maria left the Noviciate, and went to Rome with two holy women of the Order of St. Francis. The three made the journey on foot, and, moreover, barefooted. Pope Pius IV. heard her prayer, and, looking at her torn and bleeding feet, said to her, "Woman of strong courage, let it be as thou wilt." She returned to Granada, but both the Carmelites and the city refused her permission to found her house there, and some went so far as to threaten to have her publicly whipped. Doña Leonora de Mascareñas gave her a house in Alcalá de Henares, of which she took possession Sept. 11, 1562; but the convent, called de la Imagen, was formally constituted July 23, 1563, and subjected to the Bishop ten days after. Maria of Jesus died in the odour of sanctity at Alcalá in 1580. Fuente says that the Chronicler (*Reforma*, bk. i. ch. lix.) is in error when he asserts that this convent of Maria of Jesus was endowed.

remained with me we laid our plan for the founding of these monasteries.

2. Until I spoke to her, I never knew that our rule, before it was mitigated, required of us that we should possess nothing [3] ; nor was I going to found a convent without revenue,[4] for my intention was that we should be without anxiety about all that was necessary for us, and I did not think of the many anxieties which the possession of property brings in its train. This holy woman, taught of our Lord, perfectly understood—though she could not read— what I was ignorant of, notwithstanding my having read the Constitutions [5] so often ; and when she told me of it, I thought it right, though I feared they would never consent to this, but would tell me I was committing follies, and that I ought not to do anything whereby I might bring suffering upon others. If this concerned only myself, nothing should have kept me back,—on the contrary, it would have been my great joy to think that I was observing the counsels of Christ our Lord ; for His Majesty had already given me great longings for poverty.[6]

3. As for myself, I never doubted that this was the better part ; for I had now for some time wished it were possible in my state to go about begging, for the love of God—to have no house of my own, nor anything else. But I was afraid that others— if our Lord did not give them the same desire— might live in discontent. Moreover, I feared that it might be the cause of some distraction : for I knew some poor monasteries not very recollected, and I

---

[3] The sixth chapter of the rule is : " Nullus fratrum sibi aliquid proprium esse dicat, sed sint vobis omnia communia." Gregory IX., by a Bull of April 6, 1229, forbade the possession of land, houses, or revenues (*Bull. Carmel.* i. 4).

[4] See ch. xxxii. 13.

[5] The Constitutions in vigour in the convent of the Incarnation and elsewhere were those published by Blessed John Soreth, General (1451–1471) after the Chapter of 1462, in which no provision is made for convents of nuns, and consequently nothing is said on the subject of endowment.

[6] See *Relation* i. 10.

did not consider that their not being recollected was the cause of their poverty, and that their poverty was not the cause of their distraction : distraction never makes people richer, and God never fails those who serve Him. In short, I was weak in faith ; but not so this servant of God.

4. As I took the advice of many in everything, I found scarcely any one of this opinion—neither my confessor, nor the learned men to whom I spoke of it. They gave me so many reasons the other way, that I did not know what to do. But when I saw what the rule required, and that poverty was the more perfect way, I could not persuade myself to allow an endowment. And though they did persuade me now and then that they were right, yet, when I returned to my prayer, and saw Christ on the Cross, so poor and destitute, I could not bear to be rich, and I implored Him with tears so to order matters that I might be poor as He was.

5. I found that so many inconveniences resulted from an endowment, and saw that it was the cause of so much trouble, and even distraction, that I did nothing but dispute with the learned. I wrote to that Dominican friar [7] who was helping us, and he sent back two sheets by way of reply, full of objections and theology against my plan, telling me that he had thought much on the subject. I answered that, in order to escape from my vocation, the vow of poverty I had made, and the perfect observance of the counsels of Christ, I did not want any theology to help me, and in this case I should not thank him for his learning. If I found any one who would help me, it pleased me much. The lady in whose house I was staying was a great help to me in this matter. Some at first told me that they agreed with me ; afterwards, when they had considered the matter longer, they found in it so

[7] F. Pedro Ibañez, who was then living in the " lonely monastery " of which the Saint speaks in ch. xxxiii. 7.

many inconveniences, that they insisted on my giving it up. I told them that, though they changed their opinion so quickly, I would abide by the first.

6. At this time, because of my entreaties,—for the lady had never seen the holy friar, Peter of Alcantara, —it pleased our Lord to bring him to her house. As he was a great lover of poverty, and had lived in it for so many years, he knew well the treasures it contains, and so he was a great help to me; he charged me on no account whatever to give up my purpose.[8] Now, having this opinion and sanction,—no one was better able to give it, because he knew what it was by long experience,—I made up my mind to seek no further advice.

7. One day, when I was very earnestly commending the matter to God, our Lord told me that I must by no means give up my purpose of founding the monastery in poverty; it was His will, and the will of His Father: He would help me. I was in a trance; and the effects were such, that I could have no doubt it came from God. On another occasion, He said to me that endowments bred confusion, with other things in praise of poverty; and assured me that whosoever served Him would never be in want of the necessary means of living: and this want, as I have said,[9] I never feared myself. Our Lord changed the dispositions also of the licentiate,—I am speaking of the Dominican friar,[10]—who, as I said, wrote to me that I should not found the monastery without an endowment. Now, as I was in the greatest joy at hearing this, and having these opinions in my favour, it seemed to me nothing less than the possession of

---

[8] He also wrote a letter to St. Teresa on the same subject, dated Avila, April 14, 1562.

[9] Ch. xi. 3.

[10] F. Pedro Ibañez. St. Teresa calls him Presentado, not licentiate, a title given to those who had been chosen by the General or Provincial chapters for the degrees, as distinct from those who obtained them at the expense of their friends.

all the wealth of the world, when I had resolved to live in poverty for the love of God.

8. At this time, my Provincial withdrew the order and the obedience, in virtue of which I was staying in that house.[11]   He left it to me to do as I liked : if I wished to return, I might do so ; if I wished to remain I might also do so for a certain time.   But during that time the elections in my convent [12] would take place, and I was told that many of the nuns wished to lay on me the burden of superiorship.   The very thought of this alone was a great torment to me ; for though I was resolved readily to undergo any kind of martyrdom for God, I could not persuade myself at all to accept this ;   for, putting aside the great trouble it involved,—because the nuns were so many, —and other reasons, such as that I never wished for it, nor for any other office,—on the contrary, had always refused them,—it seemed to me that my conscience would be in great danger ;   and so I praised God that I was not then in my convent.   I wrote to my friends and asked them not to vote for me.

9. When I was rejoicing that I was not in that trouble, our Lord said to me that I was on no account to keep away ; that as I longed for a cross, there was one ready for me, and that a heavy one : that I was not to throw it away, but go on with resolution ; He would help me, and I must go at once.   I was very much distressed, and did nothing but weep, because I thought that my cross was to be the office of prioress ;   and, as I have just said, I could not persuade myself that it would be at all good for my soul—nor could I see any means by which it would be.   I told my confessor [13] of it, and he commanded me to return at once : that to do so was clearly the

---

[11] The house of Doña Luisa de la Cerda, in Toledo.
[12] The convent of the Incarnation, Avila.
[13] F. Pedro Domenech, Superior of the Jesuits at Toledo.

most perfect way ; and that, because the heat was
very great,—it would be enough if I arrived before
the election,—I might wait a few days, in order that
my journey might do me no harm.

10. But our Lord had ordered it otherwise. I
had to go at once, because the uneasiness I felt was
very great ; and I was unable to pray, and thought
I was failing in obedience to the commandments of
our Lord, and that, as I was happy and contented
where I was, I would not go to meet trouble. All
my service of God there was lip-service : why did I,
having the opportunity of living in greater perfection,
neglect it ?   If I died on the road, let me die.   Besides, my soul was in great straits, and our Lord had
taken from me all sweetness in prayer.   In short, I
was in such a state of torment, that I begged the
lady to let me go ; for my confessor, when he saw
the plight I was in, had already told me to go, God
having moved him as He had moved me.   The lady
felt my departure very much, and that was another
pain to bear ; for it had cost her much trouble, and
diverse importunities of the Provincial, to have me in
her house.

11. I considered it a very great thing for her to
have given her consent, when she felt it so much ;
but, as she was a person who feared God exceedingly,
—and as I told her, among many other reasons, that
my going away tended greatly to His service, and
held out the hope that I might possibly return,—she
gave way, but with much sorrow.   I was now not
sorry myself at coming away, for I knew that it was
an act of greater perfection, and for the service of
God.   So the pleasure I had in pleasing God took
away the pain of quitting that lady,—whom I saw
suffering so keenly,—and others to whom I owed much,
particularly my confessor of the Society of Jesus, in
whom I found all I needed.   But the greater the consolations I lost for our Lord's sake, the greater was

my joy in losing them. I could not understand it, for I had a clear consciousness of these two contrary feelings—pleasure, consolation, and joy in that which weighed down my soul with sadness. I was joyful and tranquil, and had opportunities of spending many hours in prayer ; and I saw that I was going to throw myself into a fire ; for our Lord had already told me that I was going to carry a heavy cross,— though I never thought it would be so heavy as I afterwards found it to be,—yet I went forth rejoicing. I was distressed because I had not already begun the fight, since it was our Lord's will that I should be in it. Thus His Majesty gave me strength, and established it in my weakness.[14]

12. As I have just said, I could not understand how this could be. I thought of this illustration : if I were possessed of a jewel, or any other thing which gave me great pleasure, and it came to my knowledge that a person whom I loved more than myself, and whose satisfaction I preferred to my own, wished to have it, it would give me great pleasure to deprive myself of it, because I would give all I possessed to please that person. Now, as the pleasure of giving pleasure to that person surpasses any pleasure I have in that jewel myself, I should not be distressed in giving away that or anything else I loved, nor at the loss of that pleasure which the possession of it gave me. So now, though I wished to feel some distress when I saw that those whom I was leaving felt my going so much, yet, notwithstanding my naturally grateful disposition,—which, under other circumstances, would have been enough to have caused me great pain,—at this time, though I wished to feel it, I could feel none.

13. The delay of another day was so serious a matter in the affairs of this holy house, that I know not how they would have been settled if I had waited.

[14] 2 Cor. xii. 9 : " Virtus in infirmitate perficitur."

Oh, God is great! I am often lost in wonder when I consider and see the special help which His Majesty gave me towards the establishment of this little cell of God,—for such I believe it to be,—the lodging wherein His Majesty delights; for once, when I was in prayer, He told me that this house was the paradise of His delight.[15] It seems, then, that His Majesty has chosen those whom He has drawn hither, among whom I am living very much ashamed of myself.[16] I could not have even wished for souls such as they are for the purpose of this house, where enclosure, poverty, and prayer are so strictly observed; they submit with so much joy and contentment, that every one of them thinks herself unworthy of the grace of being received into it,—some of them particularly; for our Lord has called them out of the vanity and dissipation of the world, in which, according to its laws, they might have lived contented. Our Lord has multiplied their joy, so that they see clearly how He has given them a hundredfold for the one thing they have left,[17] and for which they cannot thank His Majesty enough. Others He has advanced from well to better. To the young He gives courage and knowledge, so that they may desire nothing else, and also to understand that to live away from all things in this life is to live in greater peace even here below. To those who are no longer young, and whose health is weak, He gives—and has given—the strength to undergo the same austerities and penance with all the others.

14. O my Lord! how Thou dost show Thy power! There is no need to seek reasons for Thy will; for with Thee, against all natural reason, all things are possible: so That thou teachest clearly there is no

---

[15] See *Way of Perfection*, ch. xiii. 5.

[16] See *Foundations*, ch. i. 1.

[17] St. Matt. xix. 29: " Et omnis qui reliquerit domum . . . propter nomen Meum, centuplum accipiet, et vitam æternam possidebit."

need of anything but of loving Thee [18] in earnest, and really giving up everything for Thee, in order that Thou, O my Lord, mightest make everything easy. It is well said that Thou feignest to make Thy law difficult [19] : I do not see it, nor do I feel that the way that leadeth unto Thee is narrow. I see it as a royal road, and not a pathway ; a road upon which whosoever really enters, travels most securely. No mountain passes and no cliffs are near it : these are the occasions of sin. I call that a pass,—a dangerous pass,—and a narrow road, which has on one side a deep hollow, into which one stumbles, and on the other a precipice, over which they who are careless fall, and are dashed to pieces. He who loves Thee, O my God, travels safely by the open and royal road, far away from the precipice : he has scarcely stumbled at all, when Thou stretchest forth Thy hand to save him. One fall—yea, many falls—if he does but love Thee, and not the things of the world, are not enough to make him perish ; he travels in the valley of humility. I cannot understand what it is that makes men afraid of the way of perfection.

15. May our Lord of His mercy make us see what a poor security we have in the midst of dangers so manifest, when we live like the rest of the world ; and that true security consists in striving to advance

[18] When the workmen were busy with the building, a nephew of the Saint, the child of her sister and Don Juan de Ovalle, was struck by some falling stones and killed. The workmen took the child to his mother ; and the Saint, then in the house of Doña Guiomar de Ulloa, was sent for. Doña Guiomar took the dead boy into her arms, gave him to the Saint, saying that it was a grievous blow to the father and mother, and that she must obtain his life from God. The Saint took the body, and, laying it in her lap, ordered those around her to cease their lamentations, of whom her sister was naturally the loudest, and be silent. Then, covering her face and her body with her veil, she prayed to God, and God gave the child his life again. The little boy soon after ran up to his aunt and thanked her for what she had done. In after-years the child used to say to the Saint that, as she had deprived him of the bliss of heaven by bringing him back to life, she was bound to see that he did not suffer loss. Don Gonzalo died three years after St. Teresa, when he was twenty-eight years of age (*Reforma*, bk. i. ch. xlii. 2).

[19] Psalm xciii. 20 : " Qui fingis laborem in præcepto."

in the way of God! Let us fix our eyes upon Him, and have no fear that the Sun of Justice will ever set, or suffer us to travel to our ruin by night, unless we first look away from Him. People are not afraid of living in the midst of lions, every one of whom seems eager to tear them : I am speaking of honours, pleasures, and the like joys, as the world calls them : and herein the devil seems to make us afraid of ghosts. I am astonished a thousand times, and ten thousand times would I relieve myself by weeping, and proclaim aloud my own great blindness and wickedness, if, perchance, it might help in some measure to open their eyes. May He, who is almighty, of His goodness open their eyes, and never suffer mine to be blind again!

CHAPTER XXXVI.

THE FOUNDATION OF THE MONASTERY OF ST. JOSEPH. PERSECUTION AND TEMPTATIONS. GREAT INTERIOR TRIAL OF THE SAINT, AND HER DELIVERANCE.

She continues the same subject, and shows how the foundation of this convent of the glorious St. Joseph was finally accomplished, and the great contradictions and persecutions she had to endure after the religious had taken the habit, and the great trials and temptations through which she passed, and how God led her forth victorious to His own glory and praise.

1. HAVING now left that city,[1] I travelled in great joy, resolved to suffer most willingly whatever our Lord might be pleased to lay upon me. On the night of my arrival here,[2] came also from Rome the commission and the Brief for the erection of the mon-

---

[1] Toledo.   [2] Avila. Probably in July 1562.

astery.[3] I was astonished myself, and so were those who knew how our Lord hastened my coming, when they saw how necessary it was, and in what a moment our Lord had brought me back.[4] I found here the Bishop[5] and the holy friar, Peter of Alcantara, and that nobleman,[6] the great servant of God, in whose house the holy man was staying ; for he was a man who was in the habit of receiving the servants of God in his house. These two prevailed on the Bishop to accept the convent, which was no small thing, because it was founded in poverty ; but he was so great a lover of those whom he saw determined to serve our Lord, that he was immediately drawn to give them his protection. It was the approbation of the holy old man,[7] and the great trouble he took to make now this one, now that one, help us, that did the whole work. If I had not come at the moment, as I have just said, I do not see how it could have been done ; for the holy man was here but a short time,—I think not quite eight days,—during which he was also ill ; and almost immediately afterwards our Lord took him to Himself.[8] It seems as if His Majesty reserved him till this affair was ended, because now for some time—I think for more than two years —he had been very ill.

2. Everything was done in the utmost secrecy ; and if it had not been so, I do not see how anything could have been done at all ; for the people of the city were against us, as it appeared afterwards. Our

[3] See ch. xxxiv. 2. The Brief is dated Feb. 7, 1562, the third year of Pius IV.

[4] The Brief was addressed to Doña Aldonza de Guzman, and to Doña Guiomar de Ulloa, her daughter.

[5] Don Alvaro de Mendoza.

[6] Don Francisco de Salcedo.

[7] St. Peter of Alcantara. " Truly this is the house of St. Joseph," were the Saint's words when he saw the rising monastery ; " for I see it is the little hospice of Bethlehem." His letter to the Bishop of Avila is still treasured at the convent of St. Joseph.

[8] In less than three months, perhaps ; for St. Peter died in the sixty-third year of his age, Oct. 18, 1562, and in less than eight weeks after the foundation of the monastery of St. Joseph.

Lord ordained that one of my brothers-in-law [9] should be ill, and his wife away, and himself in such straits that my superiors gave me leave to remain with him. Nothing, therefore, was found out, though some persons had their suspicions; still, they did not believe. It was very wonderful, for his illness lasted only no longer than was necessary for our affair; and when it was necessary he should recover his health, that I might be disengaged, and he leave the house empty, our Lord restored him; and he was astonished at it himself.[10]

3. I had much trouble in persuading this person and that to allow the foundation; I had to nurse the sick man, and obtain from the workman the hasty preparation of the house, so that it might have the form of a monastery; but much remained still to be done. My friend was not here,[11] for we thought it best she should be away, in order the better to hide our purpose. I saw that everything depended on haste, for many reasons, one of which was that I was afraid I might be ordered back to my monastery at any moment. I was troubled by so many things, that I suspected my cross had been sent me, though it seemed but a light one in comparison with that which I understood our Lord meant me to carry.

4. When everything was settled, our Lord was pleased that some of us should take the habit on St. Bartholomew's Day. The most Holy Sacrament began to dwell in the house at the same time.[12] With full sanction and authority, then, our monastery of our most glorious father St. Joseph was founded in the

---

[9] Don Juan de Ovalle.

[10] When he saw that the Saint had made all her arrangements he knew the meaning of his illness, and said to her, " It is not necessary I should be ill any longer " (*Ribera*, bk. i. ch. viii.).

[11] Doña Guiomar de Ulloa was now in her native place, Ciudad Toro.

[12] The Mass was said by Gaspar Daza. See *infra*, 18; *Reforma*, bk. i. ch. xlvi. 3.

year 1562.[13]   I was there myself to give the habit,
with two nuns [14] of the house to which we belonged,
who happened then to be absent from it. As the
house which thus became a monastery was that of
my brother-in-law—I said before [15] that he had bought
it, for the purpose of concealing our plan—I was
there myself with the permission of my superiors ;
and I did nothing without the advice of learned men,
in order that I might not break, in a single point, my
vow of obedience. As these persons considered what
I was doing to be most advantageous for the whole
Order, on many accounts, they told me—though I
was acting secretly, and taking care my superiors
should know nothing—that I might go on. If they
had told me that there was the slightest imperfection
in the whole matter, I would have given up the founding of a thousand monasteries,—how much more,
then, this one ? I am certain of this ; for though I

[13] The bell which the Saint had provided for the convent weighed less
than three pounds, and remained in the monastery for a hundred years, till
it was sent by order of the General to the monastery of Pastrana, where the
general chapters were held.   There the friars assembled at the sound of the
bell, which rang for the first Mass of the Carmelite Reform (*Reforma*, bk. i.
ch. xlvi. 1).   It is now once more at the convent of St. Joseph.
[14] They were Doña Ines and Doña Ana de Tapia, cousins of the Saint.
There were present also Don Gonzalo de Aranda, Don Francisco Salcedo.
Julian of Avila, priest ; Doña Juana de Ahumada, the Saint's sister, with
her husband, Juan de Ovalle.   The Saint herself retained her own habit,
making no change, because she had not the permission of her superiors (*Reforma*, bk. i. ch. xlvi. 2).
Doña Ines de Tapia, cousin of St. Teresa, both on her father's and her
mother's side, was placed at the convent of the Incarnation under the personal care of her holy kinswoman, with whom she became very intimate.
Although present at the inauguration of the convent of St. Joseph, she
only joined it in 1567, and soon after accompanied the Saint to Medina del
Campo, of which convent she became superioress for ten years, under
the name of Agnes of Jesus.   She renounced the mitigated rule in 1571.
Having shared St. Teresa's labours in several foundations, notably that
of Palencia, she returned ultimately to Medina del Campo, where she died
on April 22, 1601.   Doña Ana de Tapia, sister of the preceding, exchanged
with her the convent of the Incarnation for that of St. Joseph, and took part
in the foundation of Medina del Campo, of which convent she became sub-
prioress.   She afterwards was the first prioress of Salamanca, where she remained fourteen years in the midst of great trials.   Called back to Medina
as prioress, she ultimately returned to Salamanca, where she died on the
same day as her sister.   Her name in the Reformed Order was Anne of the
Incarnation.   [15] Ch. xxxiii. 13.

longed to withdraw from everything more and more, and to follow my rule and vocation in the greatest perfection and seclusion, yet I wished to do so only conditionally : for if I should have learnt that it would be for the greater honour of our Lord to abandon it, I would have done so, as I did before on one occasion,[16] in all peace and contentment.

5. I felt as if I were in bliss, when I saw the most Holy Sacrament reserved, with four poor orphans,[17] —for they were received without a dowry,—and great servants of God, established in the house. It was our aim from the beginning to receive only those who, by their example, might be the foundation on which we could build up what we had in view—great perfection and prayer—and effect a work which I believed to be for the service of our Lord, and to the honour of the habit of His glorious Mother. This was my anxiety. It was also a great consolation to me that I had done that which our Lord had so often commanded me to do, and that there was one church

---

[16] Ch. xxxiii. 3.

[17] The first of these was Antonia of the Holy Ghost, whose real name was Antonia de Henao, daughter of Felipe de Arevalo and Elvira Dies de Henao, of Avila, a penitent of St. Peter of Alcantara. She wished to enter a convent far away from Avila, but St. Peter advised her to join St. Teresa. She brought to the convent a small sum of money, 17,000 maravedís, equivalent to about ten pounds sterling. She made her profession on October 21, 1564. Later on she accompanied St. Teresa (of whom she was a distant relative) on various journeys ; she became sub-prioress at Valladolid, and, after having spent some more years at Avila, she was elected for the foundations of Granada and Malaga. She died at the last-named convent, July 7, 1595.—The second, Maria de la Paz, of Ledesma, near Salamanca, was a servant of Doña Guiomar de Ulloa ; she took the name of Maria de la Cruz, and made her profession April 22, 1565. Three years later she was sent to Valladolid, where she died, February 23, 1588.—The third was Ursula de los Santos, daughter of Martin de Revilla and Maria Alvarez de Arevalo, of Avila. Gaspar Daza, under whose direction she had been living, recommended her to the Saint. She brought an alms of 300 ducats. During the time St. Teresa was detained at the convent of the Incarnation, August 24, 1562, till mid-Lent of the following year, Ursula of the Saints, though only a novice, presided over St. Joseph's convent and guided it safely through a thousand difficulties. She died February 19, 1574.—The fourth was Maria, daughter of Christobal Davila (or de Avila) and Ana de Santo Domingo, and sister of Don Julian, chaplain of the convent of St. Joseph. She took the name Maria de San José, and made her profession on July 2, 1566, being then in her forty-first year. She died July 14, 1604.

more in this city dedicated to my glorious father St. Joseph. Not that I thought I had done anything myself, for I have never thought so, and do not think so even now ; I always looked upon it as the work of our Lord. My part in it was so full of imperfections, that I look upon myself rather as a person in fault than as one to whom any thanks are due. But it was a great joy to me when I saw His Majesty make use of me, who am so worthless, as His instrument in so grand a work. I was therefore in great joy,—so much so, that I was, as it were, beside myself, lost in prayer.

6. When all was done—it might have been about three or four hours afterwards—Satan returned to the spiritual fight against me, as I shall now relate. He suggested to me that perhaps I had been wrong in what I had done ; perhaps I had failed in my obedience, in having brought it about without the commandment of the Provincial. I did certainly think that the Provincial would be displeased because I had placed the monastery under the jurisdiction of the Bishop [18] without telling him of it beforehand ; though, as he would not acknowledge the monastery himself, and as I had not changed mine, it seemed to me that perhaps he would not care much about the matter. Satan also suggested whether the nuns would be contented to live in so strict a house, whether they could always find food, whether I had not done a silly thing, and what had I to do with it, when I was already in a monastery ? All our Lord had said to me, all the opinions I had heard, and all the prayers which had been almost uninterrupted for more than two years, were completely blotted out of my memory, just as if they had never been. The only thing I remembered was my own opinion ; and every virtue, with faith itself, was then suspended within me, so that I was without strength to practise any one of them, or to defend myself against so many blows.

[18] See *Foundations*, ch. ii. 1, and ch. xxxi. 1.

7. The devil also would have me ask myself how I could think of shutting myself up in so strict a house, when I was subject to so many infirmities; how could I bear so penitential a life, and leave a house large and pleasant, where I had been always so happy, and where I had so many friends?—perhaps I might not like those of the new monastery; I had taken on myself a heavy obligation, and might possibly end in despair. He also suggested that perhaps it was he himself who had contrived it, in order to rob me of my peace and rest, so that, being unable to pray, I might be disquieted, and so lose my soul. Thoughts of this kind he put before me; and they were so many, that I could think of nothing else; and with them came such distress, obscurity, and darkness of soul as I can never describe. When I found myself in this state, I went and placed myself before the most Holy Sacrament, though I could not pray to Him; so great was my anguish that I was like one in the agony of death. I could not make the matter known to any one, because no confessor had as yet been appointed.

8. O my God, how wretched is this life! No joy is lasting; everything is liable to change. Only a moment ago, I do not think I would have exchanged my joy with any man upon earth; and the very grounds of that joy so tormented me now, that I knew not what to do with myself. Oh, if we did but consider carefully the events of our life, every one of us would learn from experience how little we ought to make either of its pleasures or of its pains! Certainly this was, I believe, one of the most distressing moments I ever passed in all my life; my spirit seemed to forecast the great sufferings in store for me, though they never were so heavy as this was, if it had continued. But our Lord would not let His poor servant suffer, for in all my troubles He never failed to succour me; so it was now. He gave me a little light, so

that I might see it was the work of the devil, and
might understand the truth, namely, that it was
nothing else but an attempt on his part to frighten
me with his lies. So I began to call to mind my great
resolutions to serve our Lord, and my desire to suffer
for His sake ; and I thought that if I carried them out,
I must not seek to be at rest ; that if I had my trials,
they would be meritorious ; and that if I had troubles,
and endured them in order to please God, it would
serve me for purgatory. What was I, then, afraid
of ? If I longed for tribulations, I had them now ;
and my gain lay in the greatest opposition. Why,
then, did I fail in courage to serve One to whom I
owed so much ?

9. After making these and other reflections, and
doing great violence to myself, I promised before the
most Holy Sacrament to do all in my power to obtain
permission to enter this house, and, if I could do it
with a good conscience, to make a vow of enclosure.
When I had done this, the devil fled in a moment, and
left me calm and peaceful, and I have continued so
ever since ; and the enclosures, penances, and other
rules of this house are to me, in their observance, so
singularly sweet and light, the joy I have is so exceedingly great, that I am now and then thinking
what on earth I could have chosen which should be
more delightful. I know not whether this may not
be the cause of my being in better health than I was
ever before, or whether it be that our Lord, because
it is needful and reasonable that I should do as all
the others do, gives me this comfort of keeping the
whole rule, though with some difficulty. However,
all who know my infirmities, are astonished at my
strength. Blessed be He Who giveth it all, and in
Whose strength I am strong !

10. Such a contest left me greatly fatigued, and
laughing at Satan ; for I saw clearly it was he. As
I have never known what it is to be discontented

because I am a nun—no, not for an instant—during more than twenty-eight years of religion, I believe that our Lord suffered me to be thus tempted, that I might understand how great a mercy He had shown me herein, and from what torment He had delivered me, and that if I saw any one in like trouble, I might not be alarmed at it, but have pity on her, and be able to console her.

11. Then, when this was over, I wished to rest myself a little after our dinner ; for during the whole of that night I had scarcely rested at all, and for some nights previously I had had much trouble and anxiety, while every day was full of toil ; for the news of what we had done had reached my convent, and was spread through the city. There arose a great outcry, for the reasons I mentioned before,[19] and there was some apparent ground for it. The prioress [20] sent for me to come to her immediately. When I received the order, I went at once, leaving the nuns in great distress. I saw clearly enough that there were troubles before me ; but as the work was really done, I did not care much for that. I prayed and implored our Lord to help me, and my father St. Joseph to bring me back to his house. I offered up to him all I was to suffer, rejoicing greatly that I had the opportunity of suffering for his honour and of doing him service. I went persuaded that I should be put in prison at once ; but this would have been a great comfort, because I should have nobody to speak to, and might have some rest and solitude, of which I was in great need ; for so much intercourse with people had worn me out.[21]

12. When I came and told the prioress what I had done, she was softened a little. They all sent for the Provincial, and the matter was reserved for

<hr>

[19] Ch. xxxiii. 1, 2.   [20] Of the Incarnation.
[21] According to the tradition of the convent of the Incarnation she actually passed a short time in the prison of the convent, which, however, was not very formidable.

him.   When he came, I was summoned to judgment,
rejoicing greatly at seeing that I had something to
offer for our Lord.   I did not think I had offended
against His Majesty, or against my Order, in anything
I had done ; on the contrary, I was striving with all
my might to exalt my Order, for which I would willingly have died,—for my whole desire was that its
rule might be observed in all perfection.   I thought
of Christ receiving sentence, and I saw how this of
mine would be less than nothing.   I confessed my
fault, as if I had been very much to blame ; and so I
seemed to every one who did not know all the reasons.
After the Provincial had rebuked me sharply—though
not with the severity which my fault deserved, nor
according to the representations made to him—I
would not defend myself, for I was determined to bear
it all ; on the contrary, I prayed him to forgive and
punish, and be no longer angry with me.

13. I saw well enough that they condemned me
on some charges of which I was innocent, for they
said I had founded the monastery that I might be
thought much of, and to make myself a name, and
for other reasons of that kind.   But on other points
I understood clearly that they were speaking the
truth, as when they said that I was more wicked than
the other nuns.   They asked, how could I, who had
not kept the rule in that house, think of keeping it
in another of stricter observance ? They said I was
giving scandal in the city, and setting up novelties.
All this neither troubled nor distressed me in the least,
though I did seem to feel it, lest I should appear to
make light of what they were saying.

14. At last the Provincial commanded me to
explain my conduct before the nuns, and I had to do
it.   As I was perfectly calm, and our Lord helped
me, I explained everything in such a way that neither
the Provincial nor those who were present found any
reason to condemn me.   Afterwards I spoke more

plainly to the Provincial alone ; he was very much
satisfied, and promised, if the new monastery pros-
pered, and the city became quiet, to give me leave to
live in it. Now the outcry in the city was very great,
as I am going to tell. Two or three days after this,
the governor, certain members of the council of the
city and of the Chapter, came together, and resolved
that the new monastery should not be allowed to exist,
that it was a visible wrong to the State, that the
most Holy Sacrament should be removed, and that
they would not suffer us to go on with our work.

15. They assembled all the Orders—that is, two
learned men from each—to give their opinion. Some
were silent, others condemned ; in the end, they
resolved that the monastery should be broken up.
Only one [22]—he was of the Order of St. Dominic, and
objected, not to the convent itself, but to the foundation of it in poverty—said that there was no reason
why it should be thus dissolved, that the matter
ought to be well considered, that there was time
enough, that it was the affair of the Bishop, with
other things of that kind. This was of great service
to us, for they were angry enough to proceed to its
destruction at once, and it was fortunate they did
not. In short, the monastery must exist ; our Lord
was pleased to have it, and all of them could do nothing
against His will. They gave their reasons, and showed

[22] F. Domingo Bañes, the great commentator on St. Thomas. On the
margin of the MS. Bañes has with his own hand written . " This was at the
end of August 1562. I was present, and gave this opinion. I am writing
this in May " (the day of the month is not legible) " 1575, and the mother
has now founded nine monasteries *en gran religion*." At this time Bañes
did not know, and had never seen, the Saint ;· he undertook her defence
simply because he saw that her intentions were good, and the means she
made use of for founding the monastery lawful, seeing that she had received
the commandment to do so from the Pope. Bañes testifies thus in the
depositions made in Salamanca in 1591, in the Saint's process. Born at
Medina del Campo, Feb. 29, 1528, he entered the Order at the age of nineteen,
taught philosophy at Salamanca, whence he was sent to the larger convent
of Santo Tomás at Avila. Here he made the acquaintance of the Saint. He
left his mark on scholastic theology. He died in his native town, Oct. 22,
1604.

their zeal for good, and thus, without offending God, made me suffer together with all those who were in favour of the monastery ; they were not many, but they suffered much persecution. The inhabitants were so excited that they talked of nothing else ; every one condemned me, and hurried to the Provincial and to my convent.

16. I was no more distressed by what they said of me than if they had said nothing ; but I was afraid the monastery would be destroyed : that was painful ; so also was it to see those persons who helped me lose their credit and suffer so much annoyance. But as to what was said of myself I was rather glad, and if I had had any faith I should not have been troubled at all ; but a slight failing in one virtue is enough to put all the others to sleep. I was therefore extremely distressed during the two days on which those assemblies of which I have spoken were held. In the extremity of my trouble, our Lord said to me : " Knowest thou not that I am the Almighty ? what art thou afraid of ? " He made me feel assured that the monastery would not be broken up, and I was exceedingly comforted. The informations taken were sent up to the king's council, and an order came back for a report on the whole matter.

17. Here was the beginning of a grand lawsuit : the city sent delegates to the court, and some must be sent also to defend the monastery : but I had no money, nor did I know what to do. Our Lord provided for us ; for the Father Provincial never ordered me not to meddle in the matter. He is so great a lover of all that is good that, though he did not help us, he would not be against our work. Neither did he authorise me to enter the house till he saw how it would end. Those servants of God who were in it were left alone, and did more by their prayers than I did with all my negotiations, though the affair needed the utmost attention. Now and then everything

seemed to fail; particularly one day, before the Provincial came, when the prioress ordered me to meddle no more with it, and to give it up altogether. I betook myself to God, and said, ''O Lord, this house is not mine; it was founded for Thee; and now that there is no one to take up the cause, do Thou protect it.'' I now felt myself in peace, and as free from anxiety as if the whole world were on my side in the matter; and at once I looked upon it as safe.[23]

18. A very great servant of God, and a lover of all perfection, a priest,[24] who had helped me always, went to the court on this business, and took great pains. That holy nobleman [25] of whom I have often spoken laboured much on our behalf, and helped us in every way. He had much trouble and persecution to endure, and I always found a father in him, and do so still. All those who helped us, our Lord filled with such fervour as made them consider our affair as their own, as if their own life and reputation were at stake; and yet it was nothing to them, except in so far as it regarded the service of our Lord. His Majesty visibly helped the priest I have spoken of before,[26] who was also one of those who gave us great help when the Bishop sent him as his representative to one of the great meetings. There he stood alone against all; at last he pacified them by means of certain propositions, which obtained us a little respite. But that was not enough; for they were ready to spend their lives if they could but destroy the monastery. This servant of God was he who gave the habit and reserved the most Holy Sacrament, and he was the object of much persecution. This attack lasted about six months : to relate in detail the heavy trials we passed through would be too tedious.

19. I wondered at what Satan did against a few poor women, and also how all people thought that

[23] See ch. xxxix. 25.　　　　　[24] Don Gonzalo de Aranda.
[25] Don Francisco de Salcedo.　　[26] Ch. xxiii. 6 ; Gaspar Daza.

merely twelve women, with a prioress, could be so
hurtful to the city,—for they were not to be more,—
I say this to those who opposed us,—and living such
austere lives ; for if any harm or error came of it, it
would all fall upon them.   Harm to the city there
could not be in any way ; and yet the people thought
there was so much in it, that they opposed us with a
good conscience.   At last they resolved they would
tolerate us if we were endowed, and in consideration
of that would suffer us to remain.   I was so distressed
at the trouble of all those who were on our side—
more than at my own—that I thought it would not
be amiss, till the people were pacified, to accept an
endowment, but afterwards to resign it.   At other
times, too, wicked and imperfect as I am, I thought
that perhaps our Lord wished it to be so, seeing that,
without accepting it, we could not succeed ; and so
I consented to the compromise.

20. The night before the settlement was to be
made, I was in prayer,—the discussion of the terms
of it had already begun,—when our Lord said to me
that I must do nothing of the kind ; for if we began
with an endowment, they would never allow us to
resign it.   He said some other things also.   The same
night, the holy friar, Peter of Alcantara, appeared to
me.   He was then dead.[27]   But he had written to
me before his death—for he knew the great opposition
and persecution we had to bear—that he was glad
the foundation was so much spoken against ; it was
a sign that our Lord would be exceedingly honoured
in the monastery, seeing that Satan was so earnest
against it ; and that I was by no means to consent
to an endowment.   He urged this upon me twice or
thrice in that letter, and said that if I persisted in
this everything would succeed according to my wish.

21. At this time I had already seen him twice

[27] He died Oct. 18, 1562.   The letter referred to was written only four
or five days before his death.

since his death, and the great glory he was in, and so I was not afraid,—on the contrary, I was very glad ; for he always appeared as a glorified body in great happiness, and the vision made me very happy too. I remember that he told me, the first time I saw him, among other things, when speaking of the greatness of his joy, that the penance he had done was a blessed thing for him, in that it had obtained so great a reward. But, as I think I have spoken of this before,[28] I will now say no more than that he showed himself severe on this occasion : he merely said that I was on no account to accept an endowment, and asked why it was I did not take his advice. He then disappeared. I remained in astonishment, and the next day told the nobleman—for I went to him in all my troubles, as to one who did more than others for us in the matter—what had taken place, and charged him not to consent to the endowment, but to let the lawsuit go on. He was more firm on this point than I was, and was therefore greatly pleased ; he told me afterwards how much he disliked the compromise.

22. After this, another personage—a great servant of God, and with good intentions—came forward, who, now that the matter was in good train, advised us to put it in the hands of learned men. This brought on trouble enough ; for some of those who helped me agreed to do so ; and this plot of Satan was one of the most difficult of all to unravel. Our Lord was my helper throughout. Writing thus briefly, it is impossible for me to explain what took place during the two years that passed between the beginning and the completion of the monastery : the last six months and the first six months were the most painful.

23. When at last the city was somewhat calm, the licentiate father, the Dominican friar [29] who helped us, exerted himself most skilfully on our behalf. Though not here at the time, our Lord brought him

[28] Ch. xxvii. 21. [29] F. Pedro Ibañez. See ch. xxxiii. 7.

here at a most convenient moment for our service, and it seems that His Majesty brought him for that purpose only. He told me afterwards that he had no reasons for coming, and that he heard of our affair as if by chance. He remained here as long as we wanted him : and on going away he prevailed, by some means, on the Father Provincial to permit me to enter this house, and to take with me some of the nuns [30]—such a permission seemed impossible in so short a time—for the performance of the Divine Office, and the training of those who were in this house : the day of our coming was a most joyful day for me.[31]

24. While praying in the church, before I went

[30] In the absence of a written permission the exact date cannot be ascertained, but must have been somewhere about the beginning of March, 1563. St. Teresa was accompanied by four professed nuns of the convent of the Incarnation, and a novice. The former were : (1) Anne of St. John (De Avila), related to the Marquis de Velada. As St. Teresa had refused the priorship, this sister acted as superioress until the Bishop of Avila, at the entreaties of the nuns, compelled the Saint to accept the dignity. Anne of St. John seems to have remained only a short time at the convent of St. Joseph, for her name is not to be found in the Patent given by the Provincial August 22, 1563, which is preserved at Avila. (2) Maria Ordoñez, daughter of Diego Ordoñez and Ana Gomez, who took the name Mary Isabelle. After some years she, too, left the Reform and returned to the Incarnation. (3) Ana Gomez, known as Anne of the Angels, sister of the preceding, was the first sub-prioress of St. Joseph's convent ; she accompanied St. Teresa to Medina del Campo, Alcalá and Malagón, where she became prioress ; afterwards she filled the same office at Toledo, where she renounced the mitigated Rule, February 9, 1572 ; in 1585 she founded the convent of Cuerva, where she died, October 2, 1605. (4) Doña Maria de Cepeda, cousin of the Saint, was obliged by ill health to return to the convent of the Incarnation, where she passed many years in the infirmary, being quite paralysed. Yet she lingered on, and even lived to witness St. Teresa's beatification in 1614. A fifth nun, Doña Isabel de la Peña, daughter of Francisco de Cepeda and Maria de Ocampo, of Torijos, was only a novice at the time, and therefore required no permission to go from the Incarnation to St. Joseph's ; she there took the name Isabelle of St. Paul, and made her profession October 21, 1564. She brought, with her habit, 200 ducats. She accompanied St. Teresa on several journeys, and assisted her in the foundations of Toledo, Pastrana and Segovia, and died at Avila, February 4, 1584, aged thirty-eight.

[31] Mid-Lent of 1563. According to tradition, St. Teresa, on her way from the convent of the Incarnation to that of St. Joseph, entered the basilica of San Vicente, where she discalced herself and exchanged her name (Doña Teresa de Ahumada) for that of Teresa de Jesús. The former appears still on the Patent of August 22, 1563, but all her own writings bear the latter. The adoption of a name of a saint in lieu of a surname was made obligatory by the General John Baptist Rubeo (1567).

into the house, and being as it were in a trance, I saw Christ ; Who, as it seemed to me, received me with great affection, placed a crown on my head, and thanked me for what I had done for His Mother. On another occasion, when all of us remained in the choir in prayer after Compline, I saw our Lady in exceeding glory, in a white mantle, with which she seemed to cover us all. I understood by that the high degree of glory to which our Lord would raise the religious of this house.

25. When we had begun to sing the Office, the people began to have a great devotion to the monastery ; more nuns were received,[32] and our Lord began to stir up those who had been our greatest persecutors to become great benefactors, and give alms to us. In this way they came to approve of what they had condemned ; and so, by degrees, they withdrew from the lawsuit, and would say that they now felt it to be a work of God, since His Majesty had been pleased

[32] These were : (1) Maria Bautista, niece of St. Teresa, whose real name was Doña Maria de Ocampo, daughter of Diego de Cepeda and Beatriz de la Cruz, of Toledo. She brought 300 ducats. Born in 1543, she lived for a time at the convent of the Incarnation as a pensioner, and as such was present at the memorable meeting which led to the establishment of the convent of St. Joseph (see ch. xxxii. 13). She joined the convent as soon as St. Teresa was established there, and made her profession October 21, 1564. Later on she became prioress of Valladolid, where she died, August 10, 1603. (2) Mary of St. Jerome, Doña Maria Davila, daughter of Alonso Alvarez Davila and Doña Mencia de Salazar. She entered the convent September 30, 1563, and brought an alms of 250 ducats, and founded the chaplaincy of the convent, which was held for many years by Don Julian. At her profession, April 22, 1565, she was twenty-four years old. After the departure of St. Teresa, with whom she was distantly related, she became superioress of the convent, under the title of sub-prioress, St. Teresa, as foundress, retaining nominally the priorship. Later on Mary of St. Jerome became prioress of Madrid, foundress of Ocaña, and finally once more prioress of St. Joseph's, Avila, where she died April 6, 1602. (3) Isabelle of St. Dominic, whose real name was Isabel de Ortega, daughter of Juan de Ortega and Maria de Vergas, of Cardeñosa. Having lost her parents at an early date she suffered great hardships, in which she was consoled and strengthened by St. Peter of Alcantara, who first told her of St. Teresa, whom she joined, October 4, 1563. She brought 600 ducats to the convent and made her profession October 21, 1565. She was the first nun of the Reform who was made prioress, viz. at Toledo, and afterwards at Pastrana and Segovia. Later on she founded the convent of Saragossa, became prioress of Ocaña, again of Segovia, and finally of Avila, where she died, June 13, 1623, at the age of eighty-four. Other nuns of this convent do not belong to this period of the life of St. Teresa.

to carry it on in the face of so much opposition. And now there is not one who thinks that it would have been right not to have founded the monastery : so they make a point of furnishing us with alms ; for without any asking on our part, without begging of any one, our Lord moves them to succour us ; and so we always have what is necessary for us, and I trust in our Lord it will always be so.[33]   As the sisters are few in number, if they do their duty as our Lord at present by His grace enables them to do, I am confident that they will always have it, and that they need not be a burden nor troublesome to anybody ; for our Lord will care for them, as He has hitherto done.

26. It is the greatest consolation to me to find myself among those who are so detached. Their occupation is to learn how they may advance in the service of God. Solitude is their delight ; and the thought of being visited by any one, even of their nearest kindred, is a trial, unless it helps them to kindle more and more their love of the Bridegroom. Accordingly, none come to this house who do not aim at this ; otherwise they neither give nor receive any pleasure from their visits. Their conversation is of God only ; and so he whose conversation is different does not understand them, and they do not understand him.

27. We keep the rule of our Lady of Carmel, not the rule of the Mitigation, but as it was settled by Fr. Hugo, Cardinal of Santa Sabina, and given in the year 1248, in the fifth year of the pontificate of Innocent IV., Pope.   All the trouble we had to go through, as it seems to me, will have been endured to good purpose.

28. And now, though the rule be somewhat severe, —for we never eat flesh except in cases of necessity, fast eight months in the year, and practise some other

[33] See *Way of Perfection*, ch. ii.

austerities besides, according to the primitive rule,[34]—yet the sisters think it light on many points, and so they have other observances, which we have thought necessary for the more perfect keeping of it. And I trust in our Lord that what we have begun will prosper more and more, according to the promise of His Majesty.

29. The other house, which the holy woman of whom I spoke before [35] laboured to establish, has been also blessed of our Lord, and is founded in Alcalá : it did not escape serious opposition, nor fail to endure many trials. I know that all duties of religion are observed in it, according to our primitive rule. Our Lord grant that all may be to the praise and glory of Himself and of the glorious Virgin Mary, whose habit we wear. Amen.

30. I think you must be wearied, my father, by the tedious history of this monastery ; and yet it is most concise, if you compare it with our labours, and the wonders which our Lord has wrought here. There are many who can bear witness to this on oath. I therefore beg of your reverence, for the love of God, should you think fit to destroy the rest of this my writing, to preserve that part of it which relates to this monastery, and give it, when I am dead, to the sisters who may then be living in it. It will encourage them greatly, who shall come here both to serve God

[34] " Jejunium singulis diebus, exceptis Dominicis, observetis a Festo Exaltationis Sanctæ Crucis usque ad diem Dominicæ Resurrectionis, nisi infirmitas vel debilitas corporis, aut alia justa causa, jejunium solvi suadeat ; quia necessitas non habet legem. Ab esu carnium abstineatis, nisi pro infirmitatis aut debilitatis remedio sumantur." This is the tenth section of the rule. The Carmelite rule, originally written by St. Albert, Patriarch of Jerusalem, about A.D. 1209, was revised by Cardinal Hugh of St. Cher, and approved by Pope Innocent IV. in 1247, not 1248, as stated in the text.

[35] See ch. xxxv. 1. Maria of Jesus had founded her house in Alcalá de Henares ; but the austerities practised in it, and the want of experience on the part of the foundress, brought the convent in a short time to the verge of ruin. Maria of Jesus begged Doña Leonora de Mascareñas to persuade St. Teresa to come to Alcalá. The Saint went there (June 1569), and was received with joy, and even entreated to take the house under her own government.

and to labour, that what has been thus begun may not fall to decay, but ever grow and thrive, when they see how much our Lord has done through one so mean and vile as I. As our Lord has been so particularly gracious to us in the foundation of this house, it seems to me that she will do very wrong, and that she will be heavily chastised of God, who shall be the first to relax the perfect observance of the rule, which our Lord has here begun and countenanced, so that it may be kept with so much sweetness : it is most evident that the observance of it is easy, and that it can be kept with ease, by the arrangement made for those who long to be alone with their Bridegroom Christ, in order to live for ever in Him.

31. This is to be the perpetual aim of those who are here, to be alone with Him alone. They are not to be more in number than thirteen : I know this number to be the best, for I have had many opinions about it ; and I have seen in my own experience, that to preserve our spirit, living on alms, without asking of any one, a larger number would be inexpedient. May they always believe one who with much labour and by the prayers of many people, accomplished that which must be for the best ! That this is most expedient for us will be seen from the joy and cheerfulness, and the few troubles, we have all had in the years we have lived in this house, as well as from the better health than usual of us all. If any one thinks the rule hard, let her lay the fault on her want of the true spirit, and not on the rule of the house, seeing that delicate persons, and those not saints,—because they have the true spirit,—can bear it all with so much sweetness. Let others go to another monastery, where they may save their souls in the way of their own spirit.

CHAPTER XXXVII.

THE EFFECTS OF THE DIVINE GRACES IN THE SOUL.   THE INESTIMABLE GREATNESS OF ONE DEGREE OF GLORY.

Of the effects which remained when God granted her some favour ; together with other very good doctrine. She shows how one ought to strive after and prize every increase in heavenly glory, and that for no trouble whatever one should neglect a good that is to be perpetual.

1. IT is painful to me to recount more of the graces which our Lord gave me than these already spoken of ; and they are so many, that nobody can believe they were ever given to one so wicked : but in obedience to our Lord, who has commanded me to do it,[1] and you, my fathers, I will speak of some of them to His glory. May it please His Majesty it may be to the profit of some soul ! For if our Lord has been thus gracious to so miserable a thing as myself, what will He be to those who shall serve Him truly ? Let all people resolve to please His Majesty, seeing that He gives such pledges as these even in this life.[2]

2. In the first place, it must be understood that, in those graces which God bestows on the soul, there are diverse degrees of joy : for in some visions the joy and sweetness and comfort of them so far exceed those of others, that I am amazed at the different degrees of fruition even in this life ; for it happens that the joy and consolation which God gives in a vision or a trance are so different, that it seems impossible for the soul to be able to desire anything more in this world : and so, in fact, the soul does

---

[1] The Saint, having interrupted her account of her interior life in order to give the history of the foundation of the monastery of St. Joseph, Avila,—the first house of the Reformed Carmelites,—here resumes that account broken off at the end of § 10 of ch. xxxii.

[2] Ephes. i, 14 : " Pignus hæreditatis nostræ,"

not desire, nor would it ask for, a greater joy. Still, since our Lord has made me understand how great a difference there is in heaven itself between the fruition of one and that of another, I see clearly enough that here also, when our Lord wills, He gives not by measure [3] ; and so I wish that I myself observed no measure in serving His Majesty, and in using my whole life and strength and health therein ; and i would not have any fault of mine rob me of the slightest degree of fruition.

3. And so I say that if I were asked which I preferred, to endure all the trials of the world until the end of it, and then receive one slight degree of glory additional, or without any suffering of any kind to enter into glory of a slightly lower degree, I would accept—oh, how willingly !—all those trials for one slight degree of fruition in the contemplation of the greatness of God ; for I know that he who understands Him best, loves Him and praises Him best. I do not mean that I should not be satisfied, and consider myself to be most blessed, to be in heaven, even if I should be in the lowest place ; for as I am one who had that place in hell, it would be a great mercy of our Lord to admit me at all ; and may it please His Majesty to bring me thither, [4] and take away His eyes from beholding my grievous sins. What I mean is this,—if it were in my power, even if it cost me everything, and our Lord gave me the grace to endure much affliction, I would not through any fault of mine lose one degree of glory. Ah, wretched that I am, who by so many faults had forfeited all !

4. It is also to be observed that, in every vision or revelation which our Lord in His mercy sent me, a great gain accrued to my soul, and that in some of the visions this gain was very great. [5] The vision of

---

[3] St. John iii. 34 : " Non enim ad mensuram dat Deus spiritum." " Causa diligendi Deum Deus est, modus sine modo diligere." (St. Bernard, *De Dilig. Deo*, i. 1.)

[4] *Rel*. ii. 16.   [5] Ch. vii. 11.

Christ left behind an impression of His exceeding
beauty, and it remains with me to this day.   One
vision alone of Him is enough to effect this ; what,
then, must all those visions have done, which our Lord
in His mercy sent me ?   One exceedingly great blessing
has resulted therefrom, and it is this,—I had one
very grievous fault, which was the source of much
evil ;   namely, whenever I found anybody well disposed towards myself, and I liked him, I used to
have such an affection for him as compelled me always
to remember and think of him, though I had no
intention of offending God : however, I was pleased
to see him, to think of him and of his good qualities.
All this was so hurtful, that it brought my soul to the
very verge of destruction.

5. But ever since I saw the great beauty [6] of our
Lord, I never saw any one who in comparison with
Him seemed even endurable, or that could occupy my
thoughts.   For if I but turn mine eyes inwardly for a
moment to the contemplation of the image which I
have within me, I find myself so free, that from that
instant everything I see is loathsome in comparison
with the excellences and graces of which I had a vision
in our Lord.   Neither is there any sweetness, nor
any kind of pleasure, which I can make any account
of, compared with that which comes from hearing but
one word from His divine mouth.   What, then, must
it be when I hear so many ?   I look upon it as impossible—unless our Lord, for my sins, should permit
the loss of this remembrance—that I should have the
power to occupy myself with anything in such a way
as that I should not instantly recover my liberty by
thinking of our Lord.

6. This has happened to me with some of my
confessors, for I always have a great affection for
those who have the direction of my soul.   As I really
saw in them only the representatives of God, I thought

[6] Ch. xxviii. 1–5.

my will was always there where it is most occupied ;
and as I felt very safe in the matter, I always showed
myself glad to see them.[7]   They, on the other hand,
servants of God, and fearing Him, were afraid that I
was attaching and binding myself too much to them,
though in a holy way, and treated me with rudeness.
This took place after I had become so ready to obey
them ; for before that time I had no affection whatever
for them.   I used to laugh to myself, when I saw
how much they were deceived.[8]   Though I was not
always putting before them how little I was attached
to anybody, as clearly as I was convinced of it myself,
yet I did assure them of it ; and they, in their further
relations with me, acknowledged how much I owed
to our Lord in the matter.   These suspicions of me
always arose in the beginning.

7. My love of, and trust in, our Lord, after I had
seen Him in a vision, began to grow, for my converse
with Him was so continual.   I saw that, though He
was God, He was man also ; that He is not surprised
at the frailties of men, that He understands our
miserable nature, liable to fall continually, because of
the first sin, for the reparation of which He had come.
I could speak to Him as to a friend, though He is my
Lord, because I do not consider Him as one of our
earthly Lords, who affect a power they do not possess,
who give audience at fixed hours, and to whom only
certain persons may speak.   If a poor man have any
business with these, it will cost him many goings and
comings, and currying favour with others, together
with much pain and labour before he can speak to
them.   Ah, if such a one has business with a king !
Poor people, not of gentle blood, cannot approach
him, for they must apply to those who are his friends,
and certainly these are not persons who tread the
world under their feet ; for they who do this speak
the truth, fear nothing, and ought to fear nothing ;

---

[7] See ch. xl. 24 ; *Way of Perfection*, ch. iv. 9.   [8] Ch. v. 9.

they are not courtiers, because it is not the custom of
a court, where they must be silent about those things
they dislike, must not even dare to think about them,
lest they should fall into disgrace.

8. O King of glory, and Lord of all kings! oh,
how Thy kingly dignity is not hedged about by trifles
of this kind! Thy kingdom is for ever. We do not
require chamberlains to introduce us into Thy presence. The very vision of Thy person shows us at
once that Thou alone art to be called Lord. Thy
Majesty is so manifest, that there is no need of a
retinue or guard to make us confess that Thou art
king. An earthly king without attendants would be
hardly acknowledged; and though he might wish
ever so much to be recognised, people will not own
him when he appears as others; it is necessary that
his dignity should be visible, if people are to believe
in it. This is reason enough why kings should affect
so much state; for if they had none, no one would
respect them; this their semblance of power is not in
themselves, and their authority must come to them
from others.

9. O my Lord! O my King! who can describe
Thy Majesty? It is impossible not to see that Thou
art Thyself the great Ruler of all, that the beholding
of Thy Majesty fills men with awe. But I am filled
with greater awe, O my Lord, when I consider Thy
humility, and the love Thou hast for such as I am.
We can converse and speak with Thee about everything whenever we will; and when we lose our
first fear and awe at the vision of Thy Majesty, we
have a greater dread of offending Thee,—not arising
out of the fear of punishment, O my Lord, for
that is as nothing in comparison with the loss of
Thee!

10. Thus far of the blessings of this vision, without
speaking of others, which abide in the soul when it is
past. If it be from God, the fruits thereof show it,

when the soul receives light ; for, as I have often said : [9]
the will of our Lord is that the soul should be in
darkness, and not see this light. It is, therefore,
nothing to be wondered at that I, knowing myself to
be so wicked as I am, should be afraid.

11. It is only just now it happened to me to be
for eight days in a state wherein it seemed that I did
not, and could not, confess my obligations to God, or
remember His mercies ; but my soul was so stupefied
and occupied with I know not what nor how : not
that I had any bad thoughts ; only I was so incapable
of good thoughts, that I was laughing at myself, and
even rejoicing to see how mean a soul can be if God
is not always working in it.[10]   The soul sees clearly
that God is not away from it in this state, and that it
is not in those great tribulations which I have spoken
of as being occasionally mine.   Though it heaps up
fuel, and does the little it can do of itself, it cannot
make the fire of the love of God burn : it is a great
mercy that even the smoke is visible, showing that it
is not altogether quenched.   Our Lord will return
and kindle it ; and until then the soul—though it
may lose its breath in blowing and arranging the fuel
—seems to be doing nothing but putting it out more
and more.

12. I believe that now the best course is to be
absolutely resigned, confessing that we can do nothing,
and so apply ourselves—as I said before [11]—to something else which is meritorious.   Our Lord, it may
be, takes away from the soul the power of praying,
that it may betake itself to something else, and learn
by experience how little it can do in its own strength.

13. It is true I have this day been rejoicing in our
Lord, and have dared to complain of His Majesty.
I said unto Him : How is it, O my God, that it is not
enough for Thee to detain me in this wretched life,

---

[9] See ch. xx. 14.   [10] See ch. xxx. 19.
[11] See ch. xxx. 18, 25.

and that I should have to bear with it for the love of
Thee, and be willing to live where everything hinders
the fruition of Thee ; where, besides, I must eat and
sleep, transact business, and converse with every one,
and all for Thy love ? how is it, then—for Thou well
knowest, O my Lord, all this to be the greatest torment
unto me,—that, in the rare moments when I am with
Thee, Thou hidest Thyself from me ? How is this
consistent with Thy compassion ? How can that
love Thou hast for me endure this ? I believe, O Lord,
if it were possible for me to hide myself from Thee, as
Thou hidest Thyself from me—I think and believe so
—such is Thy love, that Thou wouldst not endure
it at my hands. But Thou art with me, and seest me
always. O my Lord, I beseech Thee look to this ;
it must not be ; a wrong is done to one who loves
Thee so much.

14. I happened to utter these words, and others
of the same kind, when I should have been thinking
rather how my place in hell was pleasant in comparison with the place I deserved. But now and
then my love makes me foolish, so that I lose my
senses ; only it is with all the sense I have that I
make these complaints, and our Lord bears it all.
Blessed be so good a King !

15. Can we be thus bold with the kings of this
world ? And yet I am not surprised that we dare not
thus speak to a king, for it is only reasonable that
men should be afraid of him, or even to the great
lords who are his representatives. The world is now
come to such a state, that men's lives ought to be
longer than they are, if we are to learn all the new
customs and ceremonies of good breeding, and yet
spend any time in the service of God. I bless myself
at the sight of what is going on. The fact is, I did
not know how I was to live when I came into this
house. Any negligence in being much more cere-
monious with people than they deserve is not taken

as a jest ; on the contrary, they look upon it as an insult deliberately offered ; so that it becomes necessary for you to satisfy them of your good intentions, if there happens, as I have said, to have been any negligence ; and even then, God grant they may believe you.

16. I repeat it,—I certainly did not know how to live ; for my poor soul was worn out. It is told to employ all its thoughts always on God, and that it is necessary to do so if it would avoid many dangers. On the other hand, it finds it will not do to fail in any one point of the world's law, under the penalty of affronting those who look upon these things as touching their honour. I was worn out in unceasingly giving satisfaction to people ; for, though I tried my utmost, I could not help failing in many ways in matters which, as I have said, are not slightly thought of in the world.

17. Is it true that in religious houses no explanations are necessary, for it is only reasonable we should be excused these observances ? Well, that is not so ; for there are people who say that monasteries ought to be courts in politeness and instruction. I certainly cannot understand it. I thought that perhaps some saint may have said that they ought to be courts to teach those who wish to be the courtiers of heaven, and that these people misunderstood their meaning ; for if a man be careful to please God continually, and to hate the world, as he ought to do, I do not see how he can be equally careful to please those who live in the world in these matters which are continually changing. If they could be learnt once for all, it might be borne with : but as to the way of addressing letters, there ought to be a professor's chair founded, from which lectures should be given, so to speak, teaching us how to do it ; for the paper should on one occasion be left blank in one corner, and on another in another corner ; and a

man must not be addressed as the illustrious who was hitherto addressed as the magnificent.

18. I know not where this will stop : I am not yet fifty, and yet I have seen so many changes during my life, that I do not know how to live. What will they do who are only just born, and who may live many years ? Certainly I am sorry for those spiritual people who, for certain holy purposes, are obliged to live in the world ; the cross they have to carry is a dreadful one. If they could all agree together, and make themselves ignorant, and be willing to be considered so in these sciences, they would set themselves free from much trouble. But·what folly am I about ! from speaking of the greatness of God I am come to speak of the meanness of the world ! Since our Lord has given me the grace to quit it, I wish to leave it altogether. Let them settle these matters who maintain these follies with so much labour. God grant that in the next life, where there is no changing, we may not have to pay for them ! Amen.

CHAPTER XXXVIII.

CERTAIN HEAVENLY SECRETS, VISIONS, AND REVELA-
TIONS. THE EFFECTS OF THEM IN HER SOUL.

. She treats of some great mercies God showed her, even making known to her heavenly secrets by means of visions and revelations His Majesty vouchsafed to grant her. She speaks of the effects they caused, and the great improvement resulting in her soul.

1. ONE night I was so unwell that I thought I might be excused making my prayer ; so I took my rosary, that I might employ myself in vocal prayer, trying not to be recollected in my understanding, though

outwardly I was recollected, being in my oratory. These little precautions are of no use when our Lord will have it otherwise. I remained there but a few moments thus, when I was rapt in spirit with such violence that I could make no resistance whatever. It seemed to me that I was taken up to heaven ; and the first persons I saw there were my father and my mother. I saw other things also ; but the time was no longer than that in which the *Ave Maria* might be said, and I was amazed at it, looking on it all as too great a grace for me. But as to the shortness of the time, it might have been longer, only it was all done in a very short space.

2. I was afraid it might be an illusion ; but as I did not think so, I knew not what to do, because I was very much ashamed to go to my confessor about it. It was not, as it seemed to me, because I was humble, but because I thought he would laugh at me, and say : Oh, what a St. Paul !—she sees the things of heaven ; or a St. Jerome. And because these glorious Saints had had such visions, I was so much the more afraid, and did nothing but cry ; for I did not think it possible for me to see what they saw. At last, though I felt it exceedingly, I went to my confessor ; for I never dared to keep secret anything of this kind, however much it distressed me to speak of them, owing to the great fear I had of being deceived. When my confessor saw how much I was suffering, he consoled me greatly, and gave me plenty of good reasons why I should have no fear.

3. It happened, also, as time went on, and it happens now from time to time, that our Lord showed me still greater secrets. The soul, even if it would, has neither the means nor the power to see more than what He shows it ; and so, each time, I saw nothing more than what our Lord was pleased to let me see. But such was the vision, that the least part of it was enough to make my soul amazed, and to raise it so

high that it esteems and counts as nothing all the things of this life. I wish I could describe, in some measure, the smallest portion of what I saw ; but when I think of doing it, I find it impossible ; for the mere difference alone between the light we have here below, and that which is seen in a vision,—both being light,—is so great, that there is no comparison between them ; the brightness of the sun itself seems to be something exceedingly loathsome. In a word, the imagination, however strong it may be, can neither conceive nor picture to itself this light, nor any one of the things which our Lord showed me in a joy so supreme that it cannot be described ; for then all the senses exult so deeply and so sweetly, that no description is possible ; and so it is better to say nothing more.

4. I was in this state once for more than an hour, our Lord showing me wonderful things. He seemed as if He would not leave me. He said to me : " See, My daughter, what they lose who are against Me ; do not fail to tell them of it." Ah, my Lord, how little good my words will do them, who are made blind by their own conduct, if Thy Majesty will not give them light ! Some, to whom Thou hast given it, there are, who have profited by the knowledge of Thy greatness [1] ; but as they see it revealed to one so wicked and base as I am, I look upon it as a great thing if there should be any found to believe me. Blessed be Thy name, and blessed be Thy compassion ; for I can trace, at least in my own soul, a visible improvement. Afterwards I wished I had continued in that trance for ever, and that I had not returned to consciousness, because of an abiding sense of contempt for everything here below ; all seemed to be filth ; and I see how meanly we employ ourselves who are detained on earth.

5. When I was staying with that lady of whom I have been speaking,[2] it happened to me once when I

---

[1] Ch. xiii. 12.　　　[2] Ch. xxxiv. Doña Luisa de la Cerda, at Toledo.

was suffering from my heart,—for, as I have said,[3] I suffered greatly at one time, though not so much now, —that she, being a person of great charity, brought out her jewels set in gold, and precious stones of great price, and particularly a diamond, which she valued very much.   She thought this might amuse me ; but I laughed to myself, and was very sorry to see what men made much of ; for I thought of what our Lord had laid up for us, and considered how impossible it was for me, even if I made the effort, to have any appreciation whatever of such things, provided our Lord did not permit me to forget what He was keeping for us.

6. A soul in this state attains to a certain freedom, which is so complete that none can understand it who does not possess it.   It is a real and true detachment, independent of our efforts ; God effects it all Himself ; for His Majesty reveals the truth in such a way, that it remains so deeply impressed on our souls as to make it clear that we of ourselves could not thus acquire it in so short a time.

7. The fear of death, also, was now very slight in me, who had always been in great dread of it ; now it seems to me that death is a very light thing for one who serves God, because the soul is in a moment delivered thereby out of its prison, and at rest.   This elevation of the spirit, and the vision of things so high in these trances, seem to me to have a great likeness to the flight of the soul from the body, in that it finds itself in a moment in the possession of these good things.   We put aside the agonies of its dissolution, of which no great account is to be made ; for they who love God in truth, and are utterly detached from the things of this life, must die with the greater sweetness.

8. It seems to me, also, that the rapture was a great help to recognise our true home, and to see that

[3] Ch. iv. 6.

we are pilgrims here[4] ; it is a great thing to see what is going on there, and to know where we have to live ; for if a person has to go and settle in another country, it is a great help to him, in undergoing the fatigues of his journey, that he has discovered it to be a country where he may live in the most perfect peace. Moreover, it makes it easy for us to think of the things of heaven, and to have our conversation there.[5] It is a great gain, because the mere looking up to heaven makes the soul recollected ; for as our Lord has been pleased to reveal heaven in some degree, my soul dwells upon it in thought ; and it happens occasionally that they who are about me, and with whom I find consolation, are those whom I know to be living in heaven, and that I look upon them only as really alive ; while those who are on earth are so dead, that the whole world seems unable to furnish me with companions, particularly when these impetuosities of love are upon me. Everything seems a dream, and what I see with the bodily eyes an illusion. What I have seen with the eyes of the soul is that which my soul desires ; and as it finds itself far away from those things, that is death.

9. In a word, it is a very great mercy which our Lord gives to that soul to which He grants the like visions, for they help it in much, and also in carrying a heavy cross, since nothing satisfies it, and everything is against it ; and if our Lord did not now and then suffer these visions to be forgotten, though they recur again and again to the memory, I know not how life could be borne. May He be blessed and praised for ever and ever ! I implore His Majesty by that Blood which His Son shed for me, now that, of His good pleasure, I know something of these great blessings, and begin to have the fruition of them, that it may not be with me as it was with Lucifer, who by his

---

[4] i St. Peter ii. 11 : " Advenas et peregrinos."
[5] Philipp. iii. 20 : " Nostra autem conversatio in cœlis est."

own fault forfeited it all.   I beseech Thee, for Thine
own sake, not to suffer this ; for I am at times in
great fear, though at others, and most frequently, the
mercy of God reassures me, for He who has delivered
me from so many sins will not withdraw His hand
from under me, and let me be lost.   I pray you, my
father, to beg this grace for me always.

10. The mercies, then, hitherto described are not,
in my opinion, so great as those which I am now
going to speak of, on many accounts, because of the
great blessings they have brought with them, and
because of the great fortitude which my soul derived
from them ; and yet every one separately considered
is so great, that there is nothing to be compared with
them.

11. One day—it was the eve of Pentecost—I went
after Mass to a very lonely spot, where I used to pray
very often, and began to read about the feast in the
book of a Carthusian [6] ; and reading of the marks by
which beginners, proficients, and the perfect may
know that they have the Holy Ghost, it seemed to
me, when I had read of these three states, that by
the goodness of God, so far as I could understand, the
Holy Ghost was with me.   I praised God for it ; and
calling to mind how on another occasion, when I read
this, I was very deficient,—for I saw most distinctly
at that time how deficient I was then from what I
saw I was now,—I recognized herein the great mercy
of our Lord to me and so began to consider the place
which my sins had earned for me in hell, and praised
God exceedingly, because it seemed as if I did not know
my own soul again, so great a change had come over it.

12. While thinking of these things, my soul was

[6] The *Life of Christ*, by Ludolf of Saxony, translated by the Franciscan
Ambrosio de Montesino, and published in four folio vols. at Alcalá de Henares
(1520–3), and Sevilla (1537–43).   St. Teresa knew probably the latter
edition.   The passage in question occurs bk. ii. ch. lxxxiv. ; in the modern
editions, bk. iii. ch. xiv.   See also *Rel*. x.   Speaking in her Constitutions
of the books to be provided in each convent, she mentions in the first place
" buenos libros Cartujanos."

carried away with extreme violence, and I knew not why. It seemed as if it would have gone forth out of the body, for it could not contain itself, nor was it able to hope for so great a good. The impetuosity was so excessive that I had no power left, and, as I think, different from what I had been used to. I knew not what ailed my soul, nor what it desired, for it was so changed. I leaned for support, for I could not sit, because my natural strength had utterly failed.

13. Then I saw over my head a dove, very different from those we usually see, for it had not the same plumage, but wings formed of small shells shining brightly. It was larger than an ordinary dove ; I thought I heard the rustling of its wings. It hovered above me during the space of an *Ave Maria*. But such was the state of my soul, that in losing itself it lost also the sight of the dove. My spirit grew calm with such a guest ; and yet, as I think, a grace so wonderful might have disturbed and frightened it ; and as it began to rejoice in the vision, it was delivered from all fear, and with the joy came peace, my soul continuing entranced. The joy of this rapture was exceedingly great ; and for the rest of that festal time I was so amazed and bewildered that I did not know what I was doing, nor how I could have received so great a grace. I neither heard nor saw anything, so to speak, because of my great inward joy. From that day forth I perceived in myself a very great progress in the highest love of God, together with a great increase in the strength of my virtues. May He be blessed and praised for ever ! Amen.

14. On another occasion I saw that very dove above the head of one of the Dominican fathers ; but it seemed to me that the rays and brightness of the wings were far greater. I understood by this that he was to draw souls unto God.

15. At another time I saw our Lady putting a

cope of exceeding whiteness on that Licentiate of the same Order, of whom I have made mention more than once.[7]   She told me that she gave him that cope in consideration of the service he had rendered her by helping to found this house,[8] that it was a sign that she would preserve his soul pure for the future, and that he should not fall into mortal sin.   I hold it for certain that so it came to pass, for he died within a few years ; his death and the rest of his life were so penitential, his whole life and death so holy, that, so far as anything can be known, there cannot be a doubt on the subject.   One of the friars present at his death told me that, before he breathed his last, he said to him that St. Thomas was with him.[9]   He died in great joy, longing to depart out of this land of exile.

16. Since then he has appeared to me more than once in exceedingly great glory, and told me certain things.   He was so given to prayer, that when he was dying, and would have interrupted it if he could because of his great weakness, he was not able to do so ; for he was often in a trance.   He wrote to me not long before he died, and asked me what he was to do ; for as soon as he had said Mass he fell into a trance, which lasted a long time, and which he could not hinder. At last God gave him the reward of the many services of his whole life.

17. I had certain visions, too, of the great graces which our Lord bestowed upon that rector of the Society of Jesus, of whom I have spoken already more than once [10] ; but I will not say anything of them now, lest I should be too tedious.   It was his lot once

---

[7] F. Pedro Ibañez.   See ch. xxxiii. 5, ch. xxxvi. 23.   " This father died Prior of Trianos (Feb. 2, 1565)," is written on the margin of the MS. by F. Bañes.

[8] St. Joseph, Avila, where St. Teresa was living at this time.

[9] See below, § 41.

[10] F. Gaspar de Salazar : see ch. xxxiii. 9, ch. xxxiv. 2.   It appears from a letter of Feb. 10, 1578, that F. Salazar was reported to his Provincial, F. Juan Suarez, as having a desire to quit the Society for the Carmelite Order.

to be in great trouble, to suffer great persecution and distress. One day, when I was hearing Mass, I saw Christ on the Cross at the elevation of the Host. He spoke certain words to me, which I was to repeat to that father for his comfort, together with others, which were to warn him beforehand of what was coming, and to remind him of what He had suffered on his behalf, and that he must prepare for suffering. This gave him great consolation and courage ; and everything came to pass afterwards as our Lord had told me.

18. I have seen great things of members of the Order to which this father belongs, which is the Society of Jesus, and of the whole Order itself ; I have occasionally seen them in heaven with white banners in their hands, and I have had other most wonderful visions, as I am saying, about them, and therefore have a great veneration for this Order ; for I have had a great deal to do with those who are of it, and I see that their lives are conformed to that which our Lord gave me to understand about them.

19. One night, when I was in prayer, our Lord spoke to me certain words, whereby He made me remember the great wickedness of my past life. They filled me with shame and distress ; for though they were not spoken with severity, they caused a feeling and a painfulness which were too much for me : and we feel that we make greater progress in the knowledge of ourselves when we hear one of these words, than we can make by a meditation of many days on our own misery, because these words impress the truth upon us at the same time in such a way that we cannot resist it. He set before me the former inclinations of my will to vanities, and told me to make much of the desire I now had that my will, which had been so ill employed, should be fixed on Him, and that He would accept it.

20. On other occasions He told me to remember

how I used to think it an honourable thing to go against His honour ; and again, to remember my debt to Him, for when I was most rebellious He was bestowing His graces upon me. If I am doing anything wrong—and my wrong-doings are many—His Majesty makes me see it in such a way that I am utterly confounded ; and as I do so often, that happens often also. I have been found fault with by my confessors occasionally ; and on betaking myself to prayer for consolation, have received a real reprimand.

21. To return to what I was speaking of. When our Lord made me remember my wicked life, I wept ; for as I considered that I had then never done any good, I thought He might be about to bestow upon me some special grace ; because most frequently, when I receive any particular mercy from our Lord, it is when I have been previously greatly humiliated, in order that I may the more clearly see how far I am from deserving it. I think our Lord must do it for that end.

22. Almost immediately after this I was so raised up in spirit that I thought myself to be, as it were, out of the body ; at least, I did not know that I was living in it.[11] I had a vision of the most Sacred Humanity in exceeding glory, greater than I had ever seen It in before. I beheld It in a wonderful and clear way in the bosom of the Father. I cannot tell how it was, for I saw myself, without seeing, as it seemed to me, in the presence of God. My amazement was such that I remained, as I believe, some days before I could recover myself. I had continually before me, as present, the Majesty of the Son of God, though not so distinctly as in the vision. I understood this well enough ; but the vision remained so impressed on my imagination, that I could not get rid of it for some time, though it had lasted but a moment ; it is a great comfort to me, and also a great blessing.

[11] 2 Cor. xii. 2 : " Sive in corpore nescio, sive extra corpus nescio."

23. I have had this vision on three other occasions, and it is, I think, the highest of all the visions which our Lord in His mercy showed me.[12]   The fruits of it are the very greatest, for it seems to purify the soul in a wonderful way, and destroy, as it were utterly, altogether the strength of our sensual nature.   It is a grand flame of fire, which seems to burn up and annihilate all the desires of this life.   For though now —glory be to God!—I had no desires after vanities, I saw clearly in the vision how all things are vanity and how hollow are all the dignities of earth ; it was a great lesson, teaching me to raise up my desires to the Truth alone.   It impresses on the soul a sense of the presence of God such as I cannot in any way describe, only it is very different from that which it is in our own power to acquire on earth.   It fills the soul with profound astonishment at its own daring, and at any one else being able to dare to offend His most awful Majesty.

24. I must have spoken now and then of the effects of visions,[13] and of other matters of the same kind, and I have already said that the blessings they bring with them are of various degrees ; but those of this vision are the highest of all.   When I went to Communion once I called to mind the exceeding great majesty of Him I had seen, and considered that it was He who is present in the most Holy Sacrament, and very often our Lord was pleased to show Himself to me in the Host ; the very hairs on my head stood,[14] and I thought I should come to nothing.

25. O my Lord ! ah, if Thou didst not throw a veil over Thy greatness, who would dare, being so foul and miserable, to come in contact with Thy great Majesty ? Blessed be Thou, O Lord ; may the angels and all creation praise Thee, Who orderest all things according to the measure of our weakness, so

[12] Ch. xxix. 2.   [13] See ch. xxviii.
[14] Job. iv. 15 : " Inhorruerunt pili carnis meæ."

that, when we have the fruition of Thy sovereign mercies, Thy great power may not terrify us, so that we dare not, being a frail and miserable race, persevere in that fruition !

26. It might happen to us as it did to the labourer —I know it to be a certain fact—who found a treasure beyond his expectations, which were mean.   When he saw himself in possession of it, he was seized with melancholy, which by degrees brought him to his grave through simple distress and anxiety of mind, because he did not know what to do with his treasure. If he had not found it all at once, and if others had given him portions of it by degrees, maintaining him thereby, he might have been more happy than he had been in his poverty, nor would it have cost him his life.

27. O Thou Treasure of the poor ! how marvellously Thou sustainest souls, showing to them, not all at once, but by little and little, the abundance of Thy riches !   When I behold Thy great Majesty hidden beneath that which is so slight as the Host is, I am filled with wonder, ever since that vision, at Thy great wisdom ; and I know not how it is that our Lord gives me the strength and courage necessary to draw near to Him, were it not that He who has had such compassion on me, and still has, gives me strength, nor would it be possible for me to be silent, or refrain from making known marvels so great.

28. What must be the thoughts of a wretched person such as I am, full of abominations, and who has spent her life with so little fear of God, when she draws near to our Lord's great Majesty, at the moment He is pleased to show Himself to my soul ?   How can I open my mouth, that has uttered so many words against Him, to receive that most glorious Body, purity and compassion itself ?   The love that is visible in His most beautiful Face, sweet and tender, pains and distresses the soul, because it has not served Him,

more than all the terrors of His Majesty. What should have been my thoughts, then, on those two occasions when I saw what I have described ? Truly, O my Lord and my joy, I am going to say that in some way, in these great afflictions of my soul, I have done something in Thy service. Ah ! I know not what I am saying, for I am writing this as if the words were not mine,[15] because I am troubled, and in some measure beside myself, when I call these things to remembrance. If these thoughts were really mine, I might well say that I had done something for Thee, O my Lord ; but as I can have no good thought if Thou givest it not, no thanks are due to me ; I am the debtor, O Lord, and it is Thou who art the offended One.

29. Once, when I was going to Communion, I saw with the eyes of the soul, more distinctly than with those of the body, two devils of most hideous shape ; their horns seemed to encompass the throat of the poor priest ; and I beheld my Lord, in that great majesty of which I have spoken,[16] held in the hands of that priest, in the Host he was about to give me. It was plain that those hands were those of a sinner, and I felt that the soul of that priest was in mortal sin. What must it be, O my Lord, to look upon Thy beauty amid shapes so hideous ? The two devils were so frightened and cowed in Thy presence, that they seemed as if they would have willingly run away, hadst Thou but given them leave. So troubled was I by the vision, that I knew not how I could go to Communion. I was also in great fear, for I thought, if the vision was from God, that His Majesty would not have allowed me to see the evil state of that soul.[17]

30. Our Lord Himself told me to pray for that priest ; that He had allowed this in order that I might

[15] The biographers of the Saint say that she often found, on returning from an ecstasy, certain passages written, but not by herself ; this seems to be alluded to here. There is, however, no difference in the handwriting.

[16] § 22.

[17] St. John of the Cross, *Ascent of Mount Carmel*, bk. ii. ch. xxvi.

understand the power of the words of consecration, and how God failed not to be present,[18] however wicked the priest might be who uttered them ; and that I might see His great goodness in that He left Himself in the very hands of His enemy, for my good and for the good of all. I understood clearly how the priests are under greater obligations to be holy than other persons ; and what a horrible thing it is to receive this most Holy Sacrament unworthily, and how great is the devil's dominion over a soul in mortal sin. It did me a great service, and made me fully understand what I owe to God. May He be blessed for evermore !

31. At another time I had a vision of a different kind, which frightened me very much. I was in a place where a certain person died, who as I understood had led a very bad life, and that for many years. But he had been ill for two years, and in some respects seemed to have reformed. He died without confession ; nevertheless, I did not think he would be damned. When the body had been wrapped in the winding-sheet, I saw it laid hold of by a multitude of devils, who seemed to toss it to and fro, and also to treat it with great cruelty. I was terrified at the sight, for they dragged it about with great hooks. But when I saw it carried to the grave with all the respect and ceremoniousness common to all, I began to think of the goodness of God, who would not allow that person to be dishonoured, but would have the fact of his being His enemy concealed.

32. I was almost out of my senses at the sight. During the whole of the funeral service, I did not see one of the evil spirits. Afterwards, when the body was about to be laid in the grave, so great a multitude of them was therein waiting to receive it, that I was beside myself at the sight, and it required no slight courage on my part not to betray my distress. I

[18] *Rel.* ix. 20.

thought of the treatment which that soul would receive, when the devils had such power over the wretched
body.   Would to God that all who live in mortal sin
might see what I then saw,—it was a fearful sight ;
it would go, I believe, a great way towards making
them lead better lives.

33. All this made me know more of what I owe to
God, and of the evils from which He has delivered
me.   I was in great terror.   I spoke of it to my
confessor, and I thought it might be an illusion of
Satan, in order to take away my good opinion of that
person, who yet was not accounted a very good
Christian.   The truth is, that, whether it was an
illusion or not, it makes me afraid whenever I think
of it.

34. Now that I have begun to speak of the visions
I had concerning the dead, I will mention some matters
which our Lord was pleased to reveal to me in relation
to certain souls.   I will confine myself to a few for
the sake of brevity, and because they are not necessary ;
I mean that they are not for our profit.   They told
me that one who had been our Provincial [19]—he was
then of another province—was dead.   He was a man

---

[19] The first editors of the Life of St. Teresa, for whom it would have been
easy to ascertain the name of this Provincial, having unfortunately failed to
do so, the present state of the Archives of the Order renders the solution of
the question uncommonly difficult.   Fuente says the passage cannot refer
to Angel de Salazar, which is obvious, seeing that he outlived the Saint by
more than ten years.   The Spanish text says, more clearly than the English
translation, that this ex-Provincial of Castile, who had been superior for
twenty years, and had had many dealings with St. Teresa, to whom he had
shown great kindness, died while Provincial of some other province far away.
Our list of Provincials of the other Spanish provinces being defective, we
can only judge from what we know of the Provincials of Castile, assuming
the lists of these to be sufficiently complete.   And here there are two to
whom the few characteristics might apply, the first being Juan de Altamiras,
whose name occurs in 1525 and 1528 as conventual at Avila, in 1539 as Prior
of the same convent, in 1543 as conventual, from 1545 to 1548 as Provincial
of Castile, 1555 Prior, 1556 Vicar, and 1557 Prior of Avila.   The other, to
whom, in the opinion of the present writer, the balance of probabilities seems
to point, is Gregorio Fernandez, mentioned in note 8 to ch. xxxii.   But
we do not know whether the one or the other became Provincial of some
other province, nor do we know the date and place of their death, so that
the question must remain open.

of great virtue, with whom I had had a great deal to do, and to whom I was under many obligations for certain kindnesses shown me. When I heard that he was dead, I was exceedingly troubled, because I trembled for his salvation, seeing that he had been superior for twenty years. That is what I dread very much; for the cure of souls seems to me to be full of danger. I went to an oratory in great distress, and gave up to him all the good I had ever done in my whole life,—it was little enough,—and prayed our Lord that His merits might fill up what was wanting, in order that this soul might be delivered up from purgatory.

35. While I was thus praying to our Lord as well as I could, he seemed to me to rise up from the depths of the earth on my right hand, and I saw him ascend to heaven in exceeding great joy. He was a very old man then, but I saw him as if he were only thirty years old, and I thought even younger, and there was a brightness in his face. This vision passed away very quickly; but I was so exceedingly comforted by it, that I could never again mourn his death, although many persons were distressed at it, for he was very much beloved. So greatly comforted was my soul, that nothing disturbed it, neither could I doubt the truth of the vision; I mean that it was no illusion.

36. I had this vision about a fortnight after he was dead; nevertheless, I did not omit to obtain prayers for him, and I prayed myself, only I could not pray with the same earnestness that I should have done if I had not seen that vision. For when our Lord showed him thus to me, it seemed to me afterwards, when I prayed for him to His Majesty,— and I could not help it,—that I was like one who gave alms to a rich man. Later on I heard an account of the death he died in our Lord—he was far away from here; it was one of such great edification, that

he left all wondering to see how recollected, how penitent, and how humble he was when he died.

37. A nun, who was a great servant of God, died in this house.   On the next day one of the sisters was reciting the lesson in the Office of the Dead, which was said in choir for that nun's soul, and I was standing myself to assist her in singing the versicle, when, in the middle of the lesson, I saw the departed nun, as I believe, in a vision ; her soul seemed to rise on my right hand like the soul of the Provincial, and ascend to heaven.   This vision was not imaginary, like the preceding, but like those others of which I have spoken before [20] ; it is not less certain, however, than the other visions I had.

38. Another nun died in this same house of mine : she was about eighteen or twenty years of age, and had always been sickly.   She was a great servant of God, attentive in choir, and a person of great virtue. I certainly thought that she would not go to purgatory, on account of her exceeding merits, because the infirmities under which she had laboured were many. While I was saying the Office, before she was buried,— she had been dead about four hours,—I saw her rise in the same place and ascend to heaven.

39. I was once in one of the colleges of the Society of Jesus, and in one of those great sufferings which, as I have said,[21] I occasionally had, and still have, both in soul and body, and then so grievously that I was not able, as it seemed to me, to have even one good thought.   The night before, one of the brothers of that house had died in it ; and I, as well as I could, was commending his soul to God, and hearing the Mass which another father of that Society was saying for him, when I became recollected at once, and saw him go up to heaven in great glory, and our Lord with him.   I understood that His Majesty went with him by way of special grace.

[20] See ch. xxvii.   [21] Ch. xxx. 9.

40. Another brother of our Order, a good friar,[22] was very ill; and when I was at Mass, I became recollected, and saw him dead, entering into heaven without going through purgatory. He died, as I afterwards learned, at the very time of my vision. I was amazed that he had not gone to purgatory. I understood that, having become a friar and carefully kept the rule, the Bulls of the Order had been of use to him, so that he did not pass into purgatory. I do not know why I came to have this revealed to me; I think it must be because I was to learn that it is not enough for a man to be a friar in his habit—I mean, to wear the habit—to attain to that state of high perfection which that of a friar is.

41. I will speak no more of these things, because, as I have said just,[23] there is no necessity for it, though our Lord has been so gracious to me as to show me much. But in all the visions I had, I saw no souls escape purgatory except this Carmelite father, the holy friar Peter of Alcantara, and that Dominican father of whom I spoke before.[24] It pleased our Lord to let me see the degree of glory to which some souls have been raised, showing them to me in the places they occupy. There is a great difference between one place and another.

---

[22] Fray Diego de San Matia, who had been confessor to the nuns of the Incarnation. This is not, as some writers have thought, an allusion to the so-called Sabbatine Indulgence (which is quite a different matter), but to the Bulls of Honorius III. of January 30, 1226, and Innocent IV. of June 8, 1245 confirming the Carmelite Rule and enjoining its observance " in remissionem peccatorum " (*Bullar. Carmelit.* I., 1 and 6).

[23] § 34.

[24] § 15.   Fr. Pedro Ibañez.

CHAPTER XXXIX

OTHER GRACES BESTOWED ON THE SAINT. THE PRO-
MISES OF OUR LORD TO HER. DIVINE LOCUTIONS
AND VISIONS.

*She continues the same subject, mentioning great
graces granted her by God. How He promised to hear
her requests on behalf of persons for whom she should
pray. Some remarkable instances in which His Majesty
thus favoured her.*

1. I WAS once importuning our Lord exceedingly to
restore the sight of a person who had claims upon me,
and who was almost wholly blind. I was very sorry
for him, and afraid our Lord would not hear me because of my sins. He appeared to me as at other
times, and began to show the wound in His left hand ;
with the other He drew out the great nail that was
in it, and it seemed to me that, in drawing the nail,
He tore the flesh. The greatness of the pain was
manifest, and I was very much distressed thereat.
He said to me, that He who had borne that for my
sake would still more readily grant what I asked Him,
and that I was not to have any doubts about it. He
promised me there was nothing I should ask that He
would not grant ; that He knew I should ask nothing
that was not for His glory, and that He would grant
me what I was now praying for. Even during the
time when I did not serve Him, I should find, if I
considered it, I had asked nothing that He had not
granted in an ampler manner than I had known how
to ask ; how much more amply still would He grant
what I asked for, now that He knew I loved Him !
I was not to doubt. I do not think that eight days
passed before our Lord restored that person to sight.
My confessor knew it forthwith. It might be that it

was not owing to my prayer ; but, as I had had the vision, I have a certain conviction that it was a grace accorded to me. I gave thanks to His Majesty.

2. Again, a person was exceedingly ill of a most painful disease ; but, as I do not know what it was, I do not describe it by its name here. What he had gone through for two months was beyond all endurance ; and his pain was so great that he tore his own flesh. My confessor, the rector of whom I have spoken,[1] went to see him ; he was very sorry for him, and told me that I must anyhow go myself and visit him ; he was one whom I might visit, for he was my kinsman. I went, and was moved to such a tender compassion for him that I began, with the utmost importunity, to ask our Lord to restore him to health. Herein I saw clearly how gracious our Lord was to me, so far as I could judge ; for immediately, the next day, he was completely rid of that pain.

3. I was once in the deepest distress, because I knew that a person to whom I was under great obligations was about to commit an act highly offensive to God and dishonourable to himself. He was determined upon it. I was so much harassed by this that I did not know what to do in order to change his purpose ; and it seemed to me as if nothing could be done. I implored God, from the bottom of my heart, to find a way to hinder it ; but till I found it I could find no relief for the pain I felt. In my distress, I went to a very lonely hermitage,—one of those belonging to this monastery,—in which there is a picture of Christ bound to the pillar ; and there, as I was imploring our Lord to grant me this grace, I heard a voice of exceeding gentleness, speaking, as it were, in a whisper.[2]

---

[1] Ch. xxxiii. 10. F. Gaspar de Salazar.

[2] 3 Kings xix. 12 : "Sibilus auræ tenuis." The hermitage is in the garden of the convent of St. Joseph's, Avila. The Saint charged a painter with making a picture of our Lord at the pillar, which is still there. It is said to have been miraculously completed ; a replica of it is in the sacristy of the convent.

My whole body trembled, for it made me afraid. I wished to understand what was said, but I could not, for it all passed away in a moment.

4. When my fears had subsided, and that was immediately, I became conscious of an inward calmness, a joy and delight, which made me marvel how the mere hearing a voice,—I heard it with my bodily ears,—without understanding a word, could have such an effect on the soul. I saw by this that my prayer was granted ; and so it was ; and I was freed from my anxieties about a matter not yet accomplished, as it afterwards was, as completely as if I saw it done. I told my confessors of it, for I had two at this time, both of them learned men, and great servants of God.[3]

5. I knew of a person who had resolved to serve God in all earnestness,[4] and had for some days given himself to prayer, in which he had received many graces from our Lord, but who had abandoned his good resolutions because of certain occasions of sin in which he was involved, and which he would not avoid ; they were extremely perilous. This caused me the utmost distress, because the person was one for whom I had a great affection, and one to whom I owed much. For more than a month I believe I did nothing else but pray to God for his conversion. One day, when I was in prayer, I saw a devil close by in a great rage, tearing to pieces some paper which he had in his hands. That sight consoled me greatly, because it seemed that my prayer had been heard. So it was, as I learnt afterwards ; for that person had made his confession with great contrition, and returned to God so sincerely, that I trust in His Majesty he will always advance further and further. May He be blessed for ever ! Amen.

6. In answer to my prayers, our Lord has very often rescued souls from mortal sins, and led others

[3] Fr. Dominic Bañez and Fr. Garcia de Toledo, both Dominicans.
[4] *Rel.* i. 22.

on to greater perfection. But as to the delivering of souls out of purgatory, and other remarkable acts, so many are the mercies of our Lord herein, that were I to speak of them I should only weary myself and my reader. But He has done more by me for the salvation of souls than for the health of the body. This is very well known, and there are many to bear witness to it.

7. At first it made me scrupulous, because I could not help thinking that our Lord did these things in answer to my prayer ; I say nothing of the chief reason of all—His pure compassion. But now these graces are so many, and so well known to others, that it gives me no pain to think so. I bless His Majesty, and abase myself, because I am still more deeply in His debt ; and I believe that He makes my desire to serve Him grow, and my love revive.

8. But what amazes me most is this : however much I may wish to pray for those graces which our Lord sees not to be expedient, I cannot do it ; and if I try, I do so with little earnestness, force, and spirit : it is impossible to do more, even if I would. But it is not so as to those which His Majesty intends to grant. These I can pray for constantly, and with great importunity ; though I do not carry them in my memory, they seem to present themselves to me at once.[5]

9. There is a great difference between these two ways of praying, and I know not how to explain it. As to the first, when I pray for those graces which our Lord does not mean to grant,—even though they concern me very nearly,—I am like one whose tongue is tied ; who, though he would speak, yet cannot ; or, if he speaks, sees that people do not listen to him. And yet I do not fail to force myself to pray, though not conscious of that fervour which I have when praying for those graces which our Lord intends to

[5] See St. John of the Cross, *Ascent of Mount Carmel*, bk. iii. ch. 1.

give.   In the second case, I am like one who speaks clearly and intelligibly to another, whom he sees to be a willing listener.

10. The prayer that is not to be heard is, so to speak, like vocal prayer ;   the other is a prayer of contemplation so high that our Lord shows Himself in such a way as to make us feel He hears us, and that He delights in our prayer, and that He is about to grant our petition.   Blessed be He for ever who gives me so much, and to whom I give so little !   For what is he worth, O my Lord, who does not utterly abase himself to nothing for Thee ?   How much, how much, how much,—I might say so a thousand times, —I fall short of this !   It is on this account that I do not wish to live,—though there be other reasons also,—because I do not live according to the obligations which bind me to Thee.   What imperfections I trace in myself !   what remissness in Thy service !   Certainly, I could wish occasionally I had no sense, that I might be unconscious of the great evil that is in me.   May He who can do all things help me !

11. When I was staying in the house of that lady of whom I have spoken before,[6] it was necessary for me to be very watchful over myself, and keep continually in mind the intrinsic vanity of all the things of this life, because of the great esteem I was held in, and of the praises bestowed on me.   There was much there to which I might have become attached, if I had looked only to myself ;   but I looked to Him who sees things as they really are, not to let me go out of His hand.   Now that I speak of seeing things as they really are, I remember how great a trial it is for those to whom God has granted a true insight into the things of earth to have to discuss them with others. They wear so many disguises, as our Lord once told me,—and much of what I am saying of them is not from myself, but rather what my Heavenly Master

[6] Ch. xxxiv. 1.

has taught me ; and therefore, in speaking of them, when I say distinctly I understood this, or our Lord told me this, I am very scrupulous neither to add nor to take away one single syllable ; so, when I do not clearly remember everything exactly, that must be taken as coming from myself, and some things, perhaps, are so altogether. I do not call mine that which is good, for I know there is no other good in me but only that which our Lord gave me when I was so far from deserving it : I call that mine which I speak without having had it made known to me by revelation.

12. But, O my God, how is it that we too often judge even spiritual things, as we do those of the world, by our own understanding, wresting them grievously from their true meaning ?   We think we may measure our progress by the years which we have given to the exercise of prayer ; we even think we can prescribe limits to Him who bestows His gifts not by measure[7] when He wills, and who in six months can give to one more than to another in many years. This is a fact which I have so frequently observed in many persons, that I am surprised how any of us can deny it.

13. I am certainly convinced that he will not remain under this delusion who possesses the gift of discerning spirits, and to whom our Lord has given real humility ; for such a one will judge of them by the fruits, by the good resolutions and love,—and our Lord gives him light to understand the matter ; and herein He regards the progress and advancement of souls, not the years they may have spent in prayer ; for one person may make greater progress in six months than another in twenty years, because, as I said before, our Lord gives to whom He will, particularly to him who is best disposed.

[7] Ch. xxxiv. 14.   St. John iii. 34 : " Non enim ad mensuram dat Deus spiritum."

14. I see this in certain persons of tender years who have come to this monastery,—God touches their hearts, and gives them a little light and love.[8]   I speak of that brief interval in which He gives them sweetness in prayer, and then they wait for nothing further, and make light of every difficulty, forgetting the necessity even of food ; for they shut themselves up for ever in a house that is unendowed, as persons who make no account of their life, for His sake, Who, they know, loves them.   They give up everything, even their own will ; and it never enters into their mind that they might be discontented in so small a house, and where enclosure is so strictly observed. They offer themselves wholly in sacrifice to God.

15. Oh, how willingly do I admit that they are better than I am ! and how I ought to be ashamed of myself before God !   What His Majesty has not been able to accomplish in me in so many years,—it is long ago since I began to pray, and He to bestow His graces upon me,—He accomplished in them in three months, and in some of them even in three days, though He gives them much fewer graces than He gave to me : and yet His Majesty rewards them well ; most assuredly they are not sorry for what they have done for Him.

16. I wish, therefore, we reminded ourselves of those long years which have gone by since we made our religious profession.   I say this to those persons

[8] In writing this passage St. Teresa was probably thinking of Mary of St. Joseph (Davila, see ch. xxxvi., note 17) and Doña Maria de Ocampo, daughter of Diego de Cepeda and Beatriz de la Cruz, born in 1543, who made her profession on October 21, 1564, under the name of Maria Bautista ; she brought 300 ducats.   St. Teresa took her to the new foundation of Valladolid, where she spent almost her whole life, and died August 10, 1603.   And also of Isabel de Ortega, daughter of Juan de Ortega and Maria de Vergas, born in 1537.   At first she intended entering the royal convent of Franciscan nuns at Madrid, but on the advice of St. Peter of Alcantara she joined St. Teresa, took the name of Isabel of St. Dominic, and made her profession, October 21, 1565 : she brought 600 ducats.   St. Teresa relied greatly on her judgment and put her in charge of the foundations of Toledo, Pastrana, and Segovia ; at a later period she was occupied in those of Saragossa and Ocaña, but finally returned to Avila, where she died June 13, 1623.

also, who have given themselves long ago to prayer, but not for the purpose of distressing those who in a short time have made greater progress than we have made, by making them retrace their steps, so that they may proceed only as we do ourselves. We must not desire those who, because of the graces God has given them, are flying like eagles, to become like chickens whose feet are tied. Let us rather look at His Majesty, and give these souls the reins, if we see that they are humble ; for our Lord, who has had such compassion upon them, will not let them fall into the abyss.

17. These souls trust themselves in the hands of God, for the truth, which they learn by faith, helps them to do it ; and shall not we also trust them to Him, without seeking to measure them by our measure, which is that of our meanness of spirit ? We must not do it ; for if we cannot ascend to the heights of their great love and courage,—without experience none can comprehend them,—let us humble ourselves, and not condemn them ; for, by this seeming regard to their progress, we hinder our own, and miss the opportunity our Lord gives us to humble ourselves, to ascertain our own shortcomings, and learn how much more detached and more near to God these souls must be than we are, seeing that His Majesty draws so near to them Himself.

18. I have no other intention here, and I wish to have no other, than to express my preference for the prayer that in a short time results in these great effects, which show themselves at once ; for it is impossible they should enable us to leave all things only to please God, if they were not accompanied with a vehement love. I would rather have that prayer than that which lasted many years, but which at the end of the time, as well as at the beginning, never issued in a resolution to do anything for God, with the exception of some trifling services, like a grain of

salt, without weight or bulk, and which a bird might carry away in its mouth. Is it not a serious and mortifying thought that we are making much of certain services which we render our Lord, but which are too pitiable to be considered, even if they were many in number ? This is my case, and I am forgetting every moment the mercies of our Lord. I do not mean that His Majesty will not make much of them Himself, for He is good ; but I wish I made no account of them myself, or even perceived that I did them, for they are nothing worth.

19. But O, my Lord, do Thou forgive me, and blame me not, if I try to console myself a little with the little I do, seeing that I do not serve Thee at all; for if I rendered Thee any great services, I should not think of these trifles. Blessed are they who serve Thee in great deeds ; if envying these, and desiring to do what they do, were of any help to me, I should not be so far behind them as I am in pleasing Thee ; but I am nothing worth, O my Lord ; do Thou make me of some worth, Thou Who lovest me so much.

20. During one of those days, when this monastery, which seems to have cost me some labour, was fully founded by the arrival of the Brief from Rome, which empowered us to live without an endowment [9] ; and I was comforting myself at seeing the whole affair concluded, and thinking of all the trouble I had had, and giving thanks to our Lord for having been pleased to make some use of me,—it happened that I began to consider all that we had gone through. Well, so it was ; in every one of my actions, which I thought were of some service, I traced so many faults and imperfections, now and then but little courage, very frequently a want of faith ; for until this moment, when I see everything accomplished, I never abso-lutely believed ; neither, however, on the other hand, could I doubt what our Lord said to me about the

_____
[9] The one of December 5, 1562. See ch. xxxiii. 15.

foundation of this house. I cannot tell how it was ; very often the matter seemed to me, on the one hand, impossible ; and, on the other hand, I could not be in doubt ; I mean, I could not believe that it would not be accomplished. In short, I find that our Lord Himself, on his part, did all the good that was done, while I did all the evil. I therefore ceased to think of the matter, and wished never to be reminded of it again, lest I should do myself some harm by dwelling on my many faults. Blessed be He Who, when He pleases, draws good out of all my failings ! Amen.

21. I say, then, there is danger in counting the years we have given to prayer ; for, granting that there is nothing in it against humility, it seems to me to imply something like an appearance of thinking that we have merited, in some degree, by the service rendered. I do not mean that there is no merit in it at all, nor that it will not be well rewarded [10] ; yet if any spiritual person thinks, because he has given himself to prayer for many years, that he deserves any spiritual consolations, I am sure he will never attain to spiritual perfection. Is it not enough that a man has merited the protection of God, which keeps Him from committing those sins into which he fell before he began to pray, but he must also, as they say, sue God for His own money ?

22. This does not seem to me to be deep humility, and yet it may be that it is ; however, I look on it as great boldness, for I, who have very little humility, have never ventured upon it. It may be that I never asked for it, because I had never served Him ; perhaps, if I had served Him, I should have been more importunate than all others with our Lord for my reward.

23. I do not mean that the soul makes no progress

---

[10] *Imitation of Christ*, bk. i. ch. xv. 5 and ch. xxiii. 2. The *Imitation* was published in Spanish as early as 1490, but the edition known to St. Teresa under the title of *Contemptus Mundi* was that of Luis de Granada, printed at Sevilla in 1536 and again at Lisbon in 1542 and Alcalá in 1548. St. Teresa ordered each convent to have copies of it *(Constitutions, 7)*.

in time, or that God will not reward it, if its prayer has been humble ; but I do mean that we should forget the number of years we have been praying, because all that we can do is utterly worthless in comparison with one drop of blood out of those which our Lord shed for us.   And if the more we serve Him, the more we become His debtors, what is it, then, we are asking for ? for, if we pay one farthing of the debt, He gives us back a thousand ducats.   For the love of God, let us leave these questions alone, for they belong to Him.   Comparisons are always bad, even in earthly things ; what, then, must they be in that, the knowledge of which God has reserved to Himself ?   His Majesty showed this clearly enough, when those who came late and those who came early to His vineyard received the same wages.[11]

24. I have sat down so often to write, and have been so many days writing these three leaves,—for, as I have said,[12] I had, and have still, but few opportunities,—that I forgot what I had begun with, namely, the following vision.[13]

25. I was in prayer, and saw myself on a wide plain all alone.   Round about me stood a great multitude of all kinds of people, who hemmed me in on every side ; all of them seemed to have weapons of war in their hands, to hurt me ; some had spears, others swords ; some had daggers, and others very long rapiers.   In short, I could not move away in any direction without exposing myself to the hazard of death, and I was alone, without any one to take my part.   In this distress of mind, not knowing what to do, I lifted up my eyes to heaven, and saw Christ, not in heaven, but high above me in the air, holding out His hand to me, and there protecting me in such

[11] St. Matt. xx. 9–14 : " Volo autem et huic novissimo dare sicut et tibi."
[12] Ch. xiv. 12.
[13] The Saint had this vision when she was in the house of Doña Luisa de la Cerda in Toledo, and it was fulfilled in the opposition she met with in the foundation of St. Joseph of Avila. See ch. xxxvi. 18.

a way that I was no longer afraid of all that multitude, neither could they, though they wished it, do me any harm.

26. At first the vision seemed to have no results; but it has been of the greatest help to me, since I understood what it meant. Not long afterwards, I saw myself, as it were, exposed to the like assault, and I saw that the vision represented the world, because everything in it takes up arms against the poor soul. We need not speak of those who are not great servants of our Lord, nor of honours, possessions, and pleasures, with other things of the same nature; for it is clear that the soul, if it be not watchful, will find itself caught in a net,—at least, all these things labour to ensnare it; more than this, so also do friends and relatives, and—what frightens me most— even good people. I found myself afterwards so beset on all sides, good people thinking they were doing good, and I knowing not how to defend myself, nor what to do.

27. O my God, if I were to say in what way, and in how many ways, I was tried at that time, even after that trial of which I have just spoken, what a warning I should be giving to men to hate the whole world utterly! It was the greatest of all the persecutions I had to undergo. I saw myself occasionally so hemmed in on every side, that I could do nothing else but lift up my eyes to heaven, and cry unto God.[14] I recollected well what I had seen in the vision, and it helped me greatly not to trust much in any one, for there is no one that can be relied on except God. In all my great trials, our Lord—He showed it to me--sent always some one on His part to hold out his hand to help me, as it was shown to me in the vision, so that I might attach myself to nothing, but only please our Lord; and this has been enough to sustain the little

[14] 2 Paralip. xx. 12: " Hoc solum habemus residui, ut oculos nostros dirigamus ad Te."

virtue I have in desiring to serve Thee : be Thou
blessed for evermore !

28. On one occasion I was exceedingly disquieted
and troubled, unable to recollect myself, fighting and
struggling with my thoughts, running upon matters
which did not relate to perfection ; and, moreover,
I did not think I was so detached from all things as I
used to be. When I found myself in this wretched
state, I was afraid that the graces I had received from
our Lord were illusions, and the end was that a great
darkness covered my soul. In this my distress our
Lord began to speak to me : He bade me not to harass
myself, but learn, from the consideration of my
misery, what it would be if He withdrew Himself from
me, and that we were never safe while living in the
flesh. It was given me to understand how this fighting
and struggling are profitable to us, because of the
reward, and it seemed to me as if our Lord were sorry
for us who live in the world. Moreover, He bade me
not to suppose that He had forgotten me ; He would
never abandon me, but it was necessary I should do
all that I could myself.

29. Our Lord said all this with great tenderness
and sweetness ; He also spoke other most gracious
words, which I need not repeat. His Majesty, further
showing His great love for me, said to me very often :
" Thou art Mine, and I am thine." I am in the habit
of saying myself, and I believe in all sincerity : " What
do I care for myself ?—I only care for Thee, O my
Lord."

30. These words of our Lord, and the consolation
He gives me, fill me with the utmost shame, when I
remember what I am. I have said it before, I think,[15]
and I still say now and then to my confessor, that it
requires greater courage to receive these graces than
to endure the heaviest trials. When they are come,
I forget, as it were, all I have done, and there is nothing

[15] Ch. xx. 4.

before me but a picture of my wretchedness, and my understanding can make no reflections ; this, also, seems to me at times to be supernatural.

31. Sometimes I have such a vehement longing for Communion ; I do not think it can be expressed. One morning it happened to rain so much as to make it seem impossible to leave the house.[16]   When I had gone out, I was so beside myself with that longing, that if spears had been pointed at my heart, I should have rushed upon them ; the rain was nothing. When I entered the church I fell into a deep trance, and saw heaven open—not a door only, as I used to see at other times. I beheld the throne which, as I have told you, my father, I saw at other times, with another throne above it, whereon, though I saw not, I understood by a certain inexplicable knowledge that the Godhead dwelt.

32. The throne seemed to me to be supported by certain animals ; I believe I saw the form of them : I thought they might be the Evangelists. But now the throne was arrayed, and Him who sat on it I did not see, but only an exceedingly great multitude of angels, who seemed to me more beautiful, beyond all comparison, than those I had seen in heaven. I thought they were, perhaps, the seraphim or cherubim, for they were very different in their glory, and seemingly all on fire.   The difference is great, as I said before [17] ; and the joy I then felt cannot be described, either in writing or by word of mouth ; it is inconceivable to any one who has not had experience of it. I felt that everything man can desire was all there together, and I saw nothing ; they told me, but I know not who, that all I could do there was to understand that I could understand nothing, and see how everything was nothing in comparison with that. So it was ; my soul afterwards was vexed to see that it could rest

---

[16] This happened probably while she, as nun of the Incarnation, was staying with some relations of hers.   [17] Ch. xxix. 16.

on any created thing : how much more, then, if it had any affection thereto ; for everything seemed to me but an ant-hill. I communicated, and remained during Mass. I know not how it was : I thought I had been but a few minutes, and was amazed when the clock struck ; I had been two hours in that trance and joy.

33. I was afterwards amazed at this fire, which seems to spring forth out of the true love of God ; for though I might long for it, labour for it, and annihilate myself in the effort to obtain it, I can do nothing towards procuring a single spark of it myself, because it all comes of the good pleasure of His Majesty, as I said on another occasion.[18] It seems to burn up the old man, with his faults, his lukewarmness, and misery ; so that it is like the phœnix of which I have read that it comes forth, after being burnt, out of its own ashes into a new life. Thus it is with the soul : it is changed into another, whose desires are different, and whose strength is great. It seems to be no longer what it was before, and begins to walk renewed in purity in the ways of our Lord. When I was praying to Him that thus it might be with me, and that I might begin His service anew, He said to me : " The comparison thou hast made is good ; take care never to forget it, that thou mayest always labour to advance."

34. Once, when I was doubting, as I said just now,[19] whether these visions came from God or not, our Lord appeared, and, with some severity, said to me : " O children of men, how long will you remain hard of heart ? " I was to examine myself carefully on one subject,—whether I had given myself up wholly to Him, or not. If I had,—and it was so,—I was to believe that He would not suffer me to perish. I was very much afflicted when He spoke thus, but He turned to me with great tenderness and sweetness,

[18] Ch. xxix. 13.   [19] § 28.

and bade me not to distress myself, for He knew already that, so far as it lay in my power, I would not fail in anything that was for His service ; that He Himself would do what I wished,—and so He did grant what I was then praying for ; that I was to consider my love for Him, which was daily growing in me, for I should see by this that these visions did not come from Satan ; that I must not imagine that God would ever allow the devil to have so much power over the souls of His servants as to give them such clearness of understanding and such peace as I had.

35. He gave me also to understand that, when such and so many persons had told me the visions were from God, I should do wrong if I did not believe them.[20]

36. Once, when I was reciting the psalm *Quicumque vult*,[21] I was given to undeistand the mystery of One God and Three Persons with so much clearness, that I was greatly astonished and consoled at the same time. This was of the greatest help to me, for it enabled me to know more of the greatness and maivels of God ; and when I think of the most Holy Trinity, or hear It spoken of, I seem to understand the mystery, and a great joy it is.

37. One day—it was the feast of the Assumption of the Queen of the Angels, and our Lady—our Lord was pleased to grant me this grace. In a trance He made me behold her going up to heaven, the joy and solemnity of her reception there, as well as the place where she now sits. To describe it is more than I can do ; the joy that filled my soul at the sight of such great glory was excessive. The effects of the vision were great ; it made me long to endure still greater trials ; and I had a vehement desire to serve our Lady, because of her great meiits.

38. Once, in one of the Colleges of the Society of

---

[20] See ch. xxviii. 19, 20.
[21] Commonly called the Creed of St. Athanasius.

Jesus, when the brothers of the house were communicating, I saw an exceedingly rich canopy above their heads. I saw this twice ; but I never saw it when others were receiving Communion.

CHAPTER XL.

VISIONS, REVELATIONS, AND LOCUTIONS.

Continuation of the same subject of great mercies God has shown her. From some of these very good doctrines may be gathered, and this, as she declares, was, besides compliance, with obedience, her principal motive (in writing this book), namely, to enumerate such of these mercies as would be instructive to souls. This chapter brings the history of her life, written by herself, to an end. May it be for the glory of God. Amen.

1. ONE day, in prayer, the sweetness of which was so great that, knowing how unworthy I was of so great a blessing, I began to think how much I had deserved to be in that place which I had seen prepared for me in hell,—for, as I said before,[1] I never forget the way I saw myself there,—as I was thinking of this, my soul began to be more and more on fire, and I was carried away in spirit in a way I cannot describe. It seemed to me as if I had been absorbed in, and filled with, that grandeur of God which, on another occasion, I had felt.[2] In that majesty it was given me to understand one truth, which is the fulness of all truth, but I cannot tell how, for I saw nothing. It was said to me, I saw not by whom, but I knew well enough it was the Truth Itself : " This I am doing to thee is

[1] Ch. xxxii. 1.   [2] Ch. xxviii. 14.

not a slight matter ; it is one of those things for which thou owest Me much ; for all the evil in the world comes from ignorance of the truths of the holy writings in their clear simplicity, of which not one iota shall pass away."[3] I thought that I had always believed this, and that all the faithful also believed it. Then He said : " Ah, My daughter, they are few who love Me in truth ; for if men loved Me, I should not hide My secrets from them. Knowest thou what it is to love Me in truth ? It is to admit everything to be a lie which is not pleasing unto Me. Now thou dost not understand it, but thou shalt understand it clearly hereafter, in the profit it will be to thy soul."

2. Our Lord be praised, so I found it ; for after this vision I look upon everything which does not tend to the service of God as vanity and lies. I cannot tell how much I am convinced of this, nor how sorry I am for those whom I see living in darkness, not knowing the truth. I derived other great blessings also from this, some of which I will here speak of, others I cannot describe.

3. Our Lord at the same time uttered a special word of most exceeding graciousness. I know not how it was done, for I saw nothing ; but I was filled, in a way which also I cannot describe, with exceeding strength and earnestness of purpose to observe with all my might everything contained in the divine writings. I thought that I could rise above every possible hindrance put in my way.

4. Of this divine truth, which was put before me I know not how, there remains imprinted within me a truth—I cannot give it a name—which fills me with a new reverence for God ; it gives me a notion of His Majesty and power in a way which I cannot explain. I can understand that it is something very high. I had a very great desire never to speak of anything but of those deep truths which far surpass all that is

[3] St. Matt. v. 18 : " Iota unum aut unus apex non præteribit a lege."

spoken of here in the world,—and so the living in it began to be painful to me.

5. The vision left me in great tenderness, joy, and humility. It seemed to me, though I knew not how, that our Lord now gave me great things ; and I had no suspicion whatever of any illusion. I saw nothing ; but I understood how great a blessing it is to make no account of anything which does not lead us nearer unto God. I also understood what it is for a soul to be walking in the truth, in the presence of the Truth itself. What I understood is this : that our Lord gave me to understand that He is Himself the very Truth.

6. All this I am speaking of I learnt at times by means of words uttered ; at other times I learnt some things without the help of words, and that more clearly than those other things which were told me in words. I understood exceedingly deep truths concerning the Truth, more than I could have done through the teaching of many learned men. It seems to me that learned men never could have thus impressed upon me, nor so clearly explained to me, the vanity of this world.

7. The Truth of which I am speaking, and which I was given to see, is Truth Itself, in Itself. It has neither beginning nor end. All other truths depend on this Truth, as all other loves depend on this Love, and all other grandeurs on this Grandeur. I understood it all, notwithstanding that my words are obscure in comparison with that distinctness with which it pleased our Lord to show it to me. What think you must be the power of His Majesty, seeing that in so short a time it leaves so great a blessing and such an impression on the soul ? O Grandeur ! Majesty of mine ! what is it Thou art doing, O my Lord Almighty ! Consider who it is to whom Thou givest blessings so great ! Dost Thou not remember that this my soul has been an abyss of lies and a sea of vanities, and

all my fault ?   Though Thou hadst given me a natural hatred of lying, yet I did involve myself in many lying ways.   How is this, O my God ? how can it be that mercies and graces so great should fall to the lot of one who has so ill deserved them at Thy hands ?

8. Once, when I was with the whole community reciting the Office, my soul became suddenly recollected, and seemed to me all bright as a mirror, clear behind, sideways, upwards, and downwards ; and in the centre of it I saw Christ our Lord, as I usually see Him.   It seemed to me that I saw Him distinctly in every part of my soul, as in a mirror, and at the same time the mirror was all sculptured—I cannot explain it—in our Lord Himself by a most loving communication which I can never describe.   I know that this vision was a great blessing to me, and is still whenever I remember it, particularly after Communion.

9. I understood by it, that, when a soul is in mortal sin, this mirror becomes clouded with a thick vapour, and utterly obscured, so that our Lord is neither visible nor present, though He is always present in the conservation of its being.   In heretics, the mirror is, as it were, broken in pieces, and that is worse than being dimmed.   There is a very great difference between seeing this and describing it, for it can hardly be explained.   But it has done me great good ; it has also made me very sorry on account of those times when I dimmed the lustre of my soul by my sins, so that I could not see our Lord.

10. This vision seems to me very profitable to recollected persons, to teach them to look upon our Lord as being in the innermost part of their soul.   It is a method of looking upon Him which penetrates us more thoroughly, and is much more fruitful than that of looking upon Him as external to us, as I have said elsewhere,[4] and as it is laid down in books on prayer, where they speak of where we are to seek

[4] Ch. iv. 10.

God. The glorious St. Augustine,[5] in particular, says so, when he says that neither in the streets of the city, nor in pleasures, nor in any place whatever where he sought Him, did he find Him as he found Him within himself. This is clearly the best way; we need not go up to heaven, nor any further than our own selves, for that would only distress the spirit and distract the soul, and bring but little fruit.

11. I should like to point out one result of a deep trance: it may be that some are aware of it. When the time is over during which the soul was in union, wherein all its powers were wholly absorbed,—it lasts, as I have said,[6] but a moment,—the soul continues still to be recollected, unable to recover itself even in outward things; for the two powers—the memory and the understanding—are, as it were, in a frenzy, extremely disordered. This, I say, happens occasionally, particularly in the beginnings. I am thinking whether it does not result from this: that our natural weakness cannot endure the vehemence of the spirit, which is so great, and that the imagination is enfeebled. I know it to be so with some. I think it best for these to force themselves to give up prayer at that time, and resume it afterwards, when they may recover what they have lost, and not do everything at once, for in that case much harm might come of it. I know this by experience, as well as the necessity of considering what our health can bear.

12. Experience is necessary throughout, so also is a spiritual director; for when the soul has reached this point, there are many matters which must be referred

---

[5] This passage, which is also quoted in *The Way of Perfection*, ch. xxviii., and in the *Interior Castle*, M. iv. ch. iii. 3, is not from the genuine *Soliloquia* of St. Augustine, but from a medieval ascetical writing bearing the same title and wrongly attributed to the great Doctor of the Church. Printed in Latin at Venice in 1512, it was translated into Spanish and appeared at Valladolid in 1515, and again at Medina del Campo in 1553, and at Toledo in 1565; other editions followed. The words quoted by St. Teresa occur in ch. xxxi. St. John of the Cross quotes another passage of the same work in the *Ascent of Mount Carmel*, bk. i. ch. v.

[6] Ch. xx. 26.

to the director. If, after seeking such a one, the soul cannot find him, our Lord will not fail that soul, seeing that He has not failed me, who am what I am. They are not many, I believe, who know by experience so many things, and without experience it is useless to treat a soul at all, for nothing will come of it, save only trouble and distress. But our Lord will take this also into account, and for that reason it is always best to refer the matter to the director. I have already more than once said this,[7] and even all I am saying now, only I do not distinctly remember it; but I do see that it is of great importance, particularly to women, that they should go to their confessor, and that he should be a man of experience herein. There are many more women than men to whom our Lord gives these graces; I have heard the holy friar Peter of Alcantara say so, and, indeed, I know it myself. He used to say that women made greater progress in this way than men did: and he gave excellent reasons for his opinion, all in favour of women; but there is no necessity for repeating them here.

13. Once, when in prayer, I had a vision, for a moment,—I saw nothing distinctly, but the vision was most clear,—how all things are seen in God and how all things are comprehended in Him. I cannot in any way explain it, but the vision remains most deeply impressed on my soul, and is one of those grand graces which our Lord wrought in me, and one of those which put me to the greatest shame and confusion whenever I call my sins to remembrance. I believe, if it had pleased our Lord that I had seen this at an earlier time, or if they saw it who sin against Him, we should have neither the heart nor the daring to do so. I had the vision, I repeat it, but I cannot say that I saw anything; however, I must have seen something, seeing that I explain it by an illustra-

[7] Ch. xxv. 18, ch. xxvi. 4. See St. John of the Cross, *Ascent of Mount Carmel*, bk. ii. ch. xxii.

tion, only it must have been in a way so subtile and delicate that the understanding is unable to reach it, or I am so ignorant in all that relates to these visions, which seem to be not imaginary. In some of these visions there must be something imaginary, only, as the powers of the soul are then in a trance, they are not able afterwards to retain the forms, as our Lord showed them to it then, and as He would have it rejoice in them.

14. Let us suppose the Godhead to be a most brilliant diamond, much larger than the whole world, or a mirror like that to which I compared the soul in a former vision,[8] only in a way so high that I cannot possibly describe it ; and that all our actions are seen in that diamond, which is of such dimensions as to include everything, because nothing can be beyond it. It was a fearful thing for me to see, in so short a time, so many things together in that brilliant diamond, and a most piteous thing too, whenever I think of it, to see such foul things as my sins present in the pure brilliancy of that light.

15. So it is, whenever I remember it, I do not know how to bear it, and I was then so ashamed of myself that I knew not where to hide myself. Oh, that some one could make this plain to those who commit most foul and filthy sins, that they may remember their sins are not secret, and that God most justly resents them, seeing that they are wrought in the very presence of His Majesty, and that we are demeaning ourselves so irreverently before Him ! I saw, too, how completely hell is deserved for only one mortal sin, and how impossible it is to understand the exceeding great wickedness of committing it in the sight of majesty so great, and how abhorrent to His nature such actions are. In this we see more and more of His mercifulness, who, though we all know His hatred of sin, yet suffers us to live.

---

[8] § 8.   See also *Interior Castle*, M. i. ch. i. 2.

16. The vision made me also reflect, that if one such vision as this fills the souls with such awe, what will it be in the Day of Judgment, when His Majesty will appear distinctly, and when we too shall look on the sins we have committed! O my God, I have been, oh, how blind! I have often been amazed at what I have written; and you, my father, be you not amazed at anything, but that I am still living,—I, who see such things, and know myself to be what I am. Blessed for ever be He Who has borne with me so long!

17. Once, in prayer, with much recollection, sweetness, and repose, I saw myself, as it seemed to me, surrounded by angels, and was close unto God. I began to intercede with His Majesty on behalf of the Church. I was given to understand the great services which a particular Order would render in the latter days, and the courage with which its members would maintain the faith.

18. I was praying before the most Holy Sacrament one day; I had a vision of a Saint, whose Order was in some degree fallen. In his hands he held a large book, which he opened, and then told me to read certain words, written in large and very legible letters; they were to this effect: "In times to come this Order will flourish; it will have many martyrs."

19. On another occasion, when I was at Matins in choir, six or seven persons, who seemed to me to be

[9] Yepez says that the Order here spoken of is the Carmelite, and Ribera understands the Saint to refer to that of St. Dominic. The Bollandists, n. 1638–46, on the whole prefer the authority of Ribera to that of Yepez, and give good reasons for their preference, setting aside as insufficient the testimony of Fray Luis of the Assumption, who says he heard himself from the Venerable Anne of St. Bartholomew that the Order in question is the Order of our Lady of Mount Carmel. Don Vicente, the Spanish editor, rejects the opinion of Ribera, on the ground that it could not have been truly said of the Dominicans in the sixteenth century that the Order was in "some degree fallen," for it was in a most flourishing state. He therefore was inclined to believe that the Saint referred to the Augustinians or to the Franciscans. But, after he had printed this part of his book, he discovered among the MSS. in the National Library of Madrid a letter of Ven. Anne of St. Bartholomew, addressed to Fray Luis of the Assumption, in which the saintly companion of St. Teresa says that the "Order was ours." (Fuente, vol. vi. 122.)

of this Order, appeared and stood before me with swords in their hands. The meaning of that, as I think, is that they are to be defenders of the faith ; for at another time, when I was in prayer, I fell into a trance, and stood in spirit on a wide plain, where many persons were fighting ; and the members of this Order weie fighting with great zeal. Their faces were beautiful, and as it were on fire. Many they laid low on the ground defeated, others they killed. It seemed to me to be a battle with heretics.

20. I have seen this glorious Saint occasionally, and he has told me certain things, and thanked me for praying for his Order, and he has promised to pray for me to our Lord. I do not say which Orders these are,—our Lord, if it so pleased Him, could make them known,—lest the others should be aggrieved. Let every Order, or every member of them by himself, labour, that by his means our Lord would so bless his own Order that it may serve Him in the present grave necessities of His Church. Blessed are they whose lives are so spent.

21. I was once asked by a person to pray God to let him know whether his acceptance of a bishopric would be for the service of God. After Communion our Lord said to me : " When he shall have clearly and really understood that true dominion consists in possessing nothing, he may then accept it." I understood by this that he who is to be in dignity must be very far from wishing or desiring it, or at least he must not seek it.

22. These and many other graces our Lord has given, and is giving continually, to me a sinner. I do not think it necessary to speak of them, because the state of my soul can be ascertained from what I have written ; so also can the spirit which our Lord has given me. May He be blessed for ever, who has been so mindful of me !

23. Our Lord said to me once, consoling me, that

I was not to distress myself,—this He said most lovingly,—because in this life we could not continue in the same state.[10] At one time I should be fervent, at another not ; now disquieted, and again at peace, and tempted ; but I must hope in Him, and fear not.

24. I was one day thinking whether it was a want of detachment in me to take pleasure in the company of those who had the care of my soul, and to have an affection for them, and to comfort myself with those whom I see to be very great servants of God.[11] Our Lord said to me : " It is not a virtue in a sick man to abstain from thanking and loving the physician who seems to restore him to health when he is in danger of death. What should I have done without these persons ? The conversation of good people was never hurtful ; my words should always be weighed, and holy ; and I was not to cease my relations with them, for they would do me good rather than harm."

25. This was a great comfort to me, because, now and then, I wished to abstain from converse with all people ; for it seemed to me that I was attached to them. Always, in all things, did our Lord console me, even to the showing me how I was to treat those who were weak, and some other people also. Never did He cease to take care of me. I am sometimes distressed to see how little I do in His service, and how I am forced to spend time in taking care of a body so weak and worthless as mine is, more than I wish.

26. I was in prayer one night, when it was time to go to sleep. I was in very great pain, and my usual sickness was coming on.[12] I saw myself so great a slave to myself, and, on the other hand, the spirit asked for time for itself. I was so much distressed that I began to weep exceedingly, and to be very sorry. This has happened to me not once only, but,

---

[10] Job xiv. 2 : " Nunquam in eodem statu permanet."
[11] See ch. xxxvii. 4, 6. [12] See ch. vii. 18.

as I am saying, very often ; and it seems to make me weary of myself, so that at the time I hold myself literally in abhorrence. Habitually, however, I know that I do not hate myself, and I never fail to take that which I see to be necessary for me. May our Lord grant that I do not take more than is necessary !—I am afraid I do.

27. When I was thus distressed, our Lord appeared unto me. He comforted me greatly, and told me I must do this for His love, and bear it ; my life was necessary now. And so, I believe, I have never known real pain since I resolved to serve my Lord and my Consoler with all my strength ; for though He would leave me to suffer a little, yet He would console me in such a way that I am doing nothing when I long for troubles. And it seems to me there is nothing worth living for but this, and suffering is what I most heartily pray to God for. I say to Him sometimes, with my whole heart : " O Lord, either to die or to suffer ! "[13] I ask of Thee nothing else for myself." It is a comfort to me to hear the clock strike, because I seem to have come a little nearer to the vision of God, in that another hour of my life has passed away.

28. At other times I am in such a state that I do not feel that I am living, nor yet do I desire to die ; but I am lukewarm, and darkness surrounds me on every side, as I said before ;[14] for I am very often in great trouble. It pleased our Lord that the graces He wrought in me should be published abroad,[15] as He told me some years ago they should be. It was a great pain to me, and I have borne much on that account even to this day, as you, my father, know, because every man explains them in his own sense. But my comfort herein is that it is not my fault that

---

[13] This is the genuine wording of what is known as the motto of St. Teresa, " To suffer or to die." This latter form never occurs in her writings, but the former is also to be found in an undated letter to a Carmelite nun (c. 1578).

[14] Ch. xxx. 10.   [15] Ch. xxxi. 16, 17.

they are become known, for I was extremely cautious never to speak of them but to my confessors, or to persons who I knew had heard of them from them. I was silent, however, not out of humility, but because, as I said before,[16] it gave me great pain to speak of them even to my confessors.

29. Now, however,—to God be the glory!—though many speak against me, but out of a zeal for goodness, and though some are afraid to speak to me, and even to hear my confession, and though others have much to say about me, because I see that our Lord willed by this means to provide help for many souls,—and also because I see clearly and keep in mind how much He would suffer, if only for the gaining of one,—I do not care about it at all.

30. I know not why it is so, but perhaps the reason may in some measure be that His Majesty has placed me in this corner out of the way, where the enclosure is so strict, and where I am as one that is dead. I thought that no one would remember me, but I am not so much forgotten as I wish I was, for I am forced to speak to some people. But as I am in a house where none may see me, it seems as if our Lord had been pleased to bring me to a haven, which I trust in His Majesty will be secure. Now that I am out of the world, with companions holy and few in number, I look down on the world as from a great height, and care very little what people say or know about me. I think much more of one soul's advancement, even if it were but slight, than of all that people may say of me ; and since I am settled here it has pleased our Lord that all my desires tend to this.

31. He has made my life to me now a kind of sleep ; for almost always what I see seems to me to be seen as in a dream, nor have I any great sense either of pleasure or of pain. If matters occur which may occasion either, the sense of it passes away so quickly

[16] Ch. xxviii. 6.

that it astonishes me, and leaves an impression as if
I had been dreaming,—and this is the simple truth;
for if I wished afterwards to delight in that pleasure,
or be sorry over that pain, it is not in my power to do
so: just as a sensible person feels neither pain nor
pleasure in the memory of a dream that is past; for
now our Lord has roused my soul out of that state
which, because I was not mortified nor dead to the
things of this world, made me feel as I did, and His
Majesty does not wish me to become blind again.

32. This is the way I live now, my lord and father [17];
do you, my father, pray to God that He would take
me to Himself, or enable me to serve Him. May it
please His Majesty that what I have written may be
of some use to you, my father! I have so little time, [18]
and therefore my trouble has been great in writing;
but it will be a blessed trouble if I have succeeded in
saying anything that will cause one single act of praise
to our Lord. If that were the case, I should look
upon myself as sufficiently rewarded, even if you, my
father, burnt at once what I have written. I would
rather it were not burnt before those three saw it,
whom you, my father, know of, because they are,
and have been, my confessors; for if it be bad, it is
right they should lose the good opinion they have of
me; and if it be good, they are good and learned men,
and I know they will recognise its source, and give
praise to Him who hath spoken through me.

33. May His Majesty ever be your protector and
make you so great a saint that your spirit and light
may show the way to me a miserable creature, so
wanting in humility and so bold as to have ventured
to write on subjects so high! May our Lord grant I
have not fallen into any errors in the matter, for I
had the intention and the desire to be accurate and
obedient, and also that through me He might, in some

---

[17] Probably F. Garcia de Toledo. See also ch. xx. 25.
[18] See ch. xiv. 12.

measure, have glory,—because that is what I have been praying for these many years, and as my good works are inefficient for that end, I have ventured to put in order this my disordered life. Still, I have not wasted more time, nor given it more attention, than was necessary for writing it ; yet I have put down all that has happened to me with all the simplicity and sincerity possible.

34. May our Lord, Who is all-powerful, grant—and He can if He will—that I may attain to the doing of His will in all things ! May He never suffer this soul to be lost, which He so often, in so many ways, and by so many means, has rescued from hell and drawn unto Himself ! Amen.

I.H.S.

The Holy Spirit be ever with you, my father.[19] Amen. It would not be anything improper if I were to magnify my labour in writing this, to oblige you to be very careful to recommend me to our Lord ; for indeed I may well do so, considering what I have gone through in giving this account of myself, and in retracing my manifold wretchedness. But, still, I can say with truth that I felt it more difficult to speak of the graces which I have received from our Lord than to speak of my offences against His Majesty. You, my father, commanded me to write at length ; that is what I have done, on condition that you will do what you promised, namely, destroy everything in it that has the appearance of being wrong. I had not yet read it through after I had written it, when your reverence sent for it. Some things in it may not be very clearly explained, and there may be some repetitions ; for the time I could give to it was so

[19] This letter, which seems to have accompanied the " Life," is printed among the other letters of the Saint ; it was probably addressed to Fray Garcia de Toledo. See Introduction.

short, that I could not stop to see what I was writing. I entreat your reverence to correct it and have it copied, if it is to be sent on to the Father-Master, Avila,[20] for perhaps some one may recognise the handwriting. I wish very much you would order it so that he might see it, for I began to write it with a view to that. I shall be greatly comforted if he shall think that I am on a safe road, now that, so far as it concerns me, there is nothing more to be done.

Your reverence will do in all things that which to you shall seem good, and you will look upon yourself as under an obligation to take care of one who trusts her soul to your keeping. I will pray for the soul of your reverence to our Lord, so long as I live. You will, therefore, be diligent in His service, in order that you may be able to help me ; for your reverence will see by what I have written how profitable it is to give oneself, as your reverence has begun to do, wholly unto Him who gives Himself to us so utterly without measure.

Blessed be His Majesty for ever ! I hope of His mercy we shall see one another one day, when we, your reverence and myself, shall see more clearly the great mercies He has shown us, and when we shall praise Him for ever and ever. Amen.

This book was finished in June, 1562.

" This date refers to the first account which the holy Mother Teresa of Jesus wrote of her life ; it was not then divided into chapters. Afterwards she made this copy, and inserted in it many things which had taken place subsequent to this date, such as the foundation of the monastery of St. Joseph of Avila, as in p. 169.[21]—FRAY Dᵒ BAÑES."

[20] Ven. Juan de Avila, commonly called the Apostle of Andalusia.
[21] *I.e.* of the MS. See p. 303 *sqq.* of this translation.

THE

RELATIONS OR MANIFESTATIONS

OF HER

SPIRITUAL STATE

WHICH

ST. TERESA SUBMITTED TO HER CONFESSORS.

THE RELATIONS

RELATION I.

SENT TO ST. PETER OF ALCANTARA IN 1560 FROM THE MONASTERY OF THE INCARNATION, AVILA.[1]

[1] Antonius a Sancto Joseph, in his notes on this Relation, says it was written for St. Peter of Alcantara when he came to Avila in 1560, at the time when the Saint was so severely tried by her confessors and the others who examined her spirit, and were convinced that her prayer was a delusion of Satan : see the *Life*, ch. xxv. 18. The following notes were discovered among the papers of the Saint in the monastery of the Incarnation, and are supposed to refer to this Relation. The Chronicler of the Order, Francis a Sancta Maria, is inclined to the belief that they were written by St. Peter of Alcantara, to whom the Relation is addressed, and the more so because Ribera does not claim them for any member of the Society, notwithstanding the reference to them in §§ 22, 28.

" 1. The end God has in view is the drawing a soul to Himself ; that of the devil is the withdrawing it from God. Our Lord never does anything whereby any one may be separated from Him, and the devil does nothing whereby any one may be made to draw near unto God. All the visions and the other operations in the soul of this person draw her nearer unto God, and make her more humble and obedient.

" 2. It is the teaching of St. Thomas that an angel of light may be recognised by the peace and quietness he leaves in the soul. She is never visited in this way, but she afterwards abides in peace and joy ; so much so, that all the pleasures of earth together are not comparable to one of these visitations.

" 3. She never commits a fault, nor falls into an imperfection, without being instantly rebuked by Him who speaks interiorly to her.

" 4. She has never prayed for nor wished for them ; all she wishes for is to do the will of God our Lord in all things.

" 5. Everything herein is consistent with the Scriptures and the teaching of the Church, and most true, according to the most rigorous principles of scholastic theology.

" 6. This soul is most pure and sincere, with the most fervent desires of being pleasing unto God, and of trampling on every earthly thing.

" 7. She has been told that whatever she shall ask of God, being good, she shall have. She has asked much, and things not convenient to put on paper lest it should be wearisome ; all of which our Lord has granted.

1. THE method of prayer I observe at present is this : when I am in prayer, it is very rarely that I can use the understanding, because the soul becomes at once

" 8. When these operations are from God, they are always directed to the good of the recipient, to that of the community, or of some other. That she has profited by them she knows by experience, and she knows it, too, of other persons also.

" 9. No one converses with her, if he be not in evil dispositions, who is not moved thereby to devotion, even though she says nothing about it.

" 10. She is growing daily in the perfection of virtues, and learns by these things the way of a higher perfection. And thus, during the whole time in which she had visions, she was making progress, according to the doctrine of St. Thomas.

" 11. The spirit that speaks to her soul never tells her anything in the way of news, or of what is unbecoming, but only that which tends to edification.

" 12. She has been told of some persons that they were full of devils ; but this was for the purpose of enabling her to understand the state of a soul which has sinned mortally against our Lord.

" 13. The devil's method is, when he attempts to deceive a soul, to advise that soul never to speak of what he says to it ; but the spirit that speaks to this soul warns her to be open with learned men, servants of our Lord, and that the devil may deceive her if she should conceal anything through shame.

" 14. So great is the progress of her soul in this way, and the edification she ministers in the good example given, that more than forty nuns in her monastery practise great recollection.

" 15. These supernatural things occur after long praying, when she is absorbed in God, on fire with His love, or at Communion.

" 16. They kindle in her a most earnest desire to be on the right road, and to escape the delusions of Satan.

" 17. They are in her the cause of the deepest humility ; she understands that what she receives comes to her from the hand of our Lord, and how little worth she is herself.

" 18. When they are withheld, anything that occurs is wont to pain and distress her ; but when she is in this state, she remembers nothing ; all she is conscious of is a great longing for suffering, and so great is it that she is amazed at it.

" 19. They are to her sources of joy and consolation in her troubles, when people speak ill of her, and in her infirmities,—and she has fearful pains about the heart, sicknesses, and many other afflictions, all of which leave her when she has these visions.

" 20. With all this, she undergoes great penances, fasting, the discipline, and mortifications.

" 21. All that on earth may give her any pleasure, and her trials, which are many, she bears with equal tranquillity of mind, without losing the peace and quiet of her soul.

" 22. Her resolution never to offend our Lord is so earnest that she has made a vow never to leave undone what she knows herself, or is told by those who understand the matter better, to be the more perfect. And though she holds the members of the Society to be saints, and believes that our Lord made use of them to bestow on her graces so great, she told me that, if she knew it would be more perfect to have nothing more to do with them, she would never speak to them again, nor see them, notwithstanding the fact that it was through them that her mind had been quieted and directed in these things.

recollected, remains in repose, or falls into a trance, so that I cannot in any way have the use of the faculties and the senses,—so much so, that the hearing alone is left ; but then it does not help me to understand anything.

2. It often happens, when I am not even thinking of the things of God, but engaged in other matters, and when prayer seems to be beyond my power, whatever efforts I might make, because of the great aridity I am in, bodily pains contributing thereto, that this recollection or elevation of spirit comes upon me so suddenly that I cannot withstand it, and the fruits and blessings it brings with it are in a moment

" 23. The sweetnesses she commonly receives, her sense of God, her languishing with love, are certainly marvellous, and through these she is wont to be enraptured the whole day long.

" 24. She frequently falls into a trance when she hears God spoken of with devotion and earnestness, and cannot resist the rapture, do what she can ; and in that state her appearance is such that she excites very great devotion.

" 25. She cannot bear to be directed by any one who will not tell her of her faults, and rebuke her ; all that she accepts with great humility.

" 26. Moreover, she cannot endure people who are in a state of perfection, if they do not labour to become perfect, according to the spirit of their rule.

" 27. She is most detached from her kindred, has no desire to converse with people, and loves solitude. She has a great devotion to the saints, and on their feasts, and on the days on which the Church celebrates the mysteries of the faith, is filled with most fervent affections for our Lord.

" 28. If all the members of the Society, and all the servants of God upon earth, tell her that her state is an effect of the operations of Satan, or were to say so, she is in fear and trembling before the visions occur ; but as soon as she is in prayer, and recollected, she cannot be persuaded, were they to tear her into a thousand pieces, that it is any other than God who is working in her and speaking to her.

" 29. God has given her a most wonderfully strong and valiant spirit : she was once timid ; now she tramples on all the evil spirits. She has put far away from herself all the littleness and silliness of women ; she is singularly free from scruples, and most sincere.

" 30. Besides, our Lord has given her the gift of most sweet tears, great compassion for her neighbours, the knowledge of her own faults, a great reverence for good people, and self-abasement ; and I am certain that she has done good to many, of whom I am one.

" 31. She is continually reminding herself of God, and has a sense of His presence. All the locutions have been verified, and every one of them accomplished ; and this is a very great test.

" 32. Her visions are a source of great clearness in her understanding, and an admirable illumination in the things of God.

" 33. It was said to her that she should lead those who were trying her spirit to look into the Scriptures, and that they would not find that any soul desirous of pleasing God had been so long deceived."

mine : and this, without my having had a vision, or heard anything, or knowing where I am, except that when the soul seems to be lost [2] I see it make great progress, which I could not have made if I had laboured for a whole year, so great is my gain.

3. At other times certain excessive impetuosities occur, accompanied with a certain fainting away of the soul for God, so that I have no control over myself [3] ; my life seems to have come to an end, and so it makes me cry out and call upon God ; and this comes upon me with great vehemence. Sometimes I cannot remain sitting, so great is the oppression of the heart ; and this pain comes on without my doing anything to cause it, and the nature of it is such that my soul would be glad never to be without it while I live. And the longings I have are longings not to live ; and they come on because it seems as if I must live on without being able to find any relief, for relief comes from the vision of God, which comes by death, and death is what I cannot take ; and with all this my soul thinks that all except itself are filled with consolations, and that all find help in their troubles, but not itself. The distress thus occasioned is so intense that, if our Lord did not relieve it by throwing it into a trance, whereby all is made calm, and the soul rests in great quiet and is satisfied, now by seeing something of that which it deserves, now by hearing other things, it would seem to be impossible for it to be delivered from this pain.

4. At other times there come upon me certain desires to serve God, with a vehemence so great that I cannot describe it, and accompanied with a certain pain at seeing how unprofitable I am. It seems to me then that there is nothing in the world, neither death, nor martyrdom, that I could not easily endure. This conviction, too, is not the result of any reflection,

[2] That is, so absorbed as to lose the use of its faculties.
[3] See *Life*, ch. xxix. 9–13.

but comes in a moment.   I am wholly changed, and
I know not whence cometh such great courage.   I
think I should live to raise my voice, and publish to
all the world how important it is for men not to be
satisfied with the common way, and how great the
good is that God will give us if we prepare ourselves
to receive it.   I say it again, these desires are such
that I am melted away in myself, for I seem to desire
what I cannot have.   The body seems to me to hold
me in prison, through its inability to serve God and
my state [4] in anything ;   for if it were not for the
body, I might do very great things, so far as my
strength would allow ;   and thus, because I see myself
without any power whatever to serve God, I feel this
pain in a way wholly indescribable ;   the issue is
delight, recollection, and the consolation of God.

5. Again, it has happened, when these longings to
serve Him come upon me, that I wish to do penance,
but I am not able.   It would be a great relief to me,
and it does relieve and cheer me, though what I do is
almost nothing, because of my bodily weakness ;   and
yet, if I were to give way to these my longings, I
believe I should observe no moderation.

6. Sometimes, if I have to speak to any one, I am
greatly distressed, and I suffer so much that it makes
me weep abundantly ;   for my whole desire is to be
alone, and solitude comforts me, though at times I
neither pray nor read, and conversation—particularly of kindred and connections—seems oppressive,
and myself to be as a slave, except when I speak to
those whose conversation is of prayer and matters of
the soul,—in these I find comfort and joy [5] ;   yet these
occasionally are too much for me, and I would rather
not see them, but go where I might be alone :   though
this is not often the case, for those especially who
direct my conscience always console me.

[4] Fuente thinks she means the religious state.   See *Foundations*, i. 6.
[5] See *Life*, ch. xxiv. 8, and ch. xxxi. 22.

7. At other times it gives me much pain that I must eat and sleep, and that I see I cannot forgo these things, being less able to do so than any one. I submit that I may serve God, and thus I offer up those actions to Him. Time seems to me too short, and that I have not enough for my prayer, for I should never be tired of being alone. I am always wishing I had time for reading, for I have been always fond of reading. I read very little, for when I take up a book I become recollected through the pleasure it gives me, and thus my reading is turned into prayer : and it is but rarely, for I have many occupations ; and though they are good, they do not give me the pleasure which reading would give. And thus I am always wishing for more time, and everything becomes disagreeable, so I believe, because I see I cannot do what I wish and desire.

8. All these desires, with an increase in virtue, have been given me by our Lord since He raised me to this prayer of quiet, and sent these raptures. I find myself so improved that I look on myself as being a mass of perdition before this. These raptures and visions leave me in possession of the blessings I shall now speak of ; and I maintain that if there be any good in me, they are the occasions of it.

9. I have made a very strong resolution never to offend God, not even venially. I would rather die a thousand deaths than do anything of the kind knowingly. I am resolved never to leave undone anything I may consider to be the more perfect, or more for the honour of our Lord, if he who has the care of my soul and directs me tells me I may do it. Cost me what pain it might, I would not leave such an act undone for all the treasures of the world. If I were to do so, I do not think I could have the face to ask anything of God our Lord, or to make my prayer ; and yet, for all this, I have many faults and imperfections. I am

obedient to my confessor,[6] though imperfectly ; but if I know that he wishes or commands anything, I would not leave that undone, so far as I understand it ; if I did so, I should think myself under a grievous delusion.

10. I have a longing for poverty, though not free from imperfection ; however, I believe, if I had wealth, I would not reserve any revenue, nor hoard money for myself, nor do I care for it ; I wish to have only what is necessary Nevertheless, I feel that I am very defective in this virtue ; for, though I desire nothing for myself, I should like to have something to give away : still, I desire no revenue, nor anything for myself.[7]

11. In almost all the visions I have had, I have found good, if it be not a delusion of Satan ; herein I submit myself to the judgment of my confessors.

12. As to fine and beautiful things, such as water, fields, perfume, music, etc., I think I would rather not have them, so great is the difference between them and what I am in the habit of seeing, and so all pleasure in them is gone from me.[8]   Hence it is that I care not for them, unless it be at the first sight : they never make any further impression ; to me they seem but dirt.

13. If I speak or converse with people in the world—for I cannot help it—even about prayer, and if the conversation be long, though to pass away the time, I am under great restraint if it be not necessary, for it gives me much pain.

14. Amusements, of which I used to be fond, and worldly things, are all disagreeable to me now, and I cannot look at them.

15. The longings, which I said I have,[9] of loving and serving and seeing God, are not helped by any

[6] At that time Balthasar Alvarez. See *Life*, ch. xxiii. 19.
[7] See *Life*, ch. xxxv. 2.
[8] See *Life*, ch. ix. 6, and ch. xiv. 7.
[9] See § 3 above.

reflections, as formerly, when I thought I was very devout, and shed many tears ; but they flow out of a certain fire and heat so excessive that, I repeat it, if God did not relieve them by throwing me into a trance, wherein the soul seems to find itself satisfied, I believe my life would come to an end at once.

16. When I see persons making great progress, and thus resolved, detached, and courageous, I love them much ; and I should like to have my conversation with such persons, and I think they help me on.   People who are afraid, and seemingly cautious in those things, the doing of which is perfectly reasonable here, seem to vex me, and drive me to pray to God and the saints to make them undertake such things as these which now frighten us.   Not that I am good for anything myself, but because I believe that God helps those who, for His sake, apply themselves to great things, and that He never abandons any one who puts his trust in Him only.   And I should like to find any one who would help me to believe so, and to be without thought about food and raiment, but leave it all in the hands of God.[10]

17. This leaving in the hands of God the supply of all I need is not to be understood as excluding all labour on my part, but merely solicitude—I mean, the solicitude of care.[11]   And since I have attained to this liberty, it goes well with me, and I labour to forget myself as much as I can.   I do not think it is a year ago since our Lord gave me this liberty.

18. Vainglory [12]—glory be to God !—so far as I know, there is no reason why I should have any ; for I see plainly that in these things which God sends me I have no part myself ; on the contrary, God makes me conscious of my own wretchedness ; for whatever reflections I might be able to make, I could never come

---

[10] St. Matt. vi. 31 : " Nolite ergo solliciti esse, dicentes : Quid manducabimus . . . aut quo operiemur ? "

[11] Ribera says that these words were afterwards added by St. Teresa.

[12] See *Life*, ch. vii. 2.

to the knowledge of such deep truths as I attain to in a single rapture.

19. When I speak of these things a few days after, they seem to me as if they had happened to another person. Previously, I thought it a wrong to me that they should be known to others ; but I see now that I am not therefore any the better, but rather worse, seeing that I make so little progress after receiving mercies so great. And certainly, in every way, it seems to me that there was not in the world anybody worse than myself [13] ; and so the virtues of others seem to me much more meritorious than mine, and that I do nothing myself but receive graces, and that God must give to others at once all that He is now giving unto me ; and I pray Him not to reward me in this life ; and so I believe that God has led me along this way because I am weak and wicked.

20. When I am in prayer, and even almost always when I am able to reflect at all, I cannot, even if I tried, pray to God for rest, or desire it ; for I see that His life was one of suffering, and that I ask Him to send me, giving me first the grace to bear it.

21. Everything of this kind, and of the highest perfection, seems to make so deep an impression on me in prayer, that I am amazed at the sight of truths so great and so clear that the things of the world seem to be folly ; and so it is necessary for me to take pains to reflect on the way I demeaned myself formerly in the things of the world, for it seems to me folly to feel for deaths and the troubles of the world,—at least, that sorrow for, or love of, kindred and friends should last long. I say I have to take pains when I am considering what I was, and what I used to feel.

22. If I see people do anything which clearly seems to be sin, I cannot make up my mind that they have offended God ; and if I dwell upon this at all,—which happens rarely or never,—I never can make up my

---

[13] See *Life*, ch. xxx. 10, 11.

mind, though I see it plainly enough. It seems to me that everybody is as anxious to serve God as I am. And herein God has been very gracious to me, for I never dwell on an evil deed, to remember it afterwards ; and if I do remember it, I see some virtue or other in that person. In this way these things never weary me, except generally : but heresies do ; they distress me very often, and almost always when I think of them they seem to me to be the only trouble which should be felt. And also I feel, when I see people who used to give themselves to prayer fall away ; this gives me pain, but not much, because I strive not to dwell upon it.[14]

23. I find also, that I am improved in the matter of that excessive neatness which I was wont to observe,[15] though not wholly delivered from it. I do not discern that I am always mortified in this ; sometimes, however, I do.

24. All this I have described, together with a very constant dwelling in thought on God, is the ordinary state of my soul, so far as I can understand it. And if I must be busy about something else, without my seeking it, as I said before,[16] I know not who makes me awake,—and this not always, only when I am busy with things of importance ; and such—glory be to God !—only at intervals demand my attention, and do not occupy me at all times.

25. For some days—they are not many, however —for three, or four, or five, all my good and fervent thoughts, and my visions, seem to be withdrawn, yea, even forgotten, so that, if I were to seek for it, I know of no good that can ever have been in me. It seems to have been all a dream or, at least, I can call nothing to mind. Bodily pains at the same time distress me. My understanding is troubled, so that I cannot think at all about God, neither do I know under what law

[14] See *Life*, ch. xxxix. 4.   [15] See *Life*, ch. ii. 2.
[16] § 2 above.

I live. If I read anything, I do not understand it ;
I seem to be full of faults, and without any resolution
whatever to practise virtue ; and the great resolution
I used to have is come to this, that I seem to be unable
to resist the least temptation or slander of the world.
It suggests itself to me then that I am good for nothing, if any one would have me undertake more than
the common duties. I give way to sadness, thinking
I have deceived all those who trusted me at all. I
should like to hide myself where nobody could see
me ; but my desire for solitude arises from want of
courage, not from love of virtue. It seems to me that
I should like to dispute with all who contradict me ;
I am under the influence of these impressions, only
God has been so gracious unto me, that I do not offend
more frequently than I was wont to do, nor do I ask
Him to deliver me from them, but only, if it be His
will I should always suffer thus, to keep me from offending Him ; and I submit myself to His will with my
whole heart, and I see that it is a very great grace
bestowed upon me that He does not keep me constantly
in this state.

26. One thing astonishes me : it is that, while I
am in this state, through a single word of those I am
in the habit of hearing, or a single vision, or a little
self-recollection, lasting but an *Ave Maria*, or through
my drawing near to communicate, I find my soul and
body so calm, so sound, the understanding so clear,
and myself possessing all the strength and all the
good desires I usually have. And this I have had
experience of very often—at least when I go to Communion ; it is more than six months ago that I felt a
clear improvement in my bodily health,[17] and that
occasionally brought about through raptures, and I
find it last sometimes more than three hours, at other
times I am much stronger for a whole day ; and I
do not think it is fancy, for I have considered the

[17] See *Life*, ch. xx. 29.

matter, and reflected on it.   Accordingly, when I am thus recollected, I fear no illness.   The truth is, that when I pray, as I was accustomed to do before, I feel no improvement.

27. All these things of which I am speaking make me believe that it comes from God ; for when I see what once I was, that I was in the way of being lost, and that soon, my soul certainly is astonished at these things, without knowing whence these virtues came to me ; I did not know myself, and saw that all was a gift, and not the fruit of my labours.   I understand in all truthfulness and sincerity, and see that I am not deluded, that it has been not only the means of drawing me to God in His service, but of saving me also from hell.   This my confessors know, who have heard my general confession.

28. Also, when I see any one who knows anything about me, I wish to let him know my whole life,[18] because my honour seems to me to consist in the honour of our Lord, and I care for nothing else.   This He knows well, or I am very blind[19] ; for neither honour, nor life, nor praise, nor good either of body or of soul can interest me, nor do I seek or desire any advantage, only His glory.   I cannot believe that Satan has sought so many means of making my soul advance, in order to lose it after all.   I do not hold him to be so foolish.   Nor can I believe it of God, though I have deserved to fall into delusions because of my sins, that He has left unheeded so many prayers of so many good people for two years, and I do nothing else but ask everybody to pray to our Lord that He would show me if this be for his glory, or lead me by another way.[20]   I do not believe that these things would have been permitted by His Majesty to be

---

[18] See *Life*, ch. xxxi. 17.

[19] Ribera and the earlier editors have, instead of " or I am very blind," " and of this I am quite certain."   It all depends whether the Saint wrote " ciega " (blind) or " cierta " (certain).

[20] See *Life*, ch. xxv. 20.

always going on if they were not His work. These
considerations, and the reasons of so many saintly
men, give me courage when I am under the pressure
of fear that they are not from God, I being so wicked
myself. But when I am in prayer, and during those
days when I am in repose, and my thoughts fixed on
God, if all the learned and holy men in the world
came together and put me to all conceivable tortures,
and I, too, desirous of agreeing with them, they could
not make me believe that this is the work of Satan, for
I cannot. And when they would have had me believe
it, I was afraid, seeing who it was that said so ; and
I thought that they must be saying what was true,
and that I, being what I was, must have been deluded.
But all they had said to me was destroyed by the
first word, or recollection, or vision that came, and I
was able to resist no longer, and believed it was from
God.[21]

29. However, I can think that Satan now and
then may intermeddle here, and so it is, as I have seen
and said ; but he produces different results, nor can
he, as it seems to me, deceive any one possessed of
any experience. Nevertheless, I say that, though I
do certainly believe this to be from God, I would never
do anything, for any consideration whatever, that is
not judged by him who has the charge of my soul to
be for the better service of our Lord, and I never had
any intention but to obey without concealing anything, for that is my duty. I am very often rebuked
for my faults, and that in such a way as to pierce me
to the very quick ; and I am warned when there is,
or when there may be, any danger in what I am doing.
These rebukes and warnings have done me much
good, in often reminding me of my former sins, which
made me exceedingly sorry.

30. I have been very long, but this is the truth,—
that, when I rise from my prayer, I see that I have

[21] See *Life*, ch. xxv. 18, 22.

received blessings which seem too briefly described. Afterwards I fall into many imperfections, and am unprofitable and very wicked. And perhaps I have no perception of what is good, but am deluded ; still, the difference in my life is notorious, and compels me to think over all I have said—I mean, that which I verily believe I have felt. These are the perfections which I feel our Lord has wrought in me who am so wicked and so imperfect. I refer it all to your judgment, my father, for you know the whole state of my soul.

RELATION II.

TO ONE OF HER CONFESSORS, FROM THE HOUSE OF DOÑA LUISA DE LA CERDA, IN 1562.[1]

JESUS.

I THINK it is more than a year since this was written ; God has all this time protected me with His hand, so that I have not become worse ; on the contrary, I see a great change for the better in all I have to say : may He be praised for it all !

1. The visions and revelations have not ceased, but they are of a much higher kind. Our Lord has taught me a way of prayer, wherein I find myself far more advanced, more detached from the things of this life, more courageous, and more free.[2] I fall into a trance more frequently, for these ecstasies at times come upon me with great violence, and in such a way as to be outwardly visible, I having no power to resist them ; and even when I am with others—for they come in such a way as admits of no disguising them, unless it be by letting people suppose that, as I am subject to disease of the heart, they are fainting-

---

[1] Addressed, it is believed, to her confessor, Fr. Pedro Ibañez. This Relation corresponds with ch. xxxiv. of the *Life*.

[2] See *Life*, ch. xxvii.

fits ; I take great pains, however, to resist them when they are coming on—sometimes I cannot do it.

2. As to poverty, God seems to have wrought great things in me ; for I would willingly be without even what is necessary, unless given me as an alms ; and therefore my longing is extreme that I may be in such a state as to depend on alms alone for my food.[3] It seems to me that to live, when I am certain of food and raiment without fail, is not so complete an observance of my vow or of the counsel of Christ as it would be to live where no revenue is possessed, and I should be in want at times ; and as to the blessings that come with true poverty, they seem to me to be great, and I would not miss them. Many times do I find myself with such great faith, that I do not think God will ever fail those who serve Him, and without any doubt whatever that there is, or can be, any time in which His words are not fulfilled : I cannot persuade myself to the contrary, nor can I have any fear ; and so, when they advise me to accept an endowment, I feel it keenly, and betake myself unto God.

3. I think I am much more compassionate towards the poor than I used to be, having a great pity for them and a desire to help them ; for if I regarded only my good will, I should give them even the habit I wear. I am not fastidious with respect to them, even if I had to do with them or touched them with my hands,—and this I now see is a gift of God ; for though I used to give alms for His love, I had no natural compassion. I am conscious of a distinct improvement herein.

4. As to the evil speaking directed against me,— which is considerable, and highly injurious to me, and done by many,—I find myself herein also very much the better. I think that what they say makes scarcely any more impression upon me than it would

---

[3] See *Life*, ch. xxxv. 2, how the Saint came to found her convent in strict poverty.

upon an idiot. I think at times, and nearly always, that it is just. I feel it so little that I see nothing in it that I might offer to God, as I learn by experience that my soul gains greatly thereby ; on the contrary, the evil speaking seems to be a favour. And thus, the moment I go to prayer, I have no ill-feeling against them ; the first time I hear it, it creates in me a little resistance, but it neither disturbs nor moves me ; on the contrary, when I see others occasionally disturbed, I am sorry for them.[4] So it is, I put myself out of the question ; for all the wrongs of this life seem to me so light that it is not possible to feel them, because I imagine myself to be dreaming, and see that all this will be nothing when I awake.

5. God is giving me more earnest desires, a greater love of solitude, a much greater detachment, as I said, with the visions ; by these He has made me know what all that is, even if I gave up all the friends I have, both men and women and kindred. This is the least part of it : my kindred are rather a very great weariness to me ; I leave them in all freedom and joy, provided it be to render the least service unto God ; and thus on every side I find peace.

6. Certain things, about which I have been warned in prayer, have been perfectly verified. Thus, considering the graces received from God, I find myself very much better ; but, considering my service to Him in return, I am exceedingly worthless, for I have received greater consolation than I have given, though sometimes that gives me grievous pain. My penance is very scanty, the respect shown me great, much against my own will very often.[5] However, in a word, I see that I live an easy, not a penitential, life ; God help me, as He can ![6]

---

[4] Instead of " I am sorry for them," Ribera's edition has, " I laugh within myself."

[5] See *Life*, ch. xxxi. 15.

[6] The last two lines are not in Ribera and the other old editions. The sequel was written at the convent of St. Joseph, Avila, in the course of 1563.

7. It is now nine months, more or less, since I wrote this with my own hand ; since then I have not turned my back on the graces which God has given me ; I think I have received, so far as I can see, a much greater liberty of late.   Hitherto I thought I had need of others, and I had more reliance on worldly helps.   Now I clearly understand that all men are bunches of dried rosemary, and that there is no safety in leaning on them, for if they are pressed by contradictions or evil speaking they break down. And so I know by experience that the only way not to fall is to cling to the cross, and put our trust in Him who was nailed thereto.   I find Him a real Friend, and with Him I find myself endowed with such might that, God never failing me, I think I should be able to withstand the whole world if it were against me.

8. Having a clear knowledge of this truth, I used to be very fond of being loved by others ; now I do not care for that, yea, rather, their love seems to weary me in some measure, excepting theirs who take care of my soul, or theirs to whom I think I do good. Of the former I wish to be loved, in order that they may bear with me ; and of the latter, that they may be more inclined to believe me when I tell them that all is vanity.

9. In the very grievous trials, persecutions, and contradictions of these months,[7] God gave me great courage ;   and the more grievous they were, the greater the courage, without weariness in suffering. Not only had I no ill-feeling against those who spoke evil of me, but I had, I believe, conceived a deeper affection for them.   I know not how it was ; certainly it was a gift from the hand of our Lord.

10. When I desire anything, I am accustomed naturally to desire it with some vehemence ; now my desires are so calm, that I do not even feel that I am

---

[7] The Saint refers to the troubles she endured during the foundation of the monastery of St. Joseph.

pleased when I see them fulfilled. Sorrow and joy, excepting in that which relates to prayer, are so moderated, that I seem to be without sense, and in that state I remain for some days.

11. The vehement longings to do penance which come, and have come, upon me are great ; and if I do any penance, I feel it to be so slight in comparison with that longing, that I regard it sometimes, and almost always, as a special consolation ; however, I do but little, because of my great weakness.

12. It is a very great pain to me very often, and at this moment most grievous, that I must take food, particularly if I am in prayer. It must be very great, for it makes me weep much, and speak the language of affliction, almost without being aware of it, and that is what I am not in the habit of doing, for I do not remember that I ever did so in the very heaviest trials of my life : I am not a woman in these things, for I have a hard heart.

13. I feel in myself a very earnest desire, more so than usual, that God may find those who will serve Him, particularly learned men, in all detachment, and who will not cleave to anything of this world, for I see it is all a mockery ; for when I see the great needs of the Church, I look upon it as a mockery to be distressed about aught else.[8] I do nothing but pray to God for such men, because I see that one person, who is wholly perfect in the true fervour of the love of God, will do more good than many who are lukewarm.

14. In matters concerning the faith, my courage seems to me much greater. I think I could go forth alone by myself against the Lutherans, and convince them of their errors. I feel very keenly the loss of so many souls. I see many persons making great progress ; I see clearly it was the pleasure of God that such progress should have been helped by me ; and

---

[8] See *Life*, ch. xxxiv. 19, with respect to F. Garcia de Toledo. *Way of Perfection*, i. 1.

I perceive that my soul, of His goodness, grows daily more and more in His love.

15. I think I could not be led away by vainglory, even if I seriously tried, and I do not see how I could imagine any one of my virtues to be mine, for it is not long since I was for many years without any at all ; and now, so far as I am concerned, I do nothing but receive graces, without rendering any service in return, being the most worthless creature in the world. And so it is that I consider at times how all, except myself, make progress ; I am good for nothing in myself. This is not humility only, but the simple truth ; and the knowledge of my being so worthless makes me sometimes think with fear that I must be under some delusion. Thus I see clearly that all my gain has come through the revelations and the raptures, in which I am nothing myself, and do no more to effect them than the canvas does for the picture painted on it. This makes me feel secure and be at rest ; and I place myself in the hands of God, and trust my desires ; for I know for certain that my desires are to die for Him, and to lose all ease, and that whatever may happen.

16. There are days wherein I remember times without number the words of St. Paul,[9]—though certainly they are not true of me,—that I have neither life, nor speech, nor will of my own, but that there is One in me by Whom I am directed and made strong ; and I am, as it were, beside myself, and thus life is a very grievous burden to me. And the greatest oblation I make to God, as the highest service on my part, is that I, when I feel it so painfully to be absent from Him, am willing to live on for the love of Him. I would have my life also full of great tribulations and persecutions ; now that I am unprofitable, I should like to suffer ; and I would endure all the tribulations in the world to gain ever so little

---

[9] Gal. ii. 20 : " Vivo autem, jam non ego ; vivit vero in me Christus."

more merit—I mean, by a more perfect doing of His will.[10]

17. Everything that I have learnt in prayer, though it may be two years previously, I have seen fulfilled. What I see and understand of the grandeurs of God, and of the way He has shown them, is so high, that I scarcely ever begin to think of them but my understanding fails me,—for I am as one that sees things far higher than I can understand,—and I become recollected.

18. God so keeps me from offending Him that I am verily amazed at times. I think I discern the great care He takes of me, without my taking scarcely any care at all, being as I was, before these things happened to me, a sea of wickedness and sins, and without a thought that I was mistress enough of myself to leave them undone. And the reason why I would have this known is that the great power of God might be made manifest. Unto Him be praise for ever and ever! Amen.

JESUS.

This Relation here set forth, not in my handwriting, is one that I gave to my confessor,[11] and which he with his own hand copied without adding or diminishing a word. He was a most spiritual man and a theologian : I discussed the state of my soul with him, and he with other learned men, among whom was Father Mancio.[12] They found nothing in it that is not in perfect agreement with the holy writings. This makes me calm now, though, while God is leading me by this way, I feel that it is necessary for me to put no trust whatever in myself. And so I have always done, though it is painful enough.

[10] See *Life*, ch. xxxvii. 3.
[11] Probably Fr. Pedro Ibañez.
[12] A Dominican, who had studied at the Sorbonne and filled during sixteen years the chair of divinity at Alcalá, and for eleven years that of Salamanca. He was equally renowned as preacher.

You, my father, will be careful that all this goes under the seal of confession, according to my request.

RELATION III.

OF VARIOUS GRACES GRANTED TO THE SAINT FROM THE YEAR 1568 TO 1571 INCLUSIVE.

1. WHEN I was in the monastery of Toledo, and some people were advising me not to allow any but noble persons to be buried there,[1] our Lord said to me : " Thou wilt be very inconsistent, My daughter, if thou regardest the laws of the world. Look at Me, poor and despised of men : are the great people of the world likely to be great in My eyes ; or is it descent or virtue that is to make you esteemed ? " [1569 or 1570.]

2. After Communion, the second day of Lent, in St. Joseph of Malagon, our Lord Jesus Christ appeared to me in an imaginary vision, as He is wont to do ; and when I was looking upon Him I saw that He had on His head, instead of the crown of thorns, a crown of great splendour, over the part where the wounds of that crown must have been. And as I have a great devotion to the crowning with thorns, I was exceedingly consoled, and began to think how great the pain must have been because of the many wounds, and to be sorrowful. Our Lord told me not to be sad because of those wounds, but for the many wounds which men inflict upon Him now. I asked Him what I could do by way of reparation ; for I was resolved to do anything. He replied : " This is not the time for rest " ; that I must hasten on the foundations, for He would take His rest with the souls which entered the monasteries ; that I must admit all who offered themselves, because there were many souls that did not serve Him

---

[1] Alonzo Ramirez wished to have the right of burial in the new monastery, but the nobles of Toledo looked on his request as unreasonable. See *Foundations*, chs. xv. and xvi.

because they had no place wherein to do it ; that those monasteries which were to be founded in small towns should be like this ; that the merit of those in them would be as great, if they only desired to do that which was done in the other houses ; that I must contrive to put them all under the jurisdiction of one superior,[2] and take care that anxieties about means of bodily maintenance did not destroy interior peace, for He would help us, so that we should never be in want of food. Especial care was to be had of the sick sisters ; the prioress who did not provide for and comfort the sick was like the friends of Job : He sent them sickness for the good of their souls, and careless superiors risked the patience of their nuns. I was to write the history of the foundation of the monasteries. I was thinking how there was nothing to write about in reference to the foundation of Medina, when He asked me, what more did I want to see than that the foundation there was miraculous ? By this He meant to say that He alone had done it, when it seemed impossible.[3] I resolved to execute His commands. [1570.]

3. Our Lord told me something I was to tell another, and as I was considering how I did not understand it at all,—though I prayed to Him, and was thinking it might be from Satan,—He said to me that it was not, and that He Himself would warn me when the time came.[4] [1570 or 1571.]

[2] See *Way of Perfection*, ch. v. 4.

[3] See *Book of the Foundations*, ch. iii.

[4] St. Teresa had a great reluctance to deliver such messages. One day she said to our Lord, " Why doest Thou give me this trouble ? Canst Thou not speak directly to that person ? Why charge me with such a mission ? " Our Lord answered : " Since thou canst not do great things for Me, I wish thee at least to help others to serve Me. Moreover, the person in question has not the necessary dispositions that I should speak to him Myself, and if I did it he, little given to prayer, would not believe Me." On another occasion she said to the Divine Master : " Lord, are there not others—for instance, theologians—who would carry out this mission better than I, a wretched sinner, if Thou didst but speak to them ? " He answered : " Theologians will do nothing to enter into personal communication with me. Repulsed by them, I must choose women to open to them My heart and speak of My affairs " (*Ribera*, iv. 5).

4. Once, when I was thinking how much more purely they live who withdraw themselves from all business, and how ill it goes with me, and how many faults I must be guilty of, when I have business to transact, I heard this : " It cannot be otherwise, My daughter ; but strive thou always after a good intention in all things, and detachment ; lift up thine eyes to Me, and see that all thine actions may resemble Mine." [1570 or 1571.]

5. Thinking how it was that I scarcely ever fell into a trance of late in public, I heard this : " It is not necessary now ; thou art sufficiently esteemed for My purpose ; we are considering the weakness of the wicked." [5] [1570 or 1571.]

6. One Tuesday after the Ascension,[6] having prayed for awhile after Communion in great distress, because I was so distracted that I could fix my mind on nothing, I complained of our poor nature to our Lord. The fire began to kindle in my soul, and I saw, as it seemed to me, the most Holy Trinity[7] distinctly present in an intellectual vision, whereby my soul understood, through a certain representation, as a figure of the truth, so far as my dulness could understand, how God is Three and One ; and thus it seemed to me that all the Three Persons spoke to me, that They were distinctly present in my soul, saying unto me " that from that day forth I should see that my soul had grown better in three ways, and that each one of the Three Persons had bestowed on me a distinct grace,—in charity, in suffering joyfully, in a sense of that charity in my soul, accompanied with fervour." I learnt the meaning of those words of our Lord, that the Three Divine Persons will dwell in the soul that is in a state of grace.[8] Afterwards

---

[5] *Interior Castle*, M. vii. ch. iii. 10.

[6] May 29, 1571, at St. Joseph's, at Avila.

[7] *Life*, ch. xxvii. 10.

[8] St. John xiv. 23 : " Ad eum veniemus, et mansionem apud eum faciemus."

giving thanks to our Lord for so great a mercy, and finding myself utterly unworthy of it, I asked His Majesty with great earnestness how it was that He, after showing such mercies to me, let me go out of His hand, and allowed me to become so wicked ; for on the previous day I had been in great distress on account of my sins, which I had set before me. I saw clearly then how much our Lord on His part had done, ever since my infancy, to draw me to Himself by means most effectual, and yet that all had failed. Then I had a clear perception of the surpassing love of God for us, in that He forgives us all this when we turn to Him, and for me more than for any other, for many reasons. The vision of the Three Divine Persons—one God—made so profound an impression on my soul, that if it had continued it would have been impossible for me not to be recollected in so divine a company. What I saw and heard besides is beyond my power to describe.

7. Once, when I was about to communicate,—it was shortly before I had this vision,—the Host being still in the ciborium, for It had not yet been given me, I saw something like a dove, which moved its wings with a sound. It disturbed me so much, and so carried me away out of myself, that it was with the utmost difficulty I received the Host. All this took place in St. Joseph of Avila. It was Father Francis de Salcedo who was giving me the most Holy Sacrament. Hearing Mass another day, I saw our Lord glorious in the Host ; He said to me that his sacrifice was acceptable unto Him.

8. I heard this once : " The time will come when many miracles will be wrought in this church ; it will be called the holy church." It was in St. Joseph of Avila, in the year 1571.

9. I retain to this day, which is the Commemoration of St. Paul, the presence of the Three Persons of

which I spoke in the beginning [9] ; they are present almost continually in my soul. I, being accustomed to the presence of Jesus Christ only, always thought that the vision of the Three Persons was in some degree a hindrance, though I know the Three Persons are but one God. To-day, while thinking of this, our Lord said to me " that I was wrong in imagining that those things which are peculiar to the soul can be represented by those of the body ; I was to understand that they were very different, and that the soul had a capacity for great fruition." It seemed to me as if this were shown to me thus : as water penetrates and is drunk in by the sponge, so, it seemed to me, did the Divinity fill my soul, which in a certain sense had the fruition and possession of the Three Persons. And I heard Him say also : " Labour thou not to hold Me within thyself enclosed, but enclose thou thyself within Me." It seemed to me that I saw the Three Persons within my soul, and communicating Themselves to all creatures abundantly without ceasing to be with me. [June 30, 1571, Medina del Campo.]

10. A few days after this, thinking whether they were right who disapproved of my going out to make new foundations, and whether it would not be better for me if I occupied myself always with prayer, I heard this : " During this life, the true gain consists not in striving after greater joy in Me, but in doing My will." It seemed to me, considering what St. Paul says about women, how they should stay at home,[10]— people reminded me lately of this, and, indeed, I had heard it before,—it might be the will of God I should do so too. He said to me : " Tell them they are not to follow one part of the Scripture by itself, without looking to the other parts also ; perhaps, if they could, they would like to tie My hands." [Beginning of July 1571, same place.]

---

[9] See § 6, *Relation* ix. 12.
[10] Titus ii. 5 : " Sobrias, domus curam habentes."

11. One day after the octave of the Visitation, in one of the hermitages of Mount Carmel, praying to God for one of my brothers, I said to our Lord,— I do not know whether it was only in thought or not, for my brother was in a place where his salvation was in peril, —" If I saw one of Thy brethren, O Lord, in this danger, what would I not do to help him!" It seemed to me there was nothing that I could do which I would not have done. Our Lord said to me: "O daughter, daughter! the nuns of the Incarnation are thy sisters, and thou holdest back. Take courage, then. Behold, this is what I would have thee do: it is not so difficult as it seems; and though it seems to thee that by going thither thy foundations will be ruined, yet it is by thy going that both these and the monastery of the Incarnation will gain; resist not, for My power is great." [11]   [July 10, 1571, same place.]

12. Once, when thinking of the great penance practised by Doña Catalina de Cardona, [12] and how I might have done more, considering the desires which our Lord had given me at times, if it had not been for my obedience to my confessors, I asked myself whether it would not be as well if I disobeyed them for the future in this matter. Our Lord said to me: "No, my daughter; thou art on the sound and safe road. Seest thou all her penance? I think more of thy obedience." [1572.]

13. Once, when I was in prayer, He showed me by a certain kind of intellectual vision the condition of a soul in a state of grace: in its company I saw by intellectual vision the most Holy Trinity, from whose companionship the soul derived a power which was a dominion over the whole earth. I understood the meaning of those words in the Canticle: "Let my

[11] This took place in 1571, when the Saint had been appointed prioress of the monastery of the Incarnation at Avila; the very house she had left in order to found that of St. Joseph, to keep the rule in its integrity.

[12] See *Book of the Foundations*, ch. xxviii. Ribera quotes a letter of St. Teresa to Fr. Martin Gutierrez, Rector at Salamanca, on the same subject.

Beloved come into His garden and eat." [13]   He showed me also the condition of a soul in sin, utterly powerless, like a person tied and bound and blindfold, who, though anxious to see, yet cannot, being unable to walk or to hear, and in grievous obscurity.   I was so exceedingly sorry for such souls, that, to deliver only one, any trouble seemed to me light.   I thought it impossible for any one who saw this as I saw it,—and I can hardly explain it,—willingly to forfeit so great a good or continue in so evil a state.   [1571.]

14. One day, in very great distress about the state of the Order, and casting about for means to succour it, our Lord said to me : " Do thou what is in thy power, and leave Me to Myself, and be not disquieted by anything ; rejoice in the blessing thou hast received, for it is a very great one.   My Father is pleased with thee, and the Holy Ghost loves thee."   [1570 or 1571.]

15. " Thou art ever desiring trials, and, on the other hand, declining them.   I order things according to what I know thy will is, and not according to thy sensuality and weakness.   Be strong, for thou seest how I help thee ; I have wished thee to gain this crown. Thou shalt see the Order of the Virgin greatly advanced in thy days." [14]   I heard this from our Lord about the middle of February, 1571.   [Salamanca.]

16. On the eve of St. Sebastian, the first year of my being in the monastery of the Incarnation [15] as prioress there, at the beginning of the *Salve*, I saw the Mother of God descend with a multitude of angels to the stall of the prioress, where the image of our Lady is, and sit there herself.   I think I did not see the image then, but only our Lady.   She seemed to be like that picture of her which the Countess [16] gave

[13] Cant. v. 1 : " Veniat dilectus meus in hortum suum, et comedat." See *Interior Castle*, M. vii. ch. i. 4.

[14] *Foundations*, i. 7.

[15] Jan. 19, 1572.

[16] Maria de Velasco y Aragon, Countess of Osorno ; this painting is still at the convent of St. Joseph, Avila.

me; but I had no time to ascertain this, because I
fell at once into a trance. Multitudes of angels seemed
to me to be above the canopies of the stalls, and on
the desks in front of them; but I saw no bodily forms,
for the vision was intellectual. She remained there
during the *Salve*, and said to me: "Thou hast done
well to place me here; I will be present when the
sisters sing the praises of my Son, and will offer them
to Him." After this I remained in that prayer which
I still practise, and which is that of keeping my soul
in the company of the most Holy Trinity; and it
seemed to me that the Person of the Father drew me
to Himself, and spoke to me most comfortable words.
Among them were these, while showing how He loved
me: "I give thee My Son, and the Holy Ghost, and
the Virgin: what canst thou give Me?" [17]

17. On the octave of the Holy Ghost, our Lord
was gracious unto me, and gave me hopes of this
house,[18] that it would go on improving—I mean the
souls that are in it. [May 1572.]

18. On the feast of the Magdalen, our Lord again
confirmed a grace I had received in Toledo, electing
me, in the absence of a certain person, in her place.[19]

19. In the monastery of the Incarnation, and in
the second year of my being prioress there, on the
octave of St. Martin, when I was going to Communion,
the Father, Fr. John of the Cross,[20]—divided the Host
between me and another sister. I thought it was
done, not because there was any want of Hosts, but
that he wished to mortify me because I had told him

---

[17] See *Relation* iv. 2.

[18] The monastery of the Incarnation, Avila.

[19] Yepez says that one day, on the feast of St. Magdalen, she was filled
with envy at the great love that Saint had borne our Lord. But He said
to her: "Magdalen loved Me while I was on earth, but thou lovest Me
now that I am in heaven"; and for several years He renewed this grace
on the feast of St. Magdalen. See *Relation* ix. 9.

[20] St. John of the Cross, at the instance of the Saint, was sent to Avila,
with another father of the reformed Carmelites, to be confessor of the nuns
of the Incarnation, although they did not (nor do they now) belong to the
Reform.

how much I delighted in Hosts of a large size. Yet I was not ignorant that the size of the Host is of no moment; for I knew that our Lord is whole and entire in the smallest particle. His Majesty said to me: "Have no fear, My daughter; for no one will be able to separate thee from Me,"—giving me to understand that the size of the Host mattered not.

20. Then appearing to me, as on other occasions, in an imaginary vision, most interiorly, He held out His right hand and said: "Behold this nail! it is the pledge of thy being My bride from this day forth. Until now thou hadst not merited it; from henceforth thou shalt regard My honour, not only as of one who is Thy Creator, King, and God, but as thine, My veritable bride; My honour is thine, and thine is Mine." This grace had such an effect on me, that I could not contain myself: I became as one that is foolish, and said to our Lord: "Either ennoble my vileness or cease to bestow such mercies on me, for certainly I do not think that nature can bear them." I remained thus the whole day, as one utterly beside herself. Afterwards I became conscious of great progress, and greater shame and distress to see that I did nothing in return for graces so great.

21. Our Lord said this to me one day: "Thinkest thou, My daughter, that meriting lies in fruition? No; merit lies only in doing, in suffering, and in loving. Thou hast never heard that St. Paul had the fruition of heavenly joys more than once; while he was often in sufferings.[21] Thou seest how My whole life was full of dolors, and only on Mount Tabor hast thou heard of Me in glory.[22] Do not suppose, when thou seest My Mother hold Me in her arms, that she had that joy unmixed with heavy sorrows. From the time that Simeon spoke to her, My Father made her see in clear light all I had to suffer. The grand

---

[21] 2 Cor. xi. 27: "In labore et ærumna, in vigiliis multis."
[22] St. Matt. xvii. 2: "Et transfiguratus est ante eos."

saints of the desert, as they were led by God, so also did they undergo heavy penances; besides, they waged serious war with the devil and with themselves, and much of their time passed away without any spiritual consolation whatever. Believe Me, My daughter, his trials are the heaviest whom My Father loves most; trials are the measure of His love. How can I show My love for thee better than by desiring for thee what I desired for Myself? Consider My wounds; thy pains will never reach to them. This is the way of truth; thus shalt thou help Me to weep over the ruin of those who are in the world, for thou knowest how all their desires, anxieties, and thoughts tend the other way." When I began my prayer that day, my headache was so violent that I thought I could not possibly go on. Our Lord said to me: " Behold now, the reward of suffering. As thou, on account of thy health, wert unable to speak to Me, I spoke to thee and comforted thee." Certainly, so it was; for the time of my recollection lasted about an hour and a half, more or less. It was then that He spoke to me the words I have just related, together with all the others. I was not able to distract myself, neither knew I where I was; my joy was so great as to be indescribable; my headache was gone, and I was amazed, and I had a longing for suffering. He also told me to keep in mind the words He said to His Apostles: " The servant is not greater than his Lord." [23] [November 1572.]

RELATION IV.

OF THE GRACES THE SAINT RECEIVED IN SALAMANCA AT THE END OF LENT, 1571.

1. I FOUND myself the whole of yesterday in great desolation, and, except at Communion, did not feel

[23] St. John xiii. 16: " Non est servus major domino suo."

that it was the day of the Resurrection.[1] Last night,
being with the community, I heard one [2] of them
singing how hard it is to be living away from God.
As I was then suffering, the effect of that singing on
me was such that a numbness began in my hands,
and no efforts of mine could hinder it ; but as I go
out of myself in raptures of joy, so then my soul was
thrown into a trance through the excessive pain, and
remained entranced ; and until this day I had not
felt this. A few days previously I thought that the
vehement impulses were not so great as they used to
be, and now it seems to be that the reason is what I
have described ; I know not if it is so. Hitherto the
pain had not gone so far as to make me beside myself ;
and as it is so unendurable, and as I retained the control of my senses, it made me utter loud cries beyond
my power to restrain. Now that it has grown, it has
reached this point of piercing me ; and I understand
more of that piercing which our Lady suffered ; for
until to-day, as I have just said, I never knew what
that piercing was. My body was so bruised, that I
suffer even now when I am writing this ; for my
hands are as if the joints were loosed, and in pain.
You, my father, will tell me when you see me whether
this trance be the effect of suffering, or whether I felt
it, or whether I am deceived.

2. I was in this great pain till this morning ; and,
being in prayer, I fell into a profound trance ; and it
seemed to me that our Lord had taken me up in
spirit to His Father, and said to Him : " Whom Thou
hast given to Me, I give to Thee [3] ; " and He seemed to

---

[1] St. Teresa says in this Relation it was the first day of Easter, but in the
Interior Castle, M. vi. ch. xi. 6, where she relates the same fact, she speaks
of the last of the Easter days, *i.e.* Tuesday, April 17.

[2] Isabel of Jesus, born in Segovia, and whose family name was Jimena,
told Ribera (*vide* lib. iv. cap. v.) that she was the singer, being then a novice
in Salamanca. She made her profession in 1573, accompanied the Saint to
Segovia, became prioress of Palencia and later of Salamanca, where she
died in 1614. See also *Concept. of Divine Love*, vii. 2.

[3] See *Relation* iii. § 16.

draw me near to Himself. This is not an imaginary vision, but one most certain, and so spiritually subtile that it cannot be explained. He spoke certain words to me which I do not remember. Some of them referred to His grace, which He bestows on me. He kept me by Him for some time.

3. As you, my father,[4] went away yesterday so soon, and I consider the many affairs which detain you, so that it is impossible for me to have recourse to you for comfort even when necessary,—for I see that your occupations are most urgent,—I was for some time in pain and sadness. As I was then in desolation,—as I said before,—that helped me; and as nothing on earth, I thought, had any attractions for me, I had a scruple, and feared I was beginning to lose that liberty. This took place last night; and to-day our Lord answered my doubt, and said to me " that I was not to be surprised; for as men seek for companions with whom they may speak of their sensual satisfactions, so the soul—when there is any one who understands it—seeks those to whom it may communicate its pleasures and its pains, and is sad and mourns when it can find none." He said to me: " Thou art prosperous now, and thy works please Me." As He remained with me for some time, I remembered that I had told you, my father, that these visions pass quickly away; He said to me " that there was a difference between these and the imaginary visions, and that there could not be an invariable law concerning the graces He bestowed on us; for it was expedient to give them now in one way, now in another."

4. After Communion, I saw our Lord most distinctly close beside me; and He began to comfort me with great sweetness, and said to me, among other things: " Thou beholdest Me present, My daughter,— it is I. Show me thy hands." And to me He seemed

---

[4] Fr. Martin Gutierrez, Rector of the Jesuit College of Salamanca.

to take them and to put them to His side, and said:
"Behold My wounds; thou art not without Me.
Finish the short course of thy life." By some things
He said to me, I understood that, after His Ascension, He never came down to the earth except in the
most Holy Sacrament to communicate Himself to any
one. He said to me, that when He rose again He
showed Himself to our Lady, because she was in great
trouble; for sorrow had so pierced her soul that she did
not even recover herself at once in order to have the
fruition of that joy. By this I saw how different was
my piercing.[5] But what must that of the Virgin have
been? He remained long with her then because it
was necessary to console her.

5. On Palm Sunday,[6] at Communion, I was in a
deep trance,—so much so, that I was not able even to
swallow the Host; and, still having It in my mouth,
when I had come a little to myself, I verily believed
that my mouth was all filled with Blood; and my face
and my whole body seemed to be covered with It, as
if our Lord had been shedding It at that moment.
I thought It was warm, and the sweetness I then felt
was exceedingly great; and our Lord said to me:
"Daughter, My will is that My Blood should profit
thee; and be thou not afraid that My compassion
will fail thee. I shed It in much suffering, and, as
thou seest, thou hast the fruition of It in great joy.
I reward thee well for the pleasure thou gavest me
to-day." He said this because I have been in the
habit of going to Communion, if possible, on this day
for more than thirty years, and of labouring to prepare
my soul to be the host of our Lord; for I considered
the cruelty of the Jews to be very great, after giving
Him so grand a reception, in letting Him go so far for
supper; and I used to picture Him as remaining with
me, and truly in a poor lodging, as I see now. And

[5] See above, § 1.
[6] April 8, 1571. The Saint was then at Salamanca.

thus I used to have such foolish thoughts—they must have been acceptable to our Lord, for this was one of the visions which I regard as most certain; and, accordingly, it has been a great blessing to me in the matter of Communion.

6. Previous to this I had been, I believe, for three days in that great pain, which I feel sometimes more than at others, because I am away from God; and during those days it had been very great, and seemingly more than I could bear. Being thus exceedingly wearied by it, I saw it was late to take my collation, nor could I do so,—for if I do not take it a little earlier, it occasions great weakness because of my sickness; and then, doing violence to myself, I took up some bread to prepare for collation, and on the instant Christ appeared, and seemed to be breaking the bread and putting it into my mouth. He said to me: "Eat, My daughter, and bear it as well as thou canst. I condole with thee in thy suffering; but it is good for thee now." My pain was gone, and I was comforted; for He seemed to be really with me then, and the whole of the next day; and with this my desires were then satisfied. The word "condole" made me strong; for now I do not think I am suffering at all.

RELATION V.

OBSERVATIONS ON CERTAIN POINTS OF SPIRITUALITY.

1. "What is it that distresses thee, little sinner? Am I not thy God? Doest thou not see how ill I am treated here? If thou lovest Me, why art thou not sorry for Me? Daughter, light is very different from darkness. I am faithful; no one will be lost without knowing it. He must be deceiving himself who relies on spiritual sweetnesses; the true safety lies in the witness of a

good conscience.[1] But let no one think that of himself he can abide in the light, any more than he can hinder the natural night from coming on; for that depends on My grace. The best means he can have for retaining the light is the conviction in his soul that he can do nothing of himself, and that it comes from Me; for, even if he were in the light, the instant I withdraw, night will come. True humility is this: the soul's knowing what itself can do, and what I can do. Do not neglect to write down the counsels I give thee, that thou mayest not forget them. Thou seekest to have the counsels of men in writing; why, then, thinkest thou that thou art wasting time in writing down those I give thee? The time will come when thou shalt require them all." [Date unknown.]

On Union.

2. "Do not suppose, My daughter, that to be near to Me is union; for they who sin against Me are near Me, though they do not wish it. Nor is union the joys and comforts of union,[2] though they be of the very highest kind, and though they come from Me. These very often are means of winning souls, even if they are not in a state of grace." When I heard this, I was in a high degree lifted up in spirit. Our Lord showed me what the spirit was, and what the state of the soul was then, and the meaning of those words of the *Magnificat*, "Exultavit spiritus meus." He showed me that the spirit was the higher part of the will.

3. To return to union; I understood it to be a spirit, pure and raised up above all the things of earth, with nothing remaining in it that would swerve from the will of God, being a spirit and a will resigned

---

[1] 2 Cor. i. 12: "Gloria nostra hæc est, testimonium conscientiæ nostræ."
[2] See St. John of the Cross, *Ascent of Mount Carmel*, bk. ii. ch. v. See *Relation* ix. 5.

to His will, and in detachment from all things, occupied in God in such a way as to leave no trace of any love of self, or of any created thing whatever.[3]   Thereupon, I considered that, if this be union, it comes to this, that, as my soul is always abiding in this resolution, we can say of it that it is always in this prayer of union : and yet it is true that the union lasts but a very short time.   It was suggested to me that, as to living in justice, meriting and making progress, it will be so ; but it cannot be said that the soul is in union as it is when in contemplation ; and I thought I understood, yet not by words heard, that the dust of our wretchedness, faults, and imperfections, wherein we bury ourselves, is so great, that it is not possible to live in such pureness as the spirit is in when in union with God, raised up and out of our wretched misery.   And I think, if it be union to have our will and spirit in union with the Will and Spirit of God, that it is not possible for any one not in a state of grace to attain thereto ; and I have been told so. Accordingly, I believe it is very difficult to know when the soul is in union ;   to have that knowledge is a special grace of God, because nobody can tell whether he is in a state of grace or not.[4]

4. You will show me in writing, my father, what you think of this, and how I am in the wrong, and send me this paper back.   [Year unknown.]

5. I had read in a book that it was an imperfection to possess pictures well painted,—and I would not, therefore, retain in my cell one that I had ; and also, before I had read this, I thought that it was poverty to possess none, except those made of paper,—and, as I read this afterwards, I would not have any of any other material.   I learnt from our Lord, when I was not thinking at all about this, what I am going to say : " that this mortification was not right.   Which is

---

[3] See *Foundations*, ch. v. 10.
[4] Eccl. ix. 1 : " Nescit homo utrum amore an odio dignus sit."

better, poverty or charity? But as love was the better, whatever kindled love in me, that I must not give up, nor take away from my nuns; for the book spoke of much adorning and curious devices—not of pictures.[5] What Satan was doing among the Lutherans was the taking away from them all those means by which their love might be the more quickened; and thus they were going to perdition. Those who are loyal to Me, My daughter, must now, more than ever, do the very reverse of what they do." I understood that I was under great obligations to serve our Lady and St. Joseph, because, when I was utterly lost, God, through their prayers, came and saved me. [Year unknown.]

6. One day, after the feast of St. Matthew, I was as is usual with me, after seeing in a vision the most Holy Trinity, and how It is present in a soul in a state of grace.[6] I understood the mystery most clearly, in such a way that, after a certain fashion and comparisons, I saw It in an imaginary vision. And though at other times I have seen the most Holy Trinity in an intellectual vision, for some days after the truth of it did not rest with me,—as it does now,—I mean, so that I could dwell upon it. I see now that it is just as learned men told me; and I did not understand it as I do now, though I believed them without the least hesitation; for I never had any temptations against the faith. [September 22, year unknown.]

7. It seems to us ignorant women that the Persons of the most Holy Trinity are all Three, as we see Them painted, in one Person, after the manner of those pictures, which represent a body with three faces; and thus it causes such astonishment in us that we look on it as impossible, and so there is nobody who dares to think of it; for the understanding is perplexed, is

---

[5] See St. John of the Cross, *Ascent of Mount Carmel*, bk. iii. ch. xiv. 3, ch. xxxiv.; *Way of Perfection*, ch. xxxiv. 10.

[6] See *Relation* iii. 13.

afraid it may come to doubt the truth, and that robs us of a great blessing.

8. What I have seen is this : Three distinct Persons each one by Himself visible, and by Himself speaking.[7] And afterwards I have been thinking that the Son alone took human flesh, whereby this truth is known. The Persons love, communicate, and know Themselves. Then, if each one is by Himself, how can we say that the Three are one Essence, and so believe ? That is a most deep truth, and I would die for it a thousand times. In the Three Persons there is but one will and one power and one might ; neither can One be without Another : so that of all created things there is but one sole Creator. Could the Son create an ant without the Father ? No ; because the power is all one. The same is to be said of the Holy Ghost. Thus, there is one God Almighty, and the Three Persons are one Majesty. Is it possible to love the Father without loving the Son and the Holy Ghost ? No ; for he who shall please One of the Three pleases the Three Persons ; and he who shall offend One offends All. Can the Father be without the Son and without the Holy Ghost ? No ; for They are one substance, and where One is there are the Three ; for They cannot be divided. How, then, is it that we see the Three Persons distinct ? and how is it that the Son, not the Father, nor the Holy Ghost, took human flesh ? This is what I have never understood ; theologians know it. I know well that the Three were there when that marvellous work was done, and I do not busy myself with much thinking thereon. All my thinking thereon comes at once to this : that I see God is almighty, that He has done what He would, and so can do what He will. The less I understand it, the more I believe it ; and the greater the devotion it excites in me.

---

[7] Antonius a Sancto Joseph, in his notes on this passage, is anxious to save the Thomist doctrine that one of the Divine Persons cannot be seen without the other, and so he says that the Saint speaks of the Three Persons as she saw Them—not as They are in Themselves.

May He be blessed for ever! Amen. [Year unknown.]

9. If our Lord had not been so gracious with me
as He has been, I do not think I should have had the
courage to do what has been done, nor strength to
undergo the labours endured, with the contradictions
and the opinions of men. And accordingly, since the
beginning of the foundations, I have lost the fears I
formerly had, thinking that I was under delusions,—
and I had a conviction that it was the work of God:
having this, I ventured upon difficult things, though
always with advice and under obedience. I see in this
that when our Lord willed to make a beginning of
the Order, and of His mercy made use of me, His
Majesty had to supply all that I was deficient in,
which was everything, in order that the work might
be effected and that His greatness might be the more
clearly revealed in one so wicked.

10. Antiochus was unendurable to himself, and to
those who were about him, because of the stench of
his many sins.[8]

11. Confession is for faults and sins, and not for
virtues, nor for anything of the kind relating to prayer.
These things are to be treated of out of confession
with one who understands the matter,—and let the
prioress see to this; and the nun must explain the
straits she is in, in order that the proper helps may
be found for her; for Cassian says that he who does
not know the fact, as well as he who has never seen or
learnt, that men can swim, will think, when he sees
people throw themselves into the river, that they will
all be drowned.[9]

12. Our Lord would have Joseph tell the vision to

---

[8] 2 Maccab. ix. 10, 12: "Eum nemo poterat propter intolerantiam
fœtoris portare . . . nec ipse jam fœtorem suum ferre posset."

[9] Cassian, *Collat.* lib. vii. ch. iv.: "Nec enim si quis ignarus natandi, sciens
pondus corporis sui ferre aquarum liquorem non posse, experimento suæ
voluerit imperitiæ definire, neminem penitus posse liquidis elementis solida
carne circumdatum sustineri."

his brethren, and have it known, though it was to cost Joseph so much.

13. How the soul has a sense of fear when God is about to bestow any great grace upon it; that sense is the worship of the spirit, as that of the four [10] elders spoken of in Scripture.

14. How, when the faculties are suspended, it is to be understood that certain matters are suggested to the soul, to be by it recommended to God; that an angel suggests them, of whom it is said in the Scriptures that he was burning incense and offering up the prayers of the saints. [11]

15. How there are no sins where there is no knowledge; and thus our Lord did not permit the king to sin with the wife of Abraham, for he thought that she was his sister, not his wife.

RELATION VI.

THE VOW OF OBEDIENCE TO FATHER GRATIAN WHICH THE SAINT MADE IN 1575.

1. IN the year 1575, in the month of April, when I was founding the monastery of Veas, Father Jerome of the Mother of God Gratian happened to come thither. [1] I began to go to confession to him from time to time, though not looking upon him as filling the place of the other confessors I had, so as to be wholly directed by him. One day, when I was taking food, but without any interior recollection whatever, my soul began to be recollected in such a way that I thought I must fall into a trance; and I had a vision, that passed away with the usual swiftness, like a

---

[10] Antonius a Sancto Joseph says that the Saint meant to write four-and-twenty, in allusion to Apoc. iv. 4 (*Life*, ch. xi. 18).
[11] Apoc. viii. 4.   [1] See *Foundations*, ch. xxii.

meteor. I seemed to see close beside me Jesus Christ our Lord, in the form wherein His Majesty is wont to reveal Himself, with F. Gratian on His right. Our Lord took his right hand and mine, and, joining them together, said to me that He would have me accept him in His place for my whole life, and that we were both to have one mind in all things, for so it was fitting. I was profoundly convinced that this was the work of God, though I remembered with regret two of my confessors whom I frequented in turn for a long time, and to whom I owed much; that one for whom I have a great affection especially caused a terrible resistance. Nevertheless, not being able to persuade myself that the vision was a delusion, because it had a great power and influence over me, and also because it was said to me on two other occasions that I was not to be afraid, that He wished this,—the words were different,—I made up my mind at last to act upon them, understanding it to be our Lord's will, and to follow that counsel so long as I should live. I had never before so acted with any one, though I had consulted many persons of great learning and holiness, and who watched over my soul with great care,—but neither had I received any such direction as that I should make no change; for as to my confessors, of some I understood that they would be profitable to me, and so also of these.

2. When I had resolved on this, I found myself in peace and comfort so great that I was amazed, and assured of our Lord's will; for I do not think that Satan could fill the soul with peace and comfort such as this; and so, whenever I think of it, I praise our Lord, and remember the words, " posuit fines tuos pacem," [2] and I wish I could wear myself out in the praises of God. [May 1575.]

3. It must have been about a month after this my resolve was made, on the second day after Pentecost,

[2] Psalm cxlvii. 14 : " He hath made thy borders peace."

when I was going to found the monastery in Seville, that we heard Mass in a hermitage in Ecija, and rested there during the hottest part of the day. Those who were with me remained in the hermitage while I was by myself in the sacristy belonging to it. I began to think of one great grace which I received of the Holy Ghost, on one of the vigils of His feast,[3] and a great desire arose within me of doing Him some most special service, and I found nothing that was not already done,—at least, resolved upon,—for all I do must be faulty; and I remembered that, though I had already made a vow of obedience it might be made in greater perfection, and I had an impression it would be pleasing unto Him if I promised that which I was already resolved upon, to live under obedience to the Father-Master, Fr. Jerome. On the one hand, I seemed to be doing nothing, because I was already bent on doing it; on the other hand, it would be a very serious thing, considering that our interior state is not made known to the superiors who receive our vows, and that they change, and that, if one is not doing his work well, another comes in his place; and I believed I should have none of my liberty all my life long, either outwardly or inwardly, and this constrained me greatly to abstain from making the vow. This repugnance of the will made me ashamed, and I saw that now I had something I could do for God, I was not doing it; it was a sad thing for my resolution to serve Him. The fact is, that the objection so pressed me, that I do not think I ever did anything in my life that was so hard—not even my profession— unless it be that of my leaving my father's house to become a nun.[4] The reason for this was that I had forgotten my affection for him, and his gifts for directing me; yea, rather, I was looking on it then as a strange thing, which has surprised me; feeling nothing

---

[3] The Saint refers to what she has written in her *Life*, ch. xxxviii. 11, 12 See also *Relation* ix.
[4] *Life*, ch. iv. 1.

but a great fear whether the vow would be for the
service of God or not: and my natural self—which
is fond of liberty—must have been doing its work,
though for years now I have no pleasure in it.   But
it seemed to me a far other matter to give up that
liberty by a vow, as in truth it is.   After a protracted
struggle, our Lord gave me great confidence ; and I
saw it was the better course, the more I felt about it :
if I made this promise in honour of the Holy Ghost,
He would be bound to give him light for the direction
of my soul ; and I remembered at the same time that
our Lord had given him to me as my guide.   Thereupon I fell upon my knees, and, to render this tribute
of service to the Holy Ghost, made a promise to do
whatever he should bid me do while I lived, provided
nothing were required of me contrary to the law of
God and the commands of superiors whom I am more
bound to obey.   I adverted to this, that the obligation
did not extend to things of little importance,—as if
I were to be importunate with him about anything,
and he bade me cease, and I neglected his advice and
repeated my request,—nor to things relating to my
convenience.   In a word, his commands were not to
be about trifles, done without reflection ; and I was
not knowingly to conceal from him my faults and
sins, or my interior state ; and this, too, is more than
we allow to superiors.   In a word, I promised to
regard him as in the place of God, outwardly and
inwardly.   I know not if it be so, but I seemed to
have done a great thing in honour of the Holy Ghost
—at least, it was all I could do, and very little it was
in comparison with what I owe Him.

4. I give God thanks, Who has created one capable
of this work : I have the greatest confidence that His
Majesty will bestow on him great graces ; and I
myself am so happy and free and joyous, that I seem
to be in every way free from myself ; and though I
thought that my obedience would be a burden, I have

attained to the greatest freedom. May our Lord be praised for ever! [May 23, 1575.]

RELATION VII.

MADE FOR RODRIGO ALVAREZ, S.J., IN FEBRUARY OR MARCH 1576.[1]

1. THIS nun took the habit forty years ago, and from the first began to reflect on the mysteries of the Passion of Christ our Lord, and on her own sins, for some time every day, without thinking at all of anything super-natural, but only created things, or of such subjects as suggested to her how soon the end of all things must come, discerning in creatures the greatness of God and His love for us.

2. This made her much more willing to serve Him: she was never under the influence of fear, and made no account of it, but had always a great desire to see God honoured, and His glory increased. To that end were all her prayers directed, without making any for herself; for she thought that it mattered little if she had to suffer in purgatory in exchange for the increase of His glory even in the slightest degree.

3. In this she spent about two-and-twenty years in great aridities, and never did it enter into her thoughts to desire anything else; for she regarded herself as one who, she thought, did not deserve even to think about God, except that His Majesty was very merciful to her in allowing her to remain in His pre-sence, saying her prayers, reading also in good books.

4. It must be about eighteen years since she began to arrange about the first monastery of Barefooted Carmelites which she founded. It was in Avila, three

---

[1] The autograph of this Relation, preserved at Viterbo, differs in parts from the printed versions.

or two years before,—I believe it is three,—she began to think that she occasionally heard interior locutions, and had visions and revelations interiorly. She saw with the eyes of the soul, for she never saw anything with her bodily eyes, nor heard anything with her bodily ears ; twice, she thinks, she heard a voice, but she understood not what was said. It was a sort of making things present when she saw these things interiorly ; they passed away like a meteor most frequently. The vision, however, remained so impressed on her mind, and produced such effects, that it was as if she saw those things with her bodily eyes, and more.

5. She was then by nature so very timid, that she would not dare to be alone even by day, at times. And as she could not escape from these visitations, though she tried with all her might, she went about in very great distress, afraid that it was a delusion of Satan, and began to consult spiritual men of the Society of Jesus about it, among whom were Father Araoz,[2] who was Commissary of the Society, and who happened to go to that place, and Father Francis, who was Duke of Gandía,—him she consulted twice[3] ; also a Provincial, now in Rome, called Gil Gonzalez,[4] and him also who is now Provincial of Castile,[5]— this latter, however, not so often,—Father Baltasar Alvarez,[6] who is now Rector in Salamanca ; and he

[2] Antonio Araoz, born at Vergara in 1515, was related to St. Ignatius, whose disciple he became in Rome in 1539. He was Provincial in Spain, and from 1562 to 1565 Commissary-General ; it was during this time he came into contact with St. Teresa. He died in 1573.

[3] See *Life*, ch. xxiv. 4.

[4] Gil Gonzalez d'Avila, born in 1532 at Burujon, Estramadura, was successively Provincial of three provinces, holding for thirty years the office of superior. He remained twelve years in contact with the holy mother ; during her priorship at the convent of the Incarnation he frequently visited her. His death occurred in 1596.

[5] Juan Suarez, born at Cuenca in 1525. He joined the Society in 1551, and was twice Provincial of Castile, making his journeys of inspection always on foot. By nature amiable and kind-hearted, he suffered much from depression when he became rigorous. He made St. Teresa's acquaintance during her stay at Valladolid. She wrote to him on Feb. 10, 1578 ; there exists also a note of his to the Saint. He died at Valladolid in 1595.

[6] See *Life*, ch. xxiv. 5.

heard her confession for six years at this time ; also the present Rector of Cuenca, Salazar [7] by name ; the Rector of Segovia, called Santander [8] ; the Rector of Burgos, whose name is Ripalda,[9]—and he thought very ill of her when he heard of these things, till after he had conversed with her ; the Doctor Paul Hernandez [10] in Toledo, who was a Consultor of the Inquisition [11] ; the Doctor Gutierrez,[12] who was Rector in Salamanca when she talked to him, and other fathers, some of the Society, whom she knew to be spiritual men, these she sought out, if any were in those places where she went to found monasteries.

6. With the Father Fray Peter of Alcantara, who was a holy man of the Barefooted Friars of St. Francis, she had many communications, and he it was who insisted so much upon it that her spirit should be regarded as good. They were more than six years trying her spirit minutely, as it is already described at very great length,[13] as will be shown hereafter : and

[7] Gaspar de Salazar, *Life*, ch. xxxiii. 9.   The autograph calls him Rector of Siguenza (not Cuenca).

[8] Luis Santander founded in 1559 the College of Segovia ; in 1571 he was at Valencia, but three years later the Saint met him at Segovia, and she speaks of him repeatedly with great praise.

[9] Jerome Ripalda filled various posts of superiorship, among others at Burgos, Valladolid, and Salamanca, where he met St. Teresa in 1573.   He ordered her to write the *Book of Foundations*, and she speaks of him as " my great friend of the Society " (letter to Fr. Gratian, Dec. 1576).   He gave evidence in the process of her beatification.   He was a great theologian, and composed the catechism still in use in Spain.   He died in 1618 at the age of eighty-four.

[10] Paul Hernandez, founder of the college at Seville, made the acquaintance of the Saint at Toledo in 1568.   She speaks of him in her letters as " a father of the Society, a great friend of mine," and there is also a letter of hers to him, dated Oct. 4, 1578.   He used to say, " Mother Teresa of Jesus is great from head to foot, but beyond her head she is greater still," in allusion to her supernatural gifts.

[11] The autograph adds here : " Another was called Ordoñez, who has been Rector of Avila."   She wrote to him from the convent of the Incarnation to Medina del Campo, where he resided (July 27, 1573).

[12] Martin Gutierrez.   See *Rel.* iii. 12.   Other Jesuits whom the Saint consulted were Pedro Domenech (see *Life* xxxiv. 3), Henry Enriquez, Bartholomew Perez de Nueros, Provincial of Castile, whom she knew for ten years ; Gonsalvo d'Avila, Rector of Avila in 1578 ; Juan del Aguila ; and Francis Suarez, the great theologian.

[13] See *Life*, ch. xxv. 18.

she herself in tears and deep affliction ; for the more they tried her, the more she fell into raptures, and into trances very often,—not, however, deprived of her senses.

7. Many prayers were made, and many Masses were said, that our Lord would lead her by another way,[14] for her fear was very great when she was not in prayer ; though in everything relating to the state of her soul she was very much better, and a great difference was visible : there was no vainglory, nor had she any temptation thereto, nor to pride ; on the contrary, she was very much ashamed and confounded when she saw that people knew of her state, and except with her confessors or any one who would give her light, she never spoke of these things, and it was more painful to speak of them than if they had been grave sins ;[15] for it seemed to her that people must laugh at her, and that these things were womanish imaginations, which she had always heard of with disgust.

8. About thirteen years ago, more or less, after the house of St. Joseph was founded, into which she had gone from the other monastery, came the present Bishop of Salamanca, Inquisitor, I think, of Toledo, previously of Seville, Soto by name.[16] She contrived

---

[14] See *Life*, ch. xxv. 20, and ch. xxvii. 1.

[15] See *Life*, ch. xxvi. 5.

[16] Don Francisco de Soto y Salazar was a native of Bonilla de la Sierra, and Vicar-General of the Bishops of Astorga and Avila, and Canon of Avila ; Inquisitor of Cordova, Seville, and Toledo ; Bishop, successively, of Albarracin, Segorve, and Salamanca. He died at Merida in 1576, poisoned, it was suspected, by the sect of the Illuminati, who were alarmed at his faithful zeal and holy life. " She went to the Inquisitor, Don Francisco Soto y Salazar—he was afterwards Bishop of Salamanca—and said to him : ' My lord, I am subject to certain extraordinary processes in prayer, such as ecstasies, raptures, and revelations, and do not wish to be deluded or deceived by Satan, or to do anything that is not absolutely safe. I give myself up to the Inquisition to try me, and examine my ways of going on, submitting myself to its orders.' The Inquisitor replied : ' Señora, the business of the Inquisition is not to try the spirit, nor to examine ways of prayer, but to correct heretics. Do you, then, commit your experience to writing, in all simplicity and truth, and send it to the Father-Master Avila, who is a man of great spirituality and learning, and extremely conversant with matters of prayer ; and when you shall have his answer you may be sure there is nothing to be afraid of ' " (Jerome Gratian, *Lucidario*, cap. iii.).

to have a conference with him for her greater security, and told him everything. He replied, that there was nothing in all this that concerned his office, because everything that she saw and heard confirmed her the more in the Catholic faith, in which she always was, and is, firm, with most earnest desires for the honour of God and the good of souls, willing to suffer death many times for one of them.

9. He told her, when he saw how distressed she was, to give an account of it all, and of her whole life, without omitting anything, to the Master Avila, who was a man of great learning in the way of prayer, and to rest content with the answer he should give. She did so, and described her sins and her life. He wrote to her and comforted her, giving her great security. The account I gave was such that all those learned men who saw it—they were my confessors—said that it was very profitable for instruction in spiritual things ; and they commanded her to make copies of it, and write another little book [17] for her daughters, —she was prioress,—wherein she might give them some instructions.

10. Notwithstanding all this, she was not without fears at times, for she thought that spiritual men also might be deceived like herself. She told her confessor that he might discuss these things with certain learned men, though they were not much given to prayer, for she had no other desire but that of knowing whether what she experienced was in conformity with the sacred writings or not. Now and then she took comfort in thinking that—though she herself, because of her sins, deserved to fall into delusions—our Lord would not suffer so many good men, anxious to give her light, to be led into error.

11. Having this in view, she began to communicate with fathers of the Order of the glorious St. Dominic, to which, before these things took place, she had been

[17] This book is the *Way of Perfection*, written by direction of Fr. Bañes.

to confession,—she does not say to them, but to the Order.[18]   These are they with whom she afterwards had relations.   The Father Fray Vicente Baron, at that time Consultor of the Holy Office, heard her confessions for eighteen months in Toledo, and he had done so very many years before these things began. He was a very learned man.   He reassured her greatly, as did also the Fathers of the Society spoken of before. All used to say, If she does not sin against God, and acknowledges her own misery, what has she to be afraid of?   She confessed to the Father Fray Pedro Ibañez, who was reader in Avila ; to the Father-Master Fray Dominic Bañes, who is now in Valladolid as rector of the college of St. Gregory, I confessed for six years, and whenever I had occasion to do so communicated with him by letter ; also to the Master Chaves [19] ; to the Father-Master Fray Bartholomew of Medina,[20] professor in Salamanca, of whom she knew that he thought ill of her ; for she, having heard this, thought that he, better than any other, could tell her if she was deceived, because he had so little confidence in her.   This was more than two years ago. She contrived to go to confession to him, and gave him a full account of everything while she remained there ; and he saw what she had written,[21] for the purpose of attaining to a better understanding of the matter.   He reassured her so much, and more than all the rest, and remained her very good friend.

[18] The Saint had such great affection for the Order of St. Dominic that she used to say of herself : " Yo soy la Dominica in passione," meaning thereby that she was in her heart a child of the Order.

[19] Diego de Chaves, of the convent of San Esteban of Salamanca, theologian at the Council of Trent, and professor at Compostella. For some time he lived at Avila, where he made the acquaintance of St. Teresa, who speaks of him in her letters. He died June 17, 1592, at the age of eighty-five years, of which he had spent sixty-eight in the Order of Friars Preachers.

[20] Bartholomew de Medina, born at Medina del Rioseco, was professor at Alcalá and Salamanca. When the Saint lived at Alba de Tormes in 1574 he came every morning from Salamanca (a distance of 25 kilometres) to hear her confession. He died Dec. 30, 1580.

[21] When this father had read the *Life* he had it copied, with the assent of F. Gratian, and gave the copy thus made to the Duchess of Alba.

12. She went to confession also to Fray Philip de Meneses,[22] when she founded the monastery of Valladolid, for he was Rector of the college of St. Gregory. He, having before that heard of her state, had gone to Avila, that he might speak to her,—it was an act of great charity,—being desirous of ascertaining whether she was deluded, so that he might enlighten her, and, if she was not, defend her when he heard her spoken against ; and he was much satisfied.

13. She also conferred particularly with Salinas,[23] Dominican Provincial, a man of great spirituality ; with another Licentiate named Lunar,[24] who was prior of St. Thomas of Avila ; and, in Segovia, with a Reader, Fray Diego de Yangües.[25]

14. Of these Dominicans, some never failed to give themselves greatly to prayer, and perhaps all did. Some others also she consulted ; for in so many years,

[22] Philip de Meneses, of Trujillo in Estramadura, was professor at Alcalá and Rector of San Gregorio at Valladolid. He was charged by Philip II. with the reform of several Orders, and died in 1572 in Galicia while carrying out this work.

[23] Juan de Salinas, born in 1497, died in 1569. St. Teresa saw him at Toledo. Bañez narrates that Salinas asked him one day : " Who is this Teresa of Jesus whom you seem to make so much of ? Don't trust the virtue of women." Bañez replied : " As your Reverence is going to Toledo, you can see her and form your own opinion." Some time afterwards they met again, and Bañez asked what impression the Provincial had received. He replied : " You have deceived me : you told me she was a woman, but I found her a man, even with a strong beard " (y de los muy barbados, i.e. of a strong, virile character).

[24] This passage is not in the autograph, nor is the Presentado Lunar mentioned anywhere in the writings of the Saint.

[25] Diego de Yanguas, or Yangïes, born in 1535, filled successively the chair of Divinity in several universiiies. While at Segovia he was St. Teresa's confessor, and he witnessed an ecstasy of hers in the grotto of St. Dominic beneath the Dominican convent. She entrusted to him the revision of the Book of Foundations and the Interior Castle ; it is supposed that he was the confessor who ordered her to throw her book on the Canticle of Canticles (Conceptions of Divine Love) into the fire. St. Teresa had great confidence in his learning and judgment, and consulted him orally and by letter as long as she lived. Other Dominicans with whom she was acquainted were Melchior Cano (nephew of the famous theologian), whom she knew at Avila and Segovia ; Bartholomew del Aguilar, one of her confessors at Seville (1575–76) ; Juan de la Cuevas, Provincial and afterwards Bishop of Avila, who presided at the constituent chapter of the province of Discalced Carmelites (1581) ; Pedro Fernandez, visitor of the Carmelites ; Ferdinand del Castillo, who, on behalf of the Inquisition, examined her Life, and remained her devoted friend ; and Juan Gutierrez.

and because of the fear she was in, she had opportunities
of doing so, especially as she went about founding
monasteries in so many places. Her spirit was tried
enough, for everybody wished to be able to enlighten
her, and thereby reassured her and themselves. She
always, at all times, wished to submit herself to whatever they enjoined her, and she was therefore distressed
when, as to these spiritual things, she could not obey
them. Both her own prayer and that of the nuns she
has established are always carefully directed towards
the propagation of the faith ; and it was for that
purpose, and for the good of her Order, that she began
her first monastery.

15. She used to say that, if any of these things
tended to lead her against the Catholic faith and the
law of God, she would not need to seek for learned
men nor tests, because she would see at once that they
came from Satan. She never undertook anything
merely because it came to her in prayer ; on the contrary, when her confessors bade her do the reverse,
she did so without being in the least troubled thereat,
and she always told them everything. For all that
they told her that these things came from God, she
never so thoroughly believed them that she could
swear to it herself, though it did seem to her that they
were spiritually safe, because of the effects thereof,
and of the great graces which she at times received ;
but she always desired virtues more than anything
else ; and this it is that she has charged her nuns to
desire, saying to them that the most humble and
mortified will be the most spiritual.

16. All that is told and written she communicated
to the Father-Master Fray Dominic Bañes, who is now
in Valladolid, and who is the person with whom she
has had, and has still, the most frequent communications. He sent her writings to the Holy Office in
Madrid, so it is said. In all this she submits herself
to the Catholic faith and the Roman Church. Nobody

has found fault with them, because these things are not in the power of any man, and our Lord does not require what is impossible.

17. The reason why so much is known about her is that, as she was in fear about herself, and described her state to so many, these talked to one another on the subject, and also the accident that happened to what she had written.[26]   This has been to her a very grievous torment and cross, and has cost her many tears.   She says that this distress is not the effect of humility, but of the causes already mentioned.   Our Lord seems to have given permission [27] for this torture ; for if one spoke more harshly of her than others, by little and little he spoke more kindly of her.

18. She took the greatest pains not to submit the state of her soul to any one who she thought would believe that these things came from God, for she was instantly afraid that the devil would deceive them both.   If she saw any one timid about these things, to him she laid bare her secrets with the greater joy ; though also it gave her pain when, for the purpose of trying her, these things were treated with contempt, for she thought some were really from God, and she would not have people, even if they had good cause, condemn them absolutely ;   neither would she have them believe that all were from God ;   and because she knew perfectly well that delusion was possible, therefore it was that she never thought herself altogether safe in a matter wherein there might be danger.

19. She used to strive with all her might never in any way to offend God, and was always obedient ; and by these means she thought she might obtain her deliverance, by the help of God, even if Satan were the cause.

20. Ever since she became subject to these supernatural visitations, her spirit is always inclined to seek

[26] See *Foundations*, ch. xvii. 12, note.
[27] *Life*, ch. xxiii. 15.

after that which is most perfect, and she had almost always a great desire to suffer ; and in the persecutions she underwent, and they were many, she was comforted, and had a particular affection for her persecutors. She had a great desire to be poor and lonely, and to depart out of this land of exile in order to see God. Through these effects, and others like them, she began to find peace, thinking that a spirit which could leave her with these virtues could not be an evil one, and they who had the charge of her soul said so ; but it was a peace that came from diminished weariness, not from the cessation of fear.

21. The spirit she is of never urged her to make any of these things known, but to be always obedient.[28] As it has been said already,[29] she never saw anything with her bodily eyes, but in a way so subtile and so intellectual that at first she sometimes thought that all was the effect of imagination ; at other times she could not think so. These things were not continual, but occurred for the most part when she was in some trouble : as on one occasion, when for some days she had to bear unendurable interior pains, and a restlessness of soul arising out of the fear that she was deluded by Satan, as it is described at length in the account she has given of it,[30] and where her sins, for they have been so public, are mentioned with the rest : for the fear she was in made her forget her own good name.

22. Being thus in distress such as cannot be described, at the mere hearing interiorly these words,[31] " It is I, be not afraid," her soul became so calm, courageous, and confident, that she could not understand whence so great a blessing had come ; for her confessor had not been able—and many learned men, with many words, had not been able—to give her that peace and rest which this one word had given her. And thus, at other times, some vision gave her strength,

[28] *Life*, ch. xxvi. 5.   [29] § 4.
[30] *Life*, ch. xxv. 19.   [31] *Life*, ch. xxv. 22.

for without that she could not have borne such great
trials and contradictions, together with infirmities
without number, and which she still has to bear,
though they are not so many,—for she is never free
from some suffering or other, more or less intense.
Her ordinary state is constant pain, with many other
infirmities, though since she became a nun they are
more troublesome, if she is doing anything in the
service of our Lord. And the mercies He shows her
pass quickly out of memory, though she often dwells
on those mercies,—but she is not able to dwell so long
upon these as upon her sins ; these are always a torment to her, most commonly as filth smelling foully.

23. That her sins are so many, and her service of
God so scanty, must be the reason why she is not
tempted to vainglory. There never was anything in
any of these spiritual visitations that was not wholly
pure and clean, nor does she think it can be otherwise
if the spirit be good and the visitations supernatural,
for she utterly neglects the body and never thinks of
it, being wholly intent upon God.

24. She is also living in great fear about sinning
against God, and doing His will in all things ; this is
her continual prayer. And she is, she thinks, so
determined never to swerve from this, that there is
nothing her confessors might enjoin her, which she
considers to be for the greater honour of our Lord, that
she would not undertake and perform, by the help of
our Lord. And confident that His Majesty helps
those who have resolved to advance His service and
glory, she thinks no more of herself and of her own
progress, in comparison with that, than if she did not
exist, so far as she knows herself ; and her confessors
think so too.

25. All that is written in this paper is the simple
truth, and they, and all others who have had anything
to do with her for these twenty years, can justify it.
Most frequently her spirit urged her to praise God, and

she wished that all the world gave itself up to that, even though it should cost her exceedingly. Hence the desire she has for the good of souls ; and from considering how vile are the things of this world, and how precious are interior things, with which nothing can be compared, she has attained to a contempt of the world.

26. As for the vision about which you, my father, wish to know something, it is of this kind : she sees nothing either outwardly or inwardly, for the vision is not imaginary ; but, without seeing anything, she understands what it is, and where it is, more clearly than if she saw it, only nothing in particular presents itself to her. She is like a person who feels that another is close beside her ; but because she is in the dark she sees him not, yet is certain that he is there present. Still, this comparison is not exact ; for he who is in the dark, in some way or other, through hearing a noise or having seen that person before, knows he is there, or knew it before ; but here there is nothing of the kind, for without a word, inward or outward, the soul clearly perceives who it is, where he is, and occasionally what he means.[32] Why, or how, she perceives it, she knoweth not ; but so it is ; and while it lasts, she cannot help being aware of it. And when it is over,—though she may wish ever so much to retain the image thereof,—she cannot do it, for it is then clear to her that it would be, in that case, an act of the imagination, not the vision itself,—that is not in her power ; and so it is with the supernatural things. And it is from this it comes to pass that he in whom God works these graces despises himself, and becomes more humble than he was ever before, for he sees that this is a gift of God, and that he can neither add to it nor take from it. The love and the desire become greater of serving our Lord, who is so mighty that He can do that which is more than our imagina-

---

[32] See *Life*, ch. xxvii. 5.

tion can conceive here, as there are things which men, however learned they may be, can never know. Blessed for ever and ever be He Who bestows this! Amen.

RELATION VIII.

ADDRESSED TO FATHER RODRIGO ALVAREZ (MARCH OR APRIL 1576).

1. THESE interior things of the spirit are so difficult to describe, and, still more, in such a way as to be understood,—the more so as they pass quickly away,—that, if obedience did not help me, it would be a chance if I succeeded, especially in such difficult things. I implore you, my father, to take for granted that it is not in my mind to think this to be correct, for it may well be that I do not understand the matter; but what I can assure you of is this, that I will speak of nothing I have not had experience of at times, and, indeed, often.

2. I think it will please you, my father, if I begin by discussing that which is at the root of supernatural things; for that which relates to devotion, tenderness, tears, and meditations, which is in our power here to acquire by the help of our Lord, is understood.

3. The first prayer of which I was conscious,—in my opinion, supernatural,—so I call that which no skill or effort of ours, however much we labour, can attain to, though we should prepare ourselves for it, and that preparation must be of great service,—is a certain interior recollection [1] of which the soul is sensible; the soul seems to have other senses within itself then, which bear some likeness to the exterior senses it possesses; and thus the soul, withdrawing

---

[1] *Interior Castle*, M. iv. ch. iii.

into itself, seeks to go away from the tumult of its outward senses, and accordingly it drags them away with itself ; for it closes the eyes on purpose that it may neither see, nor hear, nor understand anything but that whereon the soul is then intent, which is to be able to converse with God alone. In this prayer there is no suspension of the faculties and powers of the soul ; it retains the full use of them ; but the use of them is retained that they may be occupied with God. This will be easily understood by him whom our Lord shall have raised to this state ; but by him whom He has not, not ; at least, such a one will have need of many words and illustrations.

4. Out of this recollection grow a certain quietude and inward peace most full of comfort ; for the soul is in such a state that it does not seem to it that it wants anything ; for even speaking wearies it,—I mean by this, vocal prayer and meditation ; it would do nothing but love. This lasts some time, and even a long time.

5. Out of this prayer comes usually what is called a sleep of the faculties ; but they are not so absorbed nor so suspended as that it can be called a trance ; nor is it altogether union.

6. Sometimes, and even often, the soul is aware that the will alone is in union ; and this it sees very clearly,—that is, it seems so to it. The will is wholly intent upon God, and the soul sees that it has no power to rest on, or do, anything else ; and at the same time the two other faculties are at liberty to attend to other matters of the service of God,—in a word, Martha and Mary are together.[2] I asked Father Francis[3] if this was a delusion, for it made me stupid ; and his reply was, that it often happened.

7. When all the faculties of the soul are in union, it is a very different state of things ; for they can then do nothing whatever, because the understanding is as it

[2] See *Life*, ch. xvii. 6. [3] See *Life*, ch. xxiv. 4.

were surprised. The will loves more than the understanding knows; but the understanding does not know that the will loves, nor what it is doing, so as to be able in any way to speak of it. As to the memory, the soul, I think, has none then, nor any power of thinking, nor are the senses awake, but rather as lost, so that the soul may be the more occupied with the object of its fruition :. so it seems to me. They are lost but for a brief interval; it passes quickly away. By the wealth of humility, and other virtues and desires, left in the soul after this may be learnt how great the blessing is that flows from this grace, but it cannot be told what it is; for, though the soul applies itself to the understanding of it, it can neither understand nor explain it. This, if it be real, is, in my opinion, the greatest grace wrought by our Lord on this spiritual road,—at least, it is one of the greatest.

8. Raptures and trance, in my opinion, are all one, only I am in the habit of using the word trance instead of rapture, because the latter word frightens people; and, indeed, the union of which I am speaking may also be called a trance. The difference between union and trance is this, that the latter lasts longer and is more visible outwardly, because the breathing gradually diminishes, so that it becomes impossible to speak or to open the eyes; and though this very thing occurs when the soul is in union, there is more violence in a trance, for the natural warmth vanishes, I know not how, when the rapture is deep; and in all these kinds of prayer there is more or less of this. When it is deep, as I was saying, the hands become cold, and sometimes stiff and straight as pieces of wood; as to the body, if the rapture comes on when it is standing or kneeling, it remains so [4]; and the soul is so full of the joy of that which our Lord is setting before it, that it seems to forget to animate

[4] See *Life*, ch. xx. 23.

the body and abandons it. If the rapture lasts, the
nerves are made to feel it.

9. It seems to me that our Lord will have the soul
know more of that, the fruition of which it has, in a
trance than in union, and accordingly in a rapture
the soul receives most commonly certain revelations
of His Majesty, and the effects thereof on the soul
are great,—a forgetfulness of self, through the longing
it has that God our Lord, Who is so high, may be
known and praised. In my opinion, if the rapture be
from God, the soul cannot fail to obtain a deep conviction of its own helplessness, and of its wretchedness
and ingratitude, in that it has not served Him Who,
of His own goodness only, bestows upon it graces so
great ; for the feeling and the sweetness are so high
above all things that may be compared therewith that,
if the recollection of them did not pass away, all the
satisfactions of earth would be always loathsome to
it ; and hence comes the contempt for all the things
of the world.

10. The difference between trance and transport [5]
is this,—in a trance the soul gradually dies to outward
things, losing the senses and living unto God. A
transport comes on by one sole act of His Majesty,
wrought in the innermost part of the soul with such
swiftness that it is as if the higher part thereof were
carried away, and the soul leaving the body. Accordingly it requires courage at first to throw itself into
the arms of our Lord, that He may take it whithersoever He will ; for, until His Majesty establishes it in
peace, there whither He is pleased to take it—by take
it I mean the admitting of it to the knowledge of deep
things—it certainly requires in the beginning to be
firmly resolved to die for Him, because the poor soul
does not know what this means—that is, at first.
The virtues, as it seems to me, remain stronger after
this, for there is a growth in detachment, and the

[5] " Arrobamiento y arrebatamiento."

power of God, Who is so mighty, is the more known, so that the soul loves and fears Him. For so it is, He carries away the soul, no longer in our power, as the true Lord thereof, which is filled with a deep sorrow for having offended Him, and astonishment that it ever dared to offend a Majesty so great, with an exceedingly earnest desire that none may henceforth offend Him, and that all may praise Him. This, I think, must be the source of those very fervent desires for the salvation of souls, and for some share therein, and for the due praising of God.

11. The flight of the spirit—I know not how to call it—is a rising upwards from the very depths of the soul. I remember only this comparison, and I made use of it before, as you know, my father, in that writing where these and other ways of prayer are explained at length,[6] and such is my memory that I forget things at once. It seems to me that the soul and spirit are one and the same thing ; but only as a fire, if it is great and ready for burning ; so, like fire burning rapidly, the soul, in that preparation of itself which is the work of God, sends up a flame,—the flame ascends on high, but the fire thereof is the same as that below, nor does the flame cease to be fire because it ascends : so here, in the soul, something so subtile and so swift seems to issue from it, that ascends to the higher part, and goes thither whither our Lord wills. I cannot go further with the explanation ; it seems a flight, and I know of nothing else wherewith to compare it : I know that it cannot be mistaken, for it is most evident when it occurs, and that it cannot be hindered.

12. This little bird of the spirit seems to have escaped out of this wretchedness of the flesh, out of the prison of this body, and now, disentangled therefrom, is able to be the more intent on that which our Lord is giving it. The flight of the spirit is something

6 See *Life*, ch . xviii. 8, xx. 32, and xxi.

so fine, of such inestimable worth, as the soul perceives it, that all delusion therein seems impossible, or anything of the kind, when it occurs. It was afterwards that fear arose, because she who received this grace was so wicked ; for she saw what good reasons she had to be afraid of everything, though in her innermost soul there remained an assurance and a confidence wherein she was able to live, but not enough to make her cease from the anxiety she was in not to be deceived.

13. By impetus I mean that desire which at times rushes into the soul, without being preceded by prayer, and this is most frequently the case ; it is a sudden remembering that the soul is away from God, or of a word it has heard to that effect. This remembering is occasionally so strong and vehement that the soul in a moment becomes as if the reason were gone, just like a person who suddenly hears most painful tidings of which he knew not before, or is surprised[7] ; such a one seems deprived of the power of collecting his thoughts for his own comfort, and is as one lost. So is it in this state, except that the suffering arises from this, that there abides in the soul a conviction that it would be well worth dying in it. It seems that whatever the soul then perceives does but increase its suffering, and that our Lord will have its whole being find no comfort in anything, nor remember that it is His will that it should live : the soul seems to itself to be in great and indescribable loneliness, and abandoned of all, because the world, and all that is in it, gives it pain ; and because it finds no companionship in any created thing, the soul seeks its Creator alone, and this it sees to be impossible unless it dies ; and as it must not kill itself, it is dying to die, and there is really a risk of death, and it sees itself hanging between heaven and earth, not knowing what to do with itself. And from time to time God

---

[7] *Life*, ch. xvi. 6. *Relation* iv. 1.

gives it a certain knowledge of Himself, that it may see what it loses, in a way so strange that no explanation of it is possible ; and there is no pain in the world —at least I have felt none—that is equal or like unto this, for if it lasts but half an hour the whole body is out of joint, and the bones so racked, that I am not able to write with my hands : the pains I endure are most grievous.[8]

14. But nothing of all this is felt till the impetus shall have passed away. He to whom it comes has enough to do in enduring that which is going on within him, nor do I believe that he would feel if he were grievously tortured : he is in possession of all his senses, can speak, and even observe ; walk about he cannot,—the great blow of that love throws him down to the ground. If we were to die to have this, it would be of no use, for it cannot be except when God sends it. It leaves great effects and blessings in the soul. Some learned men say that it is this, others that it is that, but no one condemns it. The Father-Master d'Avila [9] wrote to me and said it was good, and so say all. The soul clearly understands that it is a great grace from our Lord ; were it to occur more frequently, life would not last long.

15. The ordinary impetus is, that this desire of serving God comes on with a certain tenderness, accompanied with tears, out of a longing to depart from this land of exile ; but as the soul retains its freedom, wherein it reflects that its living on is according to our Lord's will, it takes comfort in that thought, and offers its life to Him, beseeching Him that it may last only for His glory. This done, it bears all.

16. Another prayer very common is a certain kind of wounding [10] ; for it really seems to the soul as if an

---

[8] *Life*, ch. xx. 16 ; *Interior Castle*, M. vi. ch. xi. 4.
[9] See his letter (n. 6), of Sept. 12, 1568, at the end of the Introduction.
[10] See *Life*, ch. xxix. 17.

arrow were thrust through the heart, or through itself. Thus it causes great suffering, which makes the soul complain ; but the suffering is so sweet, that it wishes it never would end. The suffering is not one of sense, neither is the wound physical ; it is in the interior of the soul, without any appearance of bodily pain ; but as I cannot explain it except by comparing it with other pains, I make use of these clumsy expressions,—for such they are when applied to this suffering. I cannot, however, explain it in any other way. It is, therefore, neither to be written of nor spoken of, because it is impossible for any one to understand it who has not had experience of it,—I mean, how far the pain can go ; for the pains of the spirit are very different from those of earth. I gather, therefore, from this, that the souls in hell and purgatory suffer more than we can imagine, by considering these pains of the body.

17. At other times, this wound of love seems to issue from the inmost depth of the soul ; great are the effects of it ; and when our Lord does not inflict it, there is no help for it, whatever we may do to obtain it ; nor can it be avoided when it is His pleasure to inflict it. The effects of it are those longings after God, so quick and so fine that they cannot be described ; and when the soul sees itself hindered and kept back from entering, as it desires, on the fruition of God, it conceives a great loathing for the body, on which it looks as a thick wall which hinders it from that fruition which it then seems to have entered upon within itself, and unhindered by the body. It then comprehends the great evil that has befallen us through the sin of Adam in robbing us of this liberty.[11]

18. This prayer I had before the raptures and the great impetuosities I have been speaking of. I forgot to say that these great impetuosities scarcely ever leave me, except through a trance or great sweetness

[11] See *Life*, ch. xvii. 9.

in our Lord, whereby He comforts the soul, and gives
it courage to live on for His sake.

19. All this that I speak of cannot be the effect of
the imagination ; and I have some reasons for saying
this, but it would be wearisome to enter on them :
whether it be good or not is known to our Lord. The
effects thereof, and how it profits the soul, pass all
comprehension, as it seems to me.

20. I see clearly that the Persons are distinct, as I
saw it yesterday when you, my father, were talking
to the Father Provincial[12] ; only I saw nothing, and
heard nothing, as, my father, I have already told you.
But there is a strange certainty about it, though the
eyes of the soul see nothing ; and when the presence
is withdrawn, that withdrawal is felt. How it is, I
know not ; but I do know very well that it is not an
imagination, because I cannot reproduce the vision
when it is over, even if I were to perish in the effort ;
but I have tried to do so. So is it with all that I have
spoken of here, so far as I can see ; for, as I have been
in this state for so many years, I have been able
to observe, so that I can say so with this confidence.
The truth is,—and you, my father, should attend to
this,—that, as to the Person who always speaks, I can
certainly say which of Them He seems to me to be ;
of the others I cannot say so much. One of Them I
know well has never spoken. I never knew why, nor
do I busy myself in asking more of God than He is
pleased to give, because in that case, I believe, I should
be deluded by Satan at once ; nor will I ask now,
because of the fear I am in.

21. I think the First spoke to me at times ; but as
I do not remember that very well now, nor what it
was that He spoke, I will not venture to say so. It
is all written,—you, my father, know where,—and

[12] Diego de Acosta, one of five brothers who joined the Society. He
was student and professor at the Roman College. St. Teresa made his
acquaintance at Seville, and remained on very friendly terms with him.

more at large than it is here ; I know not whether in
the same words or not.[13] Though the Persons are
distinct in a strange way, the soul knows One only
God. I do not remember that our Lord ever seemed to
speak to me but in His Human Nature ; and—I say
it again—I can assure you that this is no imagination.

22. What, my father, you say about the water, I
know not ; nor have I heard where the earthly paradise
is. I have already said that I cannot but listen to
what our Lord tells me ; I hear it because I cannot
help myself ; but, as for asking His Majesty to reveal
anything to me, that is what I have never done. In
that case I should immediately think I was imagining
things, and that I must be in a delusion of Satan.
God be praised, I have never been curious about
things, and I do not care to know more than I do.[14]
What I have learnt, without seeking to learn, as I
have just said, has been a great trouble to me, though
it has been the means, I believe, which our Lord
made use of to save me, seeing that I was so wicked ;
good people do not need so much to make them serve
His Majesty.

23. I remember another way of prayer which I
had before the one I mentioned first,—namely, a
presence of God, which is not a vision at all. It seems
that any one, if he recommends himself to His Majesty,
even if he only prays vocally, finds Him ; every one,
at all times, can do this, if we except seasons of aridity.
May He grant I may not by my own fault lose mercies
so great, and may He have compassion on me !

[13] See *Relation* iii. 6.
[14] See St. John of the Cross, *Ascent of Mount Carmel*, bk. ii. ch. xxii.

RELATION IX

OF CERTAIN SPIRITUAL GRACES SHE RECEIVED IN
TOLEDO AND AVILA IN THE YEARS 1576 AND 1577.

1. I HAD begun to go to confession to a certain person [1]
in the city wherein I am at present staying, when he,
though he had much good-will towards me, and always
has had since he took upon himself the charge of my
soul, ceased to come here ; and one night, when I was
in prayer, and thinking how he failed me, I understood
that God kept him from coming because it was expedient for me to treat of the affairs of my soul with
a certain person on the spot. [2]   I was distressed because I had to form new relations—it might be he
would not understand me, and would disturb me—
and because I had a great affection for him who did
me this charity, though I was always spiritually
content when I saw or heard the latter preach ; also
I thought it would not do because of his many occupations.   Our Lord said to me : " I will cause him
to hear and understand thee.   Make thyself known
unto him ; it will be some relief to thee in thy troubles."
The latter part was addressed to me, I think, because
I was then so worn out by the absence of God.   His
Majesty also said that He saw very well the trouble
I was in ; but it could not be otherwise while I lived
in this land of exile : all was for my good ; and he
comforted me greatly.   So it has been : he comforts
me, and seeks opportunities to do so ; he has under-

[1] Diego de Yepes, Hieronymite, prior of Sisla, afterwards Bishop of Taras-
sona, where he died May 7, 1613, aged eighty-three, having been warned of
his impending death by an apparition of the Saint.   He is the author of a
valuable biography of St. Teresa.

[2] Don Alonzo Velasquez, Canon of Toledo, afterwards Bishop of Osma,
to whom Relation xi. is addressed.   The Saint speaks of this in a letter to
Father Gratian in September 1576, and in the *Book of Foundations*, ch. xxx. 1.

stood me, and given me great relief; he is a most learned and holy man. [August 1576.]

2. One day,—it was the Feast of the Presentation,—I was praying earnestly to God for a certain person, and thinking that after all the possession of property and of freedom was unfitting for that high sanctity which I wished him to attain to; I reflected on his weak health, and on the spiritual health which he communicated to souls; and I heard these words: "He serves Me greatly; but the great thing is to follow Me stripped of everything, as I was on the cross. Tell him to trust in Me." These last words were said because I thought he could not, with his weak health, attain to such perfection. [November 21, 1576.]

3. Once, when I was thinking of the pain it was to me to take my food and do no penance, I understood that there was at times more of self-love in that feeling than of a desire for penance. [1576.]

4. Once, when I was in great distress because of my offences against God, He said to me: "All thy sins in My sight are as if they were not. For the future, be strong[3]; for thy troubles are not over." [1576 or 1577.]

5. One day, in prayer, I felt my soul in God in such a way that it seemed to me as if the world did not exist, I was so absorbed in Him. He made me then understand that verse of the *Magnificat*, "Et exultavit spiritus meus," so that I can never forget it.[4] [1575-6.]

6. Once, when I was thinking how people sought to destroy this monastery of the Barefooted Carmelites, and that they purposed, perhaps, to bring about the destruction of them all by degrees, I heard: "They do purpose it; nevertheless, they will never

---

[3] *Foundations*, ch. xxxi. 25.

[4] Ribera says this event took place at Seville, while Fuente erroneously places it at Toledo. *Relation* v. 2.

see it done, but very much the reverse." [5]   [Seville, 1575–6.]

7. Once, in deep recollection, I was praying to God for Eliseus [6] ; I heard this : " He is My true son ; I will never fail him," or to that effect ; but I am not sure of the latter words.   [Seville, 1575.]

8. Having one day conversed with a person who had given up much for God, and calling to mind that I had given up nothing for Him, and had never served Him in anything, as I was bound to do, and then considering the many graces He had wrought in my soul, I began to be exceedingly weary ; and our Lord said to me : " Thou knowest of the betrothal between thee and Myself, and therefore all I have is thine ; and so I give thee all the labours and sorrows I endured, and thou canst therefore ask of My Father as if they were thine."   Though I have heard that we are partakers therein, [7] now it was in a way so different that it seemed as if I had become possessed of a great principality ; for the affection with which He wrought this grace cannot be described. The Father seemed to ratify the gift ; and from that time forth I look at our Lord's Passion in a very different light, as on something that belongs to me ; and that gives me great comfort.   [Seville, 1575–6.]

9. On the Feast of the Magdalene, when thinking of the great love I am bound to have for our Lord, according to the words He spoke to me in reference to this Saint, and having great desires to imitate her, our Lord was very gracious unto me, and said, I was to be henceforward strong ; for I had to serve

---

[5] The Spanish text, as printed by Fuente, says : " *Descalzas* " (Barefooted Nuns), but it appears to the present editor probable that there is some mistake.   There never was a set purpose of dissolving the convents of nuns, which had all been founded by the leave of the General.   But the General Chapter of 1575 had decreed the dissolution of three convents of Barefooted Friars founded without the General's permission.   The Saint most probably alludes to these, more especially to the convent at Triana, near Seville, in which city she was then living.

[6] Father Jerome Gratian.

[7] St, Peter iv. 13 ; " Communicantes Christi passionibus gaudete."

Him more than I had hitherto done.[8]   He filled me
with a desire not to die so soon, that I might have the
time to occupy myself therein ; and I remained with
a great resolution to suffer. [Seville, 1575.]

10. On one occasion, I understood how our Lord
was in all things, and how He was in the soul ; and
the illustration of a sponge filled with water was suggested to me.[9] [Seville, 1575–6.]

11. When my brothers came,—and I owe so much
to one of them,[10]—I remained in conversation with
him concerning his soul and his affairs, which wearied
and distressed me ; and as I was offering this up to
our Lord, and thinking that I did it all because I was
under obligations to him, I remembered that by our
Constitutions [11] we are commanded to separate ourselves from our kindred, and I was set thinking whether
I was under any obligation, our Lord said to me :
" No, My daughter ; the regulations of the Order
must be only in conformity with My law."   The truth
is, that the end of the Constitutions is, that we are
not to be attached to our kindred ; and to converse
with them, as it seems to me, is rather wearisome,
and it is painful to have anything to do with them.
[July 1575.]

12. After Communion, on St. Augustine's Day,[12] I
understood, and, as it were, saw,—I cannot tell how,
unless it was by an intellectual vision which passed
rapidly away,—how the Three Persons of the most
Holy Trinity, whom I have always imprinted in my
soul, are One.   This was revealed in a representation
so strange, and in a light so clear, that the impression
made upon me was very different from that which I

---

[8] See § 4, above. *Relation* iii. 18.

[9] *Life*, ch. xviii. 20.   *Relation* iii. 9.

[10] This was in 1575, when the Saint was founding the monastery of Seville ;
the brother was Don Lorenzo, returned from the Indies, who now placed
himself under the direction of his sister.

[11] In the chapter " De la Clausura," § 16 : " De tratar con deudos se
desvien lo mas que pudieren."

[12] See *Relation* iii. 9.

have by faith.   From that time forth I have never
been able to think of One of the Three Divine Persons
without thinking of the Three ; so that to-day, when
I was considering how, the Three being One, the Son
alone took our flesh upon Him, our Lord showed
me how, though they are One, They are also distinct.
These are marvels which make the soul desire anew to
be rid of the hindrances which the body interposes
between it and the fruition of them.   Though this
passes away in a moment, there remains a gain to the
soul incomparably greater than any it might have
made by meditation during many years ; and all
without knowing how it happens.   [August 28, 1575.]

13. I have a special joy on the Feast of our Lady's
Nativity.   When this day was come, I thought it
would be well to renew our vows ; and thereupon I
saw our Lady, by an illuminative vision ; and it
seemed as if we made them before her, and that they
were pleasing unto her.   I had this vision constantly
for some days, and our Lady was by me on my left
hand.   One day, after Communion, it seemed to me
that my soul was really one with the most Holy Body
of our Lord, then present before me ; and that wrought
a great work and blessing in me.   [September 8, 1575.]

14. I was once thinking whether I was to be sent
to reform a certain monastery [13] ; and, distressed at
it, I heard : " What art thou afraid of ?   What canst
thou lose ?—only thy life, which thou hast so often
offered to Me.   I will help thee."   This was in prayer,
which was of such a nature as to ease my soul exceedingly.

15. Once, having a desire to render some service
to our Lord, I considered that I could serve Him but
poorly, and said to myself : " Why, O Lord, doest Thou
desire my works ? "   And He answered : " To see
thy good will, My child."   [Seville, 1575 and 1576.]

[13] The monastery of Paterna, of the Calced Carmelite nuns.   This was
in 1575.

16. Once our Lord gave me light in a matter that I was very glad to understand, and I immediately forgot it, so that I was never able to call it again to mind ; and so, when I was trying to remember it, I heard : " Thou knowest now that I speak to thee from time to time. Do not omit to write down what I say ; for, though it may not profit thee, it may be that it will profit others." [14] As I was thinking whether I, for my sins, had to be of use to others, and be lost myself, He said to me : " Have no fear." [Seville, 1575–6.]

17. I was once recollected in that companionship which I ever have in my soul, and it seemed to me that God was present therein in such a way that I remembered how St. Peter said : " Thou art Christ, the Son of the living God [15] ; " for the living God was in my soul. This is not like other visions, for it overpowers faith ; so that it is impossible to doubt of the indwelling of the Trinity in our souls, by pre-sence, power, and essence.[16] To know this truth is of the very highest gain ; and as I stood amazed to see His Majesty in a thing so vile as my soul, I heard : " It is not vile, My child, for it is made in My image." [17] I also learnt something of the reason why God delights in souls more than in any other creatures ; it is so subtile that, though the understanding quickly com-prehended it, I cannot tell it. [1575.]

18. When I was in such distress, because of the illness of our father,[18] that I had no rest, and after Communion one day was making most earnestly my petition to our Lord that, as He had given him to me, I might not lose him, He said to me : " Have no fear."

19. Once, with that presence of the Three Persons

---

[14] *Relation* v. 1.

[15] St. Matt. xvi. 16 : " Tu es Christus, Filius Dei vivi."

[16] *Life*, ch. xviii. 20 ; *Relation* xi. 8.

[17] Gen. i. 26 : " Ad imaginem et similitudinem Nostram."

[18] This refers to Father Gratian, whose health caused the Saint great anxiety, especially after he had been repeatedly thrown by his mule. Mr. Lewis translated " troubles " instead of " illness," and alluded to the per-secution undergone by Father Jerome ; but this would be an anachronism

which I have in my soul, I was in light so clear that no doubt of the presence of the true and living God was possible ; and I then came to the knowledge of things which afterwards I could not speak of.   One of these things was, how the Person of the Son only took human flesh.   I cannot, as I have just said, explain it at all ; for some of these things were wrought in the secret recesses of the soul, and the understanding seems to grasp them only as one who is in his sleep, or half awake, thinks he comprehends what is told him.   I was thinking how hard it was to remain alive, seeing that it was living on that robbed us of that marvellous companionship ; and so I said to myself : " O Lord, show me some way whereby I may bear this life ! " He said unto me : " Think, my child, when life is over, thou canst not serve Me as thou art serving Me now, and eat for me, and sleep for Me.   Whatsoever thou doest, let it be done for Me as if thou wert no longer living, but I ; for that is what St. Paul said." [19] [1575.]

20. Once, after Communion, I saw how His Father within our soul accepts the most Holy Body of Christ. I have understood and seen how the Divine Persons are there, and how pleasing is this offering of His Son, because He has His joy and delight in Him, so to speak, here on earth ; for it is not the Humanity only that is with us in our souls, but the Divinity as well, and thus is it so pleasing and acceptable unto Him, and gives us graces so great.   I understood also that He accepts the sacrifice, though the priest be in sin [20] ; but then the grace of it is not communicated to his soul as it is to their souls who are in a state of grace : not that the inflowings of grace, which proceed from this Communion wherein the Father accepts the sacrifice, cease to flow in their strength, but because of his fault who has to receive them ; as it is not the fault of the sun that it does not illumine a lump of pitch,

---

[19] Galat. ii. 20 : " Vivo autem, jam non ego : vivit vero in me Christus "
[20] *Life*, ch. xxxviii. 30.

when its rays strike it, as it illumines a globe of crystal. If I could now describe it, I should be better understood ; it is a great matter to know this, because there are grand secrets within us when we are at Communion. It is sad that these bodies of ours do not allow us to have the fruition thereof. [1575.]

21. During the Octave of All Saints, I had two or three days of exceeding anguish, the result of my remembrance of my great sins, and I was also in great dread of persecutions, which had no foundation except that great accusations were brought against me, and all my resolutions to suffer anything for God failed me : though I sought to encourage myself, and made corresponding acts, and saw that all would be a great pain for me, it was to little purpose, for the fear never left me. It was a sharp warfare. I came across a letter, in which my good father [21] had written that St. Paul said that our God does not suffer us to be tempted beyond our power to bear.[22] This was a very great relief to me, but was not enough ; yea, rather, on the next day I was in great distress at his absence, for I had no one to go to in this trouble, for I seemed to be living in great loneliness. And it added to my grief to see that I now find no one but he who can comfort me, and he must be more than ever away, which is a very sore trouble. [1575.]

22. The next night after this, reading in a book I found another saying of St. Paul, with which I began to be comforted ; and being suddenly recollected, I remained thinking how I had our Lord before present within me, so that I truly saw Him to be the living God. While thinking on this He spoke to me, and I saw Him in my inmost being, as it were beside my heart, in an intellectual vision ; His words were : '' I am here, only I will have thee see how little thou

---

[21] Jerome Gratian.
[22] 1 Cor. x. 13 : '' Fidelis autem Deus est, qui non patietur vos tentari supra id quod potestis.''

canst do without Me." I was on the instant reassured, and my fears left me ; and while at Matins that very night our Lord Himself, in an intellectual vision so clear as to seem almost imaginary, laid Himself in my arms, as He is painted in the pictures of our Lady of Anguish.[23] The vision made me very much afraid, for it was so clear, and so close to me, that it made me think whether it was an illusion or not. He said to me : " Be not afraid of it, for the union of My Father with thy soul is incomparably closer than this." The vision has remained with me till now. What I have said of our Lord continued more than a month : now it has left me. [November 1575.]

23. I was one night in great distress, because it was then a long time since I had heard anything of my father [24] ; and, moreover, he was not well the last time he wrote to me. However, my distress was not so great as that I felt before, for I had hopes, and distress like that I never was in since ; but still my anxiety hindered my prayer. He appeared to me on the instant ; it could not have been the effect of imagination, for I saw a light within me, and himself coming by the way joyous, with a face all fair. It must have been the light I saw that made his face fair, for all the saints in heaven seem so ; and I considered whether it be the light and splendour proceeding from our Lord that render them thus fair. I heard this : " Tell him to begin at once without fear, for the victory is his."

24. One day, after he came, when I was at night giving thanks to our Lord for the many mercies He had given unto me, He said to me : " O my child, what canst thou ask that I have not done ? " [November 1575.]

---

[23] Don Vicente says that here is a proof—if any were wanting—that the Saint wrote this during her sojourn in Seville ; because in Avila and in Castile and Aragon the expression is, " our Lady of Dolors " ; while in Andalucia it is our Lady of Anguish—" Nuestra Señora de las Angustias."

[24] Father Jerome Gratian.

25. Our Lord said to me one day, in the monastery of Veas, that I was to present my petition to Him, for I was His bride. He promised to grant whatever I might ask of Him, and, as a pledge, gave me a very beautiful ring, with a stone set in it like an amethyst, but of a brilliancy very unlike, which He put on my finger. I write this to my own confusion, considering the goodness of God, and my wretched life; for I have deserved hell. Ah, my daughters, pray to God for me, and be devout to St. Joseph, who can do much. This folly I write . . . folly I write. . . .

26. On the eve of St. Laurence, at Communion, I was so distracted and dissipated in mind, that I had no power over it, and began to envy those who dwell in desert places; thinking that, as they see and hear nothing, they are exempt from distractions. I heard this: "Thou art greatly deceived, My daughter; on the contrary, the temptations of Satan are more violent there. Have patience; while life lasts, it cannot be helped." While dwelling on this, I became suddenly recollected, and I saw a great light within me, so that I thought I was in another world, and my spirit found itself interiorly in a forest and in a garden of delights, which made me remember those words of the Canticle [25]; "Veniat dilectus meus in hortum suum." I saw my Eliseus [26] there, not at all swarthy, but in strange beauty: around his head was a garland of precious stones; a multitude of damsels went before him with palms in their hands, all singing hymns of praise unto God. I did nothing but open my eyes, to see whether I could not distract myself from the vision, but that failed to divert my attention; and I thought there was music also,—the singing of birds and of angels,—which filled my soul with joy, though I did not hear any. My soul was in joy, and did not

[25] Cant. v. 1.
[26] This was the name given to Father Jerome Gratian when the Saint was driven, by the persecution raised against her, to distinguish her friends by other designations than those by which they were usually known.

consider that there was nobody else there. I heard these words: " He has merited to be among you, and all this rejoicing which thou beholdest will take place on the day he shall set aside for the honour of My Mother [27]; and do thou make haste, if thou wouldst reach the place where he is." This vision lasted more than an hour and a half. In this respect—differently from my other visions—I could not turn away from it, and it filled me with delight. The effect of the vision was a great affection for Eliseus, and a more frequent thinking of him in that beauty. I have had a fear of its being a temptation, for work of the imagination it could not possibly be. [Seville, 1575.]

27. The day after the presentation of the Brief,[28] as I was in the most eager expectation, which utterly disturbed me, so that I could not even pray,—for I had been told that our father was in great straits because they would not let him come away, and that there was a great tumult,—I heard these words: " O woman of little faith, be quiet; everything is going on perfectly well." It was the Feast of the Presentation of our Lady in the year 1575. I resolved within myself, if our Lady obtained from her Son that we might see ourselves and our father free of these friars, to ask him to order the solemn celebration of that feast every year in our monasteries of the Barefooted Carmelites. When I made this resolution, I did not remember what I had heard in a former vision, that he would establish this solemnity. Now, in reading again this little paper, I think this must be the feast referred to.[29] [November 1575.]

[27] See the next section.
[28] Father Jerome Gratian exhibited the Brief which made him Visitor-Apostolic to the Calced Carmelites, who were very angry thereat, and rude in their vexation.
[29] See § 26.

RELATION X.

OF A REVELATION TO THE SAINT AT AVILA (JUNE 6, 1579), AND OF CERTAIN DIRECTIONS CONCERNING THE GOVERNMENT OF THE ORDER.

In St. Joseph of Avila, on Pentecost eve, in the hermitage of Nazareth, thinking of one of the greatest graces our Lord had given me on that day some twenty years before,[1] more or less, my spirit was vehemently stirred and grew hot within me,[2] and I fell into a trance. In that profound recollection I heard our Lord say what I am now going to tell: I was to say to the Barefooted Fathers, as from Him, that they must strive to observe four things; and that so long as they observed them, the Order would increase more and more; and if they neglected them, they should know that they were falling away from their first estate.

The first is, the superiors of the monasteries are to be of one mind.

The second, even if they have many monasteries, to have but few friars in each.

The third, to converse little with people in the world, and that only for the good of their souls.

The fourth, to teach more by works than by words.

This happened in the year 1579; and because it is a great truth, I have put my name to it.

TERESA OF JESUS.

[1] See *Life*, ch. xxxviii. 11.
[2] Psalm xxxviii. 4: " Concaluit cor meum intra me."

RELATION XI.

WRITTEN FROM PALENCIA IN MAY 1581, AND ADDRESSED
TO DON ALONZO VELASQUEZ, BISHOP OF OSMA, WHO
HAD BEEN, WHEN CANON OF TOLEDO, ONE OF THE
SAINT'S CONFESSORS.[1]

JESUS.

1. OH, that I could clearly explain to your Lordship the peace and quiet my soul has found! for it has so great a certainty of the fruition of God, that it seems to be as if already in possession,[2] though the joy is withheld. I am as one to whom another has granted by deed a large revenue, into the enjoyment and use of which he is to come at a certain time, but until then has nothing but the right already given him to the revenue. In gratitude for this, my soul would abstain from the joy of it, because it has not deserved it; it wishes only to serve Him, even if in great suffering, and at times it thinks it would be very little if, till the end of the world, it had to serve Him who has given it this right; for, in truth, it is in some measure no longer subject, as before, to the miseries of this world; though it suffers more, it seems as if only the habit were struck, for my soul is, as it were, in a fortress with authority, and accordingly does not lose its peace. Still, this confidence does not remove from it its great fear of offending God, nor make it less careful to put away every hindrance to His service, yea, rather, it is more careful than before. But it is so forgetful of its own interests as to seem, in some measure, to have lost itself, so forgetful of self is it in this. Everything is directed to the honour of God, to the doing of His will more and more, and the advancement of His glory.

---

[1] This is probably the latest account of the state of her soul, for she died on Oct. 4, 1582.

[2] *Interior Castle*, M. vii. ch. ii. 3–5.

2. Though this be so, yet, in all that relates to health and the care of the body, it seems to me that I am more careful than I was, that I mortify myself less in my food, and do fewer penances: it is not so with the desires I had; they seem to be greater. All this is done that I may be the better able to serve God in other things, for I offer to Him very often, as a great sacrifice, the care I take of my body, and that wearies me much, and I try it sometimes in acts of mortification; but, after all, this cannot be done without losing health, and I must not neglect what my superiors command. Herein, and in the wish for health, much self-love also must insinuate itself; but, as it seems to me, I feel that it would give me more pleasure, and it gave me more pleasure when I was strong, to do penance, for, at least, I seemed to be doing something, and was giving a good example, and I was free from the vexation which arises out of the fact that I am not serving God at all. Your Lordship will see what it will be best to do in the matter.

3. The imaginary visions have ceased, but the intellectual vision of the Three Persons and of the Sacred Humanity seems ever present, and that, I believe, is a vision of a much higher kind; and I understand now, so I think, that the visions I had came from God, because they prepared my soul for its present state; they were given only because I was so wretched and so weak: God led me by the way which He saw was necessary; but they are, in my opinion, of great worth when they come from God.

4. The interior locutions have not left me, for, whenever it is necessary, our Lord gives me certain directions; and now, in Palencia, were it not for these, there would have been committed a great blunder, though not a sin.[3]

5. The acts and desires do not seem to be so vigor-

---

[3] This relates to the taking of the hermitage of our Lady de la Calle, in Palencia. See *Foundations*, ch. xxix. 11 sqq.

ous as they used to be, for, though they are great, I have one much greater to see the will of God accomplished and His glory increased ; for as the soul is well aware that His Majesty knoweth what is expedient herein, and is so far removed from all self-seeking, these acts and desires quickly end, and, as it seems to me, have no strength. Hence the fear I have at times, though without disquietude and pain as formerly, that my soul is dulled, and that I am doing nothing, because I can do no penance ; acts of desire for suffering, for martyrdom, and of the vision of God, have no strength in them, and, most frequently, I cannot make them. I seem to live only for eating and drinking, and avoiding pain in everything ; and yet this gives me none, except that sometimes, as I said before, I am afraid that this is a delusion ; but I cannot believe it, because, so far as I can see, I am not under the sway of any strong attachment to any created thing, not even to all the bliss of heaven, but only to the love of God ; and this does not grow less,—on the contrary, I believe it is growing together with the longing that all men may serve Him.

6. But, for all this, one thing amazes me : I have not the feelings I had formerly, so strong and so interior, which tormented me when I saw souls go to their ruin, and when I used to think I had offended God. I cannot have these feelings now, though I believe my desire that God be not sinned against is not less than it was.

7. Your Lordship must consider that in all this, in my present as well as in my previous state, I can do no more, and that it is not in my power to serve Him better : I might do so, if I were not so wicked. I may say, also, that if I were now to make great efforts to wish to die, I could not, nor can I make the acts I used to make, nor feel the pains I felt for having offended God, nor the great fears I had for so many years when I thought I was under a delusion : and

accordingly I have no need of learned men, or of speaking to anybody at all, only to satisfy myself that I am going the right road now, and whether I can do anything. I have consulted certain persons on this point, with whom I had taken counsel on the others, with Father Dominic,[4] the Master Medina,[5] and certain members of the Society.[6] I will be satisfied with the answer which you, my Lord, may give me, because of the great trust I have in your Lordship. Consider it carefully, for the love of God! Neither do I cease to learn that certain souls of people connected with me when they died are in heaven[7]: of others I learn nothing. Oh, in what solitude I find myself when I consider that the comparison of which I spoke to you, concerning the return from Egypt, does not apply to the child at my mother's breast.[8]

8. I am at peace within; and my likings and dislikings have so little power to take from me the Presence of the Three Persons, of which, while it continues, it is so impossible to doubt, that I seem clearly to know by experience what is recorded by St. John, that God will make His dwelling in the soul[9]: and not only by grace, but because He will have the soul feel that presence, and it brings with it so many blessings, particularly this, that there is no need to run after reflections to learn that God is there. This is almost always the state I am in, except when my great infirmities oppress me. Sometimes God will have me suffer without any inward comfort; but my will never swerves—not even in its first movements—from the will of God. This resignation to His will is so

---

[4] Dominic Bañez.
[5] Bartholomew de Medina. He was already dead when St. Teresa wrote this. *Relation* vii. 11.
[6] Balthasar Alvarez at Toledo and Jerome Ripalda at Valladolid. *Foundations*, ch. xxix. 4 and 5. *Relation* vii. 5.
[7] Allusion to the revelation she had while at Segovia of the death of her brother, Don Lorenzo de Cepeda, which occurred at Avila, June 26, 1580.
[8] This passage is obscure because we do not know the question the Saint had put to Velasquez.
[9] St. John xiv. 23: "Mansionem apud eum faciemus." *Life*, ch. xviii. 20.

efficacious, that I desire neither life nor death, except for some moments, when I long to see God ; and then the Presence of the Three Persons becomes so distinct as to relieve the pain of the absence, and I wish to live—if such be His good pleasure—to serve Him still longer.   And if I might help, by my prayers, to make but one soul love Him more, and praise Him, and that only for a short time, I think that of more importance than to dwell in glory.

The unworthy servant and daughter
of your Lordship,
TERESA OF JESUS.

INDEX

If you have enjoyed this book, consider making your next selection from among the following . . .

At your Bookdealer or direct from the Publisher.
Toll-Free 1-800-437-5876   Fax 815-226-7770
Tel. 815-226-7777   www.tanbooks.com

Prices subject to change.